THE ⓧ F I L E S

2—

Chapters 1 & 2
Writer: Frank Spotnitz
Artist: Brian Denham
Colors: Kelsey Shannon and Carlos Badilla
Letters: Ed Dukeshire

Chapter 3
Writer: Marv Wolfman
Artist: Brian Denham
Colors: Carlos Badilla
Letters: Ed Dukeshire

Chapter 4
Writer: Doug Moench
Artist: Brian Denham
Colors: Carlos Badilla
Letters: Ed Dukeshire

The X-Files created by Chris Carter

Collected edition cover and cover #0 by Ryan Sook
Original series covers by Tony Shasteen, Russell Walks, James Daly III
& Tim Bradstreet and Brian Denham & Kelsey Shannon

SUSTAINABLE FORESTRY INITIATIVE — Certified Fiber Sourcing
www.sfiprogram.org

PWC-SFICOC-260

THE X-FILES, published by WildStorm Productions. 888 Prospect St. #240, La Jolla, CA 92037. Compilation Copyright © 2009 Twentieth Century Fox Film Corporation. All Rights Reserved. Originally published in single magazine form as X-FILES #0-6 copyright © 2008, 2009.

THE X-FILES and all characters, the distinctive likenesses thereof and all related elements are trademarks of Twentieth Century Fox Film Corporation. WildStorm and logo are trademarks of DC Comics. The stories, characters, and incidents mentioned in this magazine are entirely fictional. Printed on recyclable paper. WildStorm does not read or accept unsolicited submissions of ideas, stories or artwork. Printed by World Color Press, Inc, St-Romuald, QC, Canada. 10/14/2009

DC Comics, a Warner Bros. Entertainment Company.

978-1-4012-2527-8

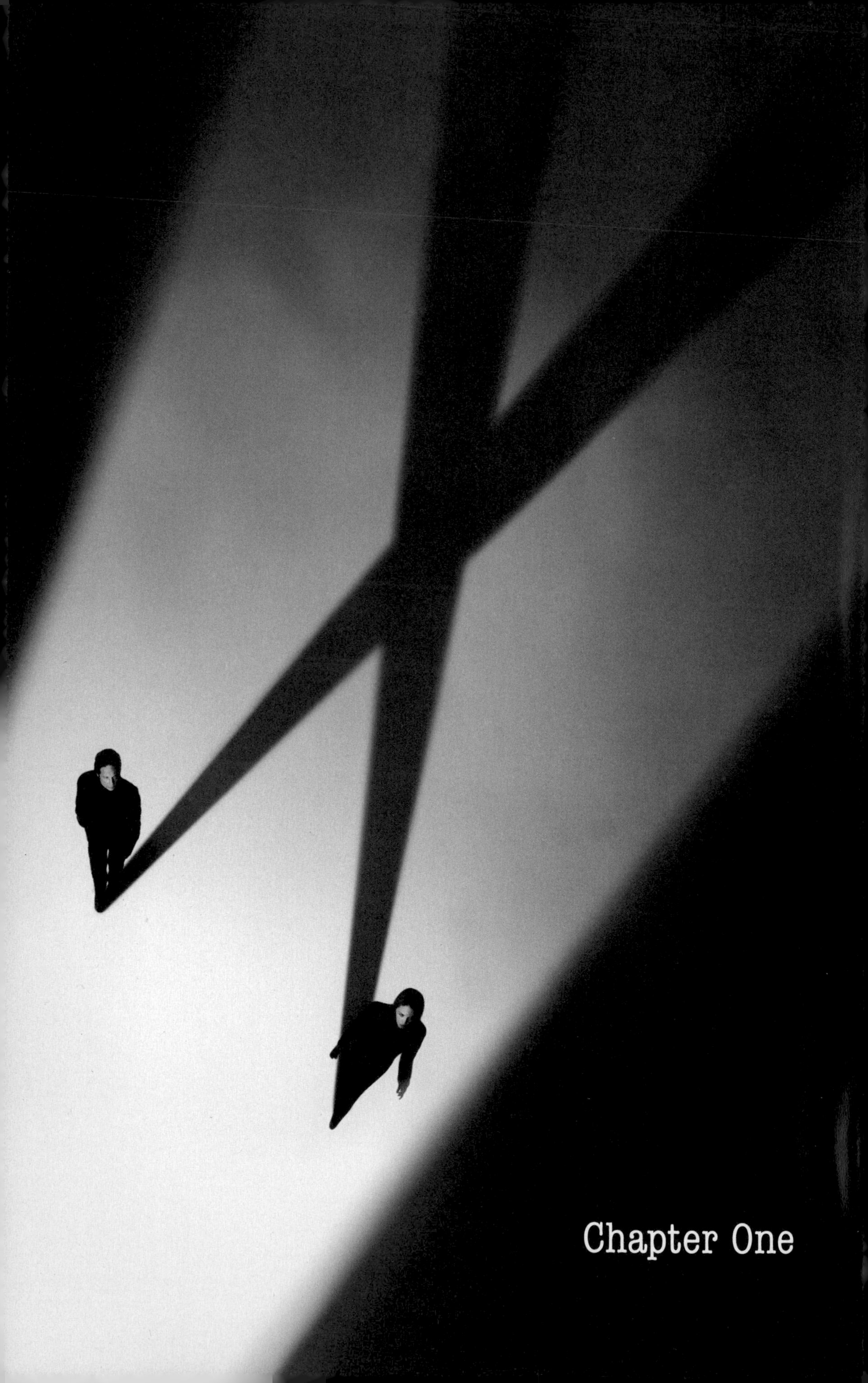

Chapter One

written by
FRANK SPOTNITZ

THE X FILES

illustrated by
BRIAN DENHAM

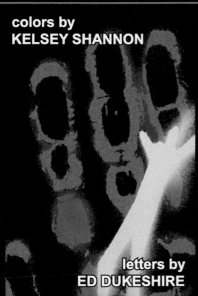

colors by
KELSEY SHANNON

edited by
SHANNON ERIC DENTON

created by
CHRIS CARTER

letters by
ED DUKESHIRE

Brick Church, Indiana
5:04 a.m.

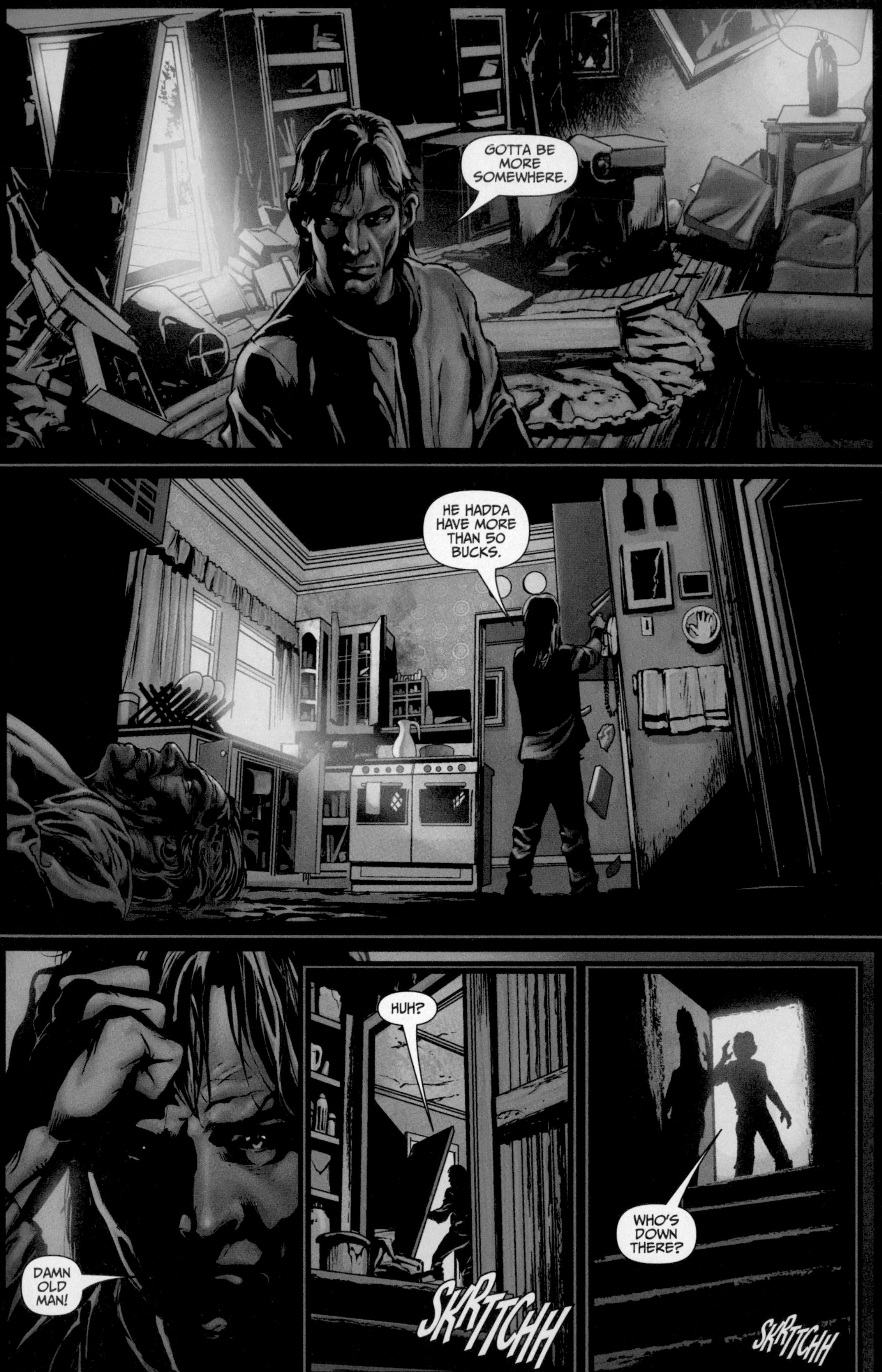
GOTTA BE MORE SOMEWHERE.
HE HADDA HAVE MORE THAN 50 BUCKS.
DAMN OLD MAN!
HUH?
SKRTTCHH
WHO'S DOWN THERE?
SKRTTCHH

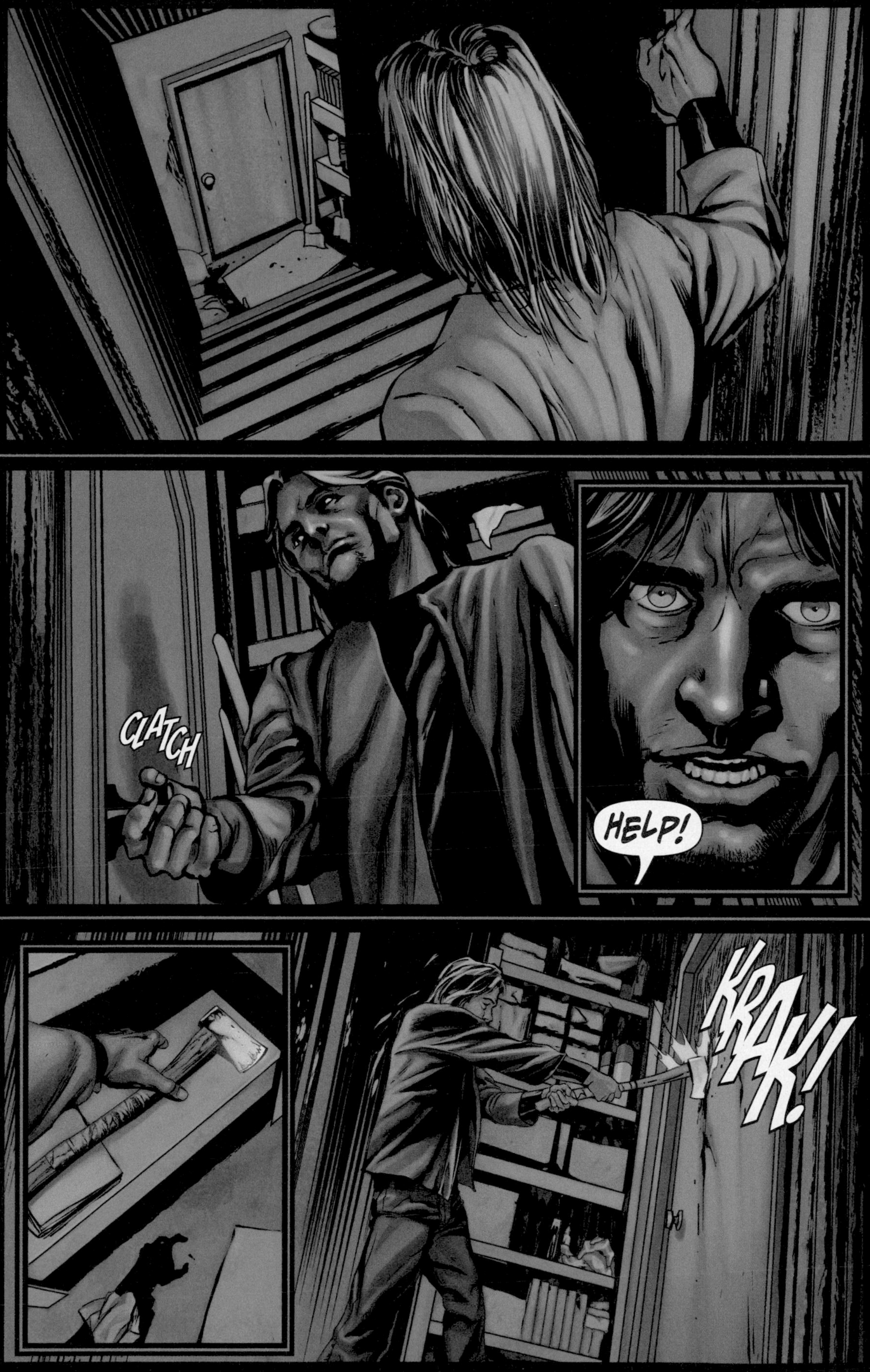
CLATCH
HELP!
KRAK!

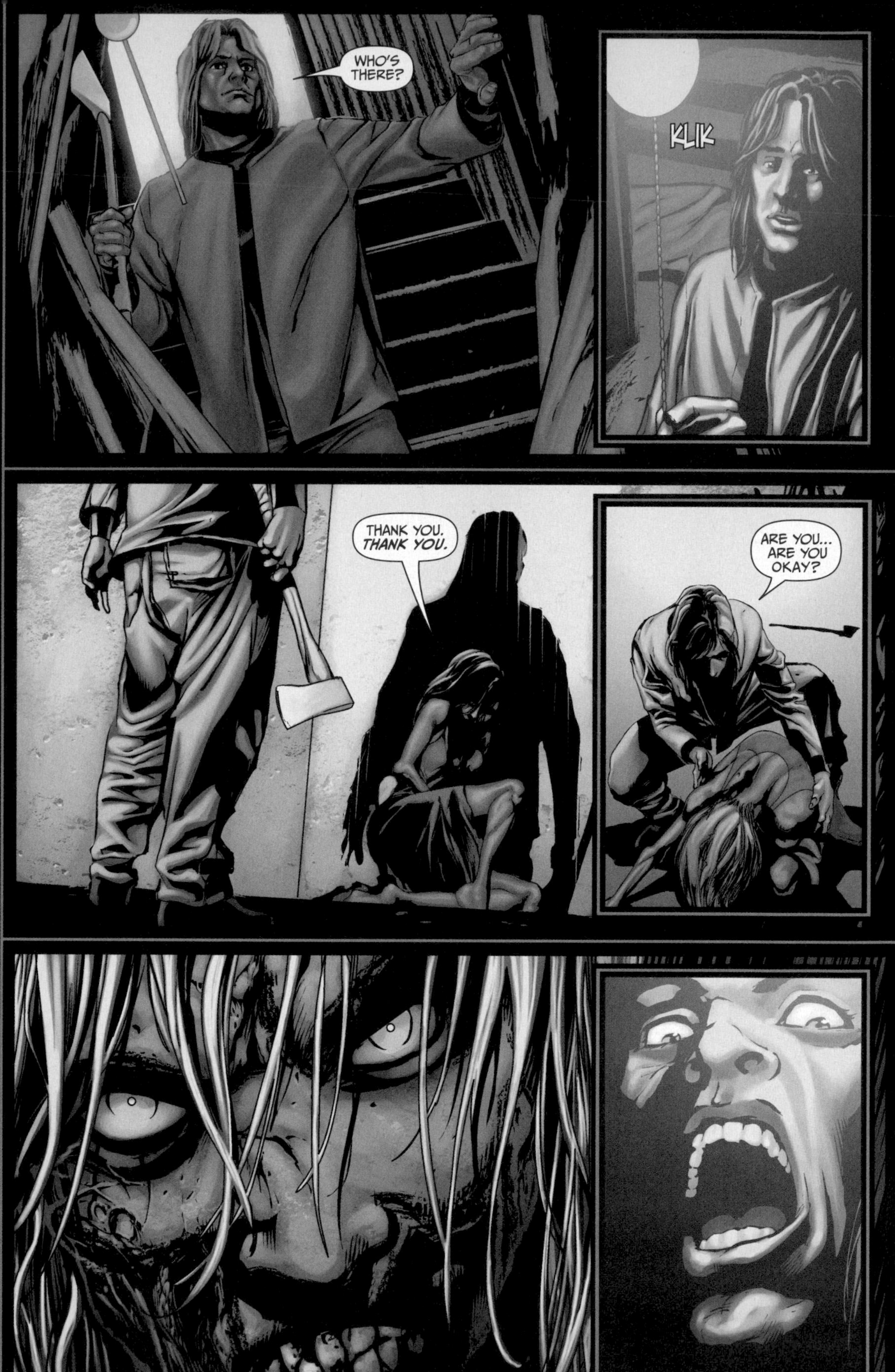
WHO'S THERE?
KLIK
THANK YOU. *THANK YOU.*
ARE YOU... ARE YOU OKAY?

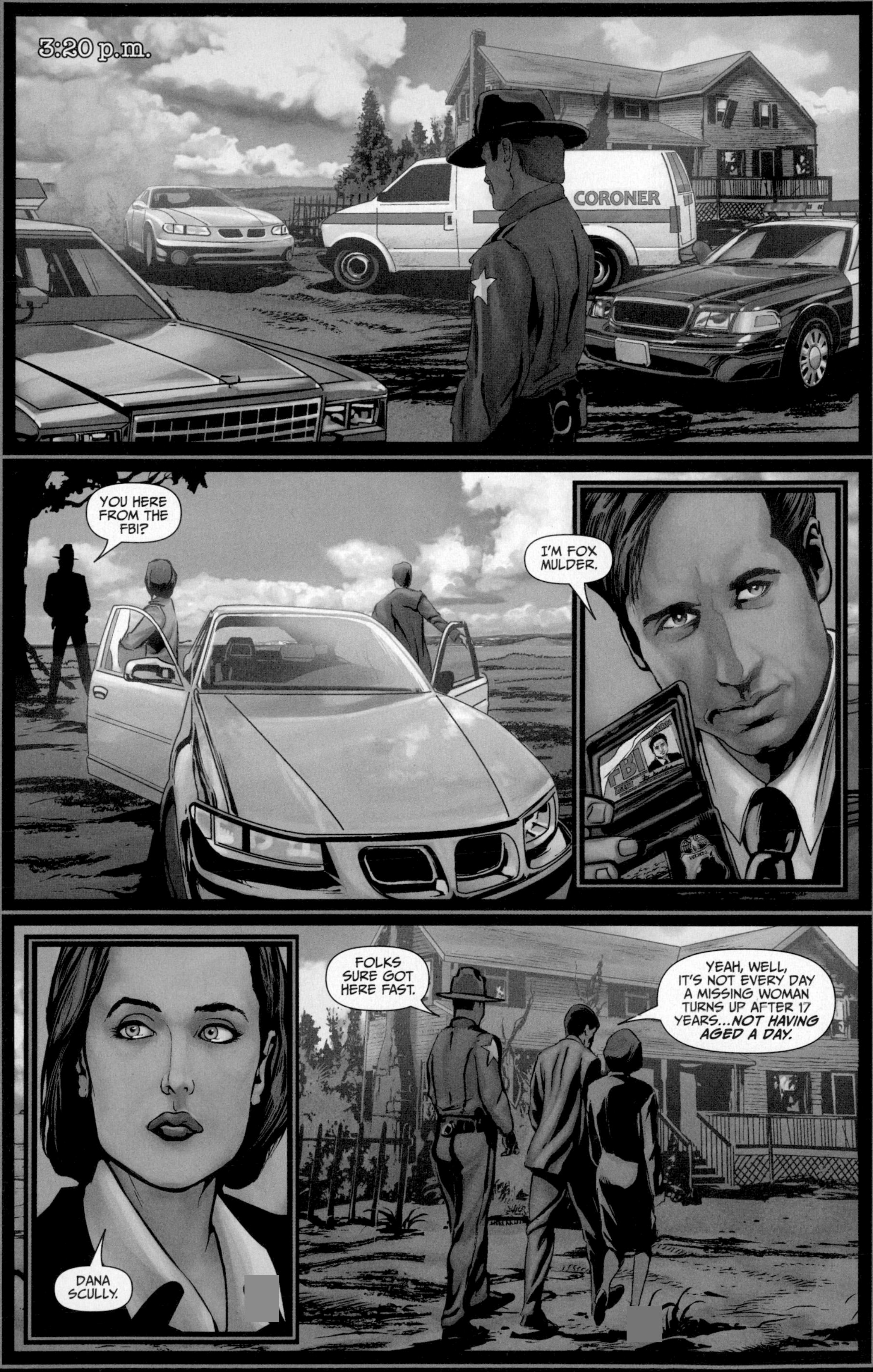
3:20 p.m.
CORONER
YOU HERE FROM THE FBI?
I'M FOX MULDER.
FBI
DANA SCULLY.
FOLKS SURE GOT HERE FAST.
YEAH, WELL, IT'S NOT EVERY DAY A MISSING WOMAN TURNS UP AFTER 17 YEARS...*NOT HAVING AGED A DAY.*

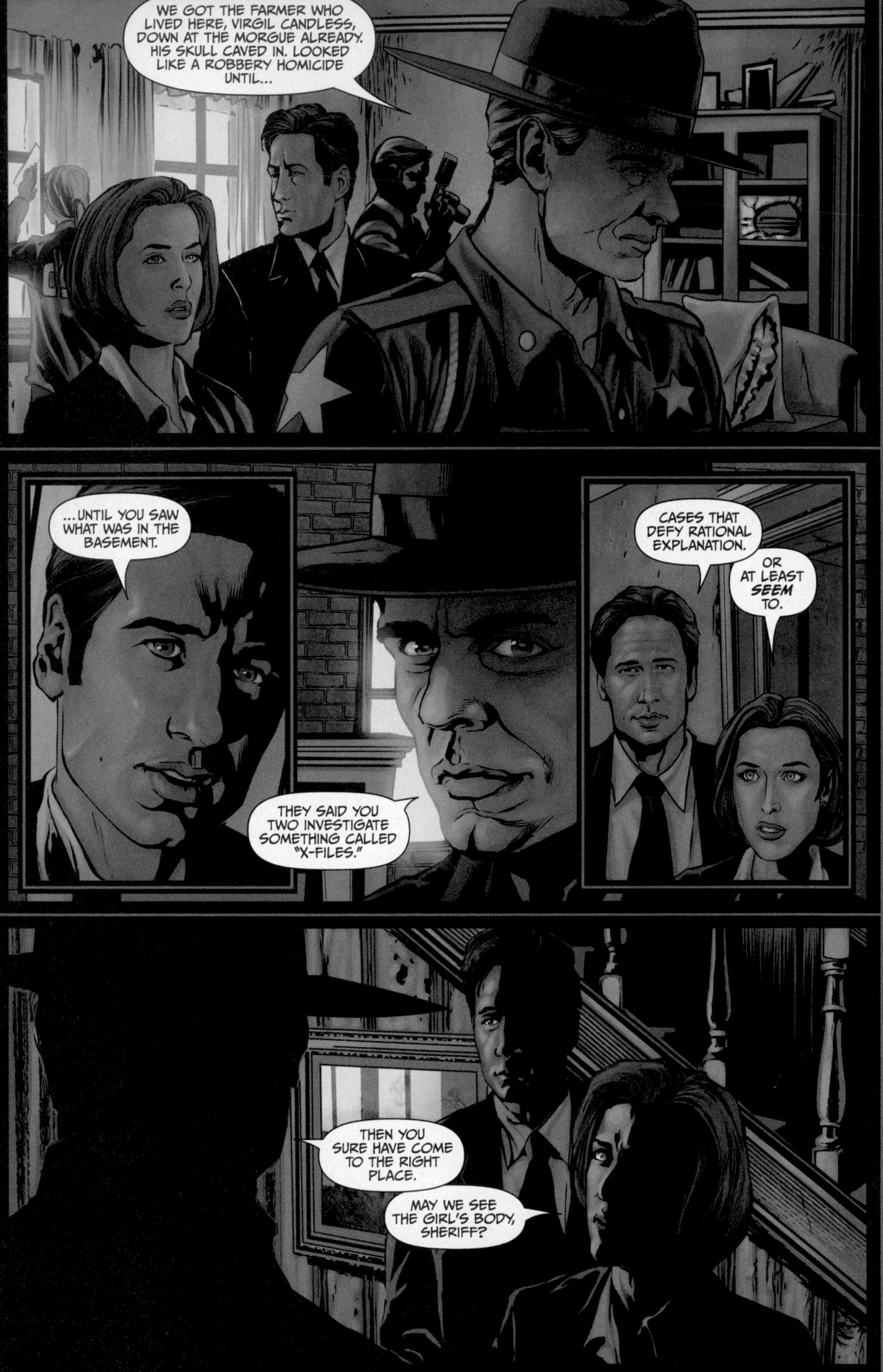
WE GOT THE FARMER WHO LIVED HERE, VIRGIL CANDLESS, DOWN AT THE MORGUE ALREADY. HIS SKULL CAVED IN. LOOKED LIKE A ROBBERY HOMICIDE UNTIL...
...UNTIL YOU SAW WHAT WAS IN THE BASEMENT.
THEY SAID YOU TWO INVESTIGATE SOMETHING CALLED "X-FILES."
CASES THAT DEFY RATIONAL EXPLANATION.
OR AT LEAST SEEM TO.
THEN YOU SURE HAVE COME TO THE RIGHT PLACE.
MAY WE SEE THE GIRL'S BODY, SHERIFF?

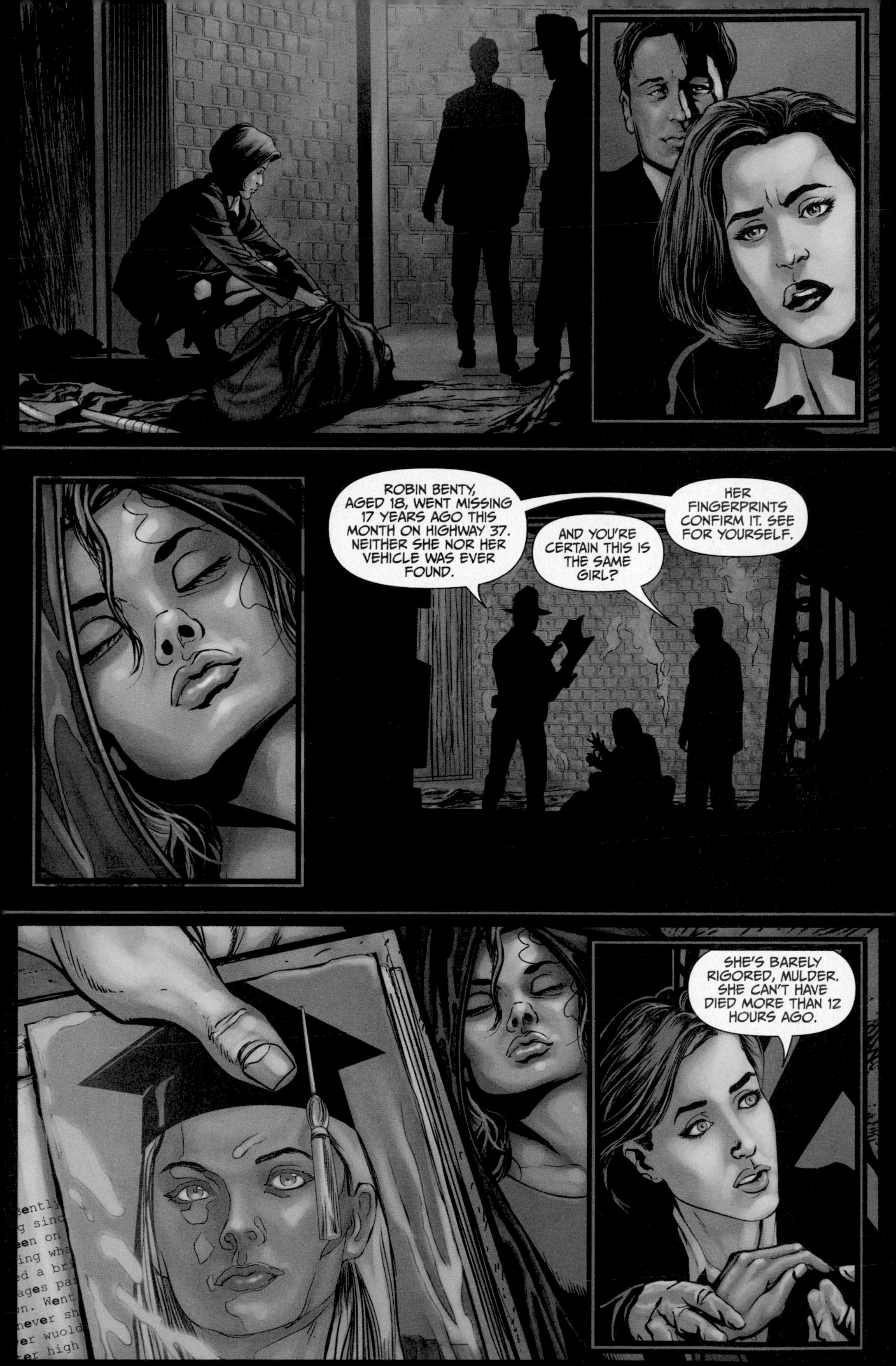
ROBIN BENTY, AGED 18, WENT MISSING 17 YEARS AGO THIS MONTH ON HIGHWAY 37. NEITHER SHE NOR HER VEHICLE WAS EVER FOUND.
AND YOU'RE CERTAIN THIS IS THE SAME GIRL?
HER FINGERPRINTS CONFIRM IT. SEE FOR YOURSELF.
SHE'S BARELY RIGORED, MULDER. SHE CAN'T HAVE DIED MORE THAN 12 HOURS AGO.

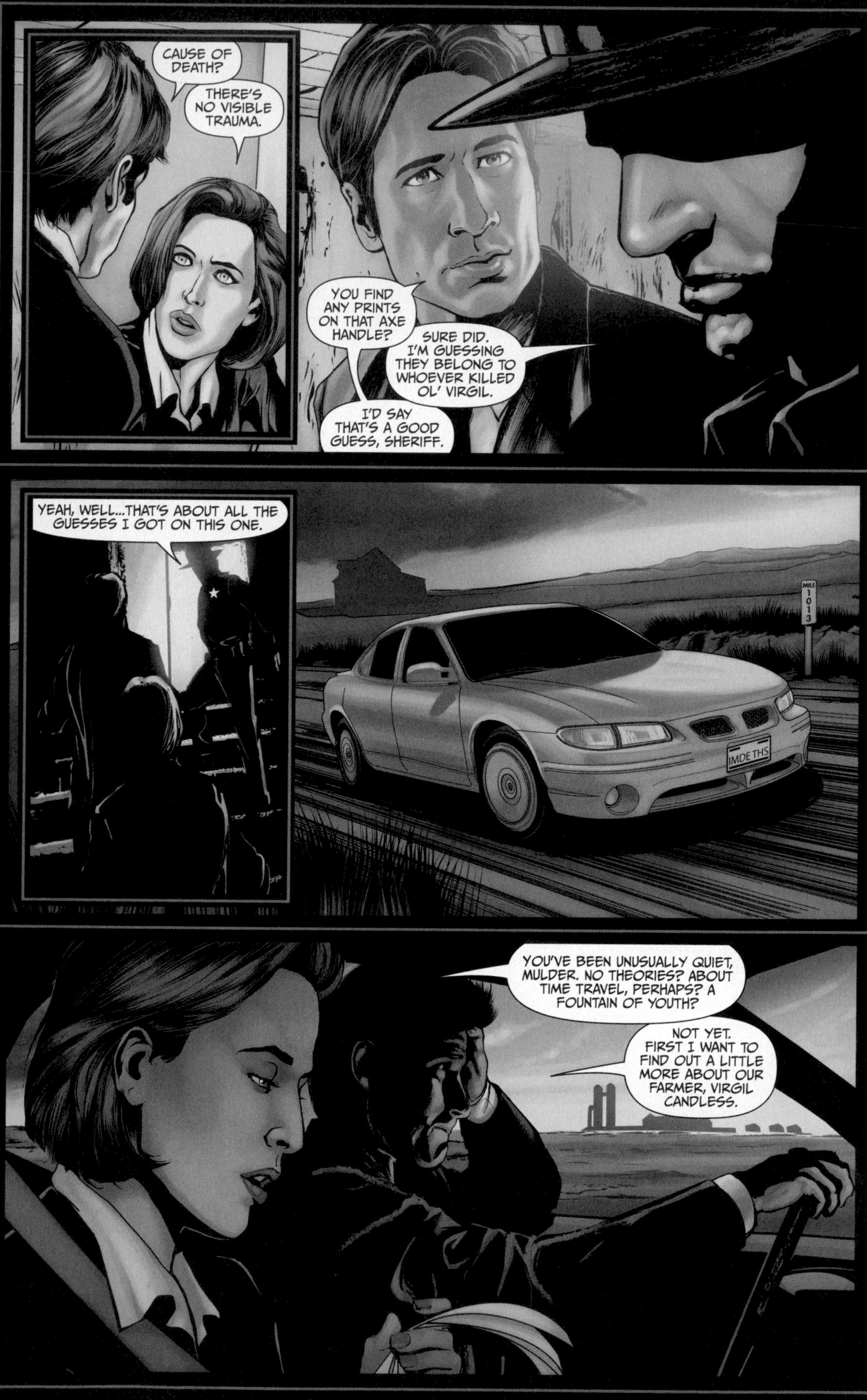
CAUSE OF DEATH?
THERE'S NO VISIBLE TRAUMA.
YOU FIND ANY PRINTS ON THAT AXE HANDLE?
SURE DID. I'M GUESSING THEY BELONG TO WHOEVER KILLED OL' VIRGIL.
I'D SAY THAT'S A GOOD GUESS, SHERIFF.
YEAH, WELL...THAT'S ABOUT ALL THE GUESSES I GOT ON THIS ONE.
MILE 1013
IMDETHS
YOU'VE BEEN UNUSUALLY QUIET, MULDER. NO THEORIES? ABOUT TIME TRAVEL, PERHAPS? A FOUNTAIN OF YOUTH?
NOT YET. FIRST I WANT TO FIND OUT A LITTLE MORE ABOUT OUR FARMER, VIRGIL CANDLESS.

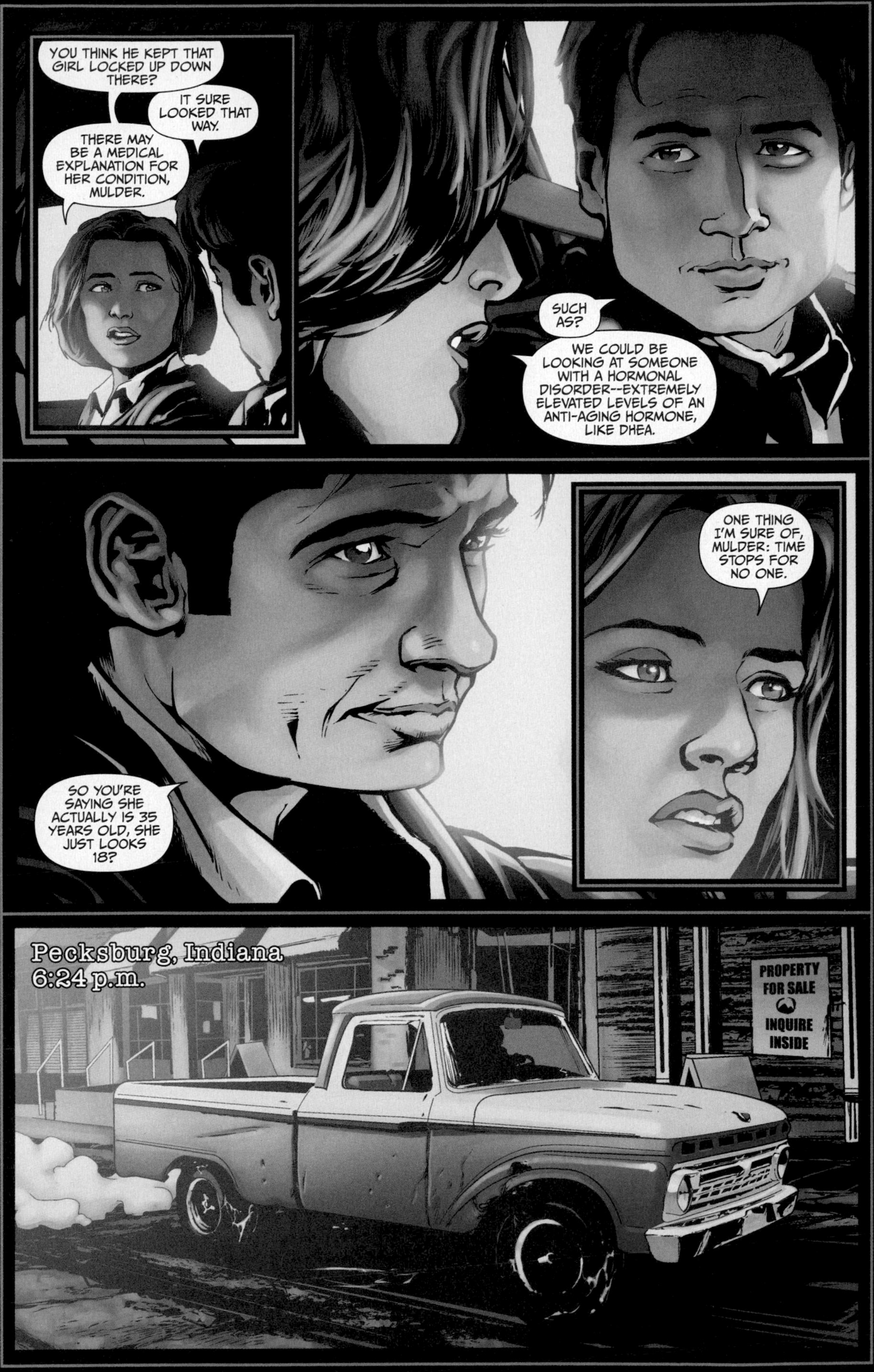
YOU THINK HE KEPT THAT GIRL LOCKED UP DOWN THERE?
IT SURE LOOKED THAT WAY.
THERE MAY BE A MEDICAL EXPLANATION FOR HER CONDITION, MULDER.
SUCH AS?
WE COULD BE LOOKING AT SOMEONE WITH A HORMONAL DISORDER--EXTREMELY ELEVATED LEVELS OF AN ANTI-AGING HORMONE, LIKE DHEA.
SO YOU'RE SAYING SHE ACTUALLY IS 35 YEARS OLD, SHE JUST LOOKS 18?
ONE THING I'M SURE OF, MULDER: TIME STOPS FOR NO ONE.
Pecksburg, Indiana
6:24 p.m.
PROPERTY FOR SALE
INQUIRE INSIDE

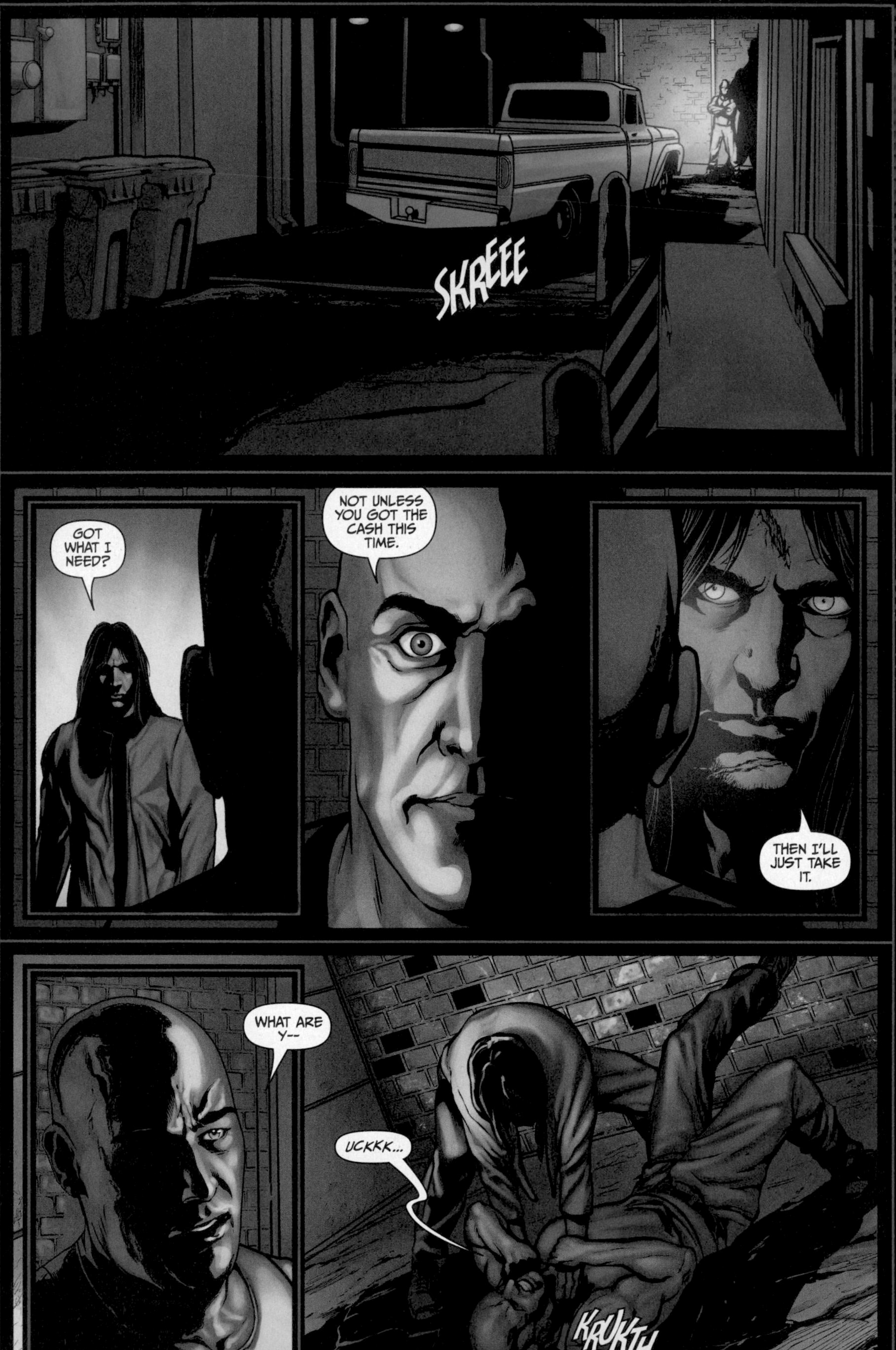
SKREEE
GOT WHAT I NEED?
NOT UNLESS YOU GOT THE CASH THIS TIME.
THEN I'LL JUST TAKE IT.
WHAT ARE Y--
UCKKK...
KRUKTH

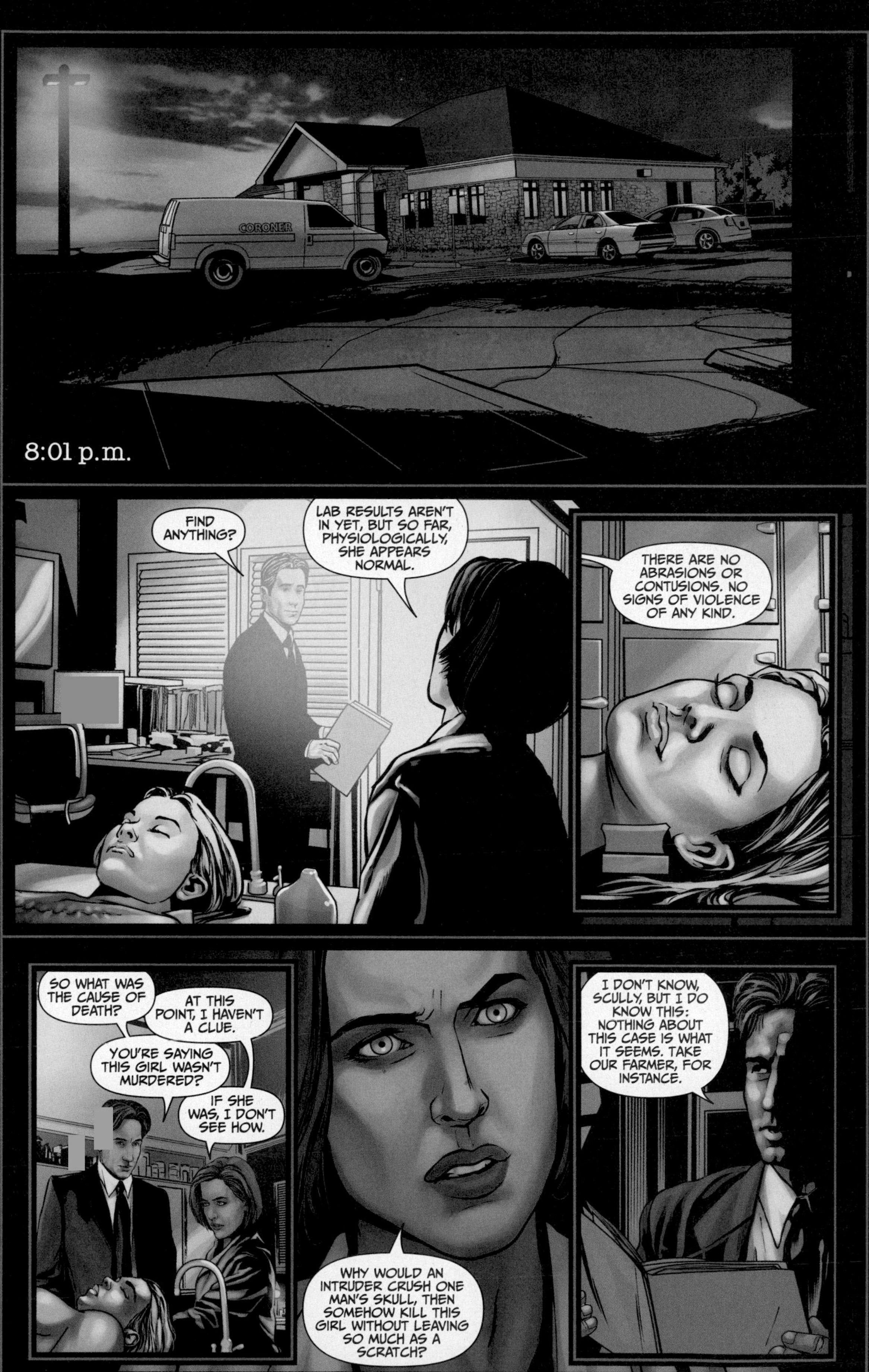
CORONER
8:01 p.m.
FIND ANYTHING?
LAB RESULTS AREN'T IN YET, BUT SO FAR, PHYSIOLOGICALLY, SHE APPEARS NORMAL.
THERE ARE NO ABRASIONS OR CONTUSIONS. NO SIGNS OF VIOLENCE OF ANY KIND.
SO WHAT WAS THE CAUSE OF DEATH?
AT THIS POINT, I HAVEN'T A CLUE.
YOU'RE SAYING THIS GIRL WASN'T MURDERED?
IF SHE WAS, I DON'T SEE HOW.
WHY WOULD AN INTRUDER CRUSH ONE MAN'S SKULL, THEN SOMEHOW KILL THIS GIRL WITHOUT LEAVING SO MUCH AS A SCRATCH?
I DON'T KNOW, SCULLY, BUT I DO KNOW THIS: NOTHING ABOUT THIS CASE IS WHAT IT SEEMS. TAKE OUR FARMER, FOR INSTANCE.

IT TURNS OUT HIS NAME WASN'T VIRGIL CANDLESS, BUT ARTHUR RAKEY.

ARTHUR RAKEY

choked until
Suffocation
wanted to br
Never was a
senter

"RAKEY WAS AWAITING TRIAL FOR A SERIES OF STRANGULATION MURDERS WHEN HE ESCAPED BY KILLING A PRISON GUARD. *IN 1991.*"

THE SAME YEAR ROBIN BENTY WAS ABDUCTED?

RAKEY ESCAPED ONLY HOURS BEFORE SHE WAS SEEN FOR THE LAST TIME.

"A WITNESS SAW HER CAR PARKED ON THE SHOULDER. AN UNIDENTIFIED MAN WAS HELPING HER WITH IT."

YOU THINK IT WAS YOUR ESCAPED CONVICT?

LIVING PEACEFULLY UNDER THE NAME VIRGIL CANDLESS WHILE ROBIN BENTY WAS IN HIS BASEMENT FOR 17 YEARS.

ROBIN BENTY DOESN'T LOOK LIKE SHE'S BEEN IMPRISONED ANYWHERE, MULDER. SHE LOOKS AS HEALTHY AS THE DAY SHE VANISHED.

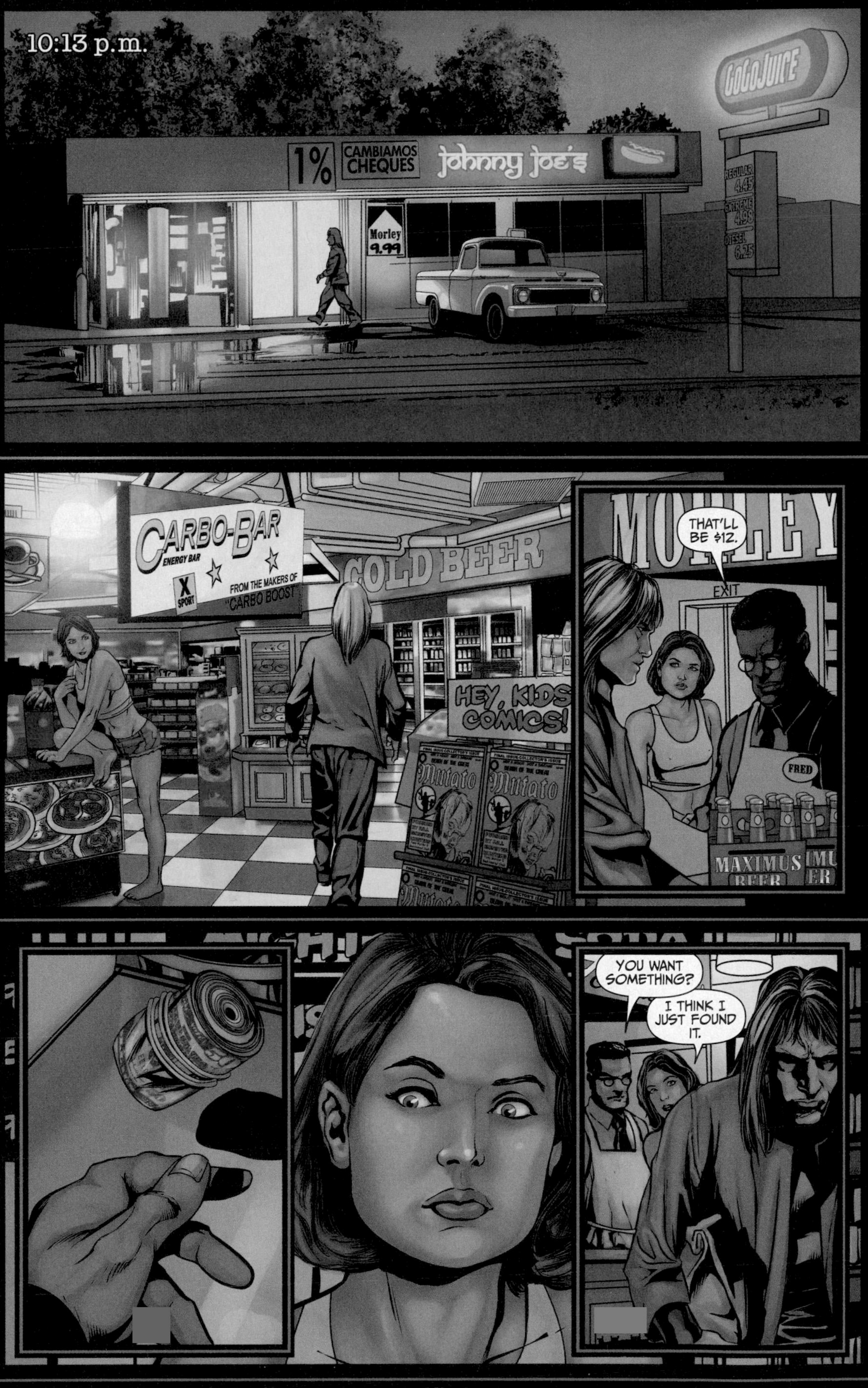
10:13 p.m.
GoGoJuice
1%
CAMBIAMOS CHEQUES
Johnny Joe's
Morley 9.99
REGULAR 4.45
EXTREME 4.98
DIESEL 6.25
CARBO-BAR
ENERGY BAR
X SPORT
FROM THE MAKERS OF "CARBO BOOST"
COLD BEER
HEY, KIDS COMICS!
Mutato
MORLEY
THAT'LL BE $12.
EXIT
FRED
MAXIMUS BEER
YOU WANT SOMETHING?
I THINK I JUST FOUND IT.

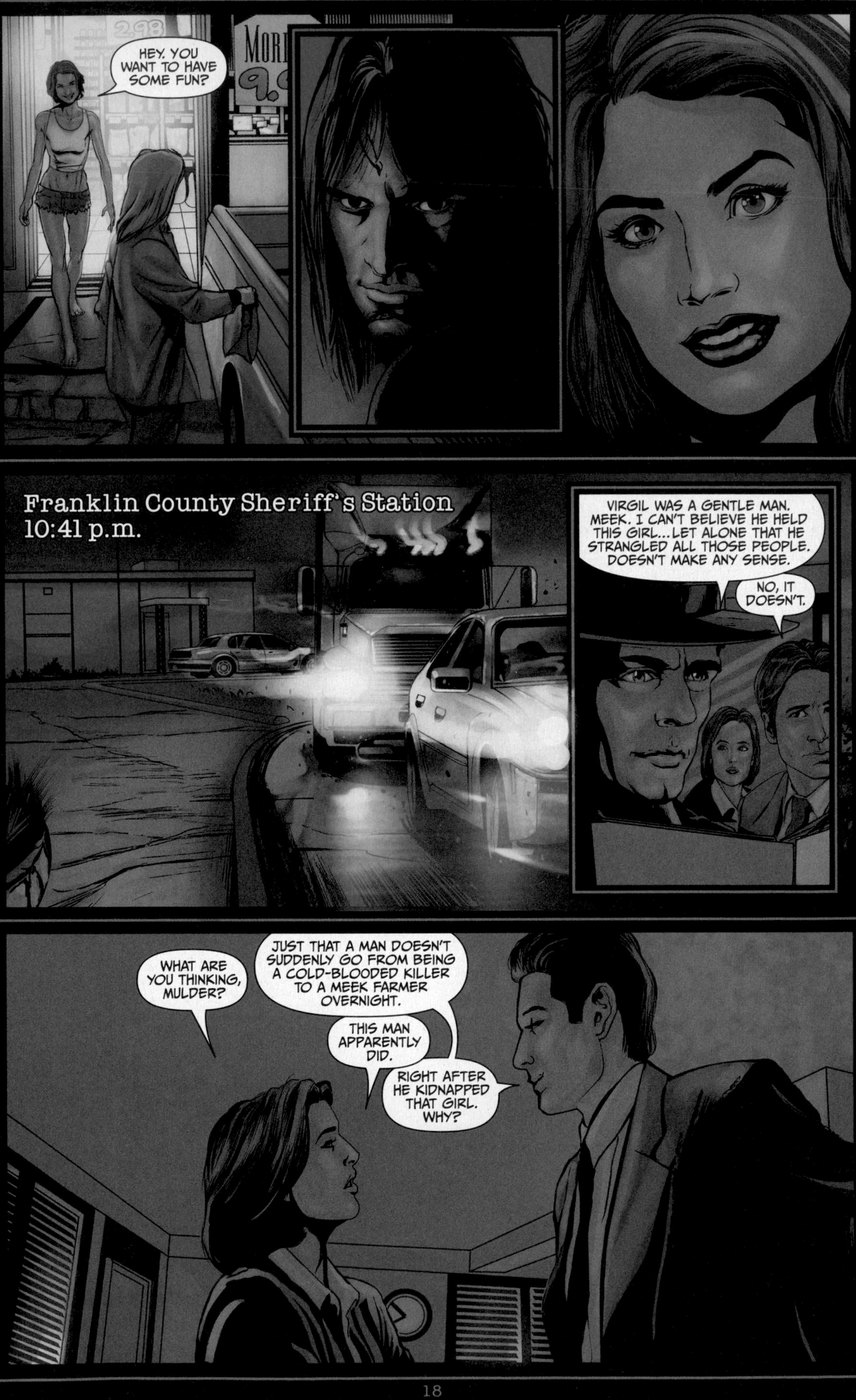

2.98
HEY. YOU WANT TO HAVE SOME FUN?
Franklin County Sheriff's Station
10:41 p.m.
VIRGIL WAS A GENTLE MAN. MEEK. I CAN'T BELIEVE HE HELD THIS GIRL... LET ALONE THAT HE STRANGLED ALL THOSE PEOPLE. DOESN'T MAKE ANY SENSE.
NO, IT DOESN'T.
WHAT ARE YOU THINKING, MULDER?
JUST THAT A MAN DOESN'T SUDDENLY GO FROM BEING A COLD-BLOODED KILLER TO A MEEK FARMER OVERNIGHT.
THIS MAN APPARENTLY DID.
RIGHT AFTER HE KIDNAPPED THAT GIRL. WHY?

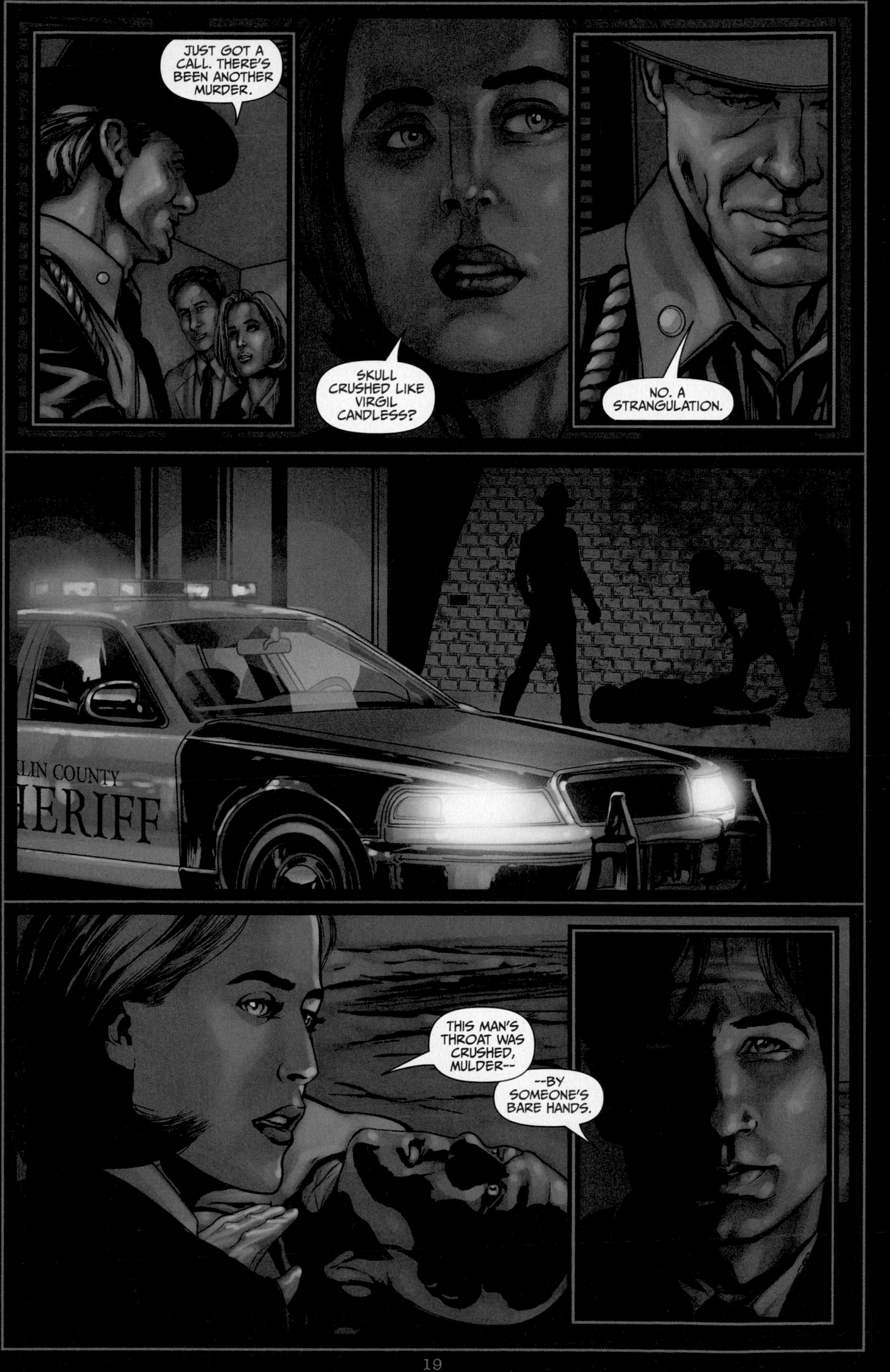
JUST GOT A CALL. THERE'S BEEN ANOTHER MURDER.
SKULL CRUSHED LIKE VIRGIL CANDLESS?
NO. A STRANGULATION.
LIN COUNTY
HERIFF
THIS MAN'S THROAT WAS CRUSHED, MULDER--
--BY SOMEONE'S BARE HANDS.

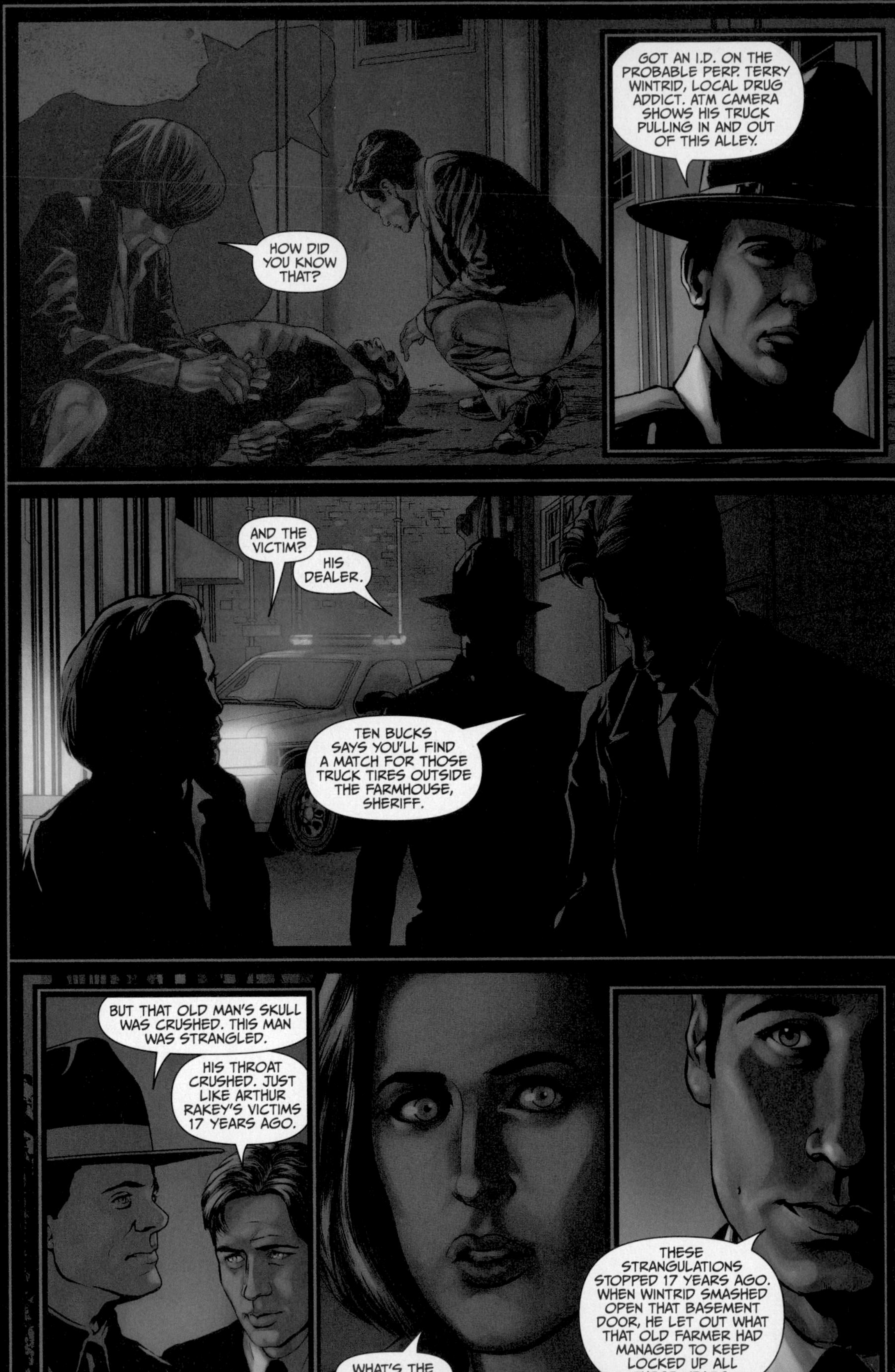
HOW DID YOU KNOW THAT?
GOT AN I.D. ON THE PROBABLE PERP. TERRY WINTRID, LOCAL DRUG ADDICT. ATM CAMERA SHOWS HIS TRUCK PULLING IN AND OUT OF THIS ALLEY.
AND THE VICTIM?
HIS DEALER.
TEN BUCKS SAYS YOU'LL FIND A MATCH FOR THOSE TRUCK TIRES OUTSIDE THE FARMHOUSE, SHERIFF.
BUT THAT OLD MAN'S SKULL WAS CRUSHED. THIS MAN WAS STRANGLED.
HIS THROAT CRUSHED. JUST LIKE ARTHUR RAKEY'S VICTIMS 17 YEARS AGO.
WHAT'S THE CONNECTION?
THESE STRANGULATIONS STOPPED 17 YEARS AGO. WHEN WINTRID SMASHED OPEN THAT BASEMENT DOOR, HE LET OUT WHAT THAT OLD FARMER HAD MANAGED TO KEEP LOCKED UP ALL THESE YEARS.

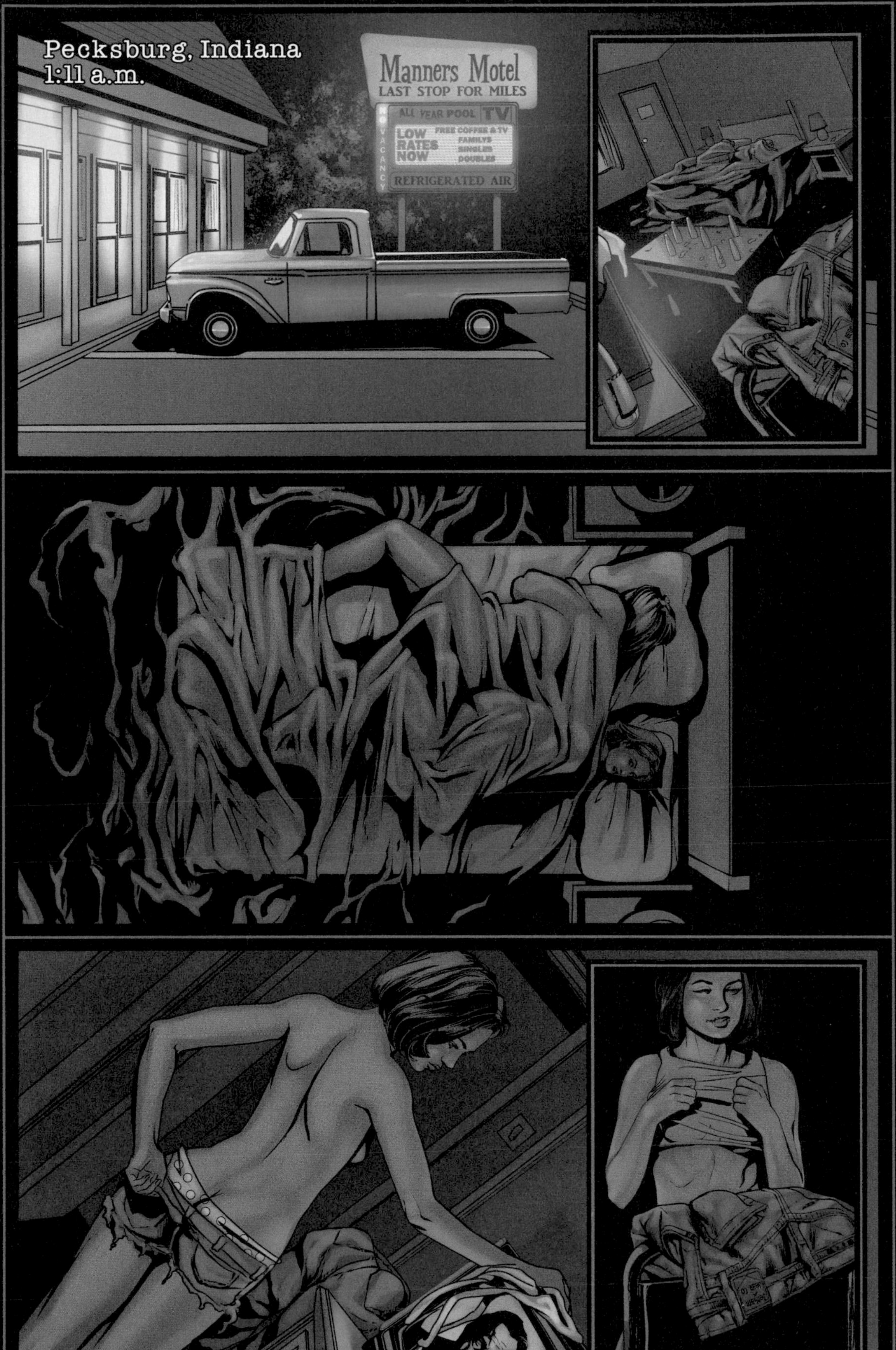
Pecksburg, Indiana
1:11 a.m.
Manners Motel
LAST STOP FOR MILES
ALL YEAR POOL
TV
LOW RATES NOW
FREE COFFEE & TV
FAMILYS
SINGLES
DOUBLES
VACANCY
REFRIGERATED AIR

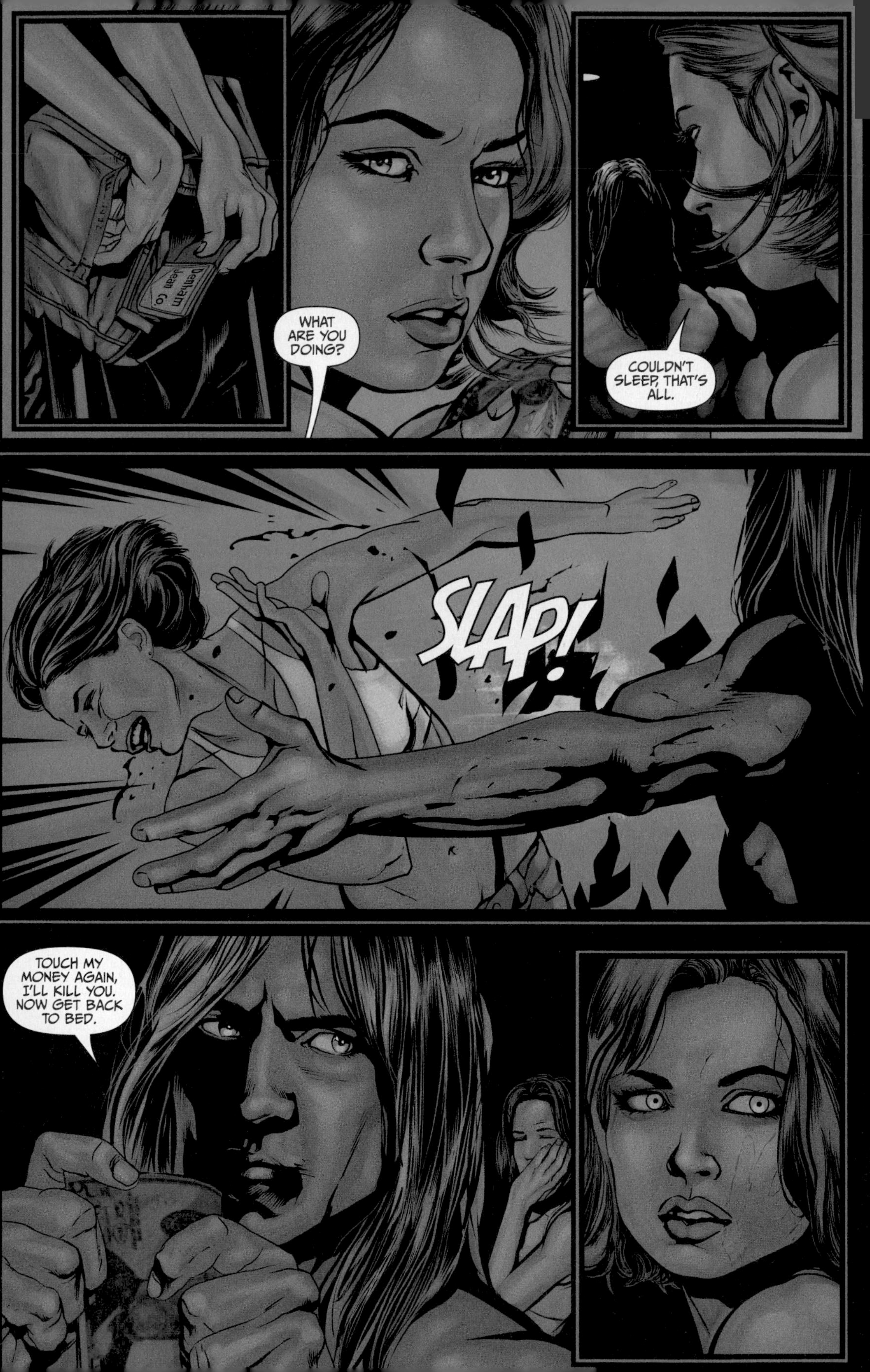
Denham Jean Co.
WHAT ARE YOU DOING?
COULDN'T SLEEP, THAT'S ALL.
SLAP!
TOUCH MY MONEY AGAIN, I'LL KILL YOU. NOW GET BACK TO BED.

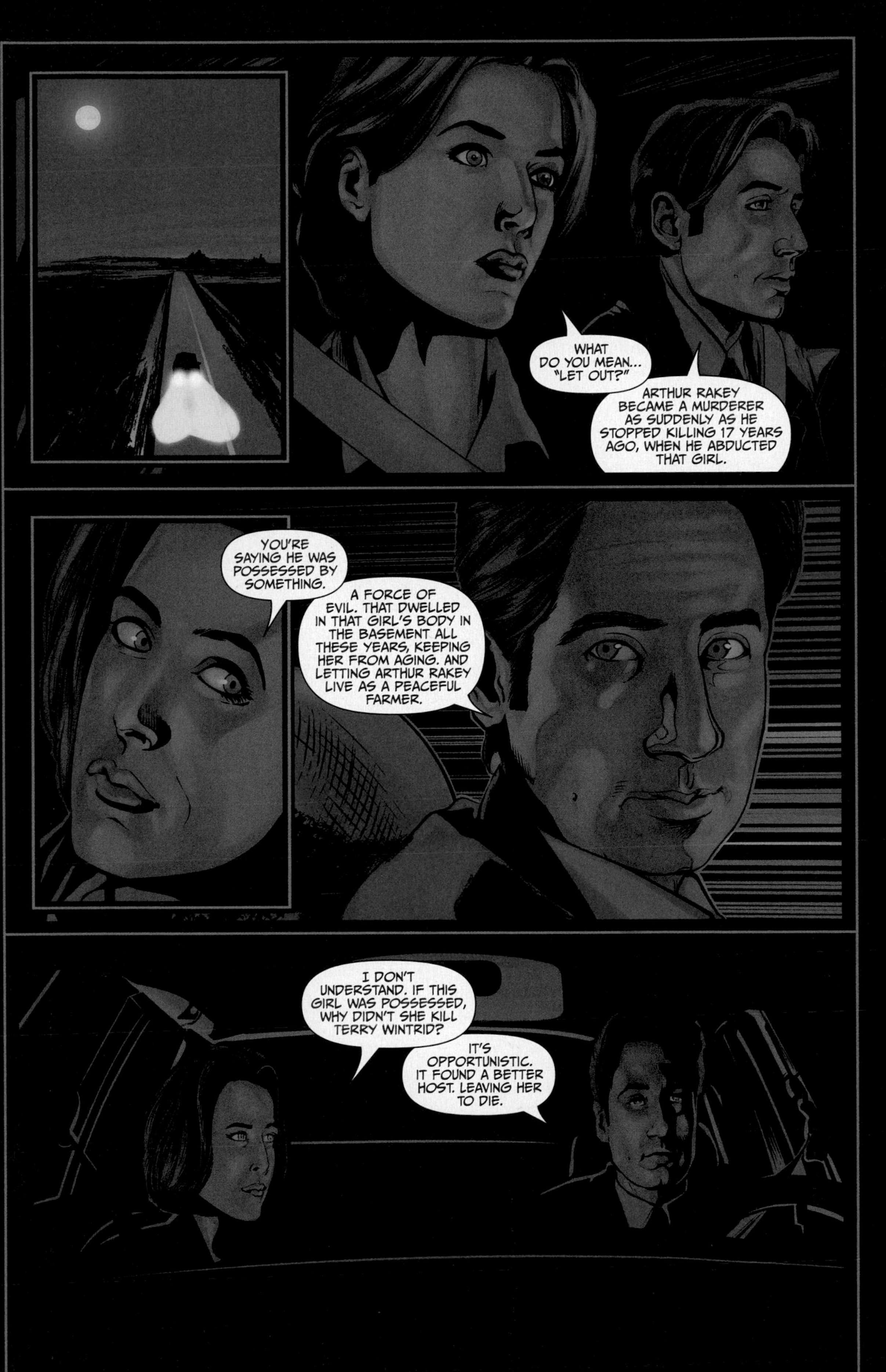
WHAT DO YOU MEAN... "LET OUT?"
ARTHUR RAKEY BECAME A MURDERER AS SUDDENLY AS HE STOPPED KILLING 17 YEARS AGO, WHEN HE ABDUCTED THAT GIRL.
YOU'RE SAYING HE WAS POSSESSED BY SOMETHING.
A FORCE OF EVIL. THAT DWELLED IN THAT GIRL'S BODY IN THE BASEMENT ALL THESE YEARS, KEEPING HER FROM AGING. AND LETTING ARTHUR RAKEY LIVE AS A PEACEFUL FARMER.
I DON'T UNDERSTAND. IF THIS GIRL WAS POSSESSED, WHY DIDN'T SHE KILL TERRY WINTRID?
IT'S OPPORTUNISTIC. IT FOUND A BETTER HOST. LEAVING HER TO DIE.

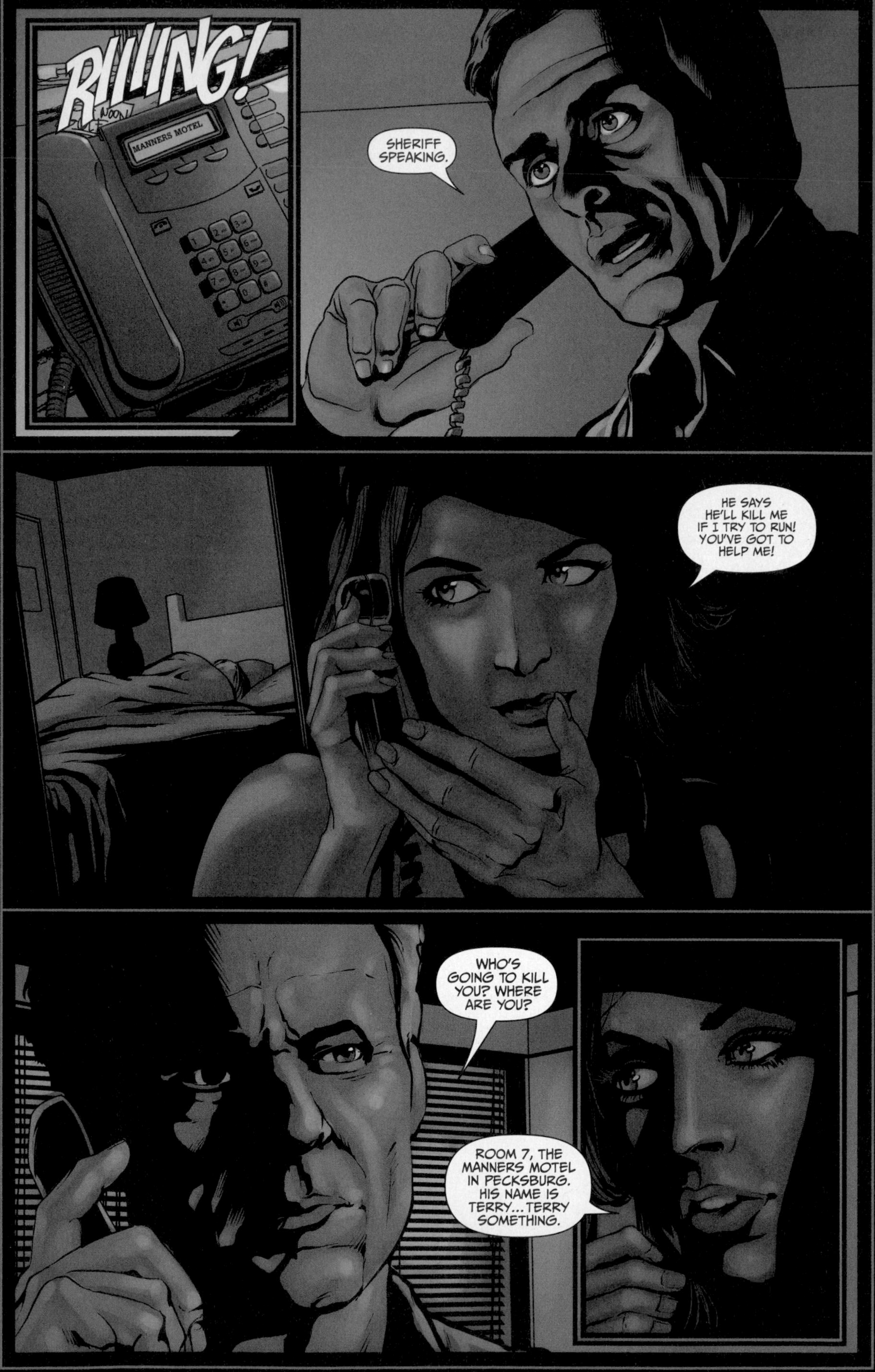
RIIIING!
MANNERS MOTEL
SHERIFF SPEAKING.
HE SAYS HE'LL KILL ME IF I TRY TO RUN! YOU'VE GOT TO HELP ME!
WHO'S GOING TO KILL YOU? WHERE ARE YOU?
ROOM 7, THE MANNERS MOTEL IN PECKSBURG. HIS NAME IS TERRY... TERRY SOMETHING.

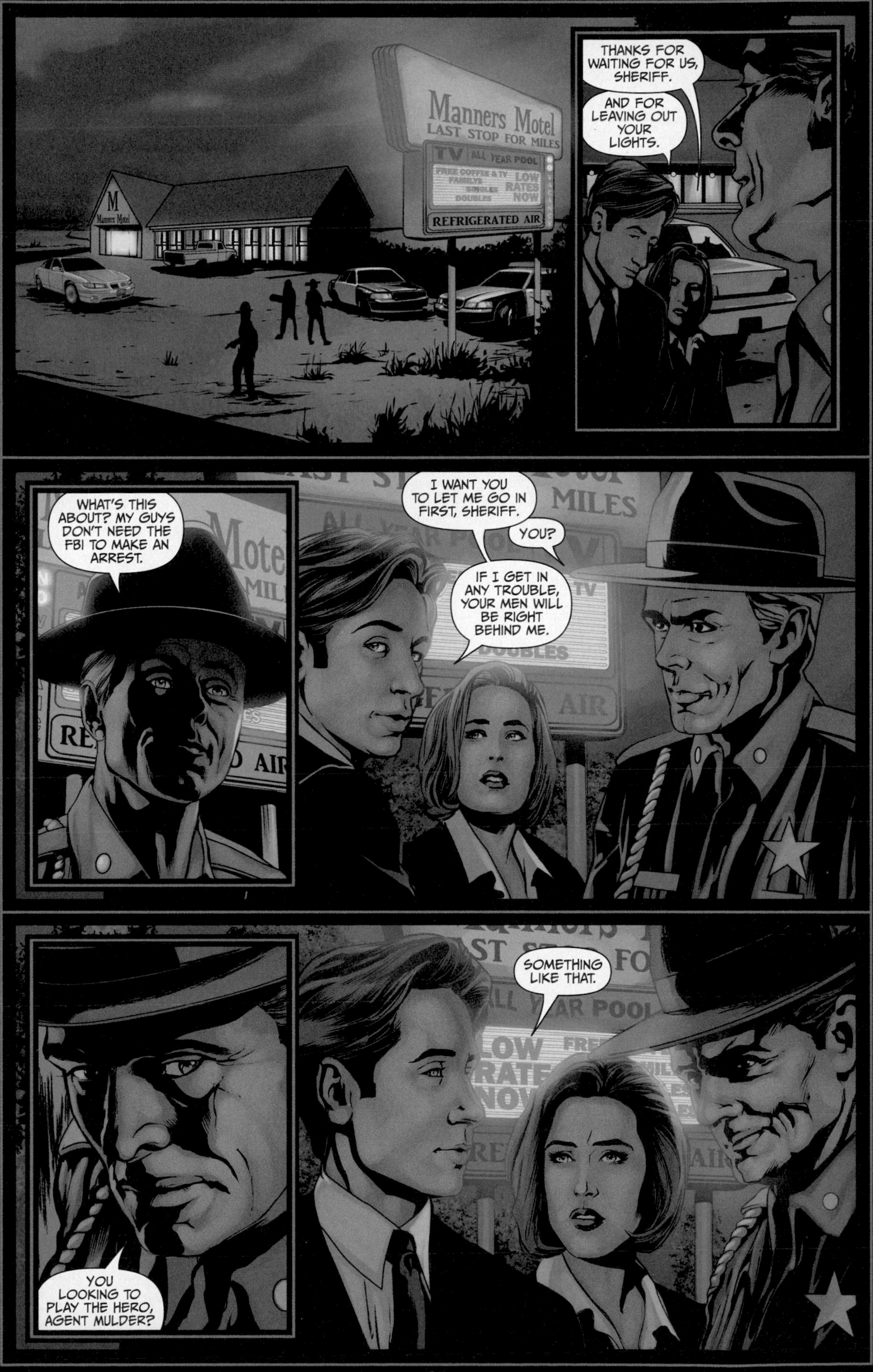
Manners Motel
LAST STOP FOR MILES
TV ALL YEAR POOL
FREE COFFEE & TV
FAMILYS
SINGLES
DOUBLES
LOW RATES NOW
REFRIGERATED AIR
THANKS FOR WAITING FOR US, SHERIFF.
AND FOR LEAVING OUT YOUR LIGHTS.
WHAT'S THIS ABOUT? MY GUYS DON'T NEED THE FBI TO MAKE AN ARREST.
I WANT YOU TO LET ME GO IN FIRST, SHERIFF.
YOU?
IF I GET IN ANY TROUBLE, YOUR MEN WILL BE RIGHT BEHIND ME.
YOU LOOKING TO PLAY THE HERO, AGENT MULDER?
SOMETHING LIKE THAT.

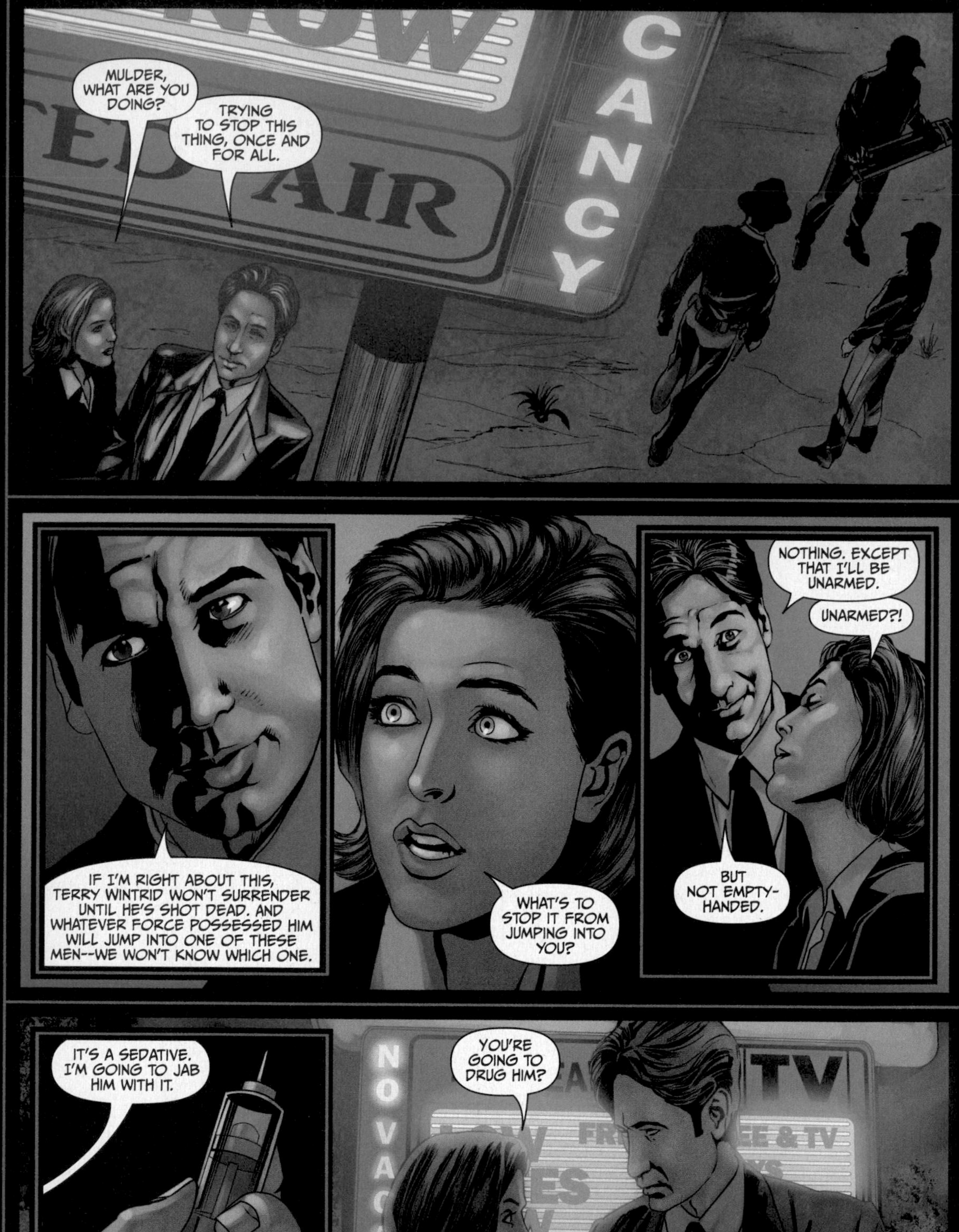
NOW
ED AIR
CANCY
MULDER, WHAT ARE YOU DOING?
TRYING TO STOP THIS THING, ONCE AND FOR ALL.
IF I'M RIGHT ABOUT THIS, TERRY WINTRID WON'T SURRENDER UNTIL HE'S SHOT DEAD. AND WHATEVER FORCE POSSESSED HIM WILL JUMP INTO ONE OF THESE MEN--WE WON'T KNOW WHICH ONE.
WHAT'S TO STOP IT FROM JUMPING INTO YOU?
NOTHING. EXCEPT THAT I'LL BE UNARMED.
UNARMED?!
BUT NOT EMPTY-HANDED.
IT'S A SEDATIVE. I'M GOING TO JAB HIM WITH IT.
YOU'RE GOING TO DRUG HIM?
NO VACANCY
TV
ANY ONE OF US COULD END UP BEING THE NEXT HOST UNLESS HE'S ISOLATED, SCULLY--JUST LIKE THAT GIRL WAS ISOLATED IN THE BASEMENT ALL THOSE YEARS.

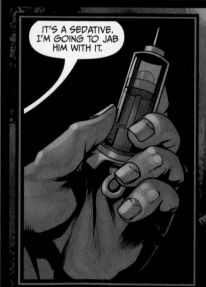

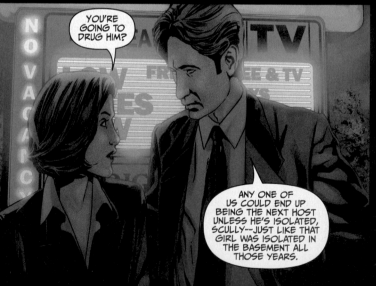

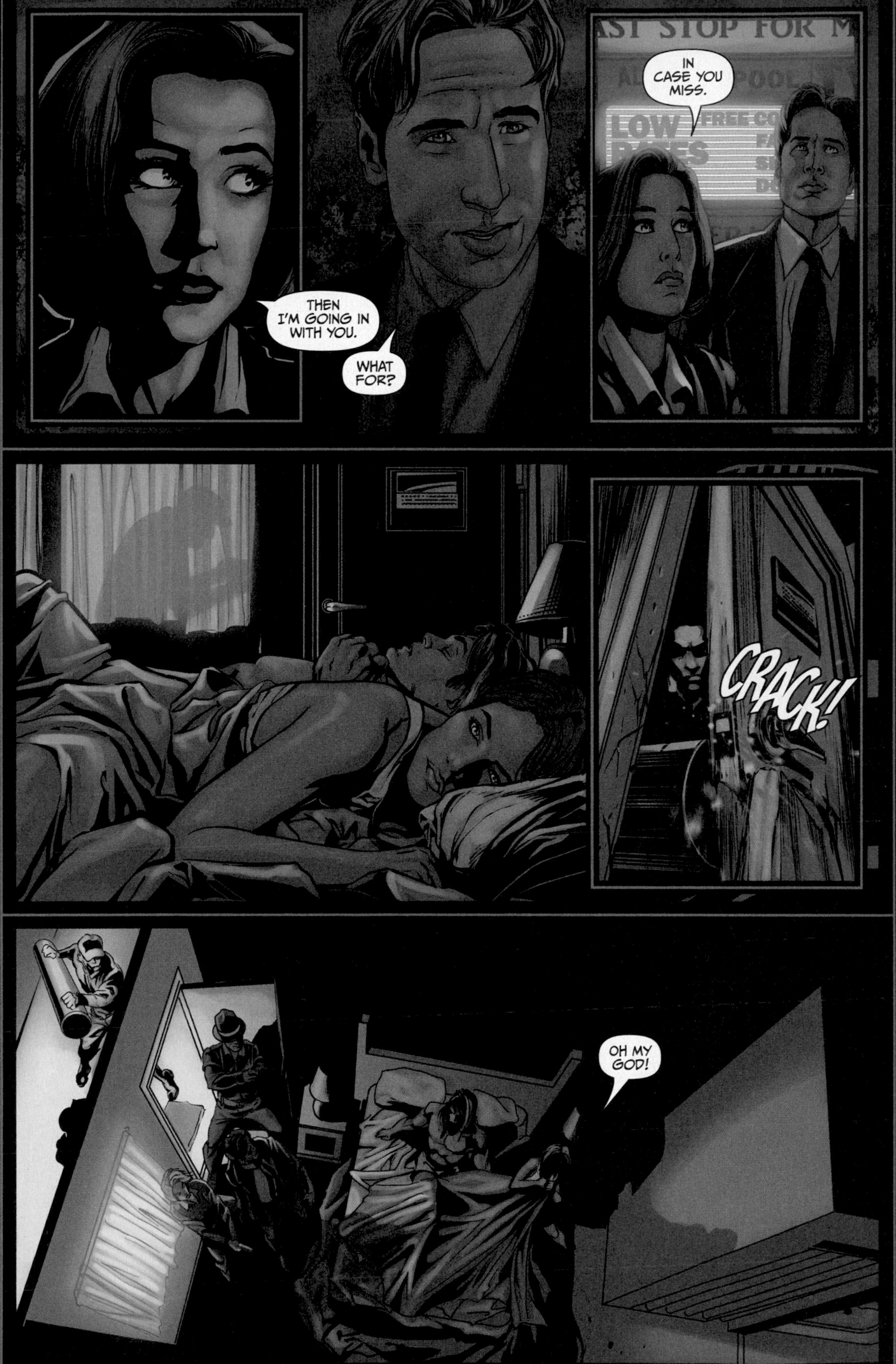
THEN I'M GOING IN WITH YOU.
WHAT FOR?
IN CASE YOU MISS.
CRACK!
OH MY GOD!

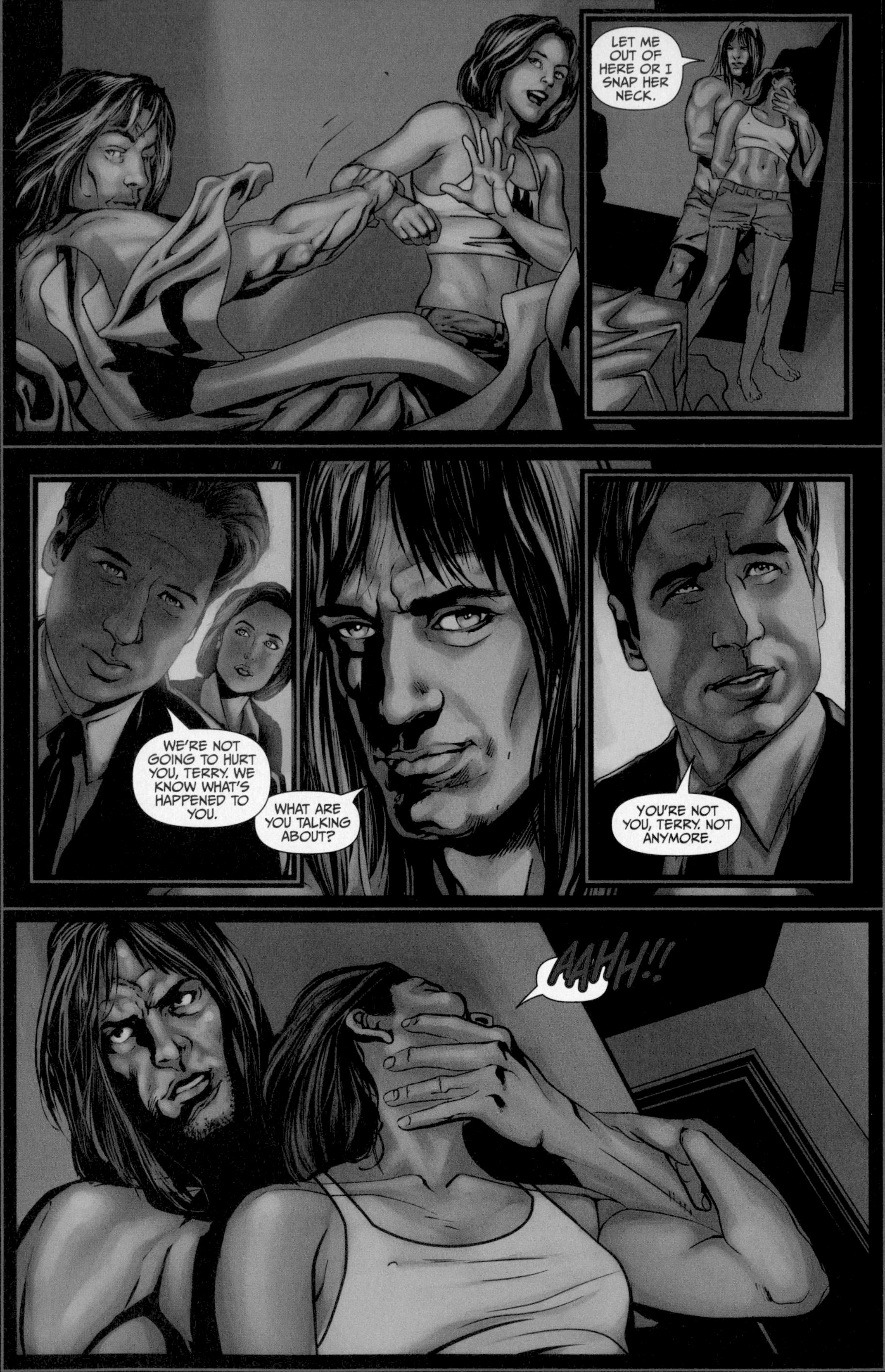
LET ME OUT OF HERE OR I SNAP HER NECK.
WE'RE NOT GOING TO HURT YOU, TERRY. WE KNOW WHAT'S HAPPENED TO YOU.
WHAT ARE YOU TALKING ABOUT?
YOU'RE NOT YOU, TERRY. NOT ANYMORE.
AAHH!!

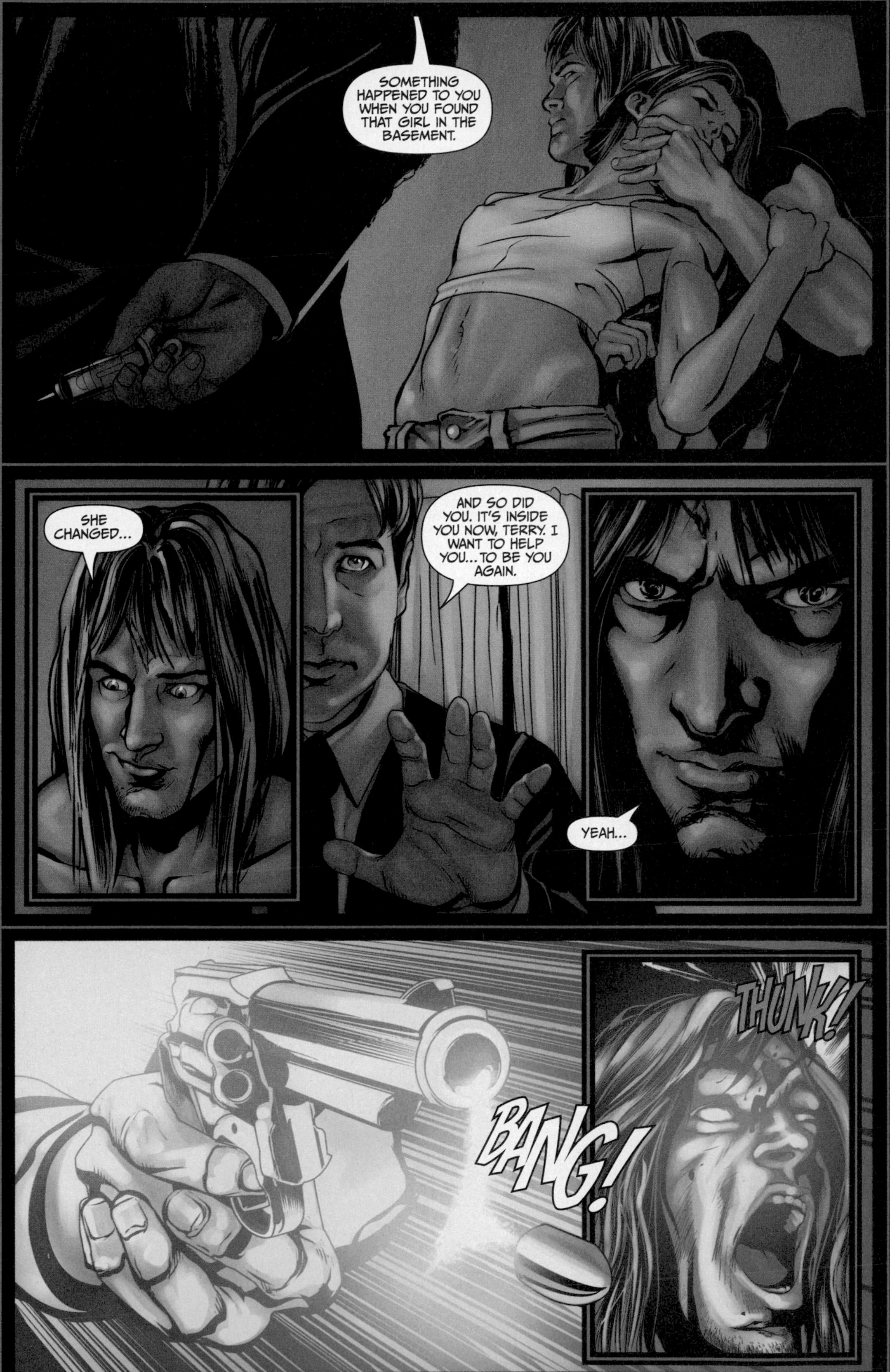
SOMETHING HAPPENED TO YOU WHEN YOU FOUND THAT GIRL IN THE BASEMENT.
SHE CHANGED...
AND SO DID YOU. IT'S INSIDE YOU NOW, TERRY. I WANT TO HELP YOU...TO BE YOU AGAIN.
YEAH...
BANG!
THUNK!

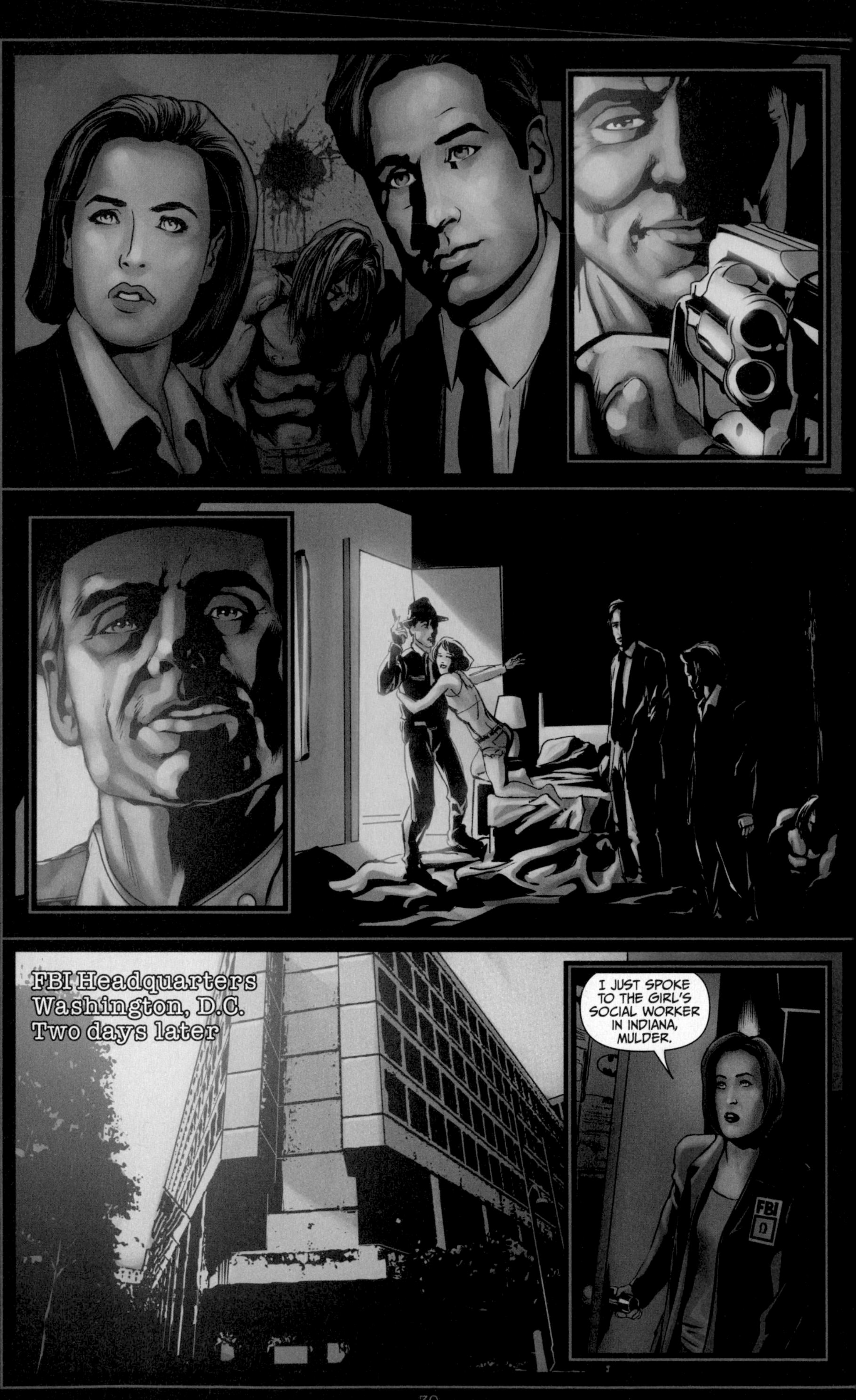
FBI Headquarters
Washington, D.C.
Two days later
I JUST SPOKE TO THE GIRL'S SOCIAL WORKER IN INDIANA, MULDER.

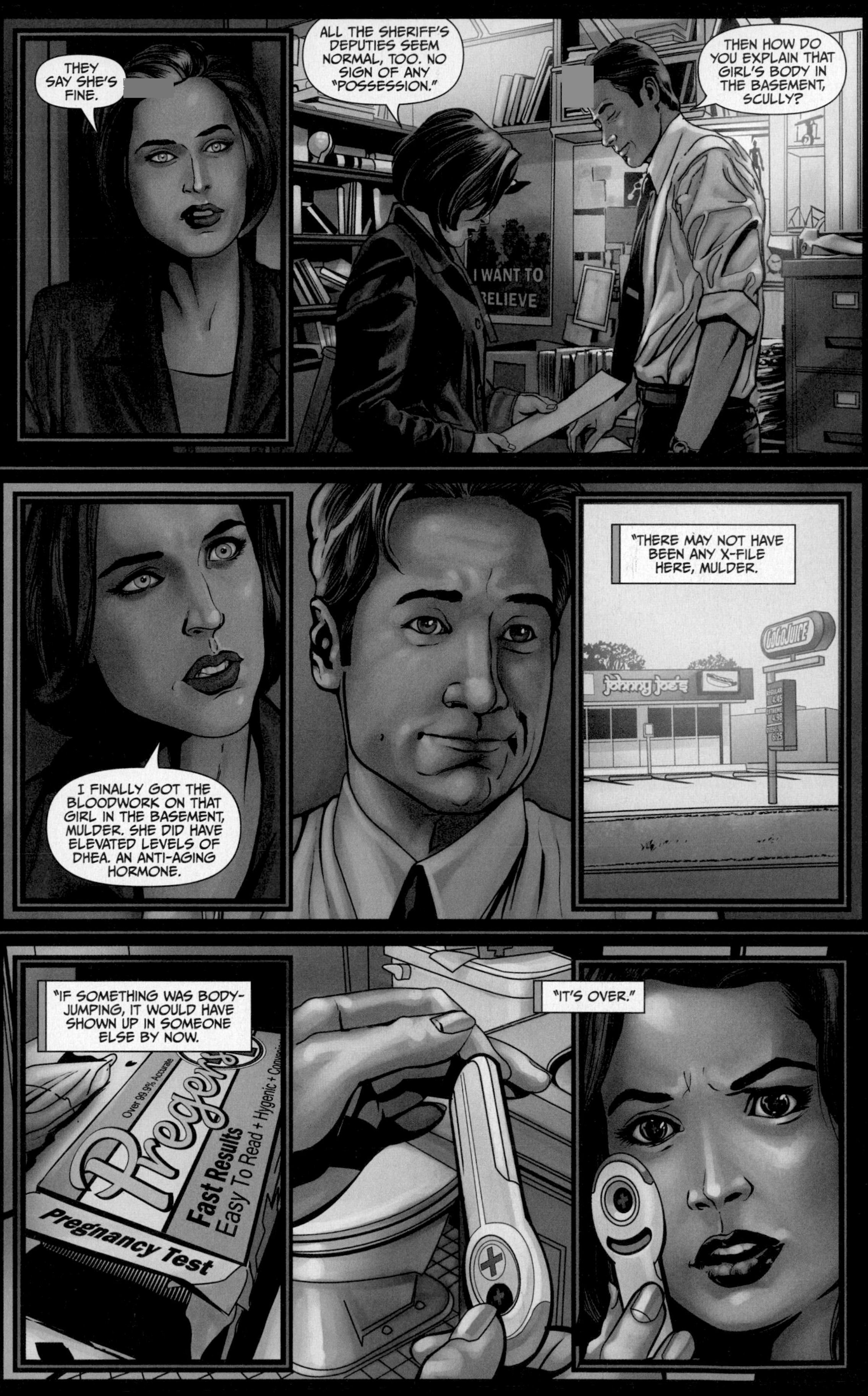
THEY SAY SHE'S FINE.
ALL THE SHERIFF'S DEPUTIES SEEM NORMAL, TOO. NO SIGN OF ANY "POSSESSION."
I WANT TO BELIEVE
THEN HOW DO YOU EXPLAIN THAT GIRL'S BODY IN THE BASEMENT, SCULLY?
I FINALLY GOT THE BLOODWORK ON THAT GIRL IN THE BASEMENT, MULDER. SHE DID HAVE ELEVATED LEVELS OF DHEA. AN ANTI-AGING HORMONE.
"THERE MAY NOT HAVE BEEN ANY X-FILE HERE, MULDER.
GoGo Juice
Johnny Joe's
"IF SOMETHING WAS BODY-JUMPING, IT WOULD HAVE SHOWN UP IN SOMEONE ELSE BY NOW.
Over 99.9% Accurate
Fast Results
Pregnancy Test
"IT'S OVER."

Chapter Two

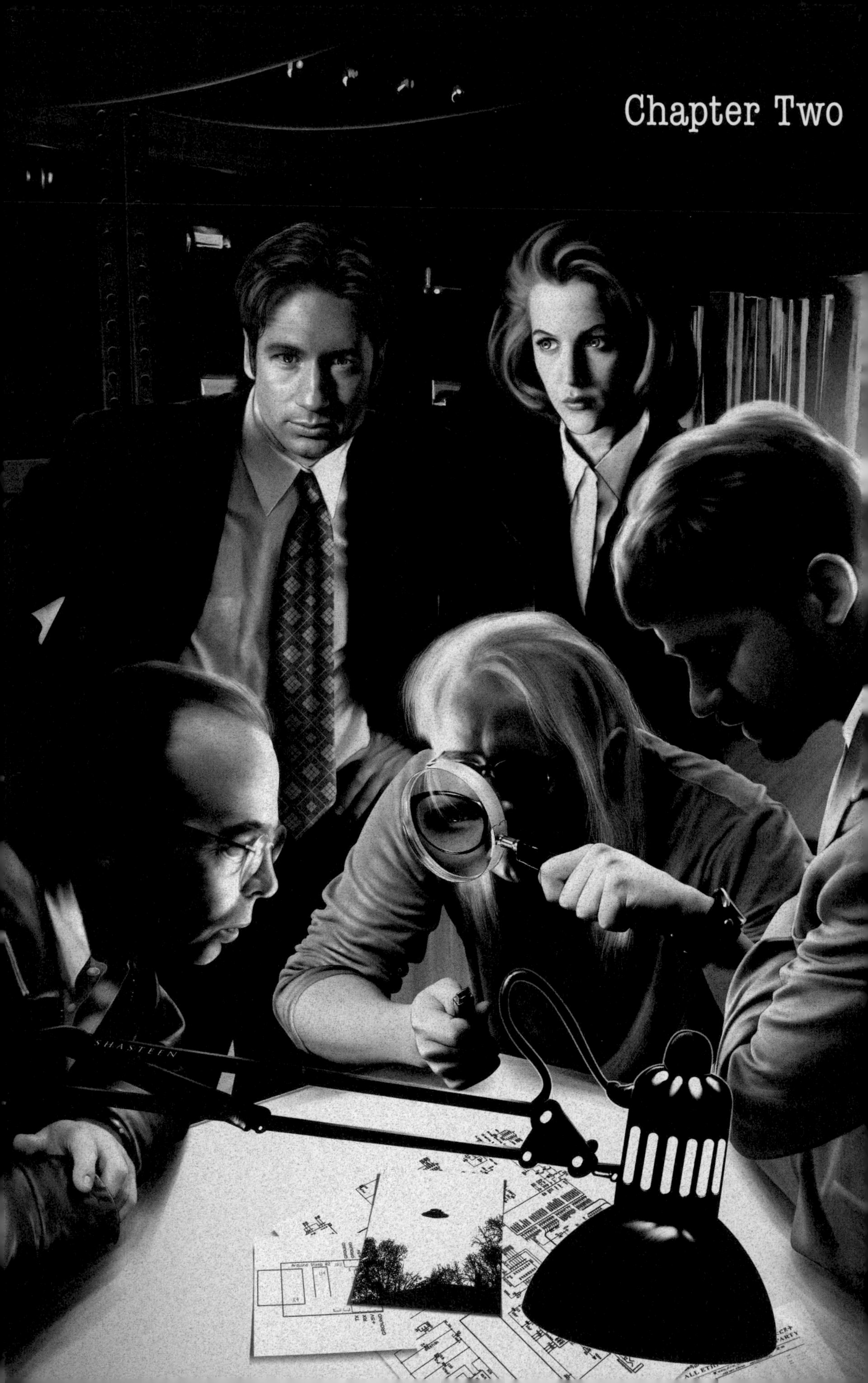
SHASTEEN

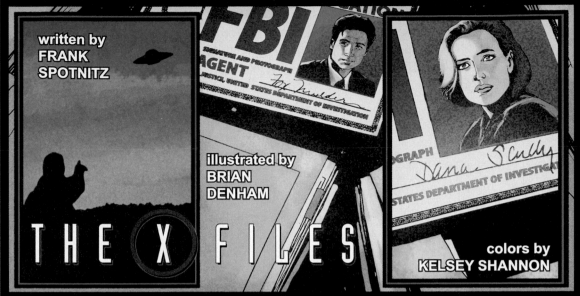

written by
FRANK SPOTNITZ
FBI
AGENT
illustrated by
BRIAN DENHAM
THE X FILES
STATES DEPARTMENT OF INVESTIGAT
colors by
KELSEY SHANNON
edited by
SHANNON ERIC DENTON
letters by
ED DUKESHIRE
created by
CHRIS CARTER
"HE COULDN'T SLEEP.
SCIENTIFIC TRAILBLAZ
Falls Church, Virginia
3:02 a.m. several weeks ago.

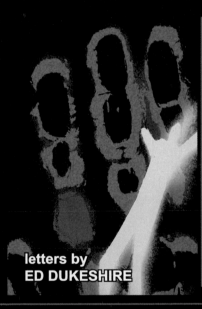

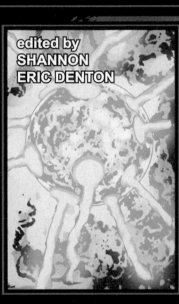

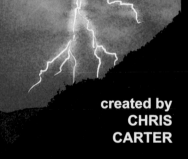

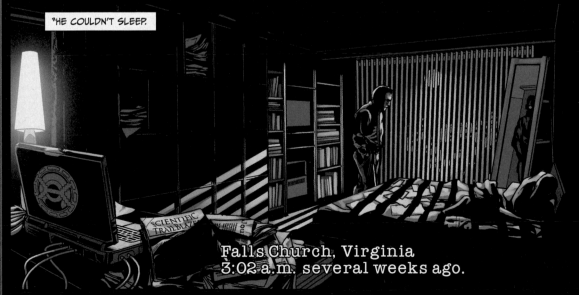

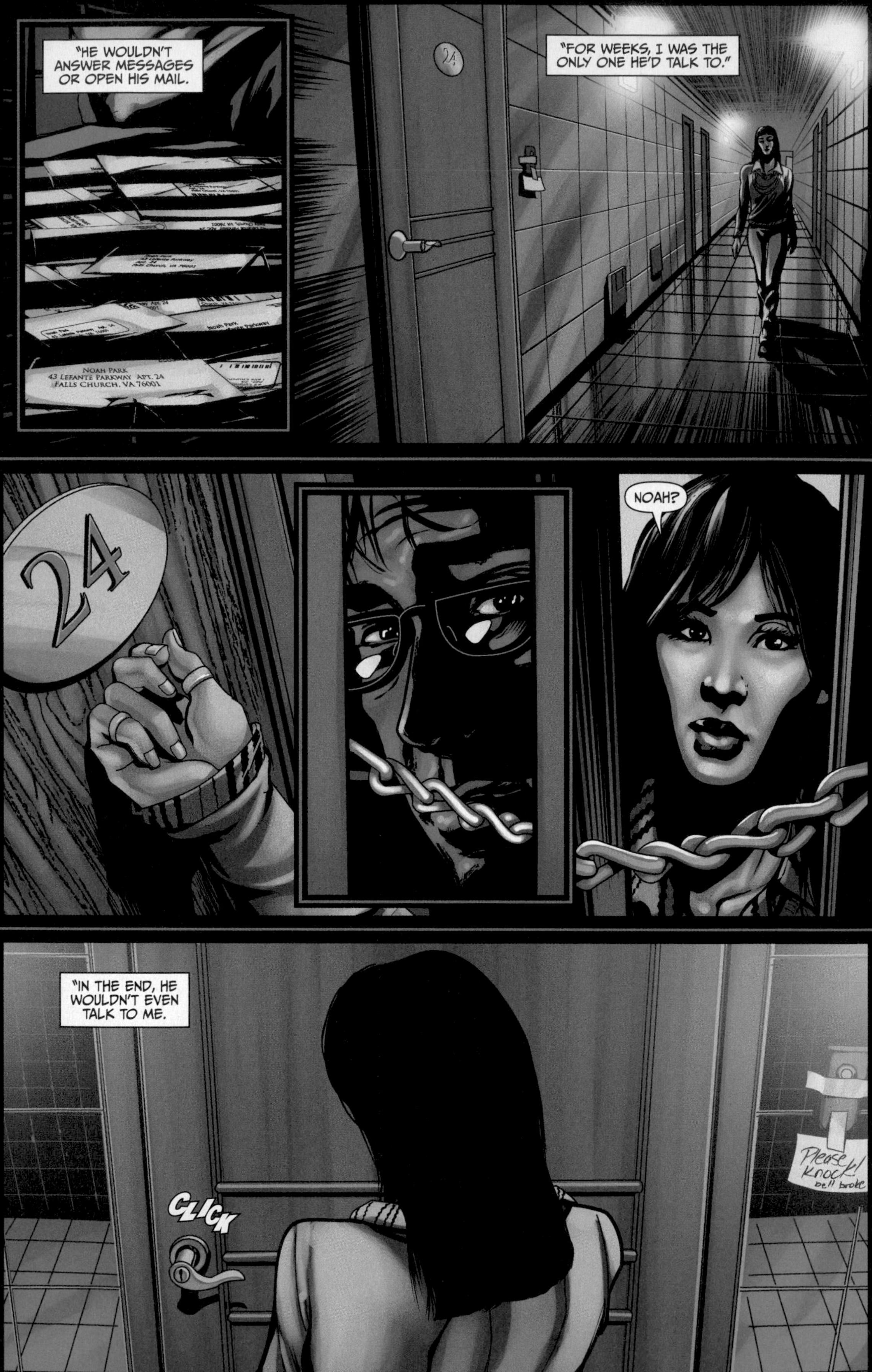
"HE WOULDN'T ANSWER MESSAGES OR OPEN HIS MAIL.
NOAH PARK
43 LEFANTE PARKWAY APT. 24
FALLS CHURCH, VA 76001
"FOR WEEKS, I WAS THE ONLY ONE HE'D TALK TO."
NOAH?
"IN THE END, HE WOULDN'T EVEN TALK TO ME.
Please! Knock! bell broke
CLICK

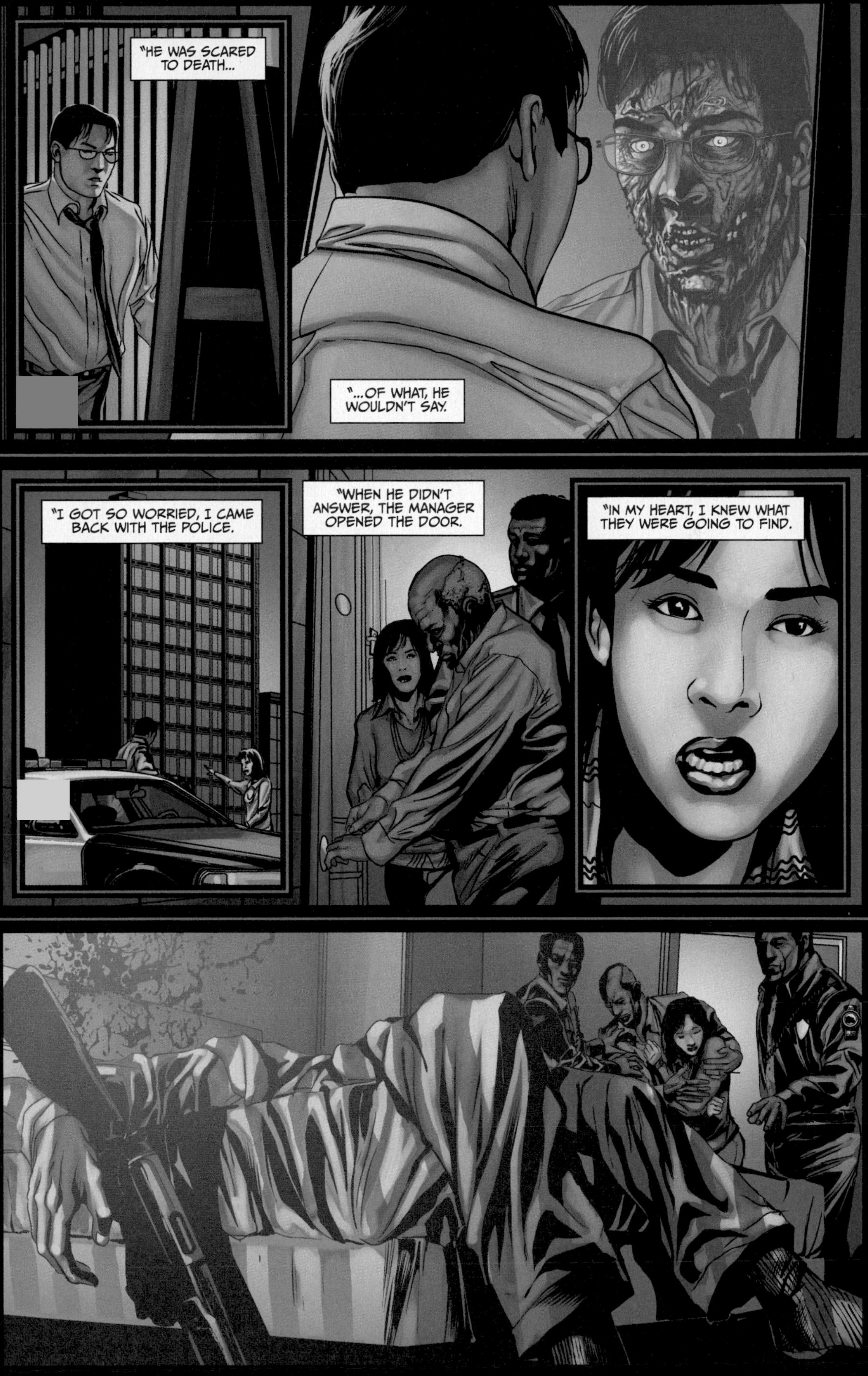
"HE WAS SCARED TO DEATH...
"...OF WHAT, HE WOULDN'T SAY.
"I GOT SO WORRIED, I CAME BACK WITH THE POLICE.
"WHEN HE DIDN'T ANSWER, THE MANAGER OPENED THE DOOR.
"IN MY HEART, I KNEW WHAT THEY WERE GOING TO FIND.

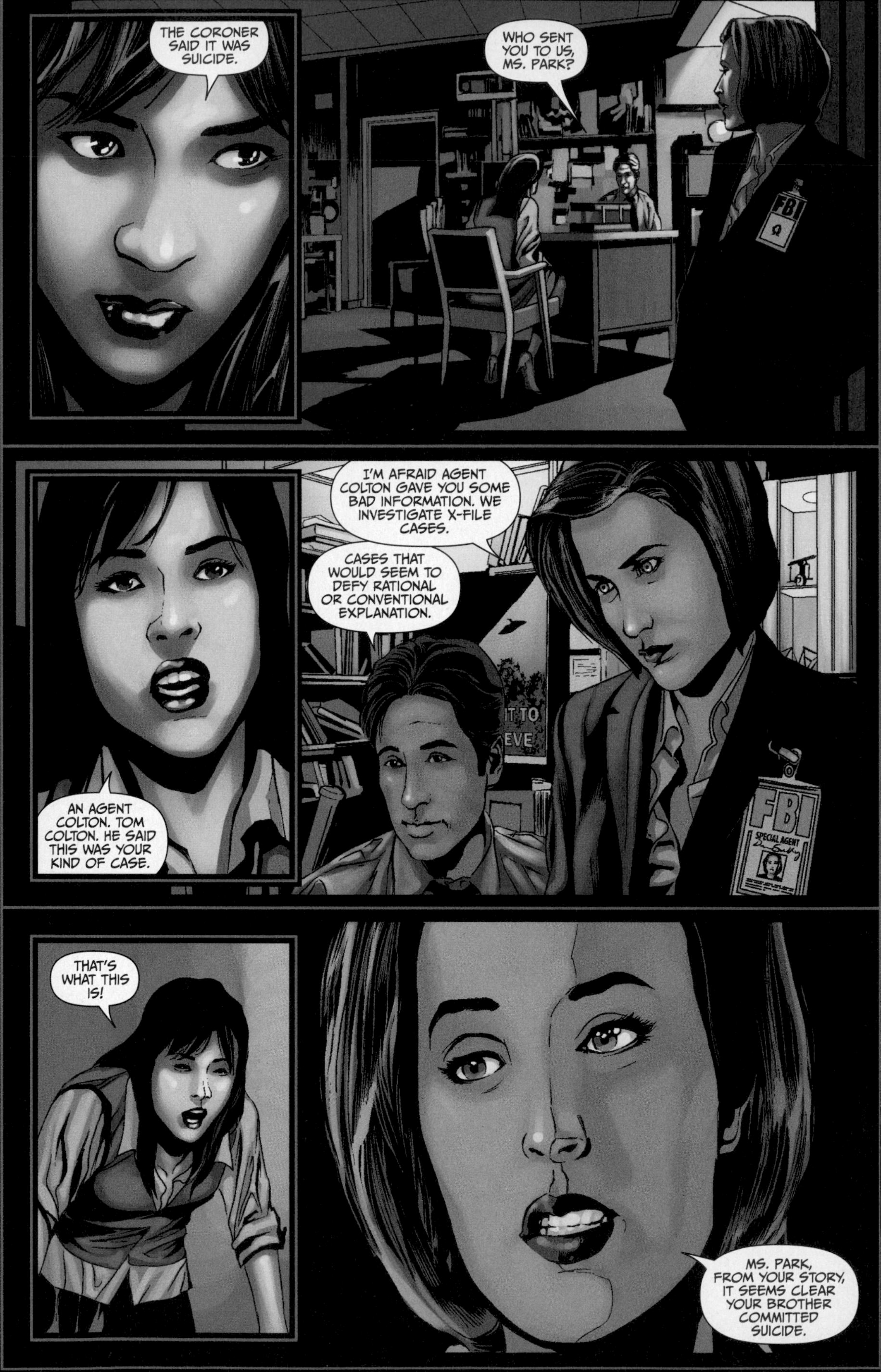
THE CORONER SAID IT WAS SUICIDE.
WHO SENT YOU TO US, MS. PARK?
AN AGENT COLTON. TOM COLTON. HE SAID THIS WAS YOUR KIND OF CASE.
I'M AFRAID AGENT COLTON GAVE YOU SOME BAD INFORMATION. WE INVESTIGATE X-FILE CASES.
CASES THAT WOULD SEEM TO DEFY RATIONAL OR CONVENTIONAL EXPLANATION.
FBI
SPECIAL AGENT
THAT'S WHAT THIS IS!
MS. PARK, FROM YOUR STORY, IT SEEMS CLEAR YOUR BROTHER COMMITTED SUICIDE.

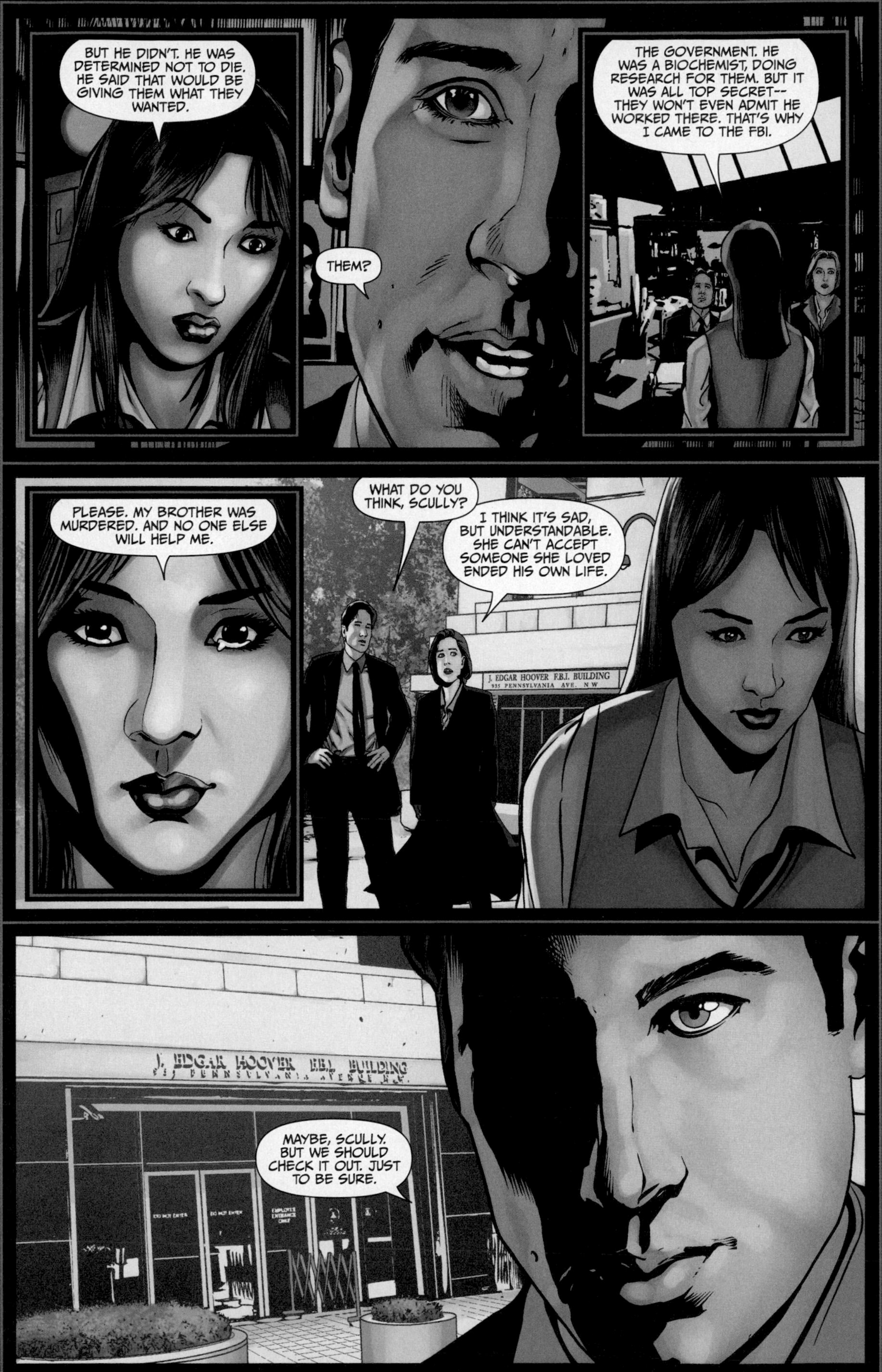

BUT HE DIDN'T. HE WAS DETERMINED NOT TO DIE. HE SAID THAT WOULD BE GIVING THEM WHAT THEY WANTED.
THEM?
THE GOVERNMENT. HE WAS A BIOCHEMIST, DOING RESEARCH FOR THEM. BUT IT WAS ALL TOP SECRET-- THEY WON'T EVEN ADMIT HE WORKED THERE. THAT'S WHY I CAME TO THE FBI.
PLEASE. MY BROTHER WAS MURDERED. AND NO ONE ELSE WILL HELP ME.
WHAT DO YOU THINK, SCULLY?
I THINK IT'S SAD, BUT UNDERSTANDABLE. SHE CAN'T ACCEPT SOMEONE SHE LOVED ENDED HIS OWN LIFE.
J. EDGAR HOOVER F.B.I. BUILDING
935 PENNSYLVANIA AVE. NW
J. EDGAR HOOVER F.B.I. BUILDING
MAYBE, SCULLY. BUT WE SHOULD CHECK IT OUT. JUST TO BE SURE.

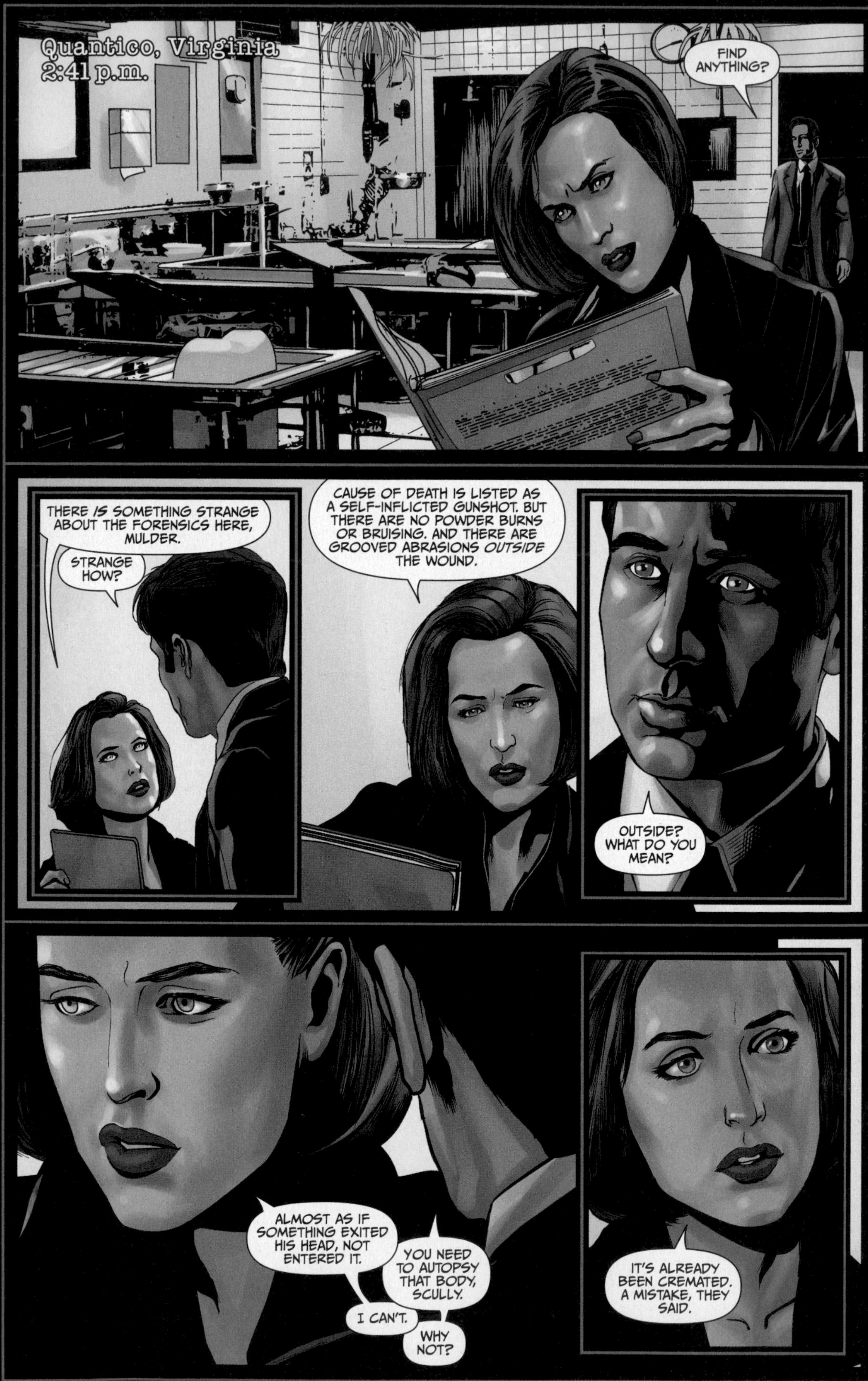
Quantico, Virginia
2:41 p.m.
FIND ANYTHING?
THERE *IS* SOMETHING STRANGE ABOUT THE FORENSICS HERE, MULDER.
STRANGE HOW?
CAUSE OF DEATH IS LISTED AS A SELF-INFLICTED GUNSHOT. BUT THERE ARE NO POWDER BURNS OR BRUISING. AND THERE ARE GROOVED ABRASIONS *OUTSIDE* THE WOUND.
OUTSIDE? WHAT DO YOU MEAN?
ALMOST AS IF SOMETHING EXITED HIS HEAD, NOT ENTERED IT.
YOU NEED TO AUTOPSY THAT BODY, SCULLY.
I CAN'T.
WHY NOT?
IT'S ALREADY BEEN CREMATED. A MISTAKE, THEY SAID.

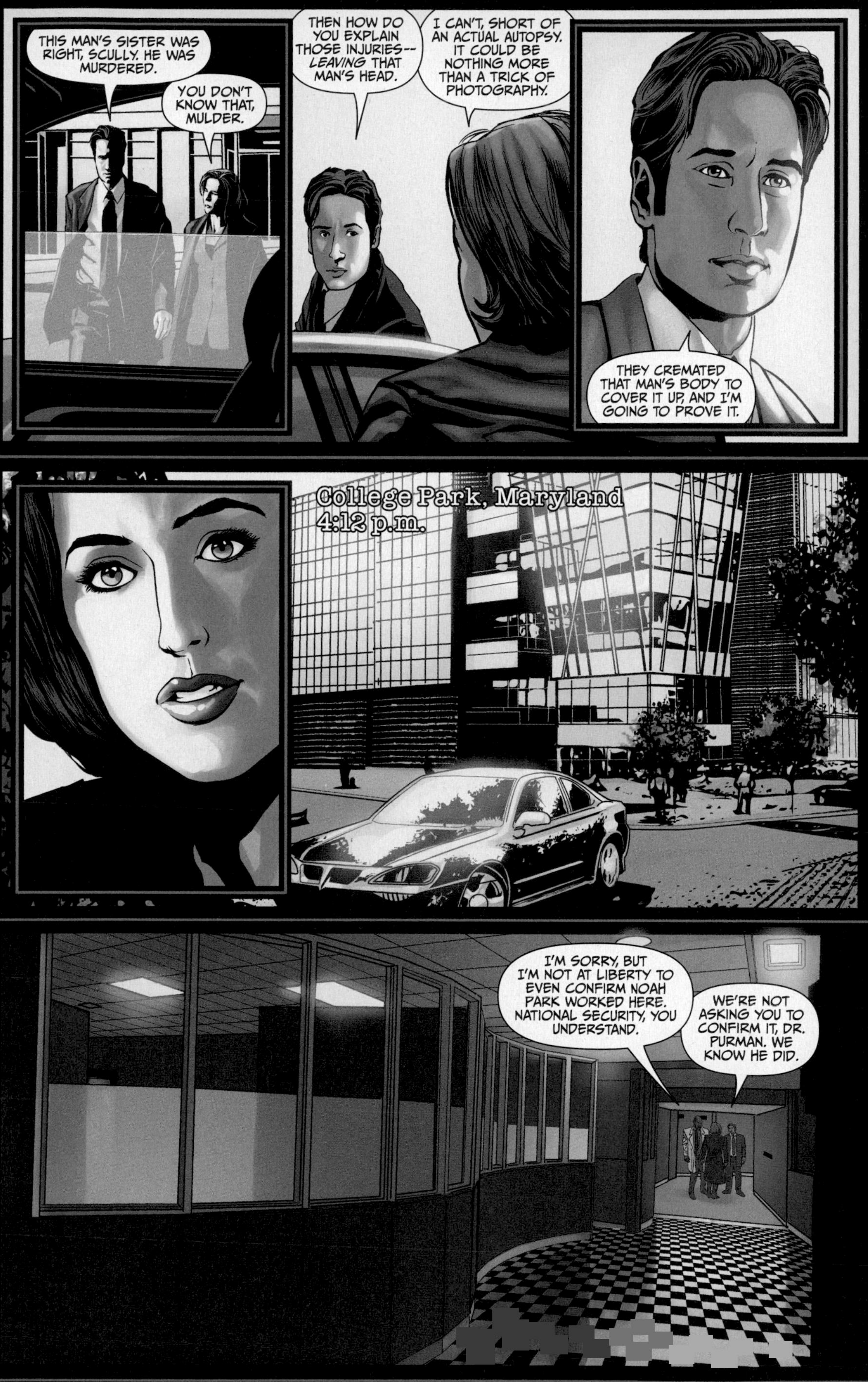

THIS MAN'S SISTER WAS RIGHT, SCULLY. HE WAS MURDERED.
YOU DON'T KNOW THAT, MULDER.
THEN HOW DO YOU EXPLAIN THOSE INJURIES-- *LEAVING* THAT MAN'S HEAD.
I CAN'T, SHORT OF AN ACTUAL AUTOPSY. IT COULD BE NOTHING MORE THAN A TRICK OF PHOTOGRAPHY.
THEY CREMATED THAT MAN'S BODY TO COVER IT UP, AND I'M GOING TO PROVE IT.
College Park, Maryland
4:12 p.m.
I'M SORRY, BUT I'M NOT AT LIBERTY TO EVEN CONFIRM NOAH PARK WORKED HERE. NATIONAL SECURITY, YOU UNDERSTAND.
WE'RE NOT ASKING YOU TO CONFIRM IT, DR. PURMAN. WE KNOW HE DID.

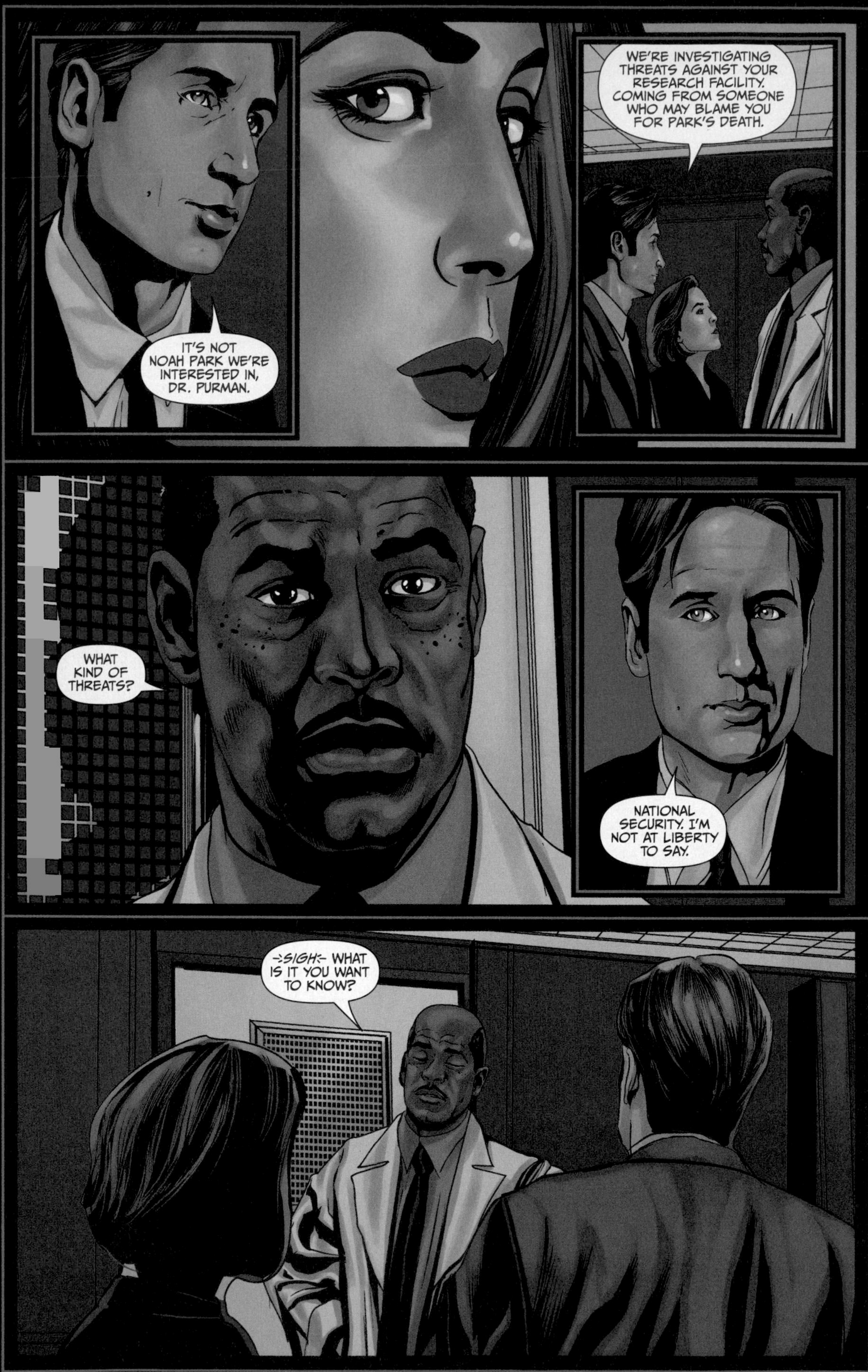
IT'S NOT NOAH PARK WE'RE INTERESTED IN, DR. PURMAN.
WE'RE INVESTIGATING THREATS AGAINST YOUR RESEARCH FACILITY. COMING FROM SOMEONE WHO MAY BLAME YOU FOR PARK'S DEATH.
WHAT KIND OF THREATS?
NATIONAL SECURITY. I'M NOT AT LIBERTY TO SAY.
-SIGH- WHAT IS IT YOU WANT TO KNOW?

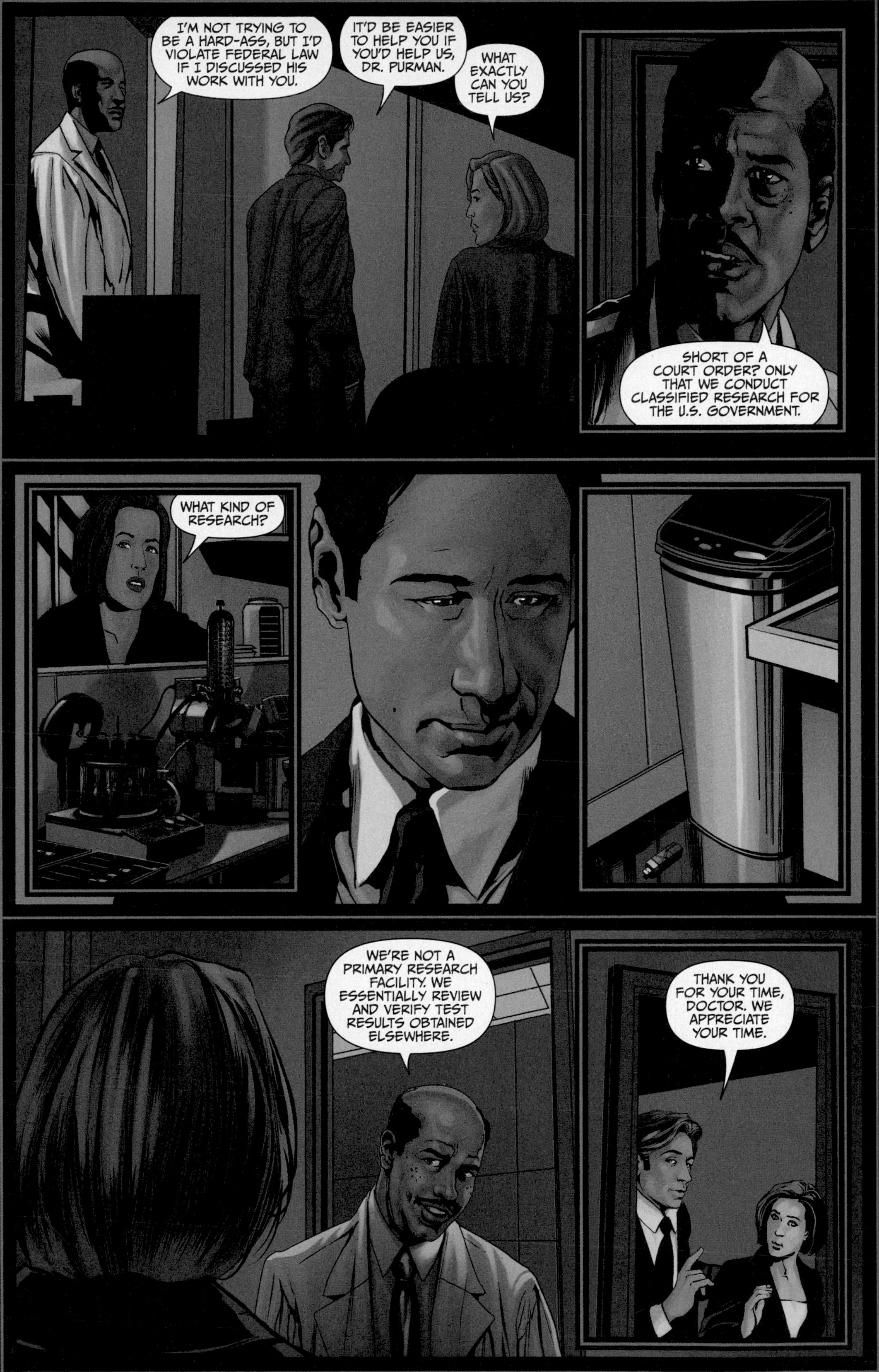
I'M NOT TRYING TO BE A HARD-ASS, BUT I'D VIOLATE FEDERAL LAW IF I DISCUSSED HIS WORK WITH YOU.
IT'D BE EASIER TO HELP YOU IF YOU'D HELP US, DR. PURMAN.
WHAT EXACTLY CAN YOU TELL US?
SHORT OF A COURT ORDER? ONLY THAT WE CONDUCT CLASSIFIED RESEARCH FOR THE U.S. GOVERNMENT.
WHAT KIND OF RESEARCH?
WE'RE NOT A PRIMARY RESEARCH FACILITY. WE ESSENTIALLY REVIEW AND VERIFY TEST RESULTS OBTAINED ELSEWHERE.
THANK YOU FOR YOUR TIME, DOCTOR. WE APPRECIATE YOUR TIME.

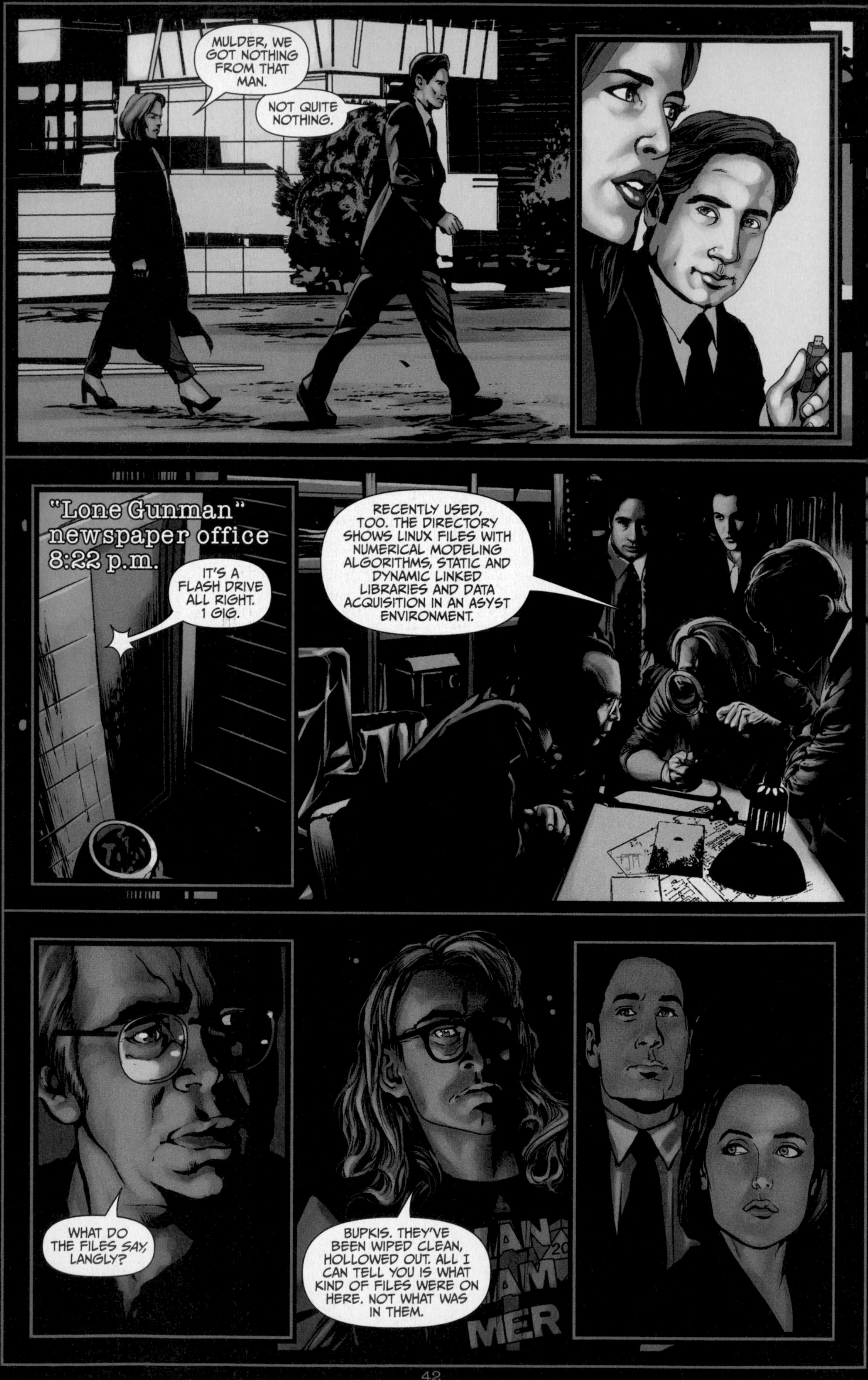
MULDER, WE GOT NOTHING FROM THAT MAN.
NOT QUITE NOTHING.
"Lone Gunman" newspaper office 8:22 p.m.
IT'S A FLASH DRIVE ALL RIGHT. 1 GIG.
RECENTLY USED, TOO. THE DIRECTORY SHOWS LINUX FILES WITH NUMERICAL MODELING ALGORITHMS, STATIC AND DYNAMIC LINKED LIBRARIES AND DATA ACQUISITION IN AN ASYST ENVIRONMENT.
WHAT DO THE FILES SAY, LANGLY?
BUPKIS. THEY'VE BEEN WIPED CLEAN, HOLLOWED OUT. ALL I CAN TELL YOU IS WHAT KIND OF FILES WERE ON HERE. NOT WHAT WAS IN THEM.

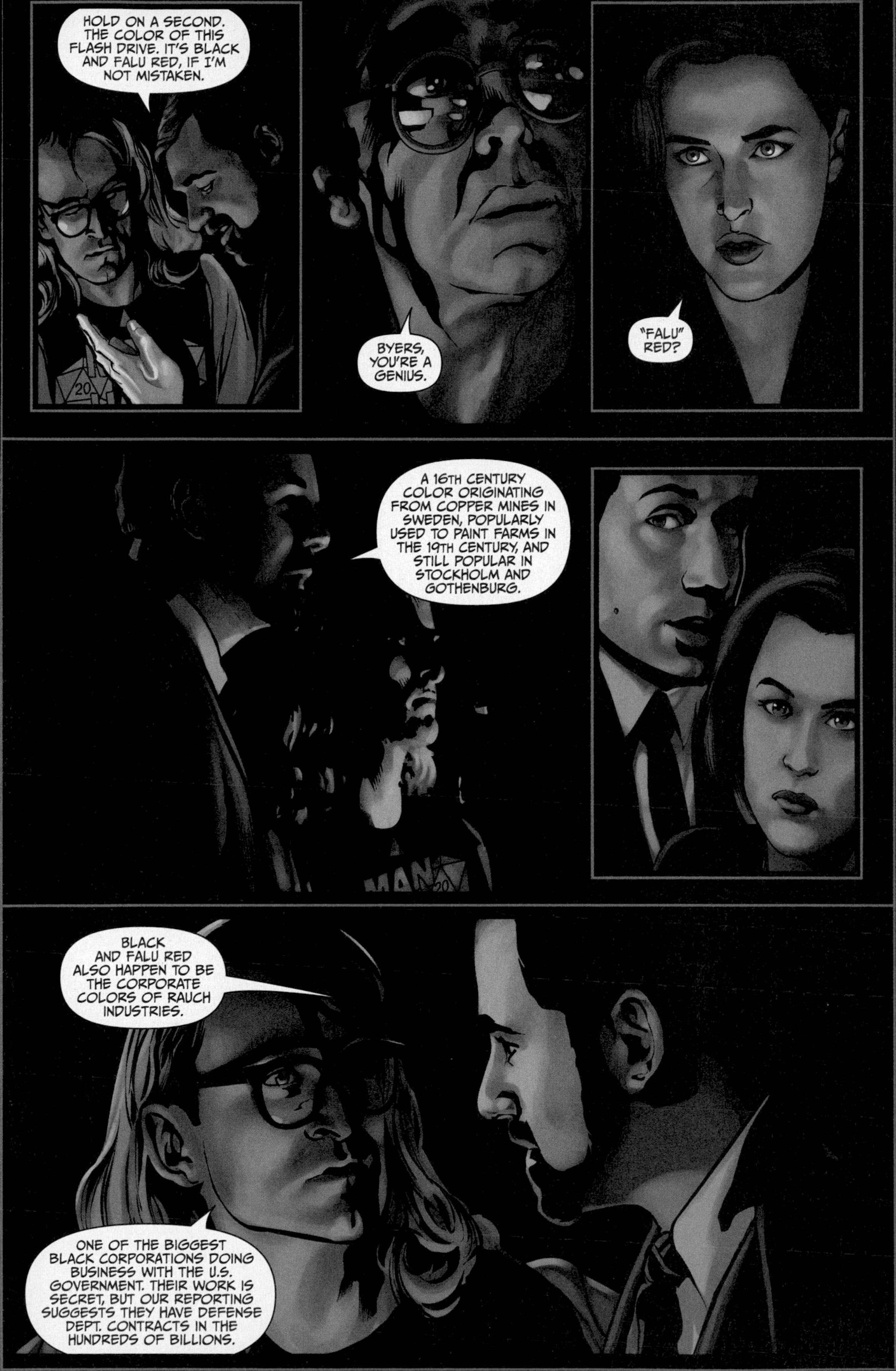
HOLD ON A SECOND. THE COLOR OF THIS FLASH DRIVE. IT'S BLACK AND FALU RED, IF I'M NOT MISTAKEN.
BYERS, YOU'RE A GENIUS.
"FALU" RED?
A 16TH CENTURY COLOR ORIGINATING FROM COPPER MINES IN SWEDEN, POPULARLY USED TO PAINT FARMS IN THE 19TH CENTURY, AND STILL POPULAR IN STOCKHOLM AND GOTHENBURG.
BLACK AND FALU RED ALSO HAPPEN TO BE THE CORPORATE COLORS OF RAUCH INDUSTRIES.
ONE OF THE BIGGEST BLACK CORPORATIONS DOING BUSINESS WITH THE U.S. GOVERNMENT. THEIR WORK IS SECRET, BUT OUR REPORTING SUGGESTS THEY HAVE DEFENSE DEPT. CONTRACTS IN THE HUNDREDS OF BILLIONS.

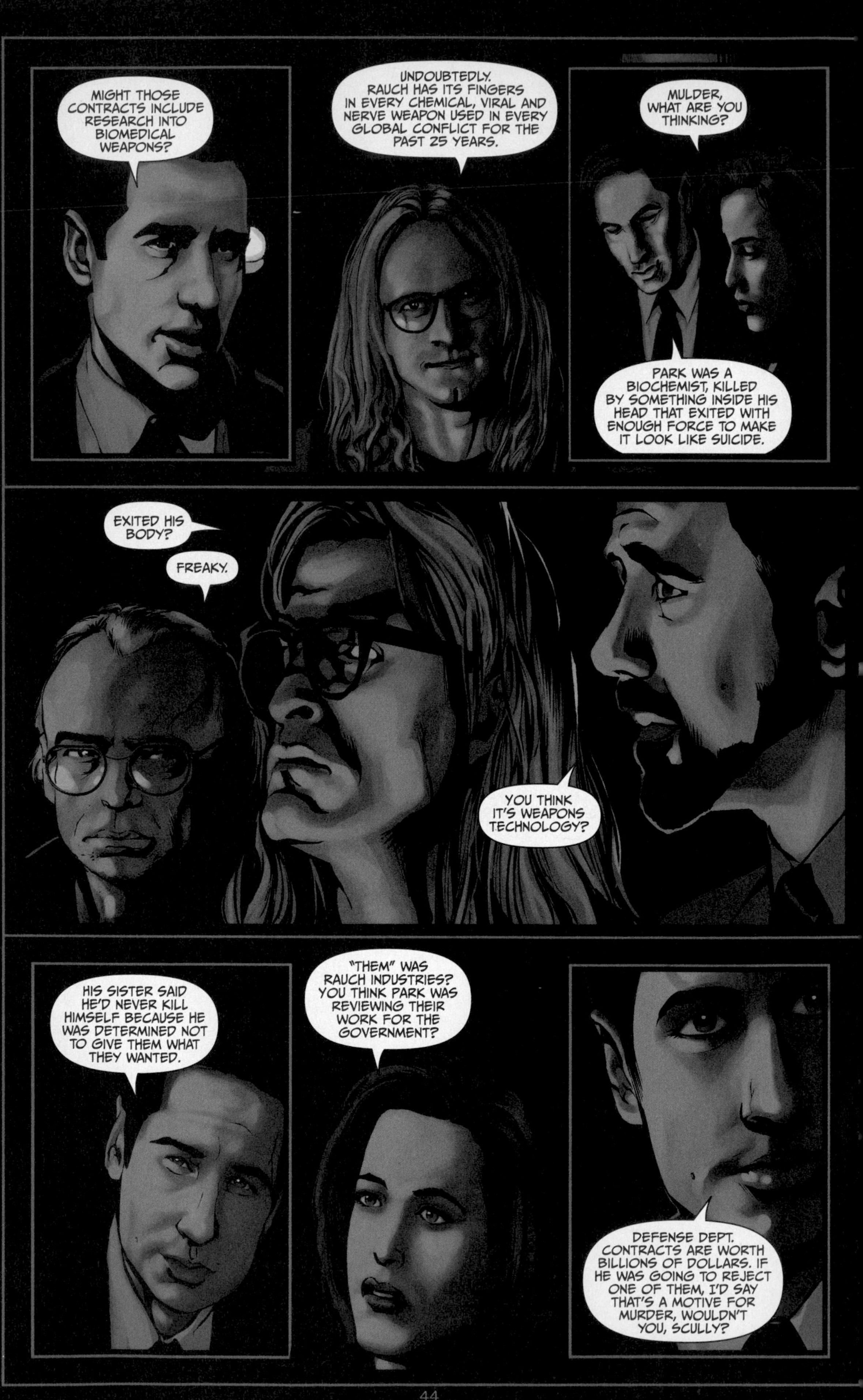
MIGHT THOSE CONTRACTS INCLUDE RESEARCH INTO BIOMEDICAL WEAPONS?
UNDOUBTEDLY. RAUCH HAS ITS FINGERS IN EVERY CHEMICAL, VIRAL AND NERVE WEAPON USED IN EVERY GLOBAL CONFLICT FOR THE PAST 25 YEARS.
MULDER, WHAT ARE YOU THINKING?
PARK WAS A BIOCHEMIST, KILLED BY SOMETHING INSIDE HIS HEAD THAT EXITED WITH ENOUGH FORCE TO MAKE IT LOOK LIKE SUICIDE.
EXITED HIS BODY?
FREAKY.
YOU THINK IT'S WEAPONS TECHNOLOGY?
HIS SISTER SAID HE'D NEVER KILL HIMSELF BECAUSE HE WAS DETERMINED NOT TO GIVE THEM WHAT THEY WANTED.
"THEM" WAS RAUCH INDUSTRIES? YOU THINK PARK WAS REVIEWING THEIR WORK FOR THE GOVERNMENT?
DEFENSE DEPT. CONTRACTS ARE WORTH BILLIONS OF DOLLARS. IF HE WAS GOING TO REJECT ONE OF THEM, I'D SAY THAT'S A MOTIVE FOR MURDER, WOULDN'T YOU, SCULLY?

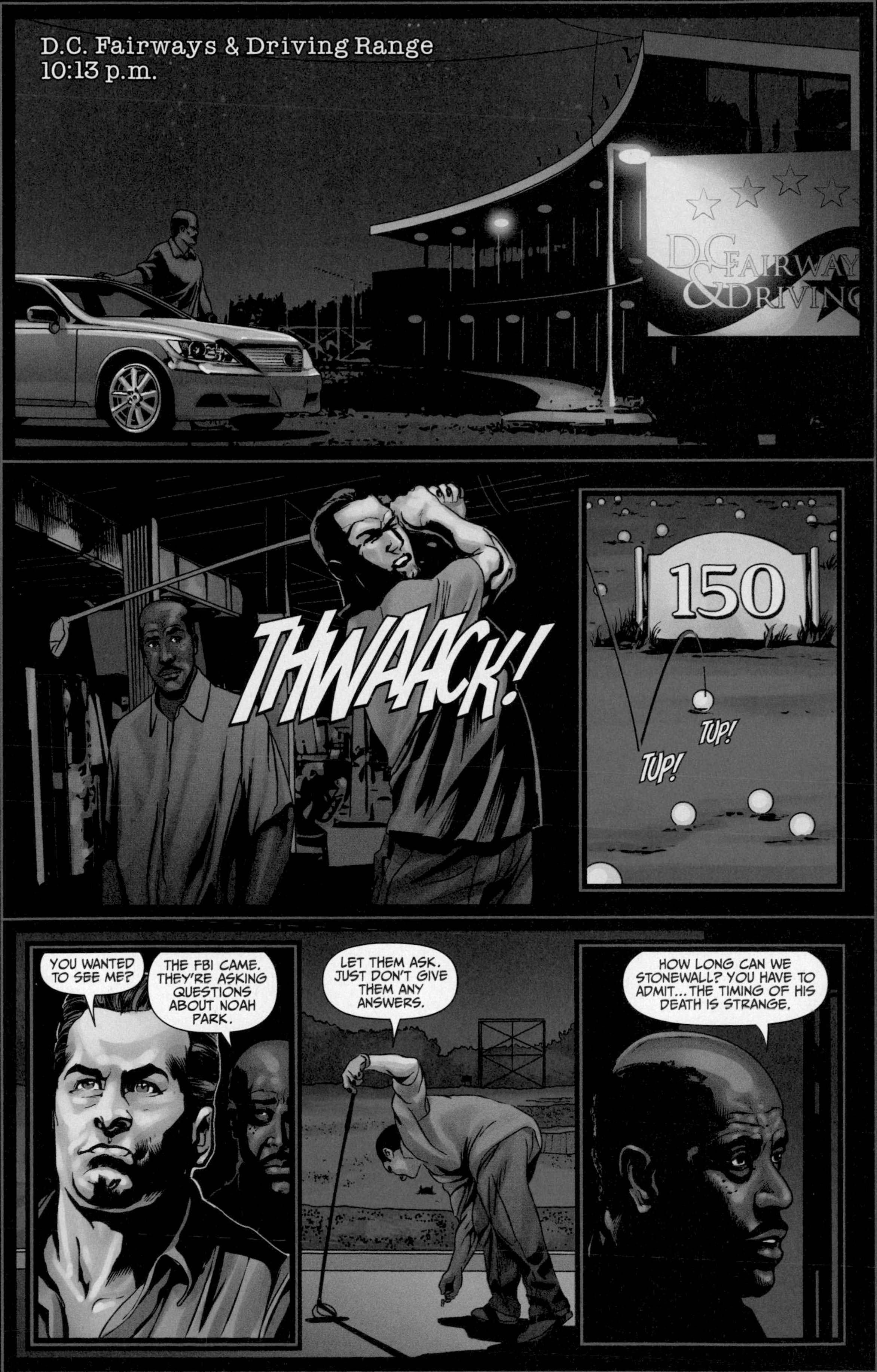
D.C. Fairways & Driving Range
10:13 p.m.
DC FAIRWAY
& DRIVING
THWAACK!
150
TUP!
TUP!
YOU WANTED TO SEE ME?
THE FBI CAME. THEY'RE ASKING QUESTIONS ABOUT NOAH PARK.
LET THEM ASK. JUST DON'T GIVE THEM ANY ANSWERS.
HOW LONG CAN WE STONEWALL? YOU HAVE TO ADMIT... THE TIMING OF HIS DEATH IS STRANGE.

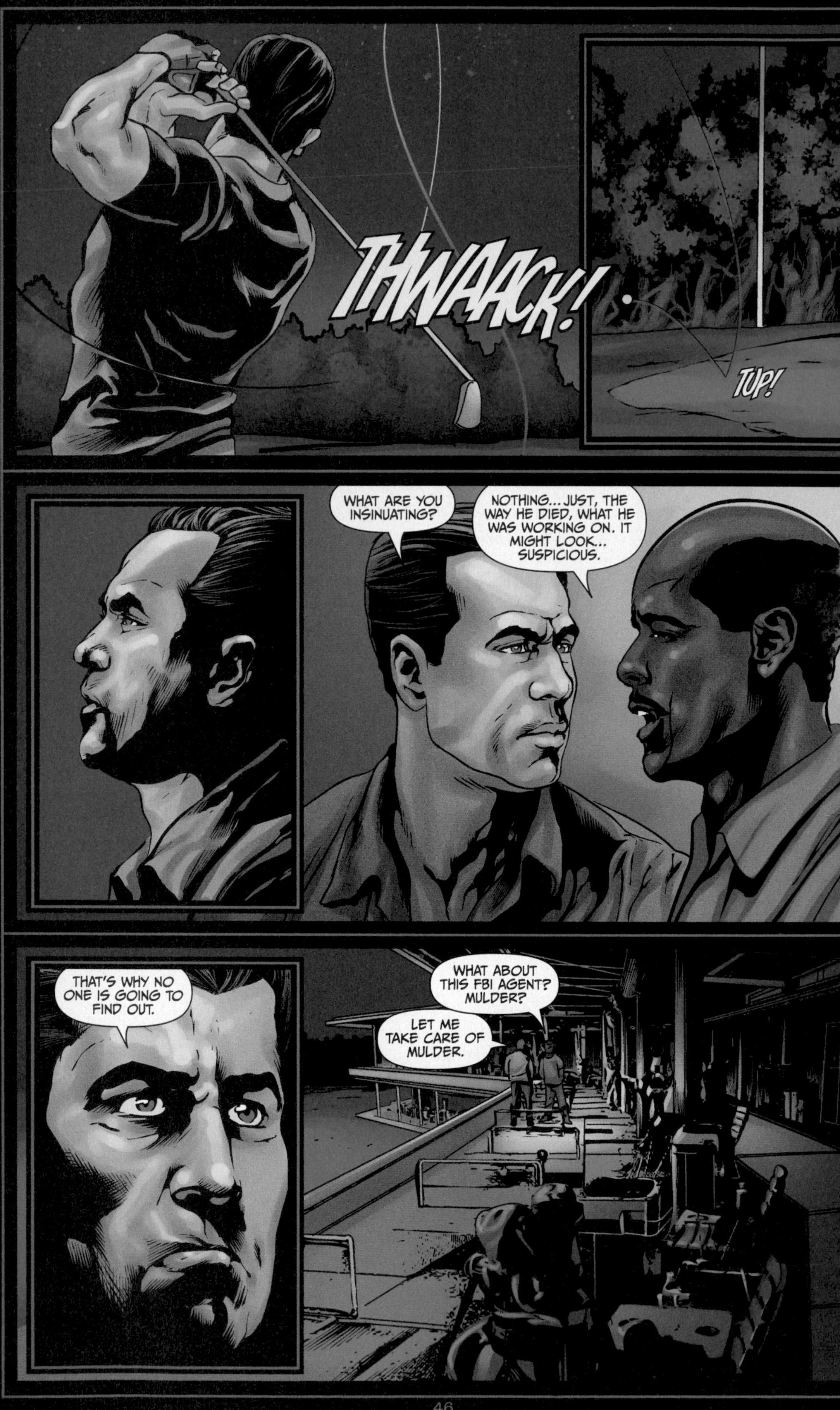
THWAAACK!
TUP!
WHAT ARE YOU INSINUATING?
NOTHING... JUST, THE WAY HE DIED, WHAT HE WAS WORKING ON. IT MIGHT LOOK... SUSPICIOUS.
THAT'S WHY NO ONE IS GOING TO FIND OUT.
WHAT ABOUT THIS FBI AGENT? MULDER?
LET ME TAKE CARE OF MULDER.

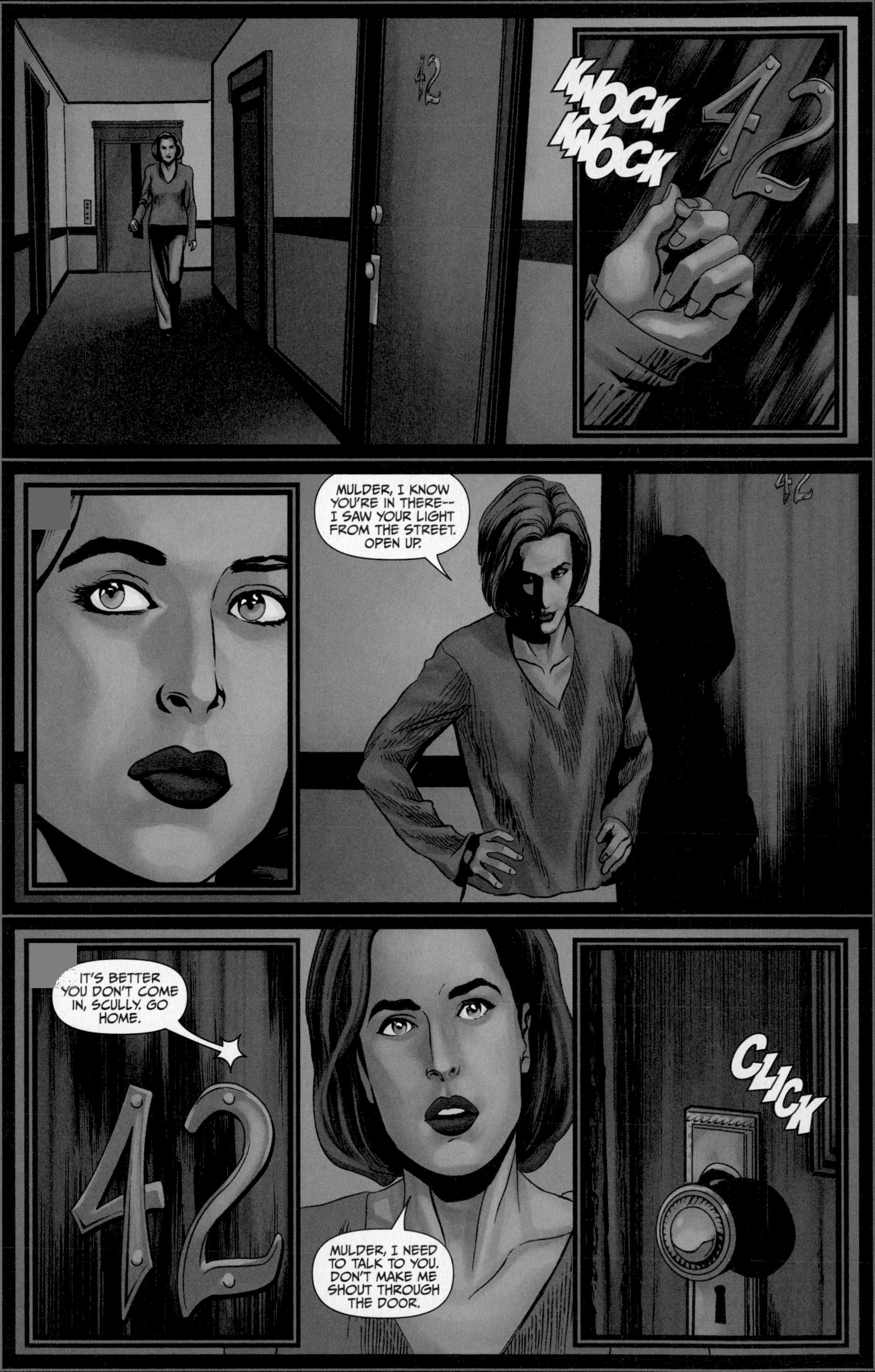
KNOCK KNOCK
MULDER, I KNOW YOU'RE IN THERE-- I SAW YOUR LIGHT FROM THE STREET. OPEN UP.
IT'S BETTER YOU DON'T COME IN, SCULLY. GO HOME.
MULDER, I NEED TO TALK TO YOU. DON'T MAKE ME SHOUT THROUGH THE DOOR.
CLICK

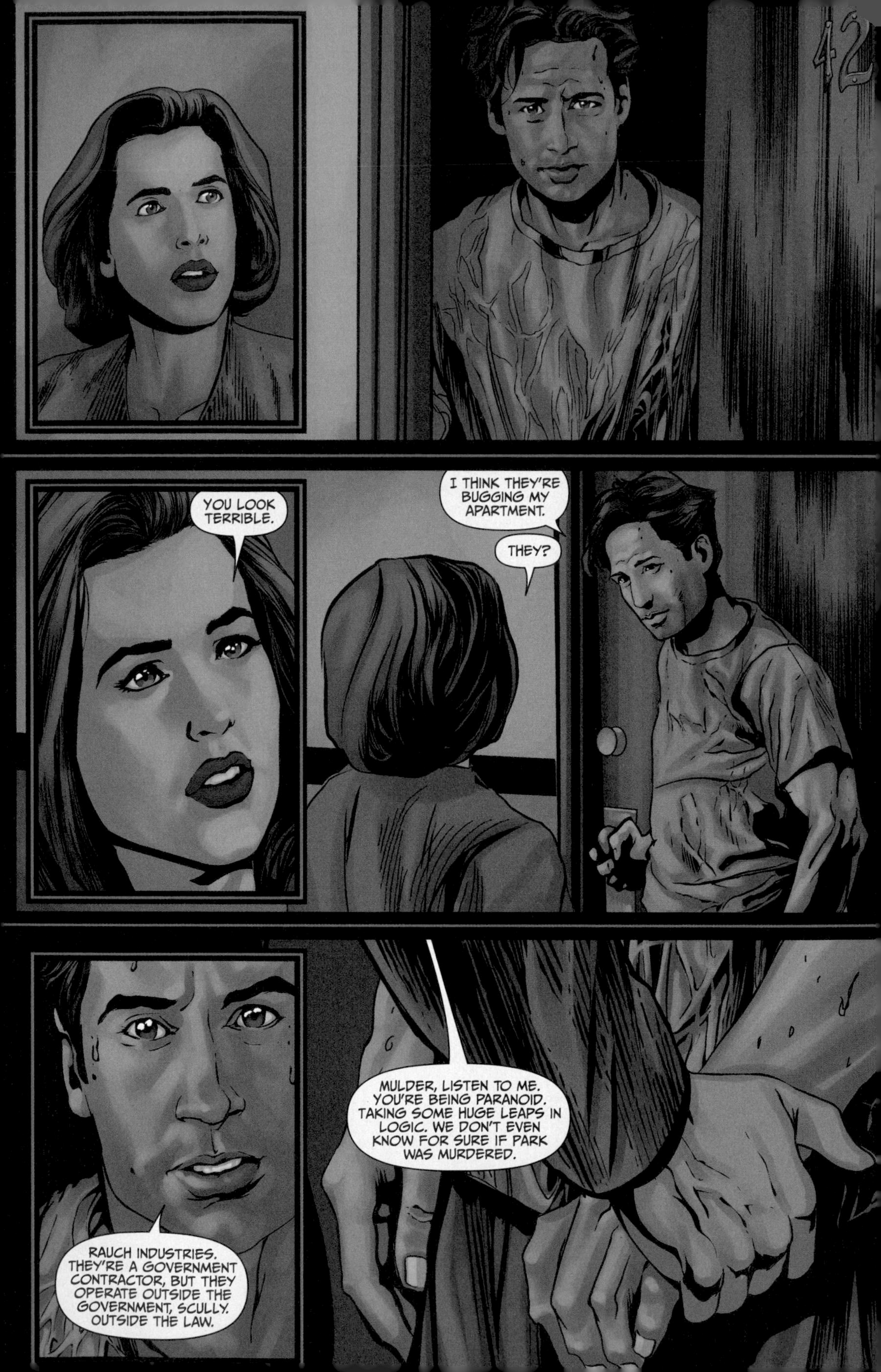
YOU LOOK TERRIBLE.
I THINK THEY'RE BUGGING MY APARTMENT.
THEY?
MULDER, LISTEN TO ME. YOU'RE BEING PARANOID. TAKING SOME HUGE LEAPS IN LOGIC. WE DON'T EVEN KNOW FOR SURE IF PARK WAS MURDERED.
RAUCH INDUSTRIES. THEY'RE A GOVERNMENT CONTRACTOR, BUT THEY OPERATE OUTSIDE THE GOVERNMENT, SCULLY. OUTSIDE THE LAW.

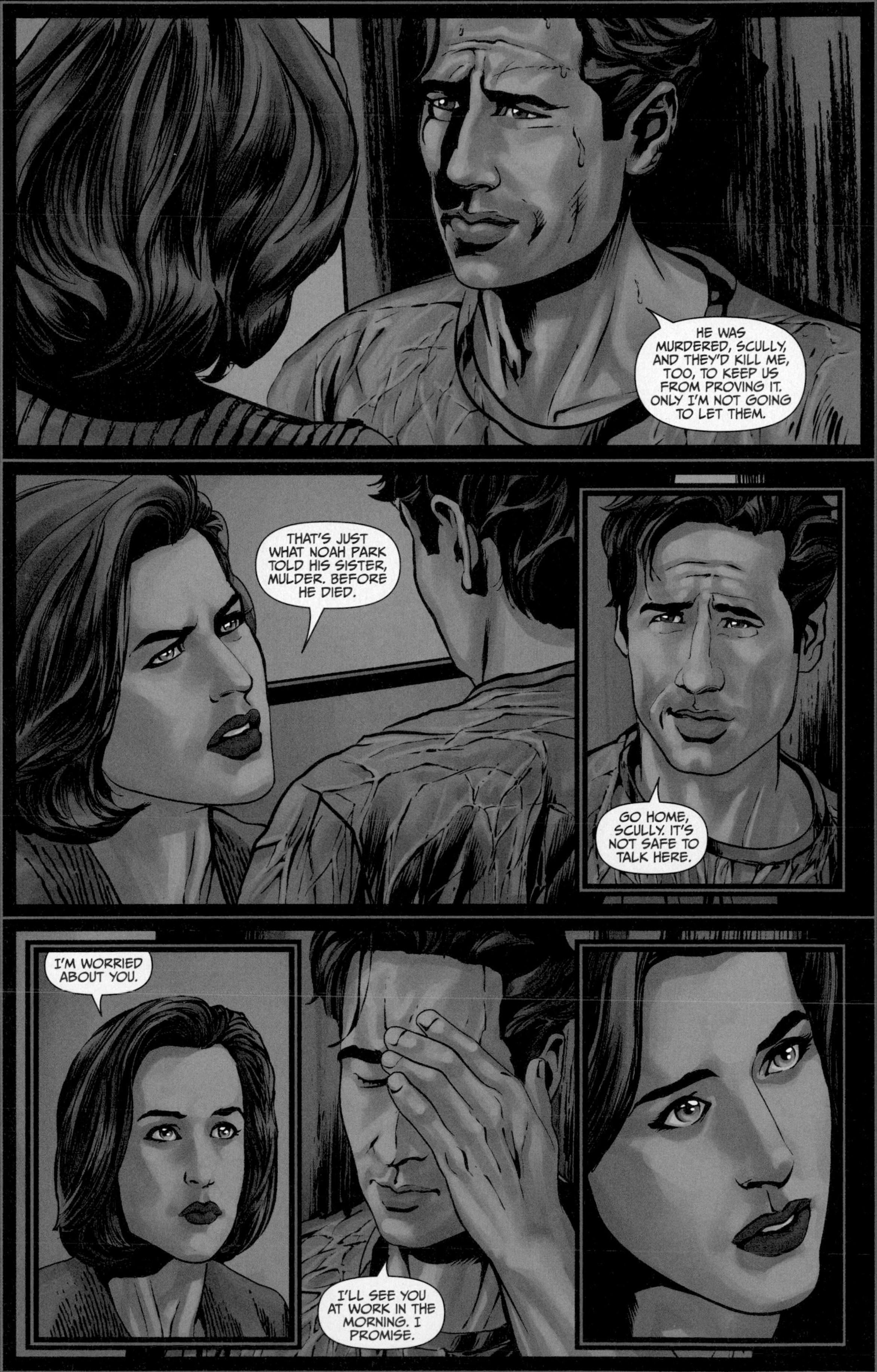
HE WAS MURDERED, SCULLY, AND THEY'D KILL ME, TOO, TO KEEP US FROM PROVING IT. ONLY I'M NOT GOING TO LET THEM.
THAT'S JUST WHAT NOAH PARK TOLD HIS SISTER, MULDER. BEFORE HE DIED.
GO HOME, SCULLY. IT'S NOT SAFE TO TALK HERE.
I'M WORRIED ABOUT YOU.
I'LL SEE YOU AT WORK IN THE MORNING. I PROMISE.

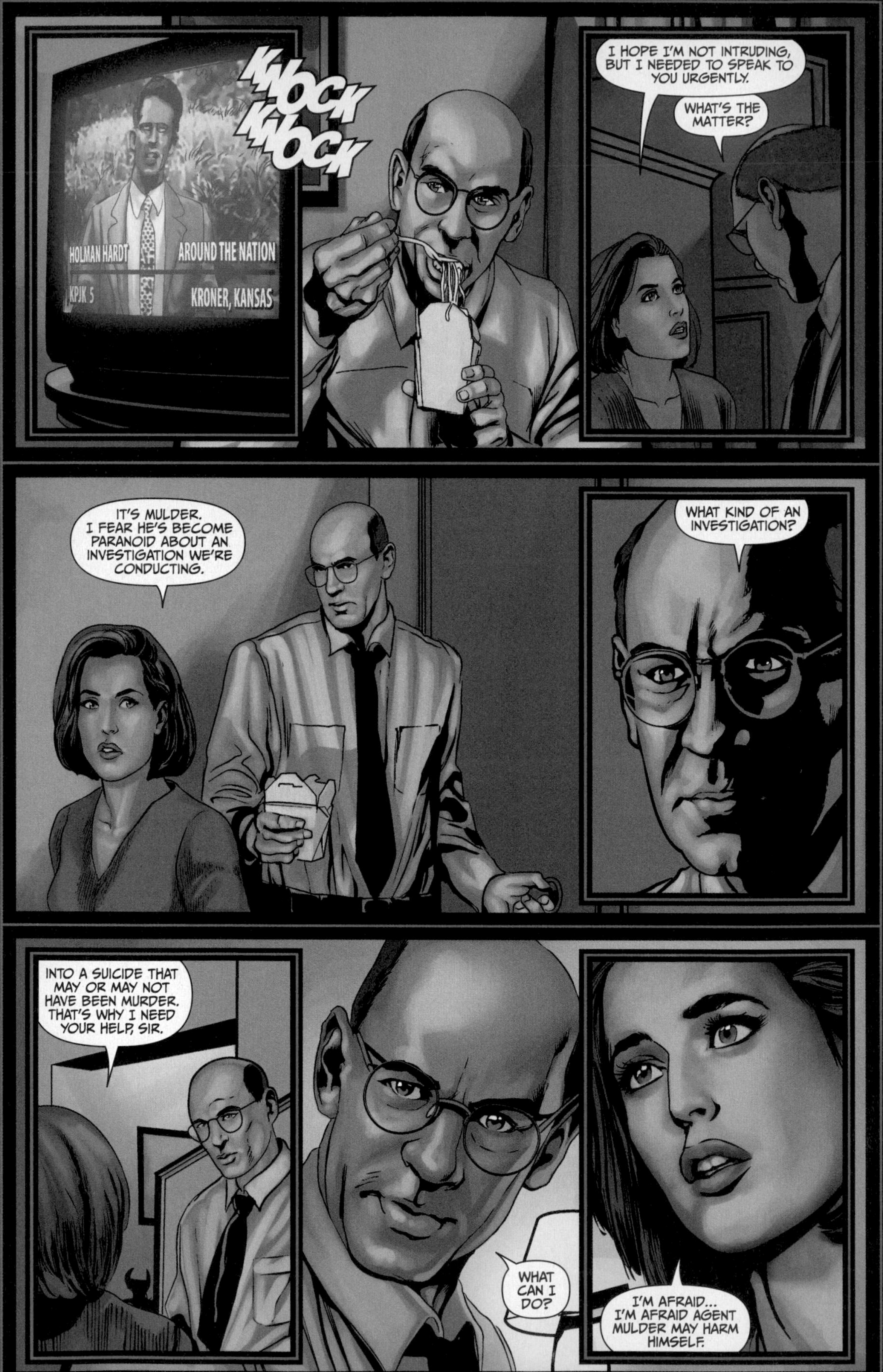
HOLMAN HARDT
AROUND THE NATION
KPJK 5
KRONER, KANSAS
KNOCK KNOCK
I HOPE I'M NOT INTRUDING, BUT I NEEDED TO SPEAK TO YOU URGENTLY.
WHAT'S THE MATTER?
IT'S MULDER. I FEAR HE'S BECOME PARANOID ABOUT AN INVESTIGATION WE'RE CONDUCTING.
WHAT KIND OF AN INVESTIGATION?
INTO A SUICIDE THAT MAY OR MAY NOT HAVE BEEN MURDER. THAT'S WHY I NEED YOUR HELP, SIR.
WHAT CAN I DO?
I'M AFRAID... I'M AFRAID AGENT MULDER MAY HARM HIMSELF.

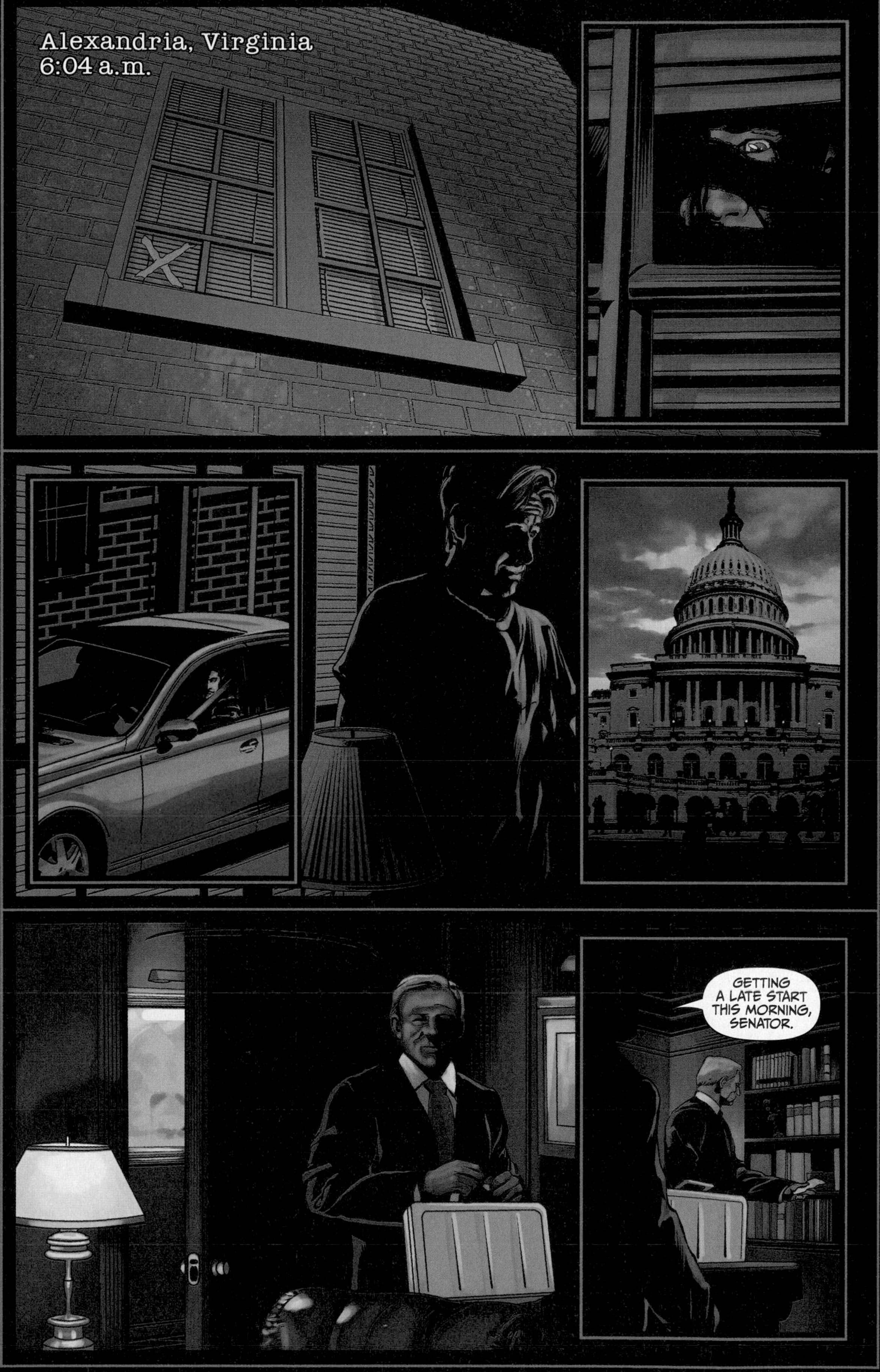
Alexandria, Virginia
6:04 a.m.
GETTING A LATE START THIS MORNING, SENATOR.

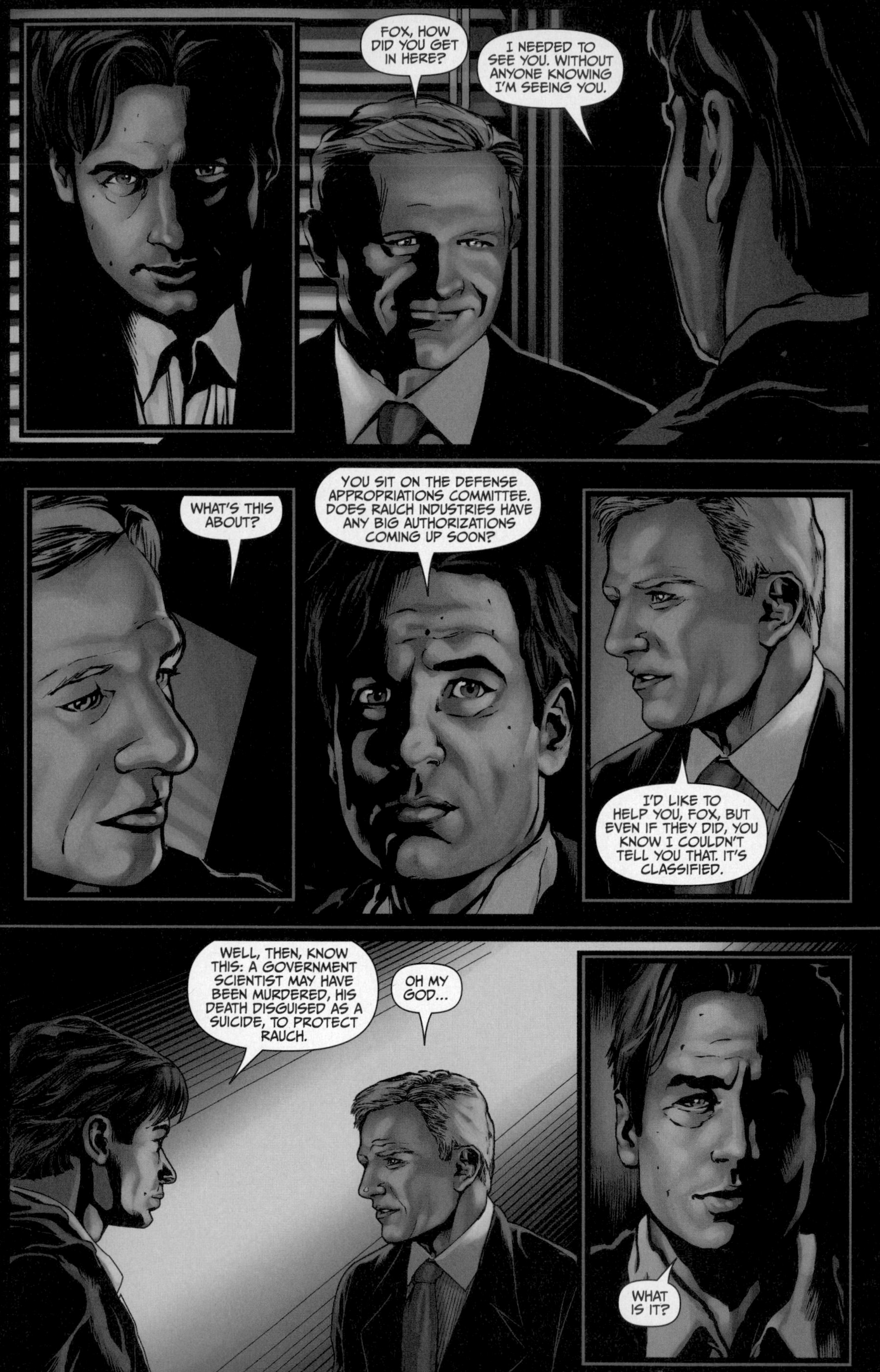

FOX, HOW DID YOU GET IN HERE?
I NEEDED TO SEE YOU. WITHOUT ANYONE KNOWING I'M SEEING YOU.
WHAT'S THIS ABOUT?
YOU SIT ON THE DEFENSE APPROPRIATIONS COMMITTEE. DOES RAUCH INDUSTRIES HAVE ANY BIG AUTHORIZATIONS COMING UP SOON?
I'D LIKE TO HELP YOU, FOX, BUT EVEN IF THEY DID, YOU KNOW I COULDN'T TELL YOU THAT. IT'S CLASSIFIED.
WELL, THEN, KNOW THIS: A GOVERNMENT SCIENTIST MAY HAVE BEEN MURDERED, HIS DEATH DISGUISED AS A SUICIDE, TO PROTECT RAUCH.
OH MY GOD...
WHAT IS IT?

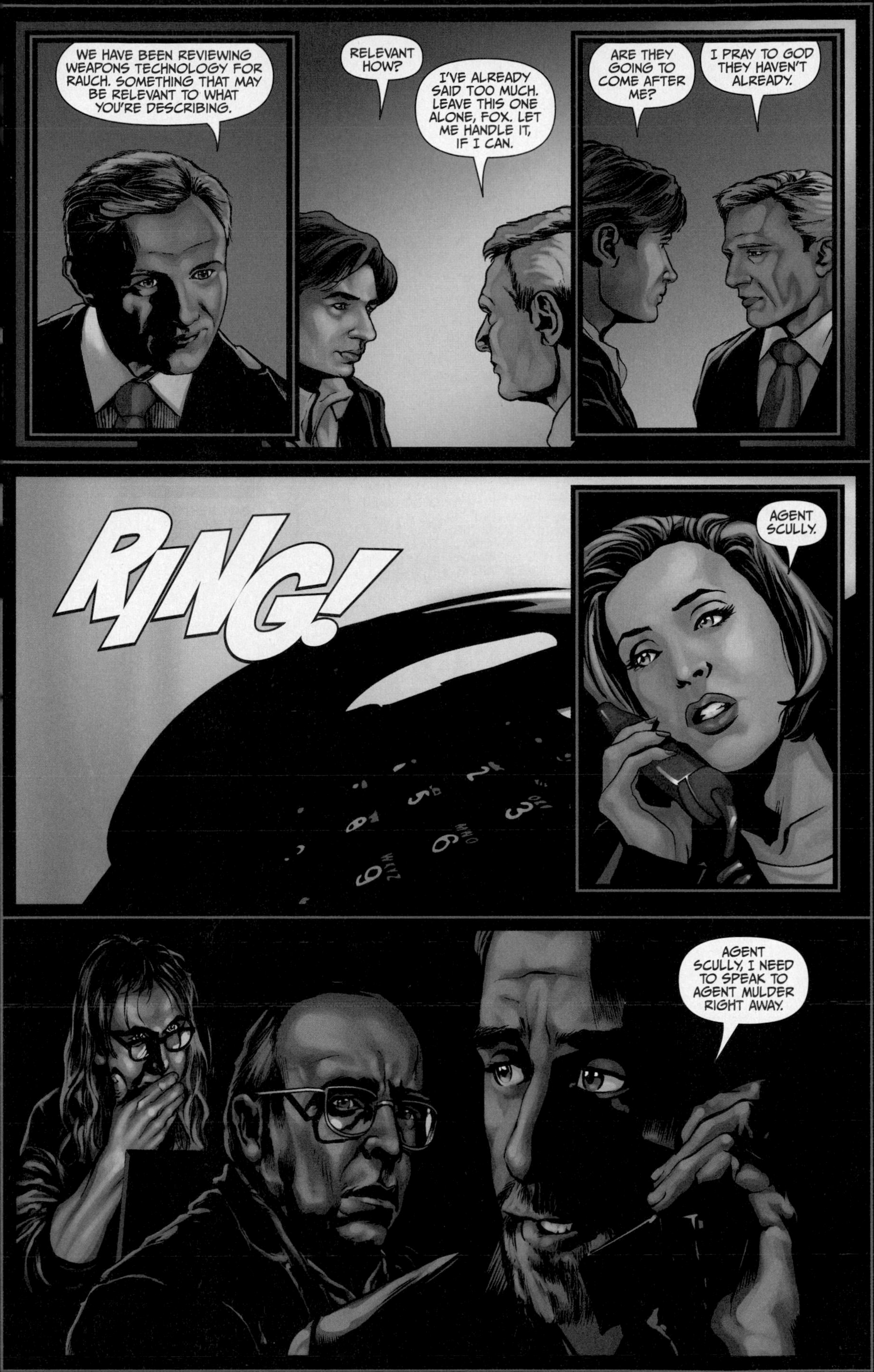
WE HAVE BEEN REVIEWING WEAPONS TECHNOLOGY FOR RAUCH. SOMETHING THAT MAY BE RELEVANT TO WHAT YOU'RE DESCRIBING.
RELEVANT HOW?
I'VE ALREADY SAID TOO MUCH. LEAVE THIS ONE ALONE, FOX. LET ME HANDLE IT, IF I CAN.
ARE THEY GOING TO COME AFTER ME?
I PRAY TO GOD THEY HAVEN'T ALREADY.
RING!
AGENT SCULLY.
AGENT SCULLY, I NEED TO SPEAK TO AGENT MULDER RIGHT AWAY.

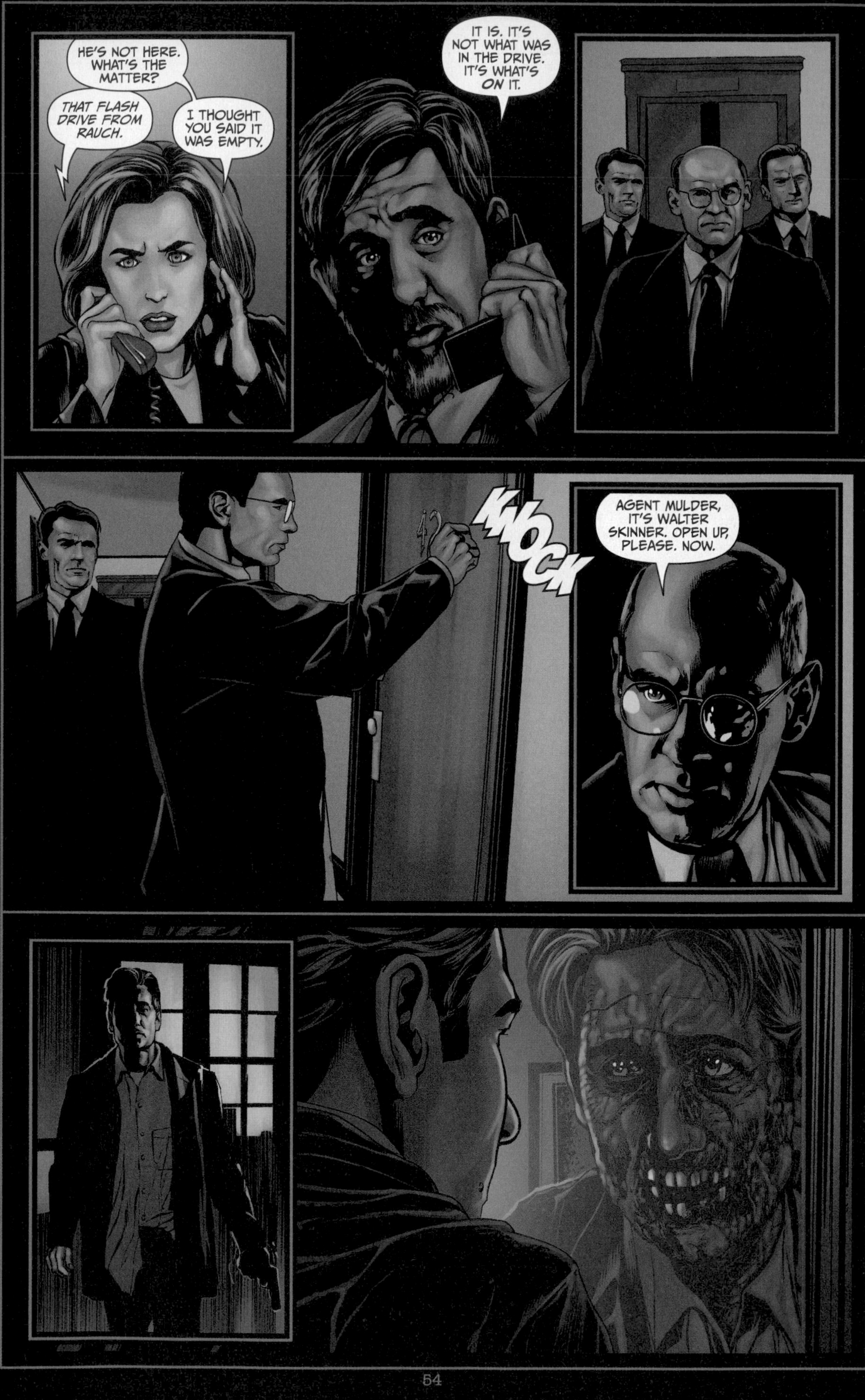

HE'S NOT HERE. WHAT'S THE MATTER?
THAT FLASH DRIVE FROM RAUCH.
I THOUGHT YOU SAID IT WAS EMPTY.
IT IS. IT'S NOT WHAT WAS IN THE DRIVE. IT'S WHAT'S ON IT.
KNOCK
AGENT MULDER, IT'S WALTER SKINNER. OPEN UP, PLEASE. NOW.

written by
FRANK
SPOTNITZ

illustrated by
BRIAN
DENHAM

THE X FILES

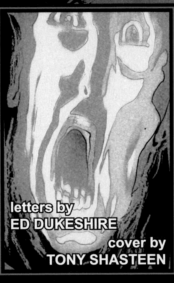

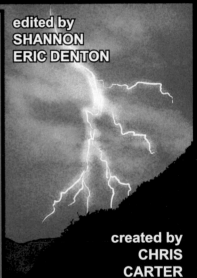

edited by
SHANNON
ERIC DENTON

colors by
KELSEY SHANNON
and CARLOS BADILLA

letters by
ED DUKESHIRE

cover by
TONY SHASTEEN

created by
CHRIS
CARTER

42

BANG!
BANG!

AGENT
MULDER,
OPEN THE
DOOR!

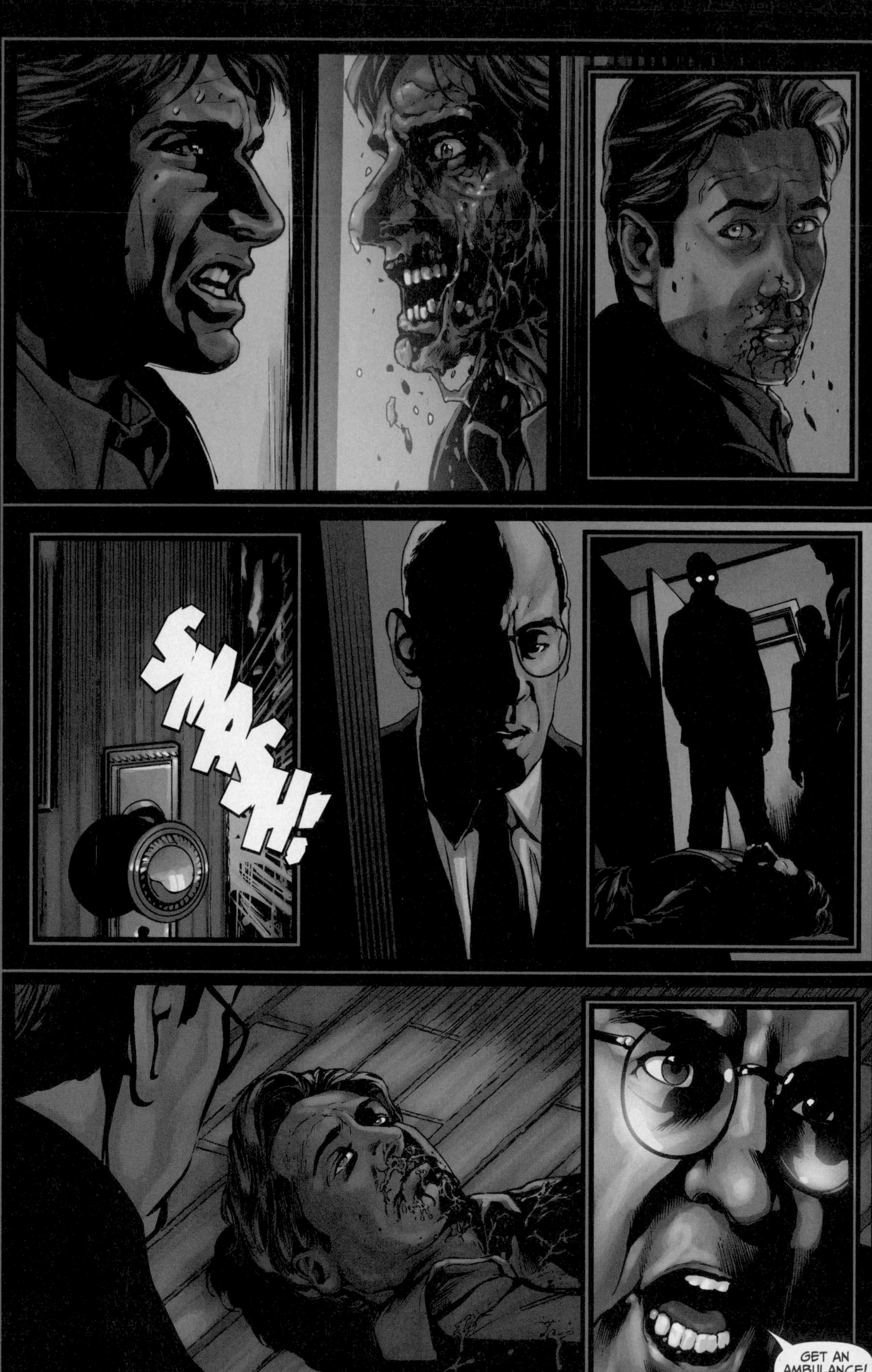
SMASH!
GET AN AMBULANCE! NOW!

WNH
WASHINGTON
NATIONAL
HOSPITAL

WAITING ROOM ▶

◀ RESTROOMS

Washington
National Hospital
7:47 a.m.

HIS CONDITION IS STABLE.

THANK GOD FOR THAT. WHAT HAPPENED TO HIM?

ACCORDING TO THE DOCTORS, NOTHING.

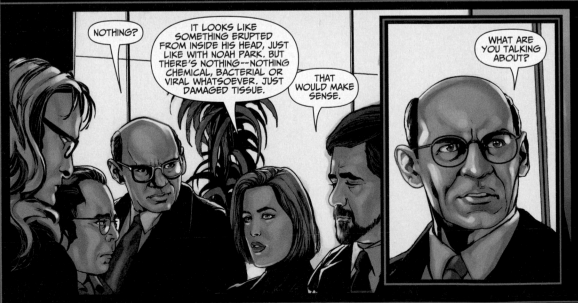

NOTHING?

IT LOOKS LIKE SOMETHING ERUPTED FROM INSIDE HIS HEAD, JUST LIKE WITH NOAH PARK. BUT THERE'S NOTHING--NOTHING CHEMICAL, BACTERIAL OR VIRAL WHATSOEVER. JUST DAMAGED TISSUE.

THAT WOULD MAKE SENSE.

WHAT ARE YOU TALKING ABOUT?

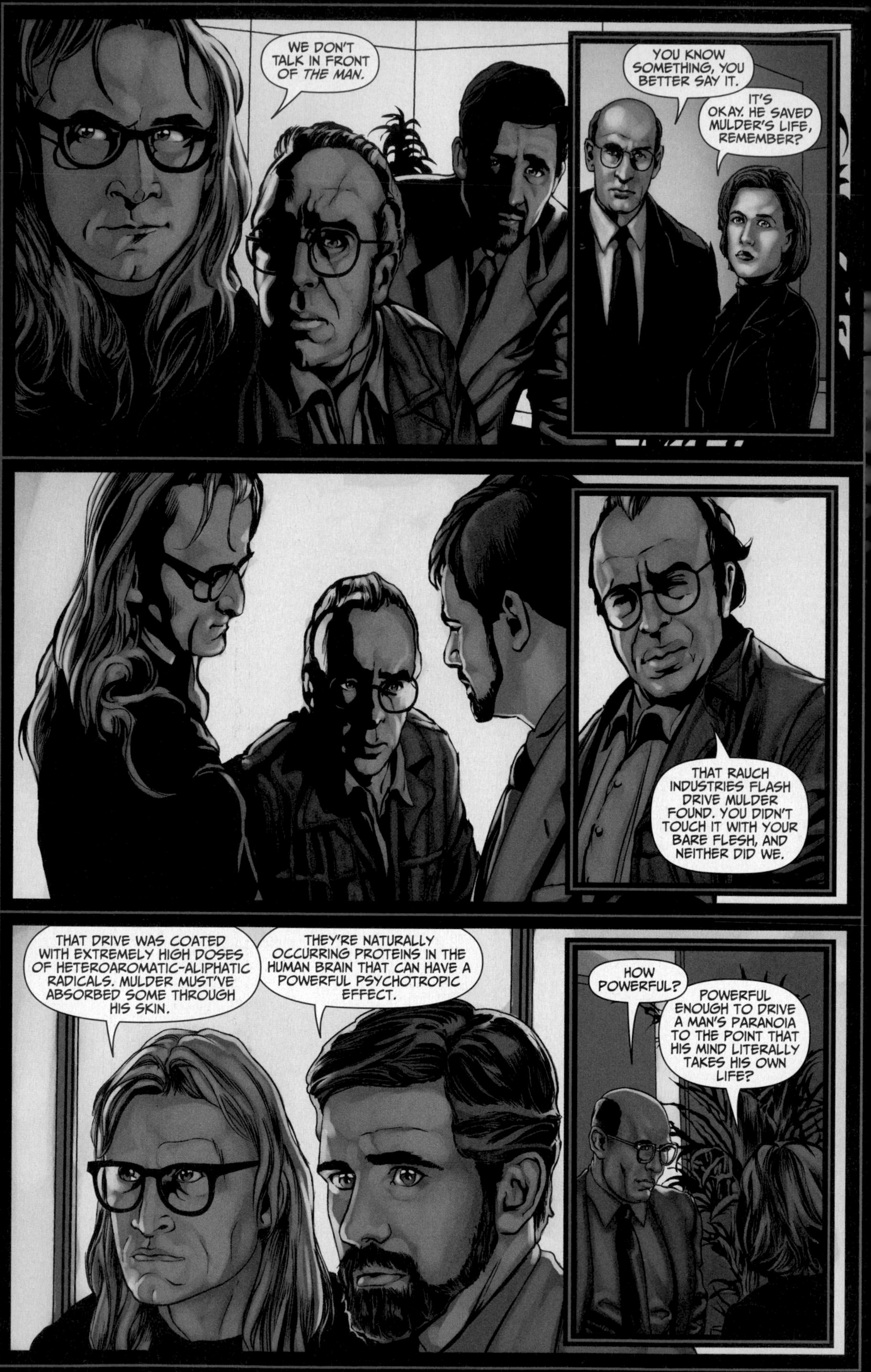
WE DON'T TALK IN FRONT OF *THE MAN.*
YOU KNOW SOMETHING, YOU BETTER SAY IT.
IT'S OKAY. HE SAVED MULDER'S LIFE, REMEMBER?
THAT RAUCH INDUSTRIES FLASH DRIVE MULDER FOUND. YOU DIDN'T TOUCH IT WITH YOUR BARE FLESH, AND NEITHER DID WE.
THAT DRIVE WAS COATED WITH EXTREMELY HIGH DOSES OF HETEROAROMATIC-ALIPHATIC RADICALS. MULDER MUST'VE ABSORBED SOME THROUGH HIS SKIN.
THEY'RE NATURALLY OCCURRING PROTEINS IN THE HUMAN BRAIN THAT CAN HAVE A POWERFUL PSYCHOTROPIC EFFECT.
HOW POWERFUL?
POWERFUL ENOUGH TO DRIVE A MAN'S PARANOIA TO THE POINT THAT HIS MIND LITERALLY TAKES HIS OWN LIFE?

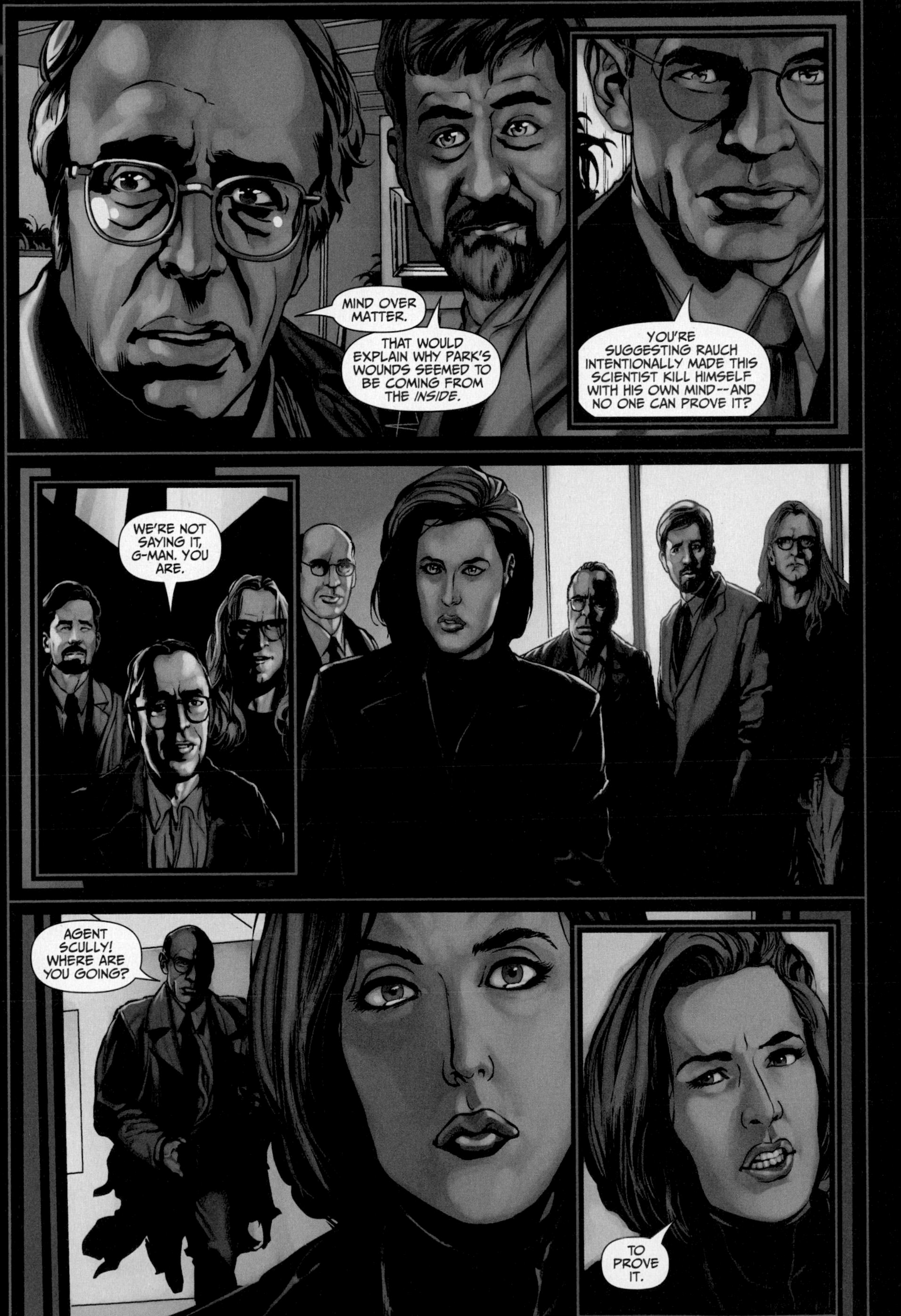
MIND OVER MATTER.
THAT WOULD EXPLAIN WHY PARK'S WOUNDS SEEMED TO BE COMING FROM THE *INSIDE*.
YOU'RE SUGGESTING RAUCH INTENTIONALLY MADE THIS SCIENTIST KILL HIMSELF WITH HIS OWN MIND--AND NO ONE CAN PROVE IT?
WE'RE NOT SAYING IT, G-MAN. YOU ARE.
AGENT SCULLY! WHERE ARE YOU GOING?
TO PROVE IT.

KAPLAN'S COFFEE SHOP

KAPLAN'S COFFEE SHOP
Since 1956

Fried Chaco
Chicken
SPECIALS
KANE'S WISCONSIN
BeeF Steak

THANK YOU FOR AGREEING TO SEE ME OUTSIDE THE OFFICE.

WHAT'S THIS ABOUT?

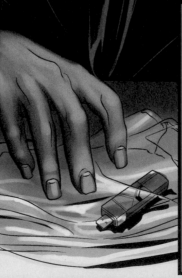

AM I SUPPOSED TO KNOW WHAT THAT IS?

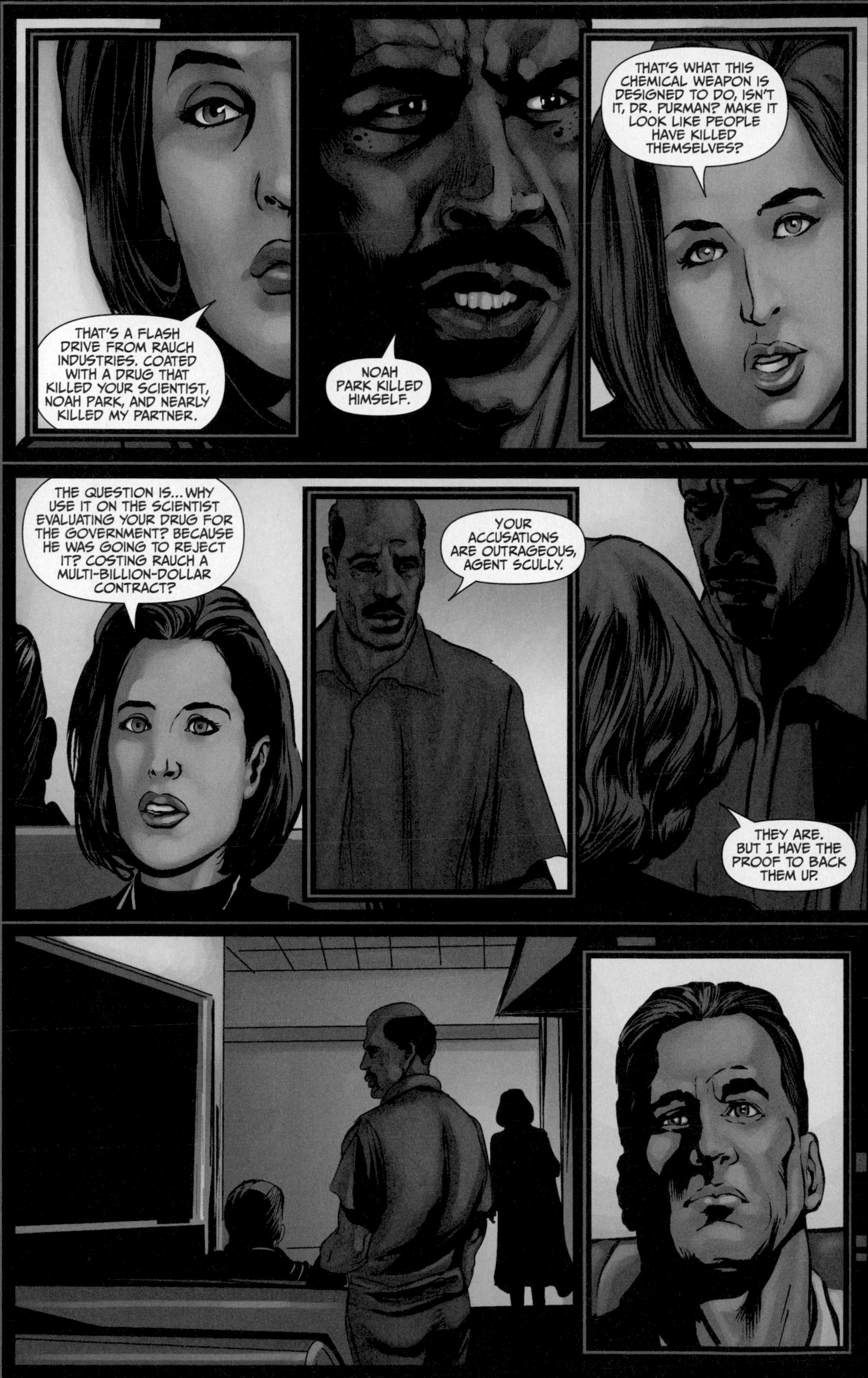
THAT'S A FLASH DRIVE FROM RAUCH INDUSTRIES. COATED WITH A DRUG THAT KILLED YOUR SCIENTIST, NOAH PARK, AND NEARLY KILLED MY PARTNER.
NOAH PARK KILLED HIMSELF.
THAT'S WHAT THIS CHEMICAL WEAPON IS DESIGNED TO DO, ISN'T IT, DR. PURMAN? MAKE IT LOOK LIKE PEOPLE HAVE KILLED THEMSELVES?
THE QUESTION IS... WHY USE IT ON THE SCIENTIST EVALUATING YOUR DRUG FOR THE GOVERNMENT? BECAUSE HE WAS GOING TO REJECT IT? COSTING RAUCH A MULTI-BILLION-DOLLAR CONTRACT?
YOUR ACCUSATIONS ARE OUTRAGEOUS, AGENT SCULLY.
THEY ARE. BUT I HAVE THE PROOF TO BACK THEM UP.

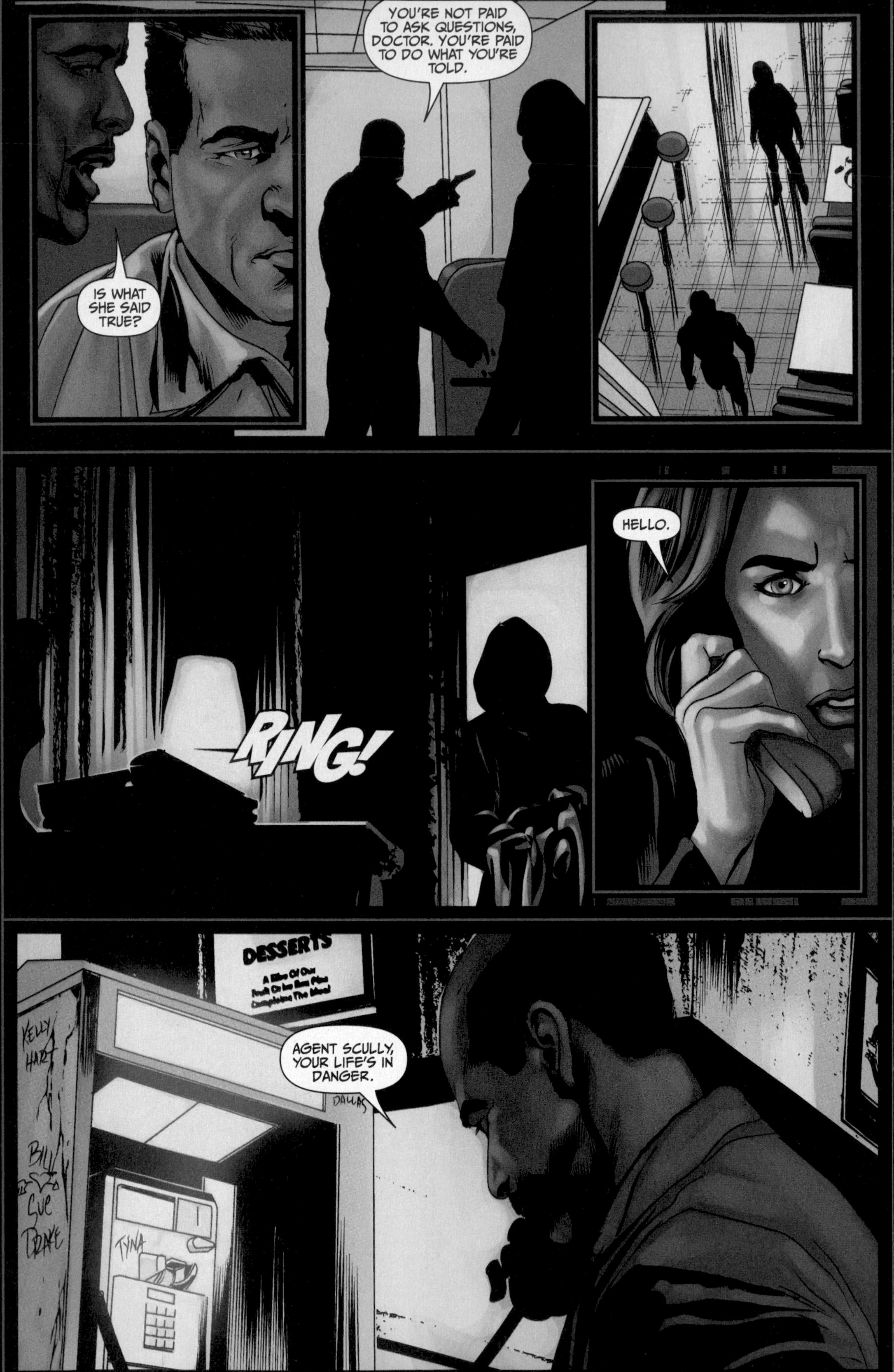
YOU'RE NOT PAID TO ASK QUESTIONS, DOCTOR. YOU'RE PAID TO DO WHAT YOU'RE TOLD.
IS WHAT SHE SAID TRUE?
RING!
HELLO.
DESSERTS
KELLY HART
DALLAS
BILL
SUE
DRAKE
TYNA
AGENT SCULLY, YOUR LIFE'S IN DANGER.

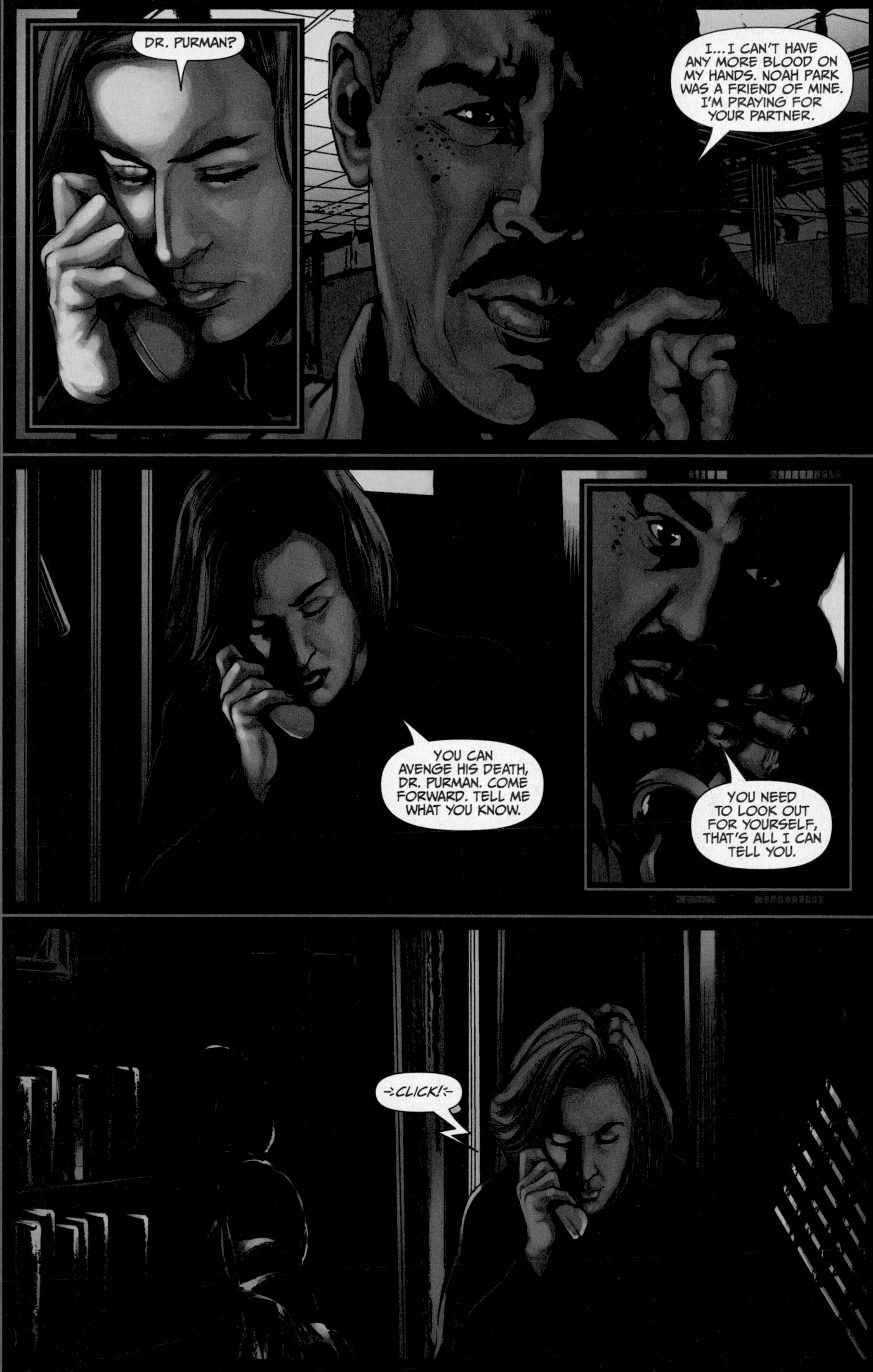
DR. PURMAN?
I...I CAN'T HAVE ANY MORE BLOOD ON MY HANDS. NOAH PARK WAS A FRIEND OF MINE. I'M PRAYING FOR YOUR PARTNER.
YOU CAN AVENGE HIS DEATH, DR. PURMAN. COME FORWARD. TELL ME WHAT YOU KNOW.
YOU NEED TO LOOK OUT FOR YOURSELF, THAT'S ALL I CAN TELL YOU.
-CLICK!-

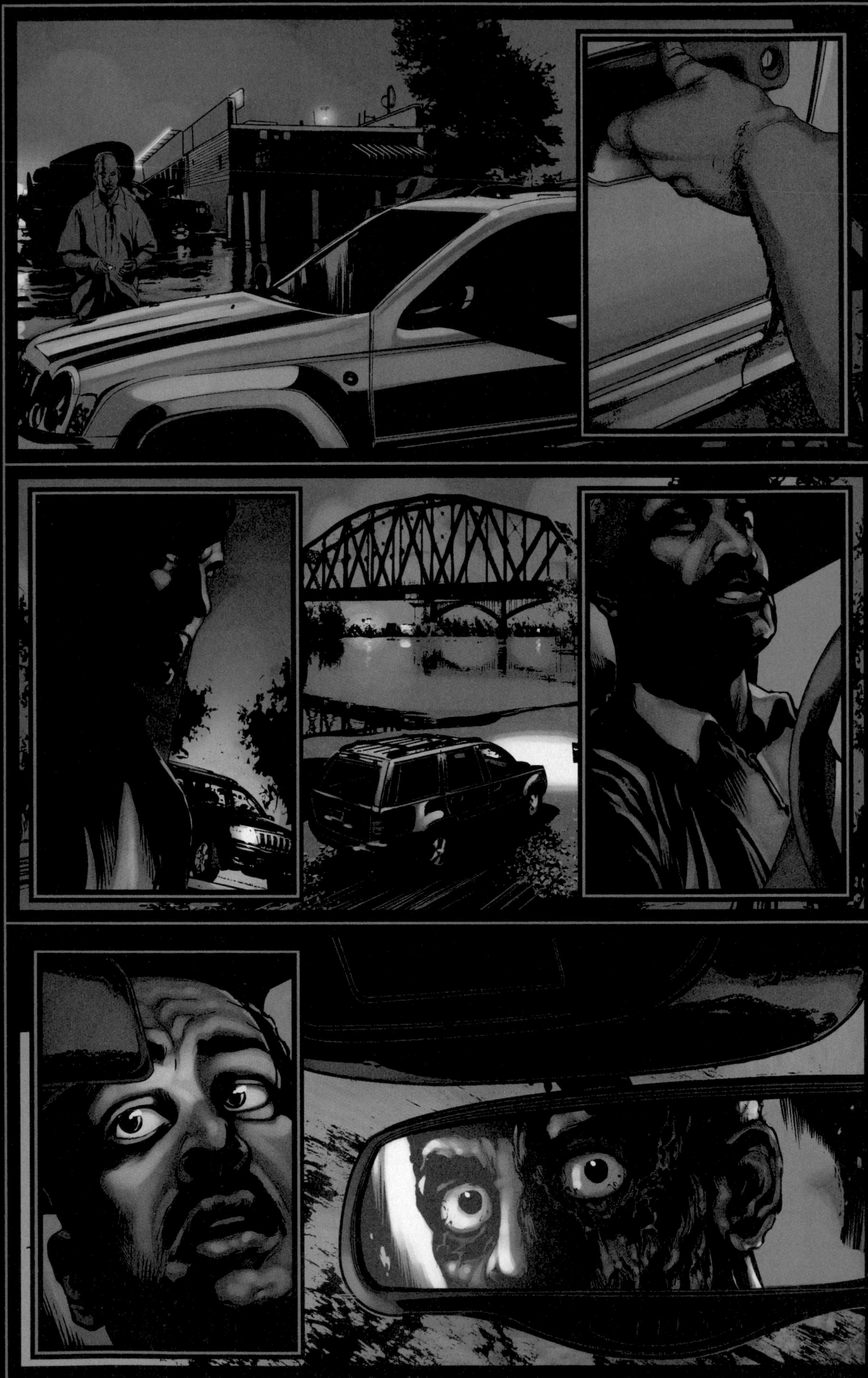

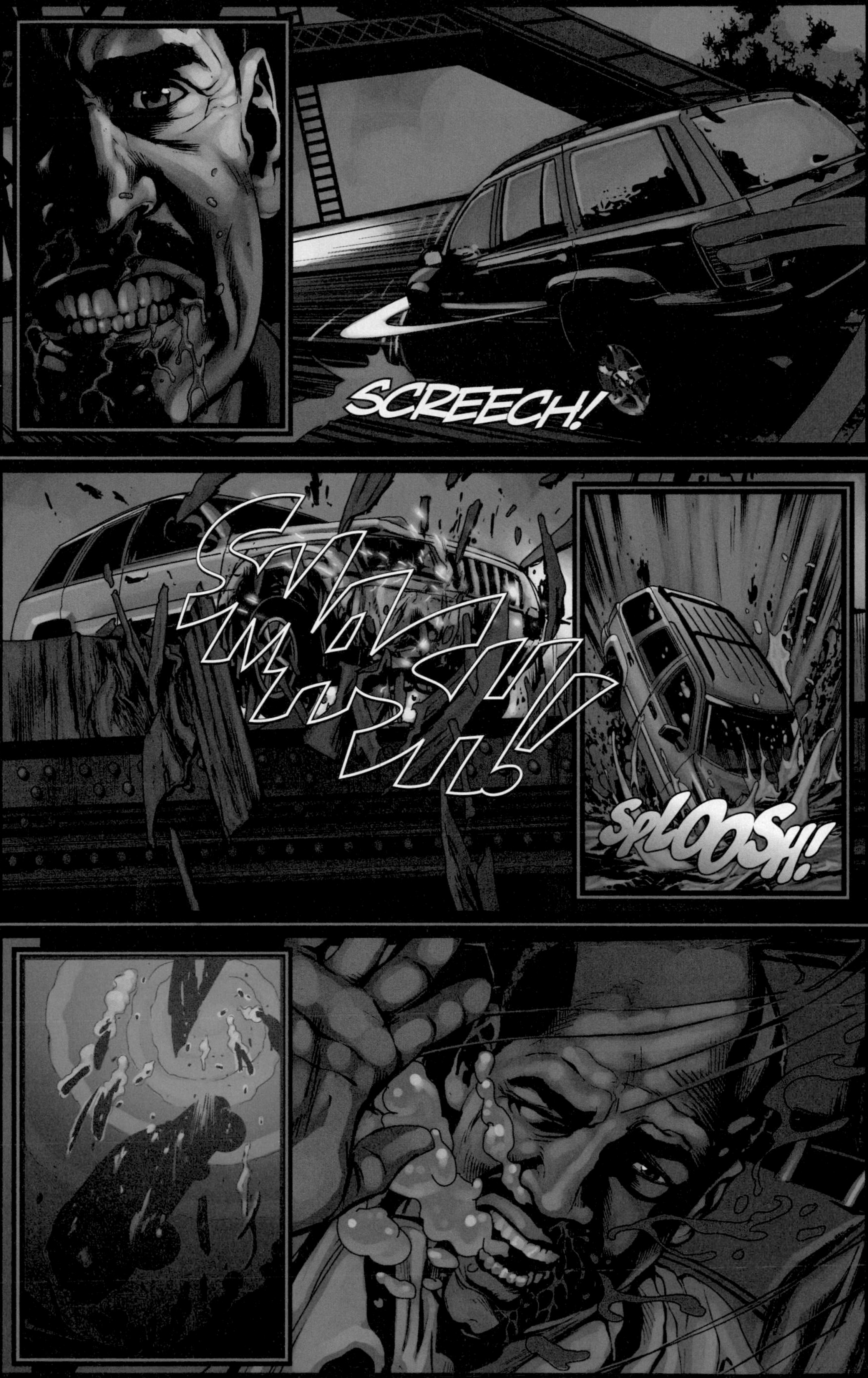
SCREECH!
SMASH!
SPLOOSH!

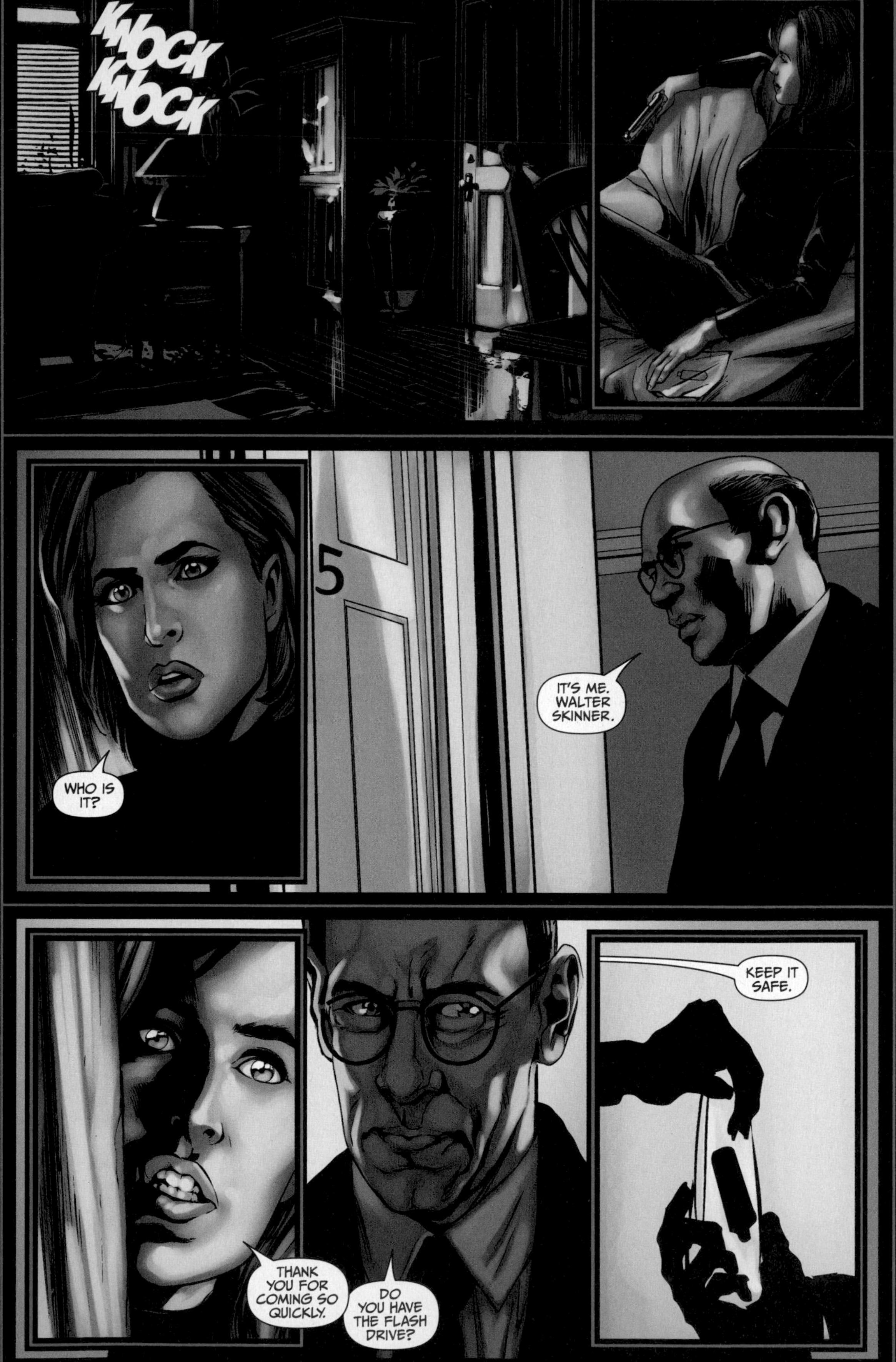
KNOCK
KNOCK
WHO IS IT?
IT'S ME. WALTER SKINNER.
THANK YOU FOR COMING SO QUICKLY.
DO YOU HAVE THE FLASH DRIVE?
KEEP IT SAFE.

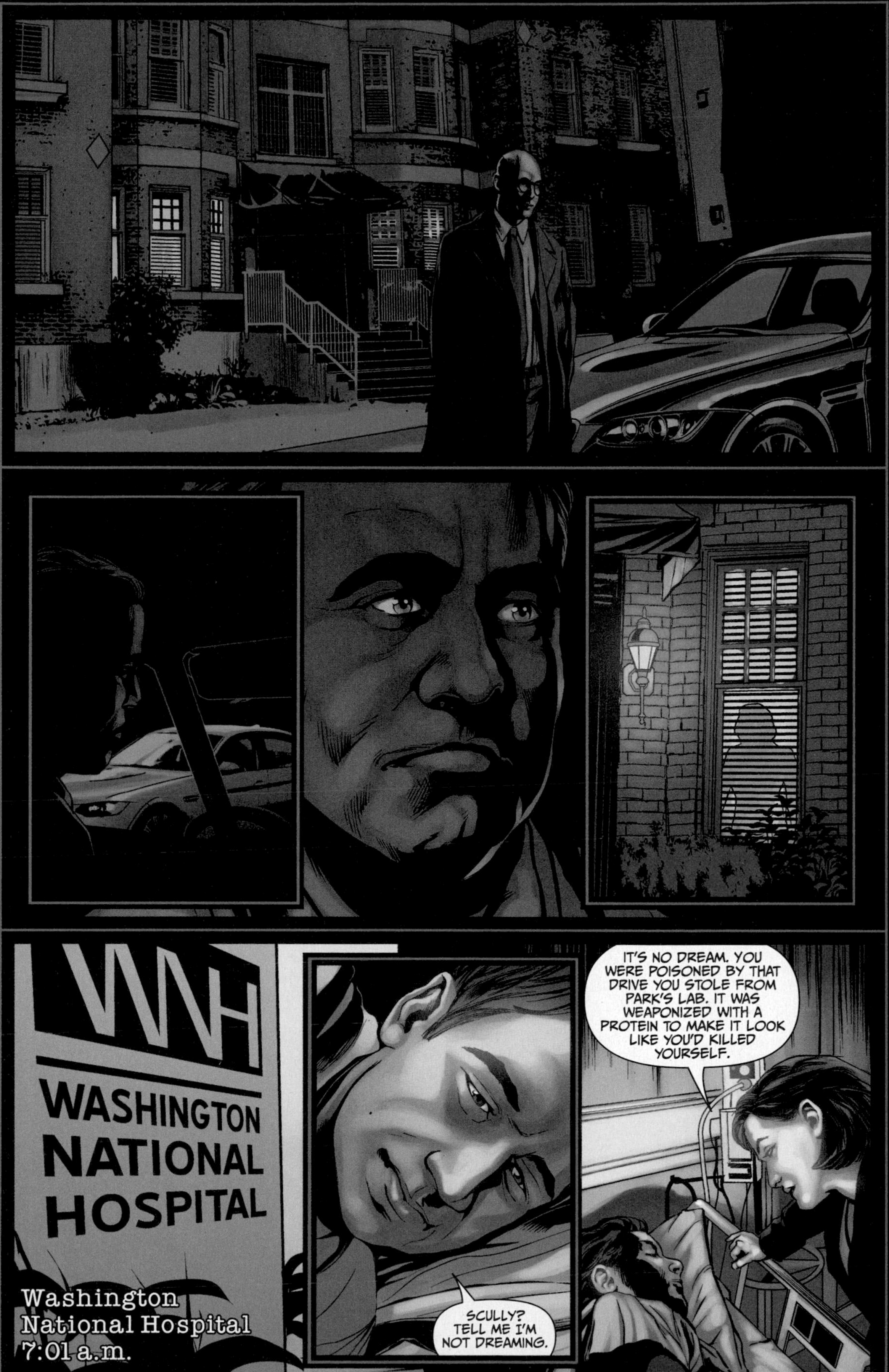
WNH
WASHINGTON NATIONAL HOSPITAL
Washington National Hospital 7:01 a.m.
SCULLY? TELL ME I'M NOT DREAMING.
IT'S NO DREAM. YOU WERE POISONED BY THAT DRIVE YOU STOLE FROM PARK'S LAB. IT WAS WEAPONIZED WITH A PROTEIN TO MAKE IT LOOK LIKE YOU'D KILLED YOURSELF.

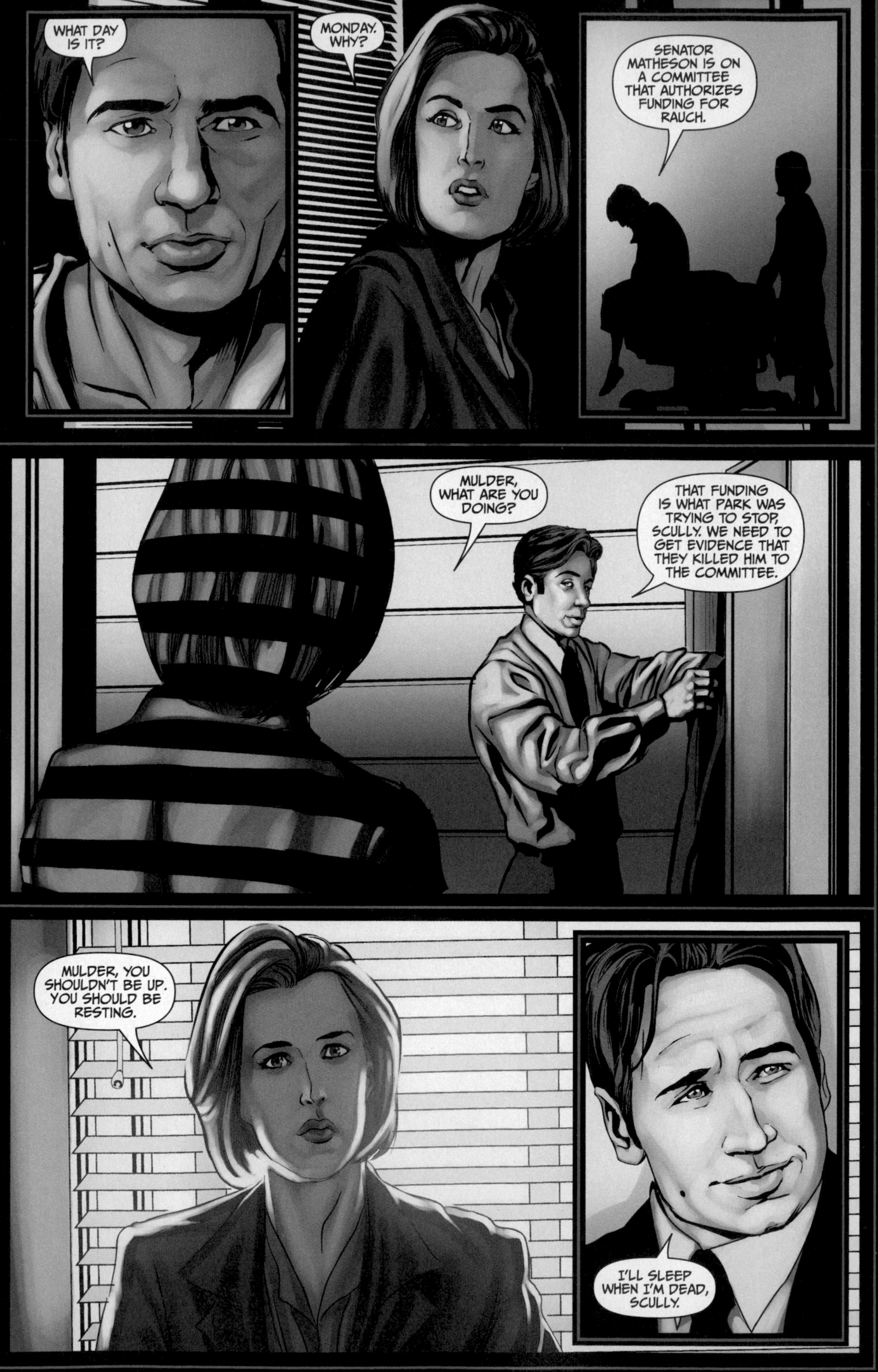
WHAT DAY IS IT?
MONDAY. WHY?
SENATOR MATHESON IS ON A COMMITTEE THAT AUTHORIZES FUNDING FOR RAUCH.
MULDER, WHAT ARE YOU DOING?
THAT FUNDING IS WHAT PARK WAS TRYING TO STOP, SCULLY. WE NEED TO GET EVIDENCE THAT THEY KILLED HIM TO THE COMMITTEE.
MULDER, YOU SHOULDN'T BE UP. YOU SHOULD BE RESTING.
I'LL SLEEP WHEN I'M DEAD, SCULLY.

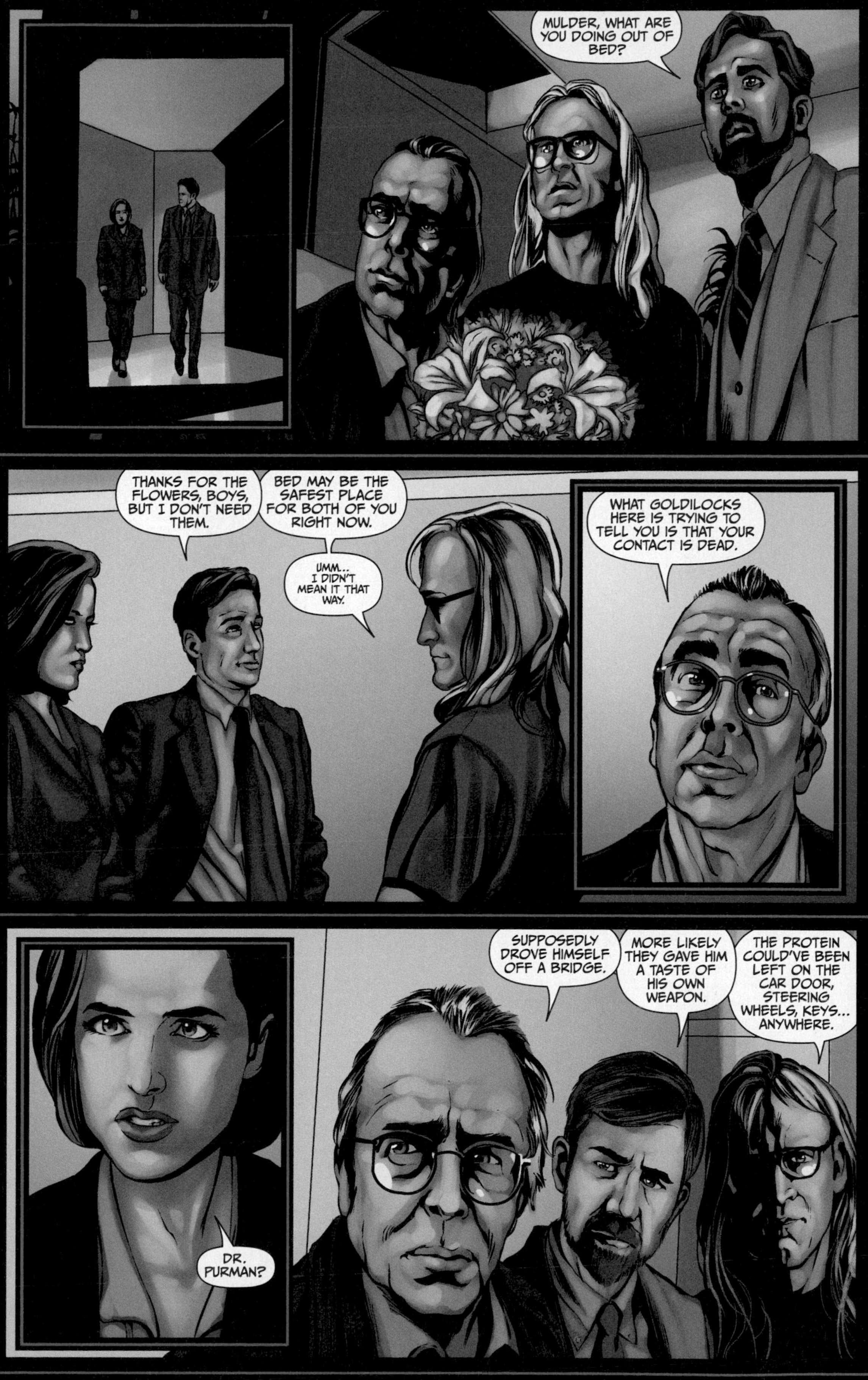
MULDER, WHAT ARE YOU DOING OUT OF BED?
THANKS FOR THE FLOWERS, BOYS, BUT I DON'T NEED THEM.
BED MAY BE THE SAFEST PLACE FOR BOTH OF YOU RIGHT NOW.
UMM... I DIDN'T MEAN IT THAT WAY.
WHAT GOLDILOCKS HERE IS TRYING TO TELL YOU IS THAT YOUR CONTACT IS DEAD.
DR. PURMAN?
SUPPOSEDLY DROVE HIMSELF OFF A BRIDGE.
MORE LIKELY THEY GAVE HIM A TASTE OF HIS OWN WEAPON.
THE PROTEIN COULD'VE BEEN LEFT ON THE CAR DOOR, STEERING WHEELS, KEYS... ANYWHERE.

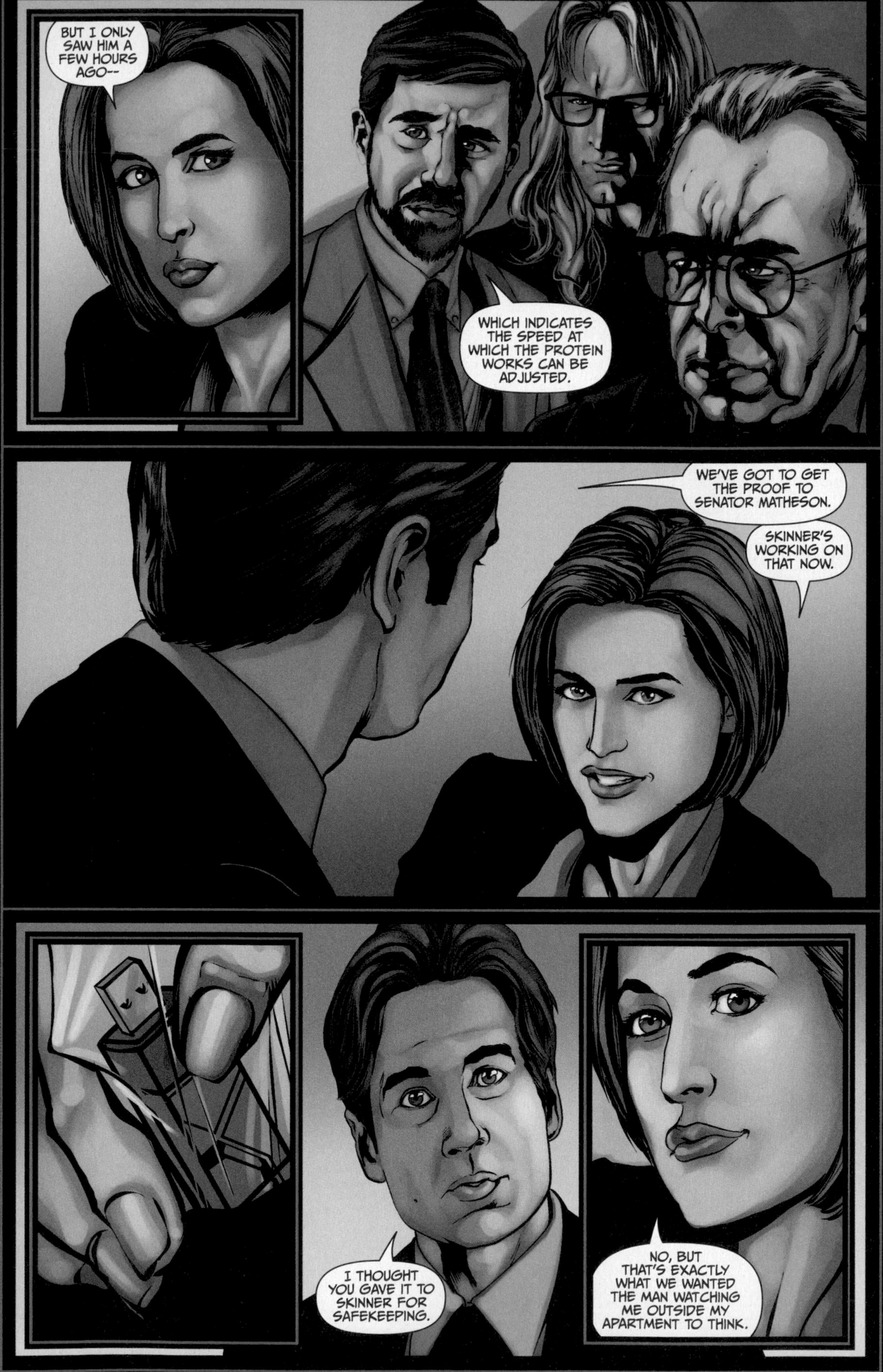
BUT I ONLY SAW HIM A FEW HOURS AGO--
WHICH INDICATES THE SPEED AT WHICH THE PROTEIN WORKS CAN BE ADJUSTED.
WE'VE GOT TO GET THE PROOF TO SENATOR MATHESON.
SKINNER'S WORKING ON THAT NOW.
I THOUGHT YOU GAVE IT TO SKINNER FOR SAFEKEEPING.
NO, BUT THAT'S EXACTLY WHAT WE WANTED THE MAN WATCHING ME OUTSIDE MY APARTMENT TO THINK.

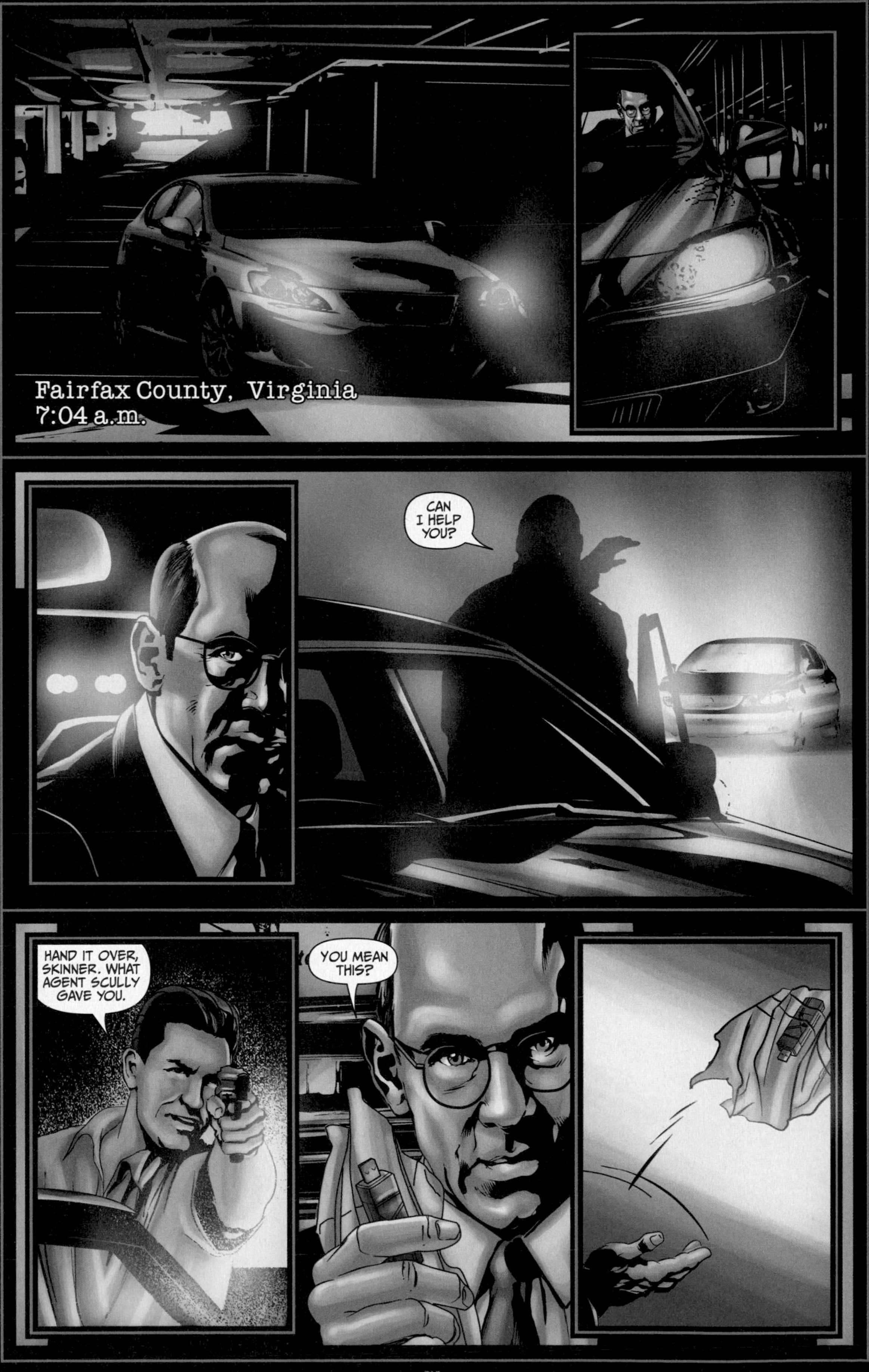
Fairfax County, Virginia
7:04 a.m.
CAN I HELP YOU?
HAND IT OVER, SKINNER. WHAT AGENT SCULLY GAVE YOU.
YOU MEAN THIS?

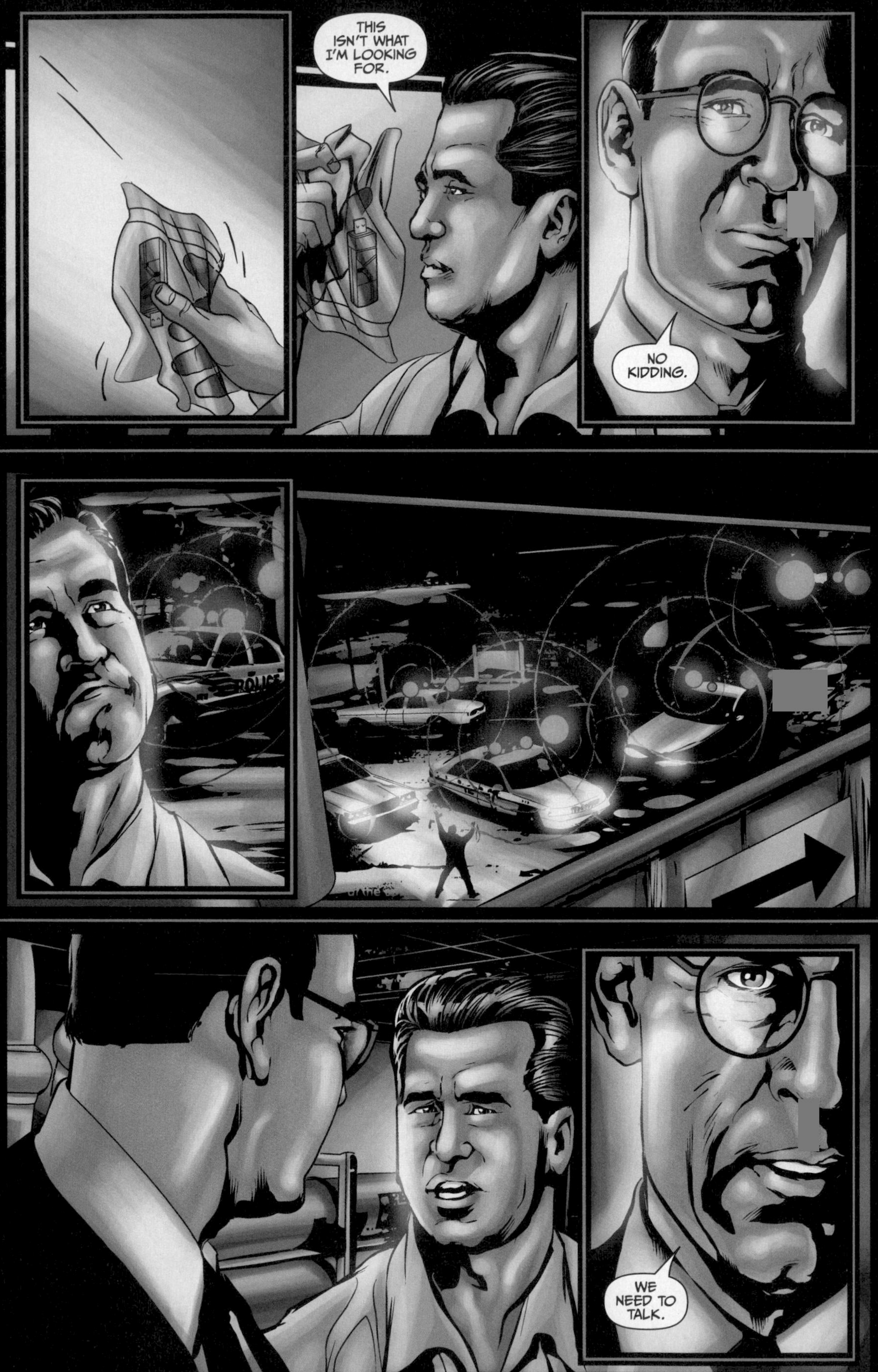
THIS ISN'T WHAT I'M LOOKING FOR.
NO KIDDING.
WE NEED TO TALK.

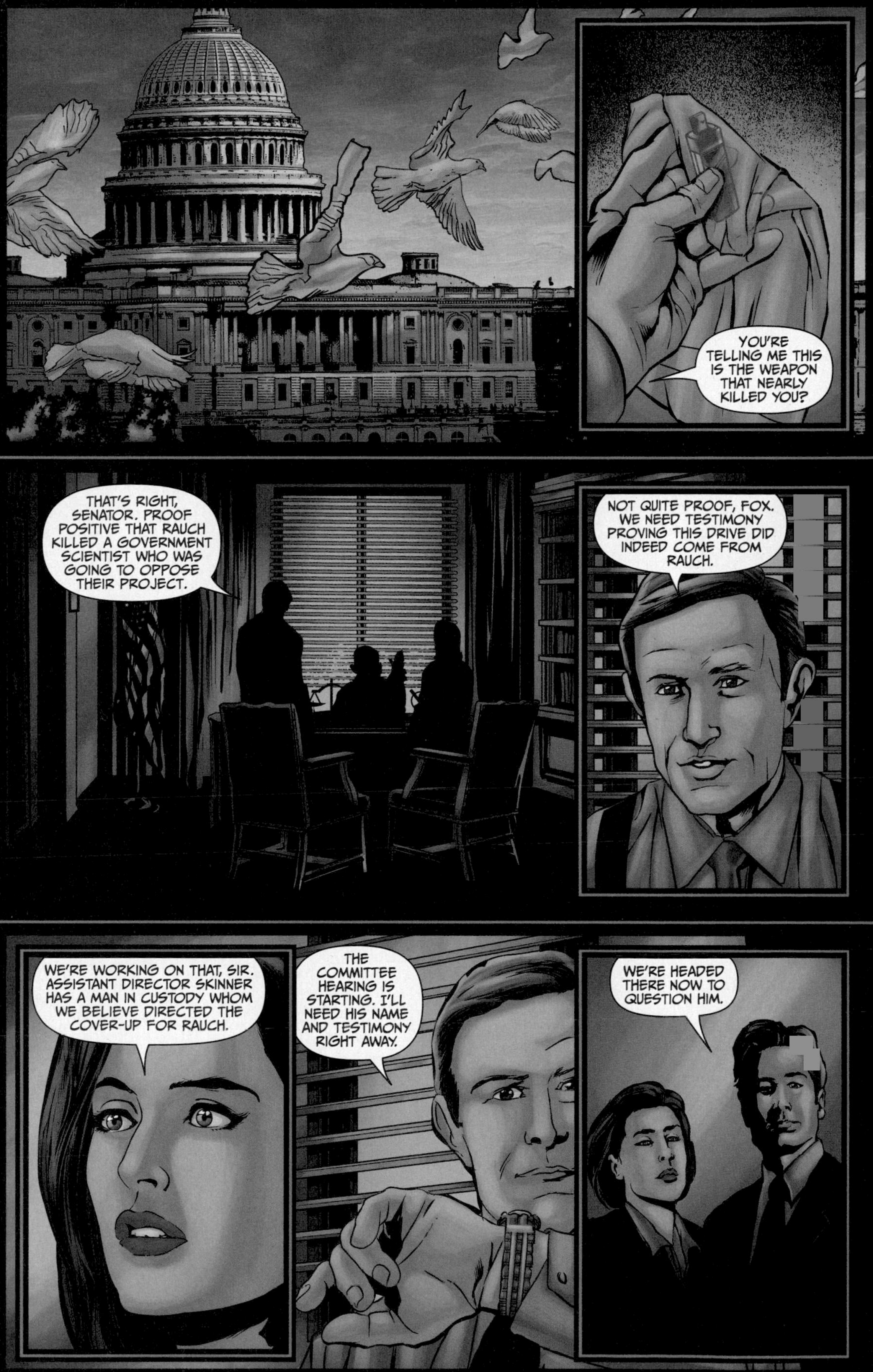
YOU'RE TELLING ME THIS IS THE WEAPON THAT NEARLY KILLED YOU?
THAT'S RIGHT, SENATOR. PROOF POSITIVE THAT RAUCH KILLED A GOVERNMENT SCIENTIST WHO WAS GOING TO OPPOSE THEIR PROJECT.
NOT QUITE PROOF, FOX. WE NEED TESTIMONY PROVING THIS DRIVE DID INDEED COME FROM RAUCH.
WE'RE WORKING ON THAT, SIR. ASSISTANT DIRECTOR SKINNER HAS A MAN IN CUSTODY WHOM WE BELIEVE DIRECTED THE COVER-UP FOR RAUCH.
THE COMMITTEE HEARING IS STARTING. I'LL NEED HIS NAME AND TESTIMONY RIGHT AWAY.
WE'RE HEADED THERE NOW TO QUESTION HIM.

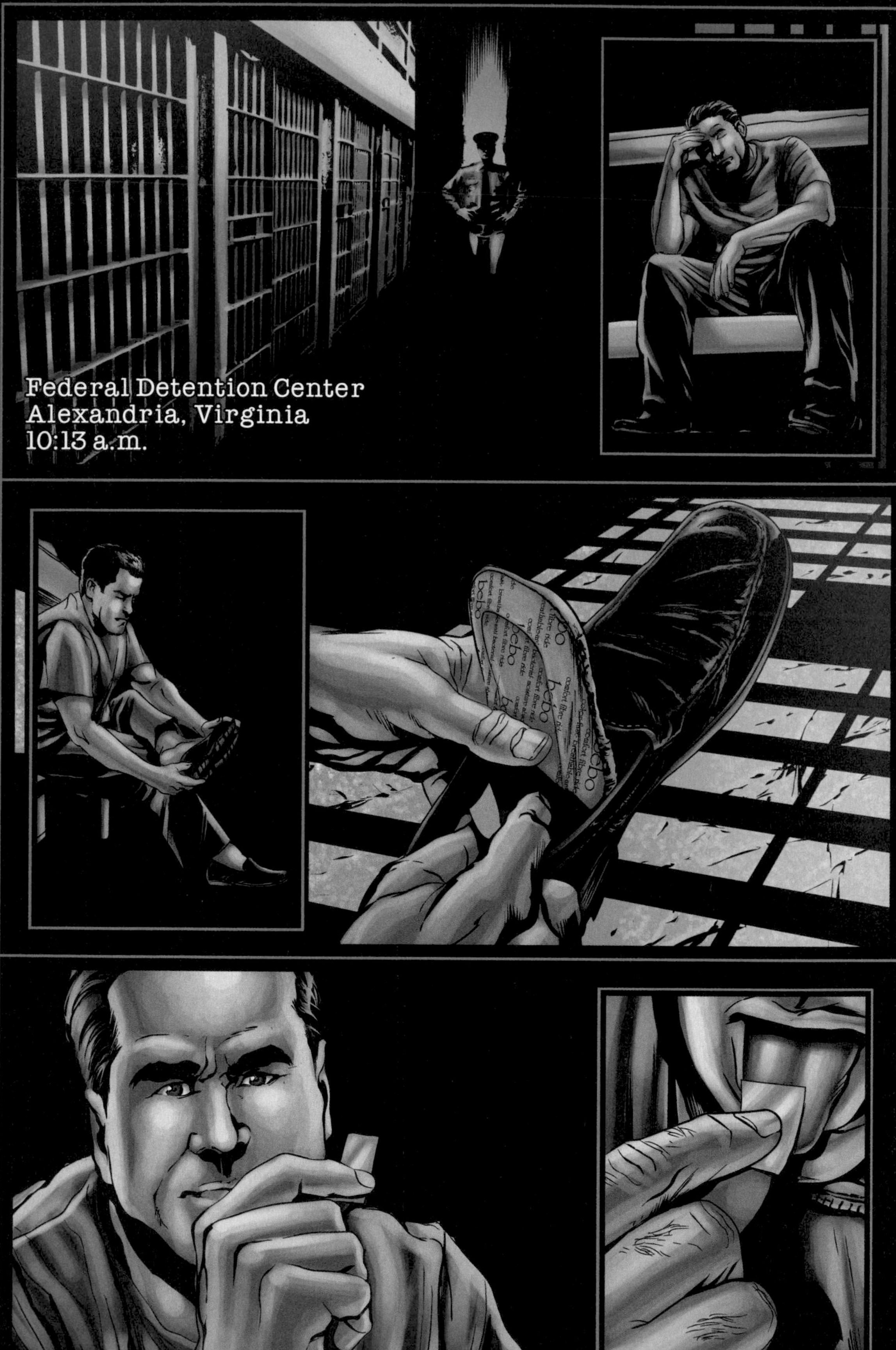
Federal Detention Center
Alexandria, Virginia
10:13 a.m.

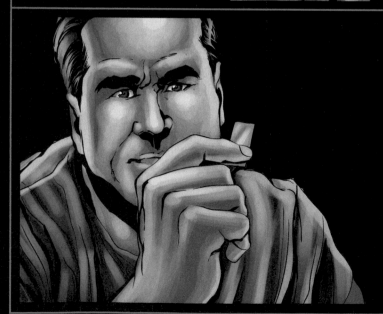

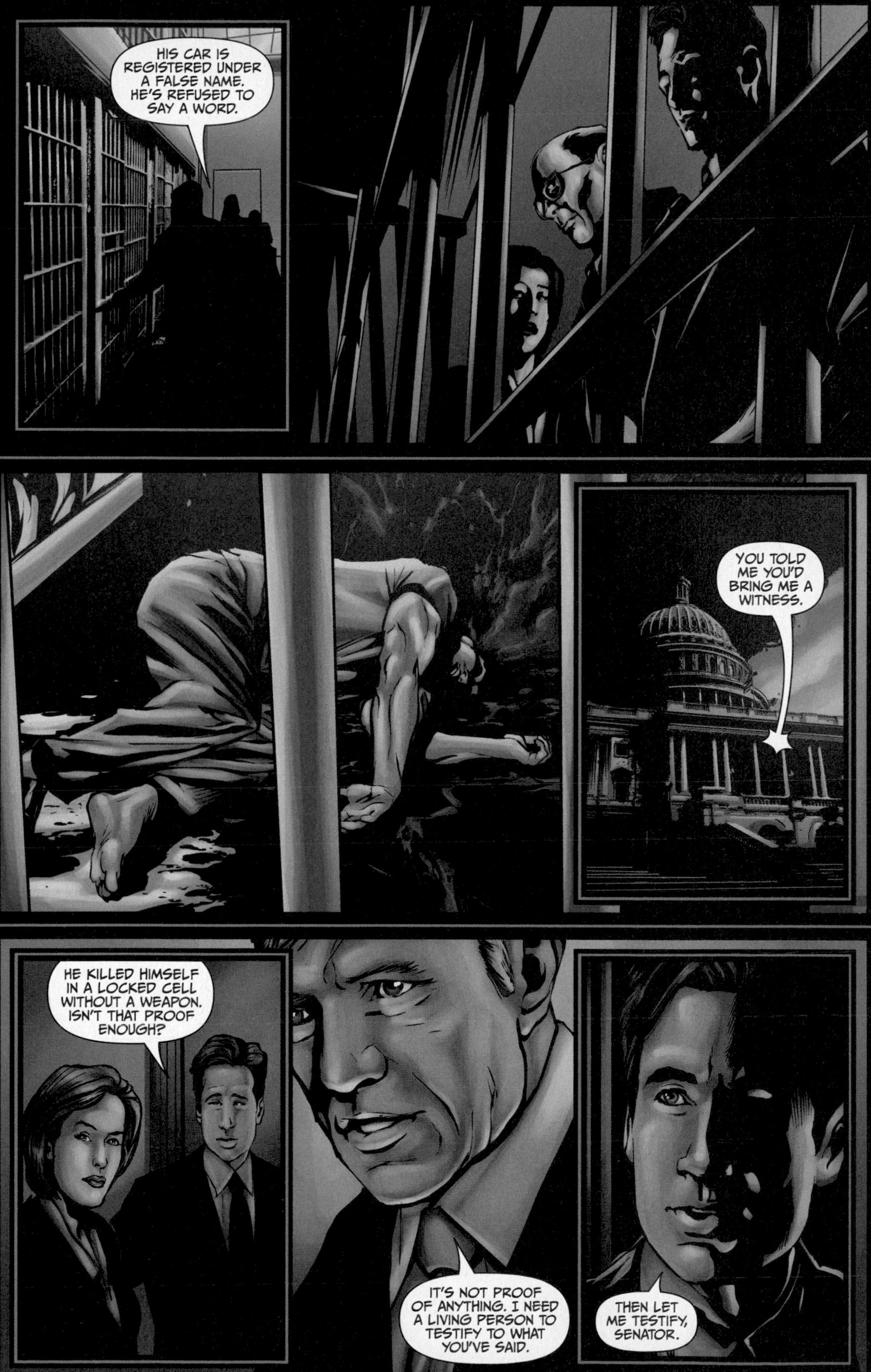
HIS CAR IS REGISTERED UNDER A FALSE NAME. HE'S REFUSED TO SAY A WORD.
YOU TOLD ME YOU'D BRING ME A WITNESS.
HE KILLED HIMSELF IN A LOCKED CELL WITHOUT A WEAPON. ISN'T THAT PROOF ENOUGH?
IT'S NOT PROOF OF ANYTHING. I NEED A LIVING PERSON TO TESTIFY TO WHAT YOU'VE SAID.
THEN LET ME TESTIFY, SENATOR.

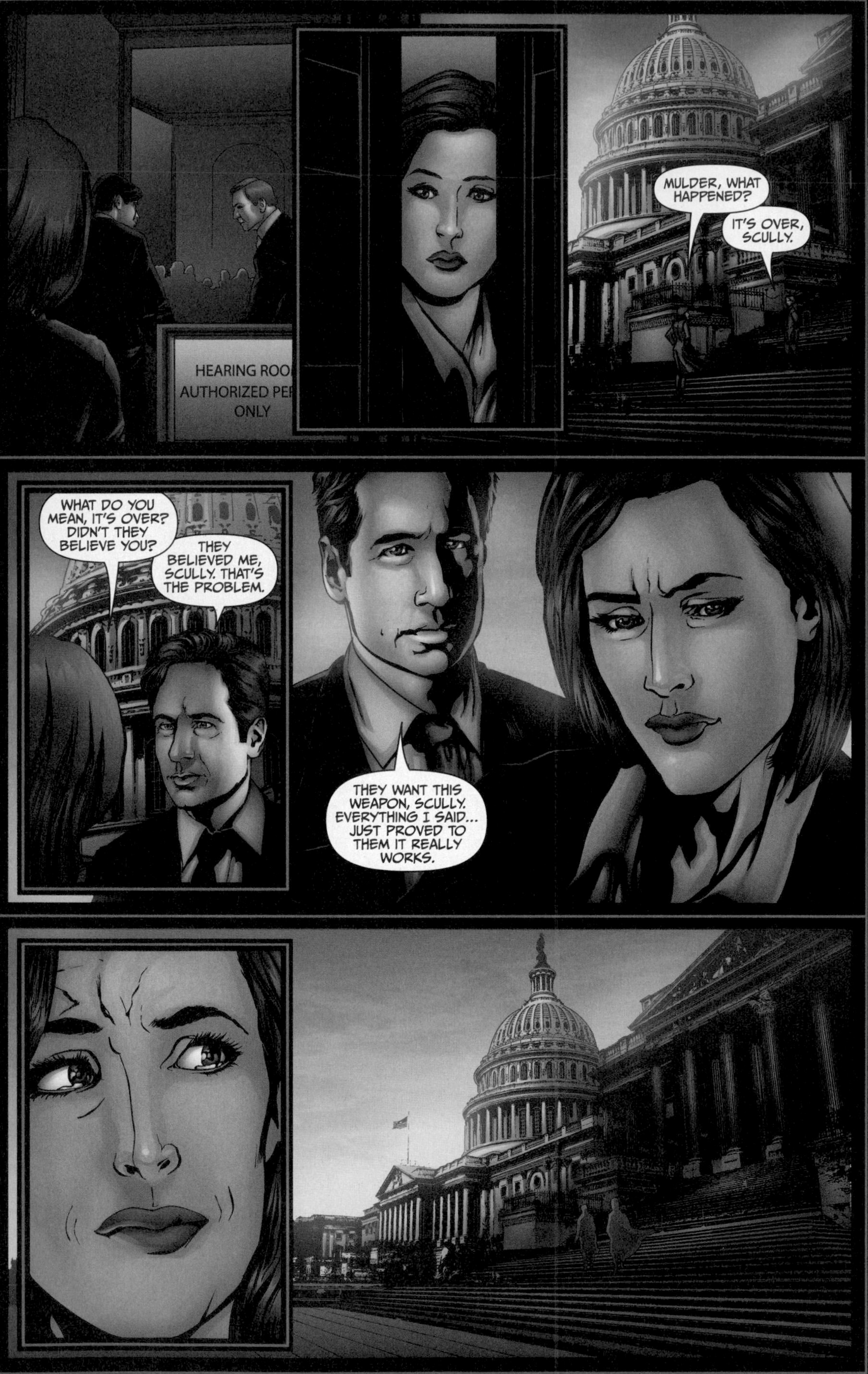
HEARING ROO
AUTHORIZED PE
ONLY
MULDER, WHAT HAPPENED?
IT'S OVER, SCULLY.
WHAT DO YOU MEAN, IT'S OVER? DIDN'T THEY BELIEVE YOU?
THEY BELIEVED ME, SCULLY. THAT'S THE PROBLEM.
THEY WANT THIS WEAPON, SCULLY. EVERYTHING I SAID... JUST PROVED TO THEM IT REALLY WORKS.

Chapter Three

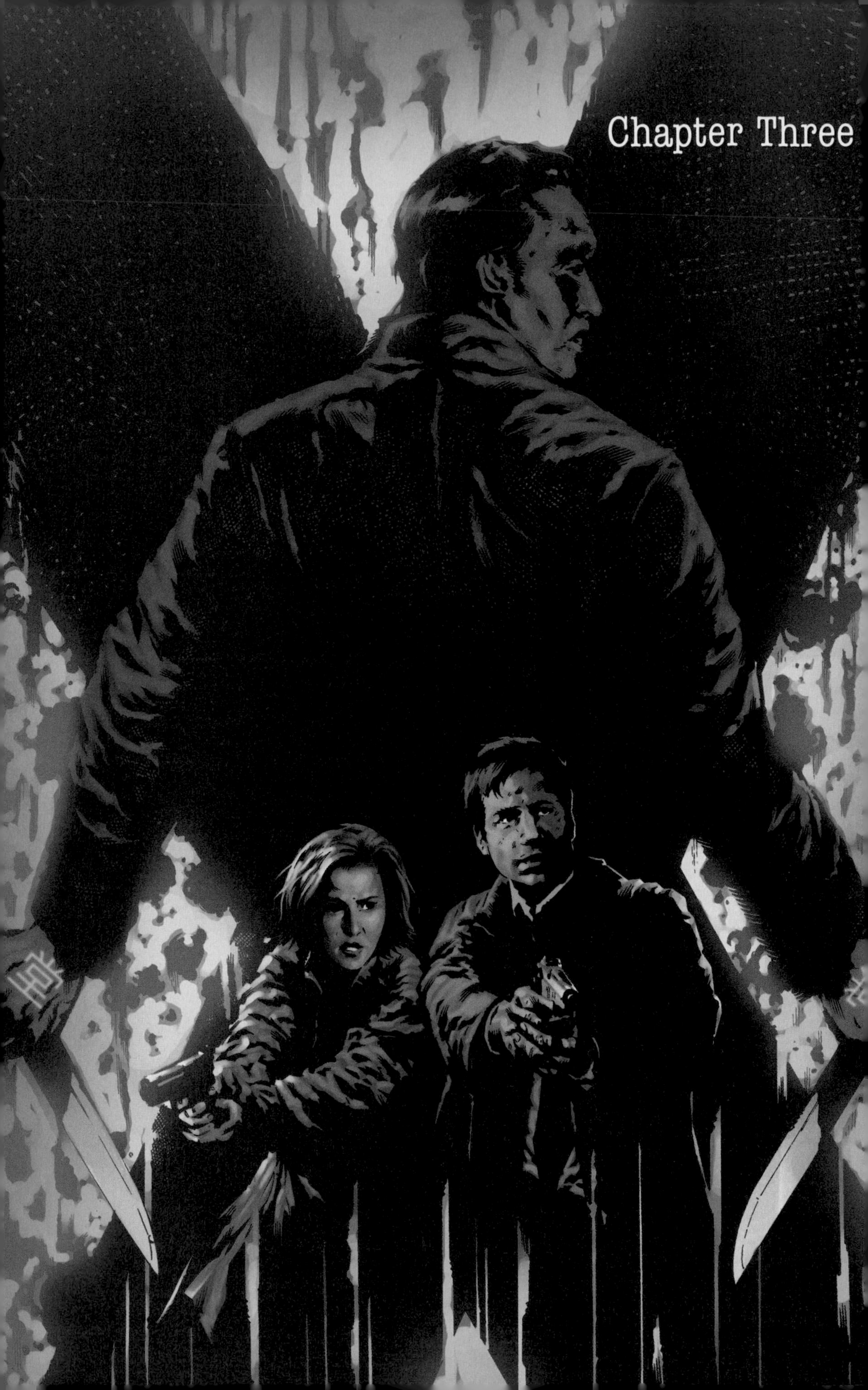

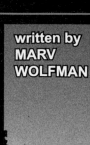

written by
MARV
WOLFMAN

illustrated by
BRIAN DENHAM

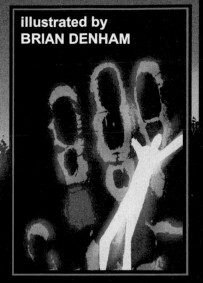

THE (X) FILES

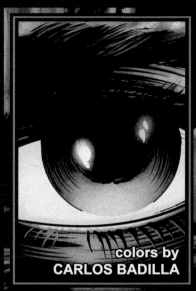

letters by
ED DUKESHIRE

edited by
SHANNON
ERIC DENTON

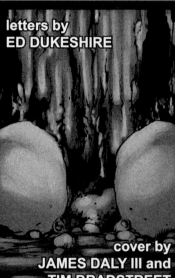

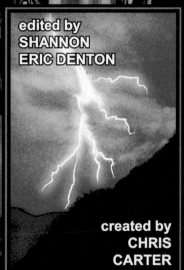

colors by
CARLOS BADILLA

cover by
JAMES DALY III and
TIM BRADSTREET

created by
CHRIS
CARTER

Chongqing, China.
January 21, 1961. 2:47 p.m.

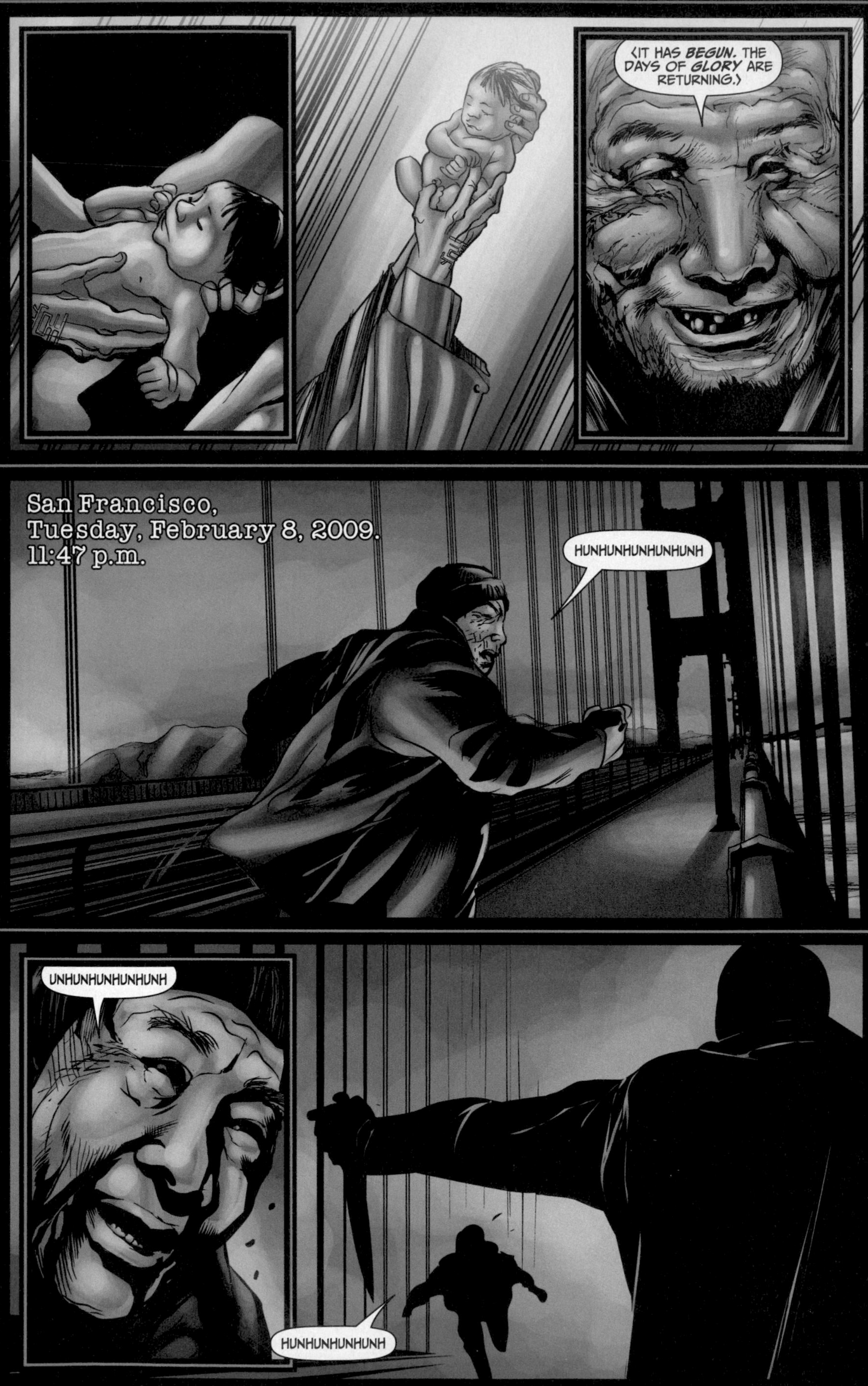

<IT HAS BEGUN. THE DAYS OF GLORY ARE RETURNING.>
San Francisco, Tuesday, February 8, 2009. 11:47 p.m.
HUNHUNHUNHUNHUNH
UNHUNHUNHUNHUNH
HUNHUNHUNHUNH

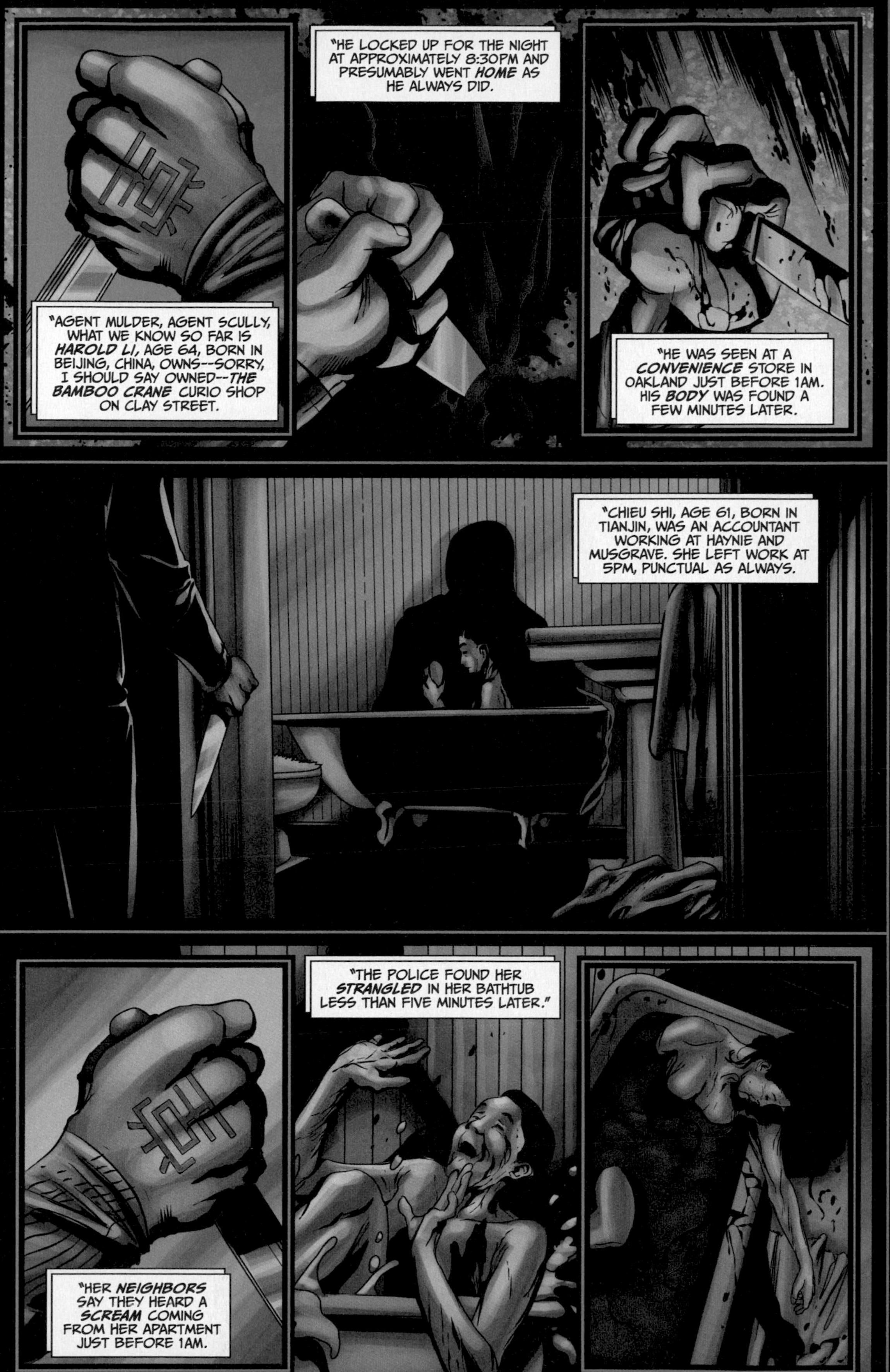
"AGENT MULDER, AGENT SCULLY, WHAT WE KNOW SO FAR IS HAROLD LI, AGE 64, BORN IN BEIJING, CHINA, OWNS--SORRY, I SHOULD SAY OWNED--THE BAMBOO CRANE CURIO SHOP ON CLAY STREET.
"HE LOCKED UP FOR THE NIGHT AT APPROXIMATELY 8:30PM AND PRESUMABLY WENT HOME AS HE ALWAYS DID.
"HE WAS SEEN AT A CONVENIENCE STORE IN OAKLAND JUST BEFORE 1AM. HIS BODY WAS FOUND A FEW MINUTES LATER.
"CHIEU SHI, AGE 61, BORN IN TIANJIN, WAS AN ACCOUNTANT WORKING AT HAYNIE AND MUSGRAVE. SHE LEFT WORK AT 5PM, PUNCTUAL AS ALWAYS.
"HER NEIGHBORS SAY THEY HEARD A SCREAM COMING FROM HER APARTMENT JUST BEFORE 1AM.
"THE POLICE FOUND HER STRANGLED IN HER BATHTUB LESS THAN FIVE MINUTES LATER."

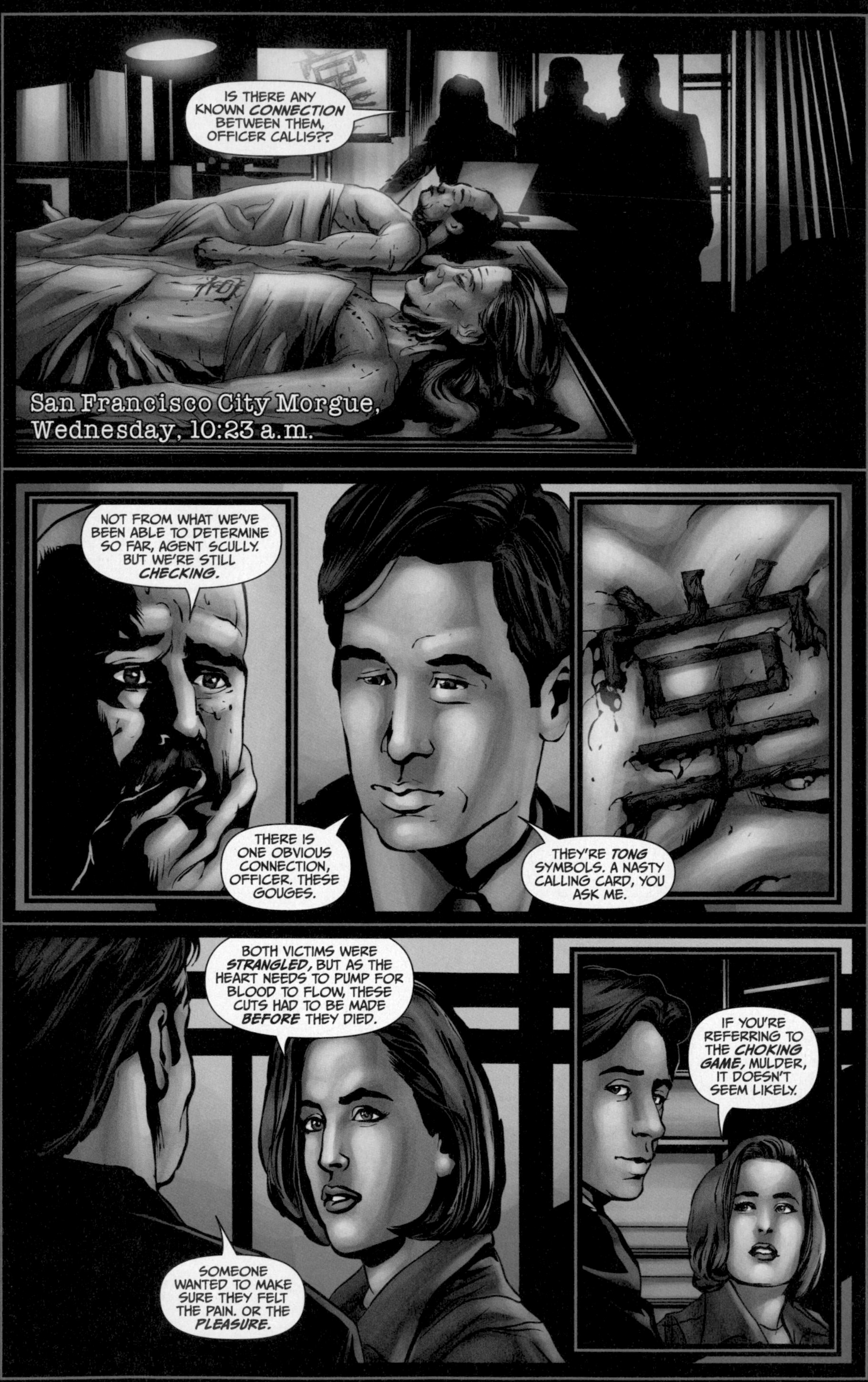
IS THERE ANY KNOWN CONNECTION BETWEEN THEM, OFFICER CALLIS??
San Francisco City Morgue, Wednesday, 10:23 a.m.
NOT FROM WHAT WE'VE BEEN ABLE TO DETERMINE SO FAR, AGENT SCULLY. BUT WE'RE STILL CHECKING.
THERE IS ONE OBVIOUS CONNECTION, OFFICER. THESE GOUGES.
THEY'RE TONG SYMBOLS. A NASTY CALLING CARD, YOU ASK ME.
BOTH VICTIMS WERE STRANGLED, BUT AS THE HEART NEEDS TO PUMP FOR BLOOD TO FLOW, THESE CUTS HAD TO BE MADE BEFORE THEY DIED.
SOMEONE WANTED TO MAKE SURE THEY FELT THE PAIN. OR THE PLEASURE.
IF YOU'RE REFERRING TO THE CHOKING GAME, MULDER, IT DOESN'T SEEM LIKELY.

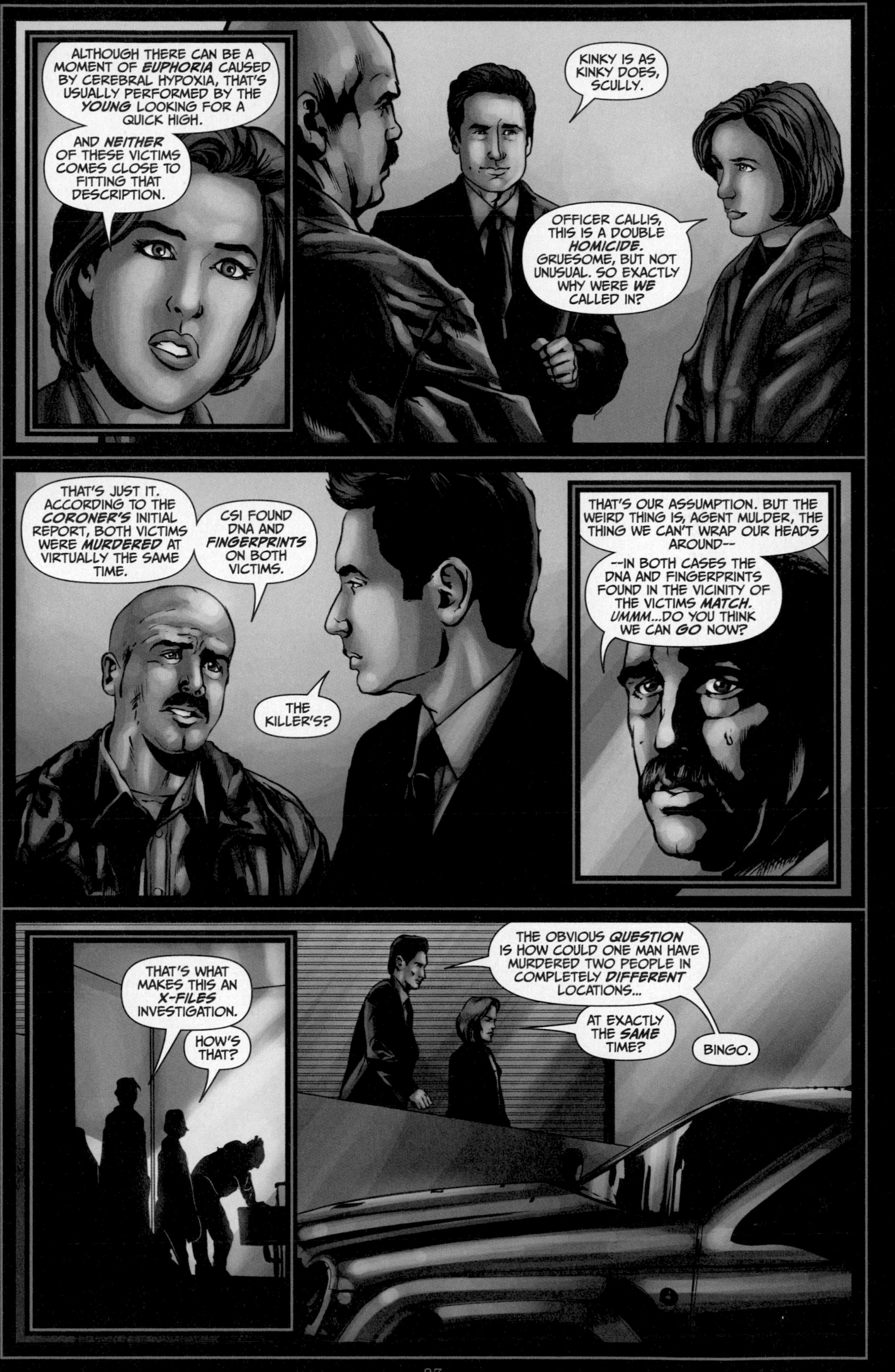
ALTHOUGH THERE CAN BE A MOMENT OF EUPHORIA CAUSED BY CEREBRAL HYPOXIA, THAT'S USUALLY PERFORMED BY THE YOUNG LOOKING FOR A QUICK HIGH.
AND NEITHER OF THESE VICTIMS COMES CLOSE TO FITTING THAT DESCRIPTION.
KINKY IS AS KINKY DOES, SCULLY.
OFFICER CALLIS, THIS IS A DOUBLE HOMICIDE. GRUESOME, BUT NOT UNUSUAL. SO EXACTLY WHY WERE WE CALLED IN?
THAT'S JUST IT. ACCORDING TO THE CORONER'S INITIAL REPORT, BOTH VICTIMS WERE MURDERED AT VIRTUALLY THE SAME TIME.
CSI FOUND DNA AND FINGERPRINTS ON BOTH VICTIMS.
THE KILLER'S?
THAT'S OUR ASSUMPTION. BUT THE WEIRD THING IS, AGENT MULDER, THE THING WE CAN'T WRAP OUR HEADS AROUND--
--IN BOTH CASES THE DNA AND FINGERPRINTS FOUND IN THE VICINITY OF THE VICTIMS MATCH. UMMM...DO YOU THINK WE CAN GO NOW?
THAT'S WHAT MAKES THIS AN X-FILES INVESTIGATION.
HOW'S THAT?
THE OBVIOUS QUESTION IS HOW COULD ONE MAN HAVE MURDERED TWO PEOPLE IN COMPLETELY DIFFERENT LOCATIONS...
AT EXACTLY THE SAME TIME?
BINGO.

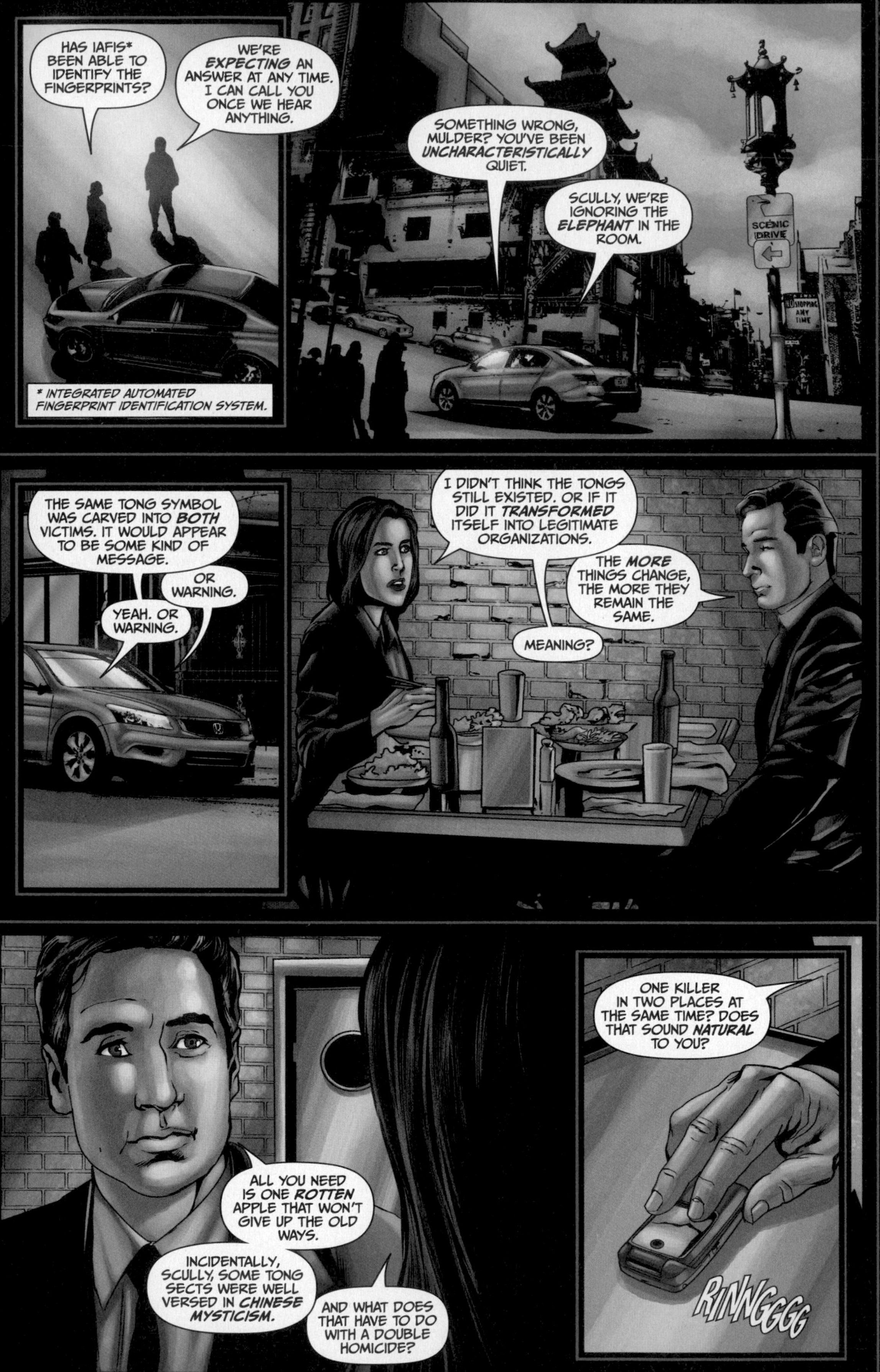

HAS IAFIS* BEEN ABLE TO IDENTIFY THE FINGERPRINTS?
WE'RE EXPECTING AN ANSWER AT ANY TIME. I CAN CALL YOU ONCE WE HEAR ANYTHING.
* INTEGRATED AUTOMATED FINGERPRINT IDENTIFICATION SYSTEM.
SOMETHING WRONG, MULDER? YOU'VE BEEN UNCHARACTERISTICALLY QUIET.
SCULLY, WE'RE IGNORING THE ELEPHANT IN THE ROOM.
SCENIC DRIVE
NO STOPPING ANY TIME
THE SAME TONG SYMBOL WAS CARVED INTO BOTH VICTIMS. IT WOULD APPEAR TO BE SOME KIND OF MESSAGE.
OR WARNING.
YEAH. OR WARNING.
I DIDN'T THINK THE TONGS STILL EXISTED. OR IF IT DID IT TRANSFORMED ITSELF INTO LEGITIMATE ORGANIZATIONS.
THE MORE THINGS CHANGE, THE MORE THEY REMAIN THE SAME.
MEANING?
ALL YOU NEED IS ONE ROTTEN APPLE THAT WON'T GIVE UP THE OLD WAYS.
INCIDENTALLY, SCULLY, SOME TONG SECTS WERE WELL VERSED IN CHINESE MYSTICISM.
AND WHAT DOES THAT HAVE TO DO WITH A DOUBLE HOMICIDE?
ONE KILLER IN TWO PLACES AT THE SAME TIME? DOES THAT SOUND NATURAL TO YOU?
RINNGGGG

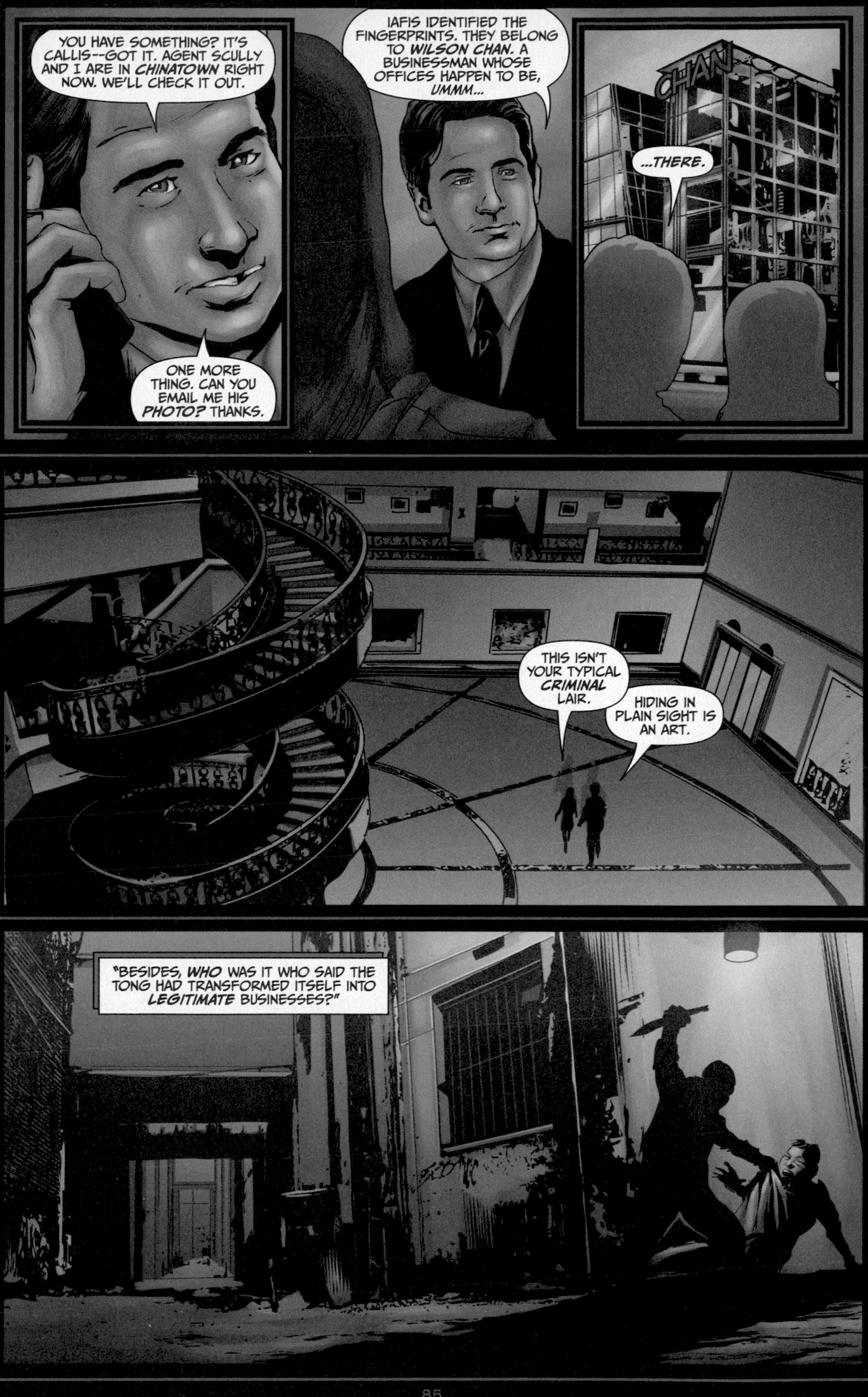
YOU HAVE SOMETHING? IT'S CALLIS--GOT IT. AGENT SCULLY AND I ARE IN CHINATOWN RIGHT NOW. WE'LL CHECK IT OUT.
ONE MORE THING. CAN YOU EMAIL ME HIS PHOTO? THANKS.
IAFIS IDENTIFIED THE FINGERPRINTS. THEY BELONG TO WILSON CHAN. A BUSINESSMAN WHOSE OFFICES HAPPEN TO BE, UMMM...
CHAN
...THERE.
THIS ISN'T YOUR TYPICAL CRIMINAL LAIR.
HIDING IN PLAIN SIGHT IS AN ART.
"BESIDES, WHO WAS IT WHO SAID THE TONG HAD TRANSFORMED ITSELF INTO LEGITIMATE BUSINESSES?"

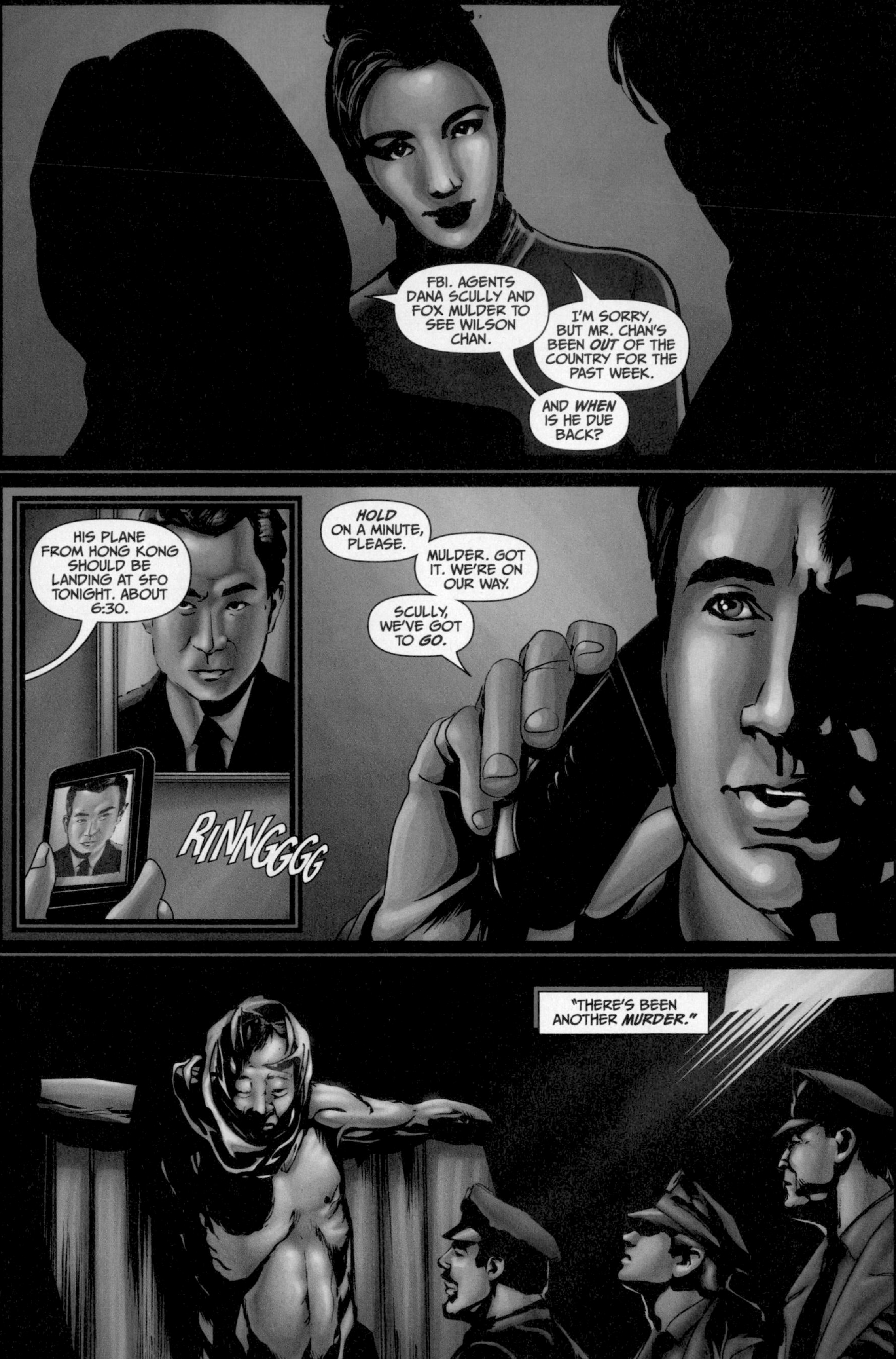
FBI. AGENTS DANA SCULLY AND FOX MULDER TO SEE WILSON CHAN.
I'M SORRY, BUT MR. CHAN'S BEEN *OUT* OF THE COUNTRY FOR THE PAST WEEK.
AND *WHEN* IS HE DUE BACK?
HIS PLANE FROM HONG KONG SHOULD BE LANDING AT SFO TONIGHT. ABOUT 6:30.
RINNGGGG
HOLD ON A MINUTE, PLEASE.
MULDER. GOT IT. WE'RE ON OUR WAY.
SCULLY, WE'VE GOT TO *GO*.
"THERE'S BEEN ANOTHER *MURDER*."

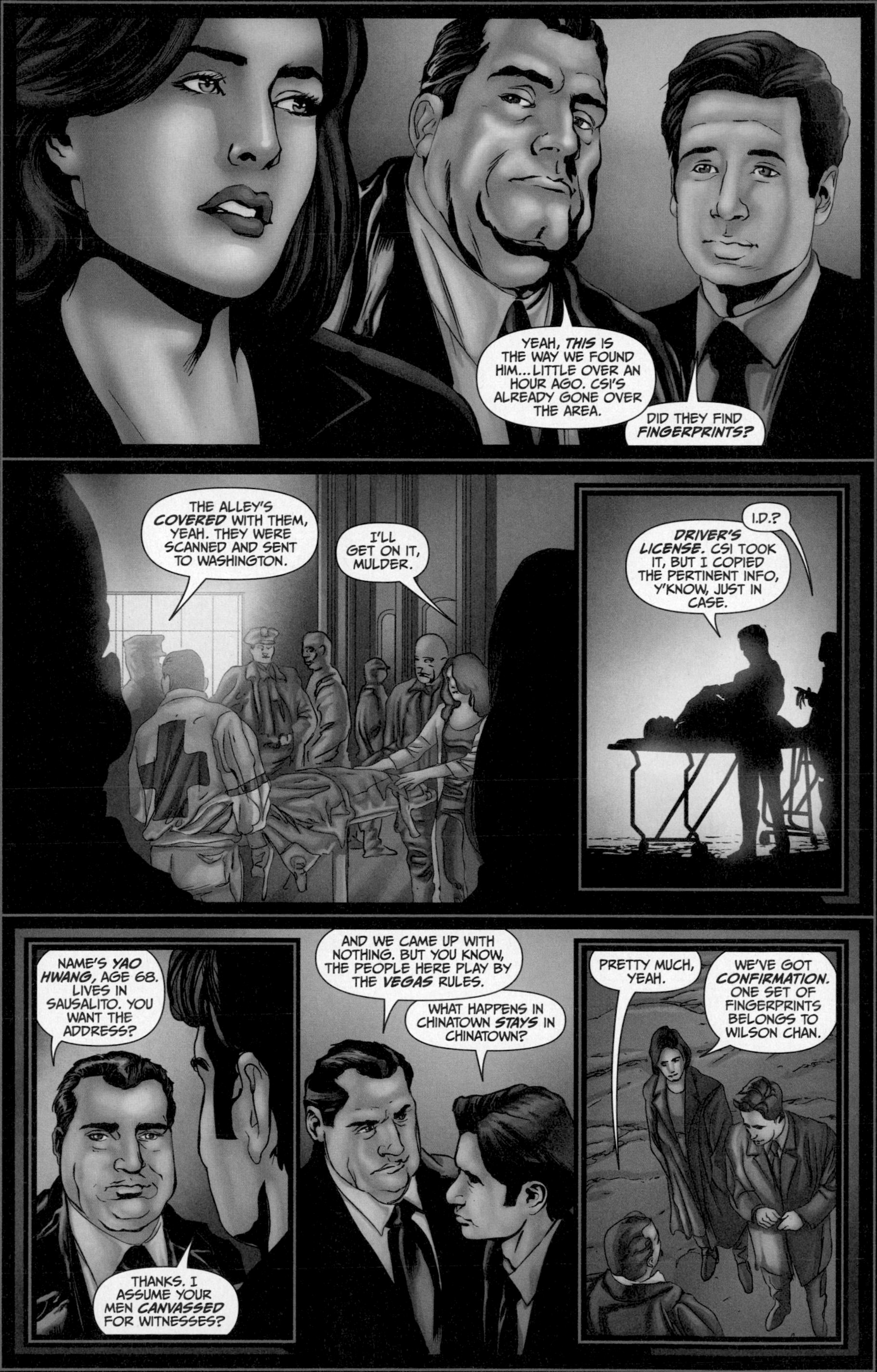
YEAH, *THIS* IS THE WAY WE FOUND HIM... LITTLE OVER AN HOUR AGO. CSI'S ALREADY GONE OVER THE AREA.
DID THEY FIND *FINGERPRINTS?*
THE ALLEY'S *COVERED* WITH THEM, YEAH. THEY WERE SCANNED AND SENT TO WASHINGTON.
I'LL GET ON IT, MULDER.
I.D.?
DRIVER'S LICENSE. CSI TOOK IT, BUT I COPIED THE PERTINENT INFO, Y'KNOW, JUST IN CASE.
NAME'S *YAO HWANG*, AGE 68. LIVES IN SAUSALITO. YOU WANT THE ADDRESS?
THANKS. I ASSUME YOUR MEN *CANVASSED* FOR WITNESSES?
AND WE CAME UP WITH NOTHING. BUT YOU KNOW, THE PEOPLE HERE PLAY BY THE *VEGAS* RULES.
WHAT HAPPENS IN CHINATOWN *STAYS* IN CHINATOWN?
PRETTY MUCH, YEAH.
WE'VE GOT *CONFIRMATION.* ONE SET OF FINGERPRINTS BELONGS TO WILSON CHAN.

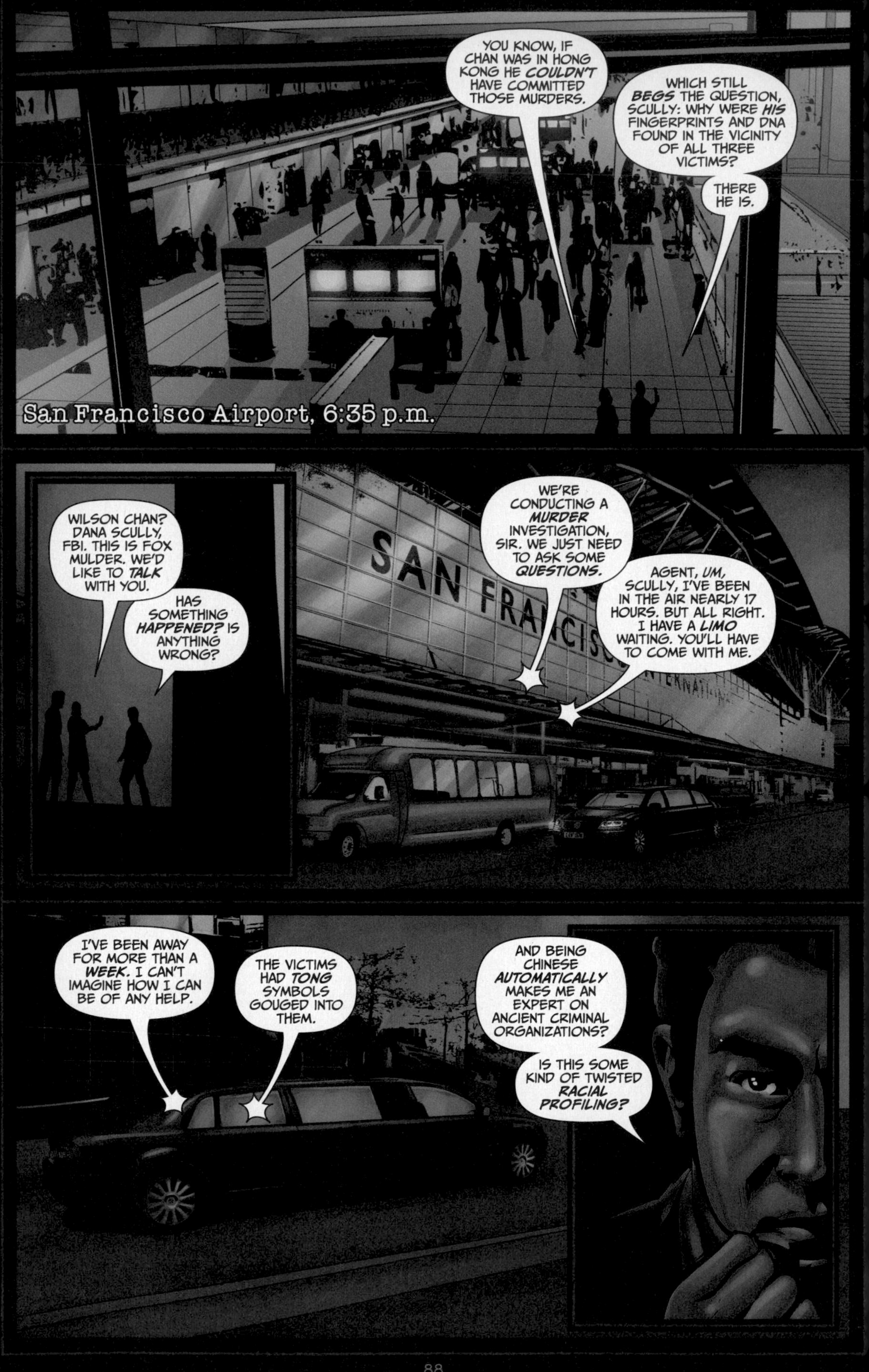
San Francisco Airport, 6:35 p.m.
YOU KNOW, IF CHAN WAS IN HONG KONG HE COULDN'T HAVE COMMITTED THOSE MURDERS.
WHICH STILL BEGS THE QUESTION, SCULLY: WHY WERE HIS FINGERPRINTS AND DNA FOUND IN THE VICINITY OF ALL THREE VICTIMS?
THERE HE IS.
WILSON CHAN? DANA SCULLY, FBI. THIS IS FOX MULDER. WE'D LIKE TO TALK WITH YOU.
HAS SOMETHING HAPPENED? IS ANYTHING WRONG?
SAN FRANCISCO
WE'RE CONDUCTING A MURDER INVESTIGATION, SIR. WE JUST NEED TO ASK SOME QUESTIONS.
AGENT, UM, SCULLY, I'VE BEEN IN THE AIR NEARLY 17 HOURS. BUT ALL RIGHT. I HAVE A LIMO WAITING. YOU'LL HAVE TO COME WITH ME.
I'VE BEEN AWAY FOR MORE THAN A WEEK. I CAN'T IMAGINE HOW I CAN BE OF ANY HELP.
THE VICTIMS HAD TONG SYMBOLS GOUGED INTO THEM.
AND BEING CHINESE AUTOMATICALLY MAKES ME AN EXPERT ON ANCIENT CRIMINAL ORGANIZATIONS?
IS THIS SOME KIND OF TWISTED RACIAL PROFILING?

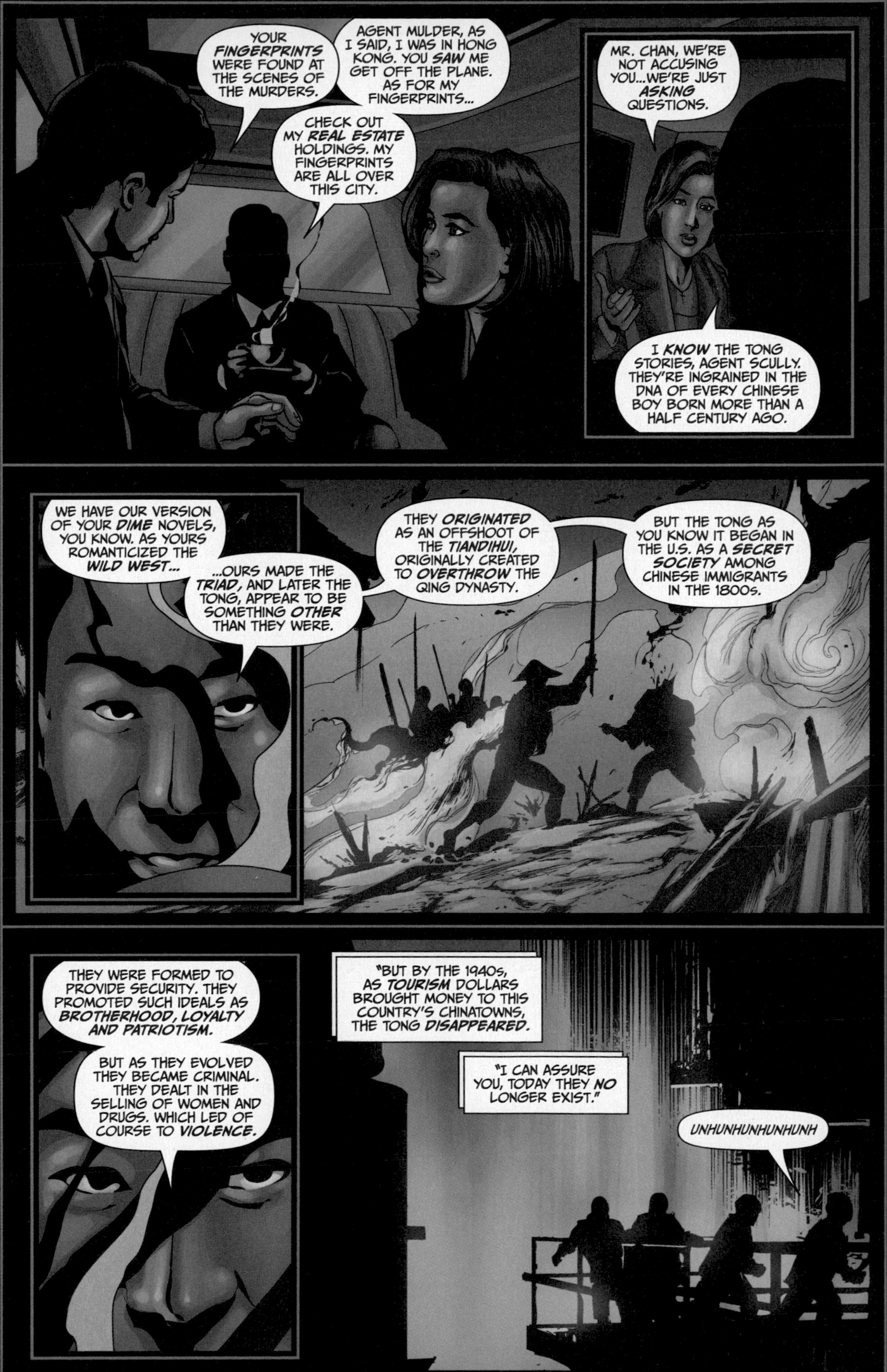
YOUR FINGERPRINTS WERE FOUND AT THE SCENES OF THE MURDERS.
AGENT MULDER, AS I SAID, I WAS IN HONG KONG. YOU SAW ME GET OFF THE PLANE. AS FOR MY FINGERPRINTS...
CHECK OUT MY REAL ESTATE HOLDINGS. MY FINGERPRINTS ARE ALL OVER THIS CITY.
MR. CHAN, WE'RE NOT ACCUSING YOU...WE'RE JUST ASKING QUESTIONS.
I KNOW THE TONG STORIES, AGENT SCULLY. THEY'RE INGRAINED IN THE DNA OF EVERY CHINESE BOY BORN MORE THAN A HALF CENTURY AGO.
WE HAVE OUR VERSION OF YOUR DIME NOVELS, YOU KNOW. AS YOURS ROMANTICIZED THE WILD WEST...
...OURS MADE THE TRIAD, AND LATER THE TONG, APPEAR TO BE SOMETHING OTHER THAN THEY WERE.
THEY ORIGINATED AS AN OFFSHOOT OF THE TIANDIHUI, ORIGINALLY CREATED TO OVERTHROW THE QING DYNASTY.
BUT THE TONG AS YOU KNOW IT BEGAN IN THE U.S. AS A SECRET SOCIETY AMONG CHINESE IMMIGRANTS IN THE 1800s.
THEY WERE FORMED TO PROVIDE SECURITY. THEY PROMOTED SUCH IDEALS AS BROTHERHOOD, LOYALTY AND PATRIOTISM.
BUT AS THEY EVOLVED THEY BECAME CRIMINAL. THEY DEALT IN THE SELLING OF WOMEN AND DRUGS. WHICH LED OF COURSE TO VIOLENCE.
"BUT BY THE 1940s, AS TOURISM DOLLARS BROUGHT MONEY TO THIS COUNTRY'S CHINATOWNS, THE TONG DISAPPEARED.
"I CAN ASSURE YOU, TODAY THEY NO LONGER EXIST."
UNHUNHUNHUNHUNH

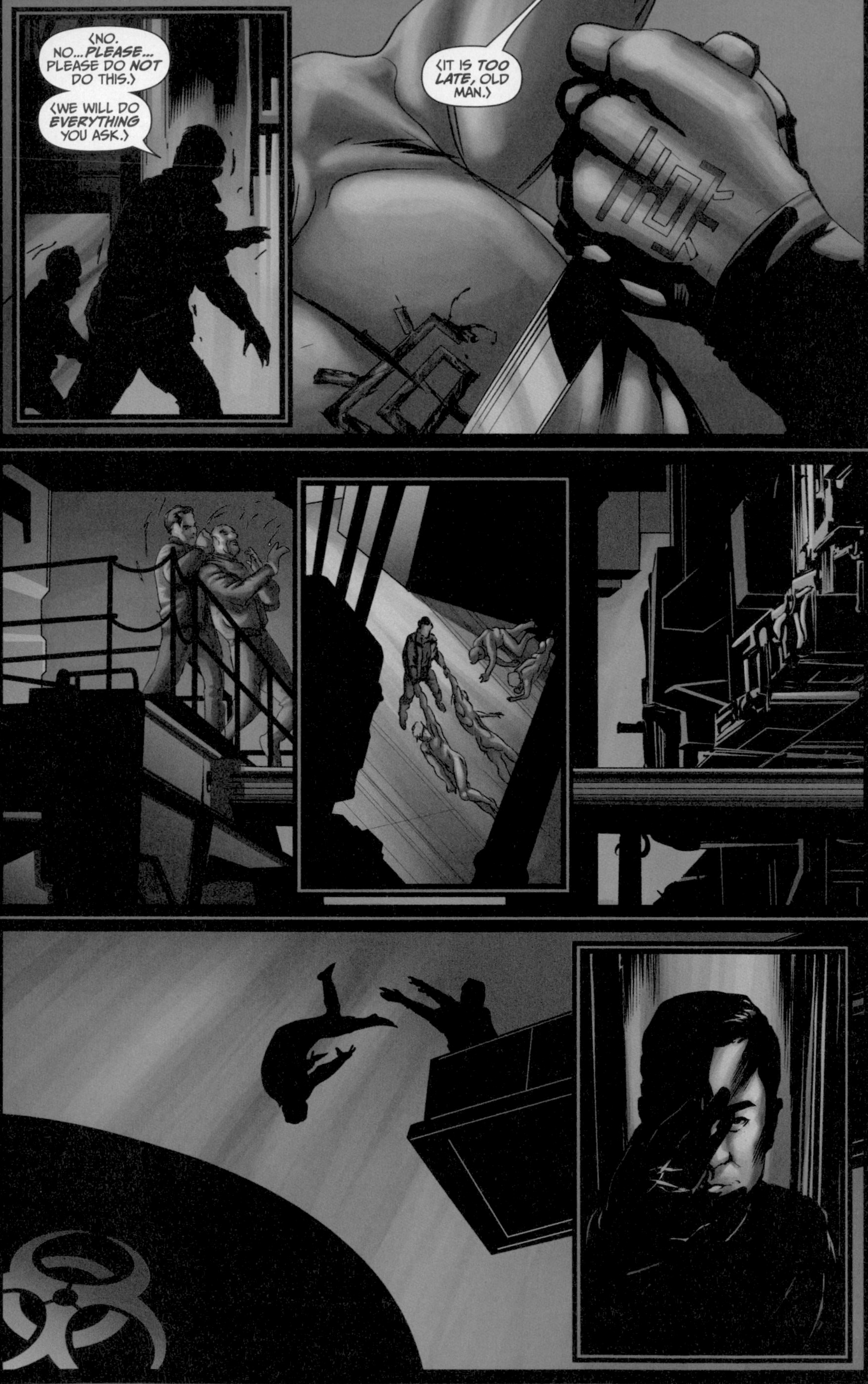
‹NO. NO...PLEASE... PLEASE DO NOT DO THIS.›
‹WE WILL DO EVERYTHING YOU ASK.›
‹IT IS TOO LATE, OLD MAN.›

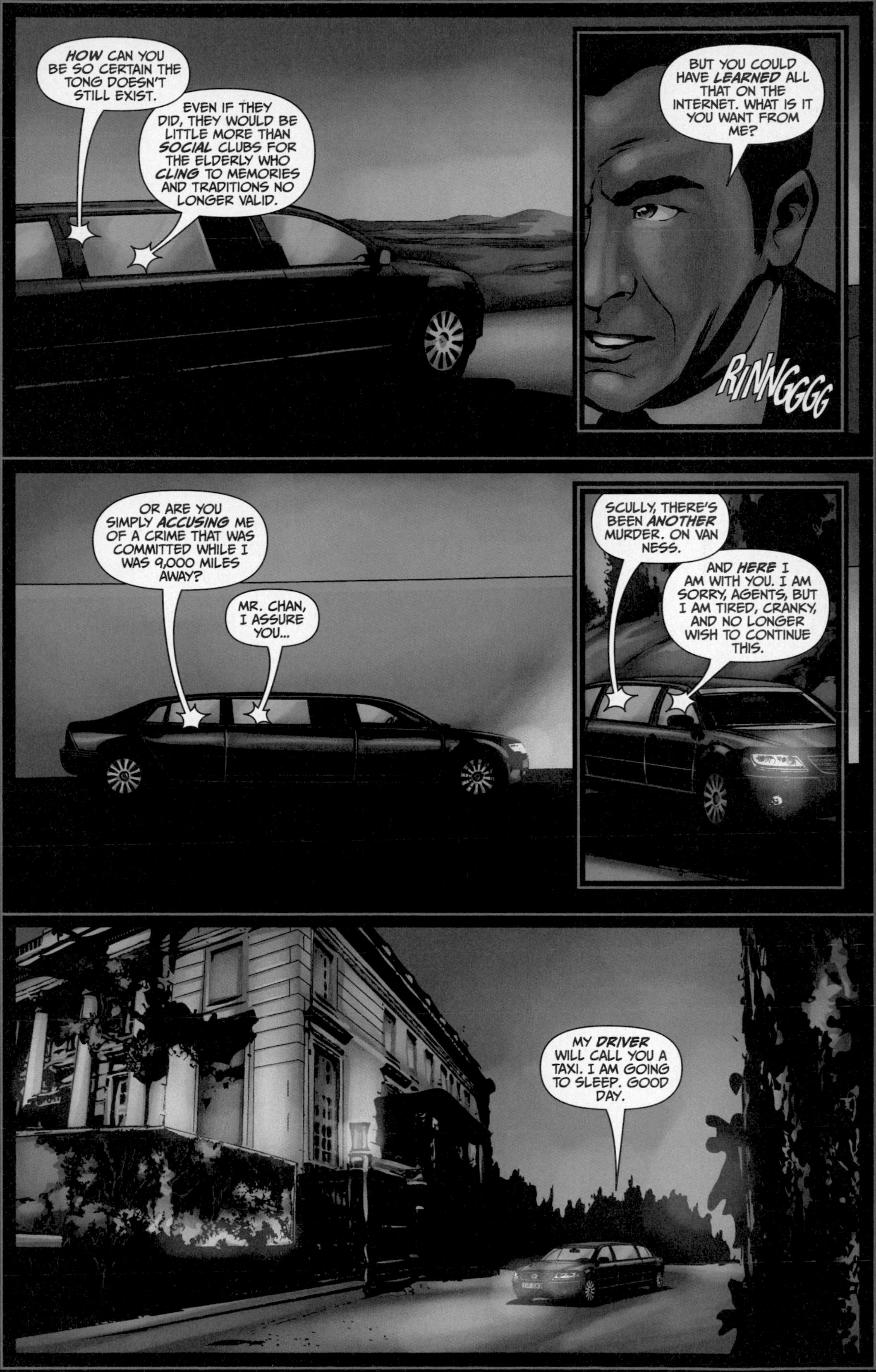
HOW CAN YOU BE SO CERTAIN THE TONG DOESN'T STILL EXIST.
EVEN IF THEY DID, THEY WOULD BE LITTLE MORE THAN SOCIAL CLUBS FOR THE ELDERLY WHO CLING TO MEMORIES AND TRADITIONS NO LONGER VALID.
BUT YOU COULD HAVE LEARNED ALL THAT ON THE INTERNET. WHAT IS IT YOU WANT FROM ME?
RINNGGGG
OR ARE YOU SIMPLY ACCUSING ME OF A CRIME THAT WAS COMMITTED WHILE I WAS 9,000 MILES AWAY?
MR. CHAN, I ASSURE YOU...
SCULLY, THERE'S BEEN ANOTHER MURDER. ON VAN NESS.
AND HERE I AM WITH YOU. I AM SORRY, AGENTS, BUT I AM TIRED, CRANKY, AND NO LONGER WISH TO CONTINUE THIS.
MY DRIVER WILL CALL YOU A TAXI. I AM GOING TO SLEEP. GOOD DAY.

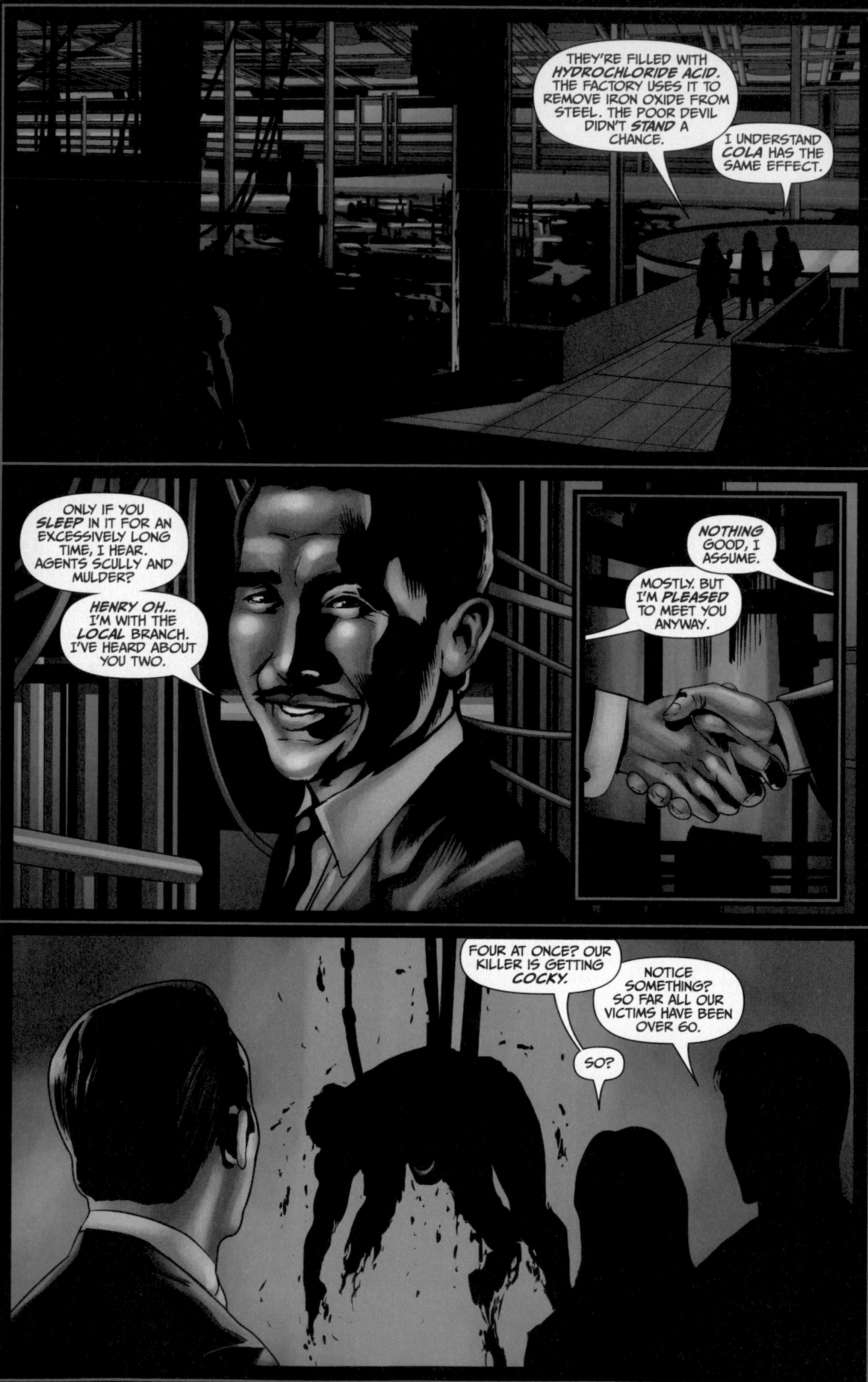
THEY'RE FILLED WITH HYDROCHLORIDE ACID. THE FACTORY USES IT TO REMOVE IRON OXIDE FROM STEEL. THE POOR DEVIL DIDN'T STAND A CHANCE.
I UNDERSTAND COLA HAS THE SAME EFFECT.
ONLY IF YOU SLEEP IN IT FOR AN EXCESSIVELY LONG TIME, I HEAR. AGENTS SCULLY AND MULDER?
HENRY OH... I'M WITH THE LOCAL BRANCH. I'VE HEARD ABOUT YOU TWO.
NOTHING GOOD, I ASSUME.
MOSTLY. BUT I'M PLEASED TO MEET YOU ANYWAY.
FOUR AT ONCE? OUR KILLER IS GETTING COCKY.
NOTICE SOMETHING? SO FAR ALL OUR VICTIMS HAVE BEEN OVER 60.
SO?

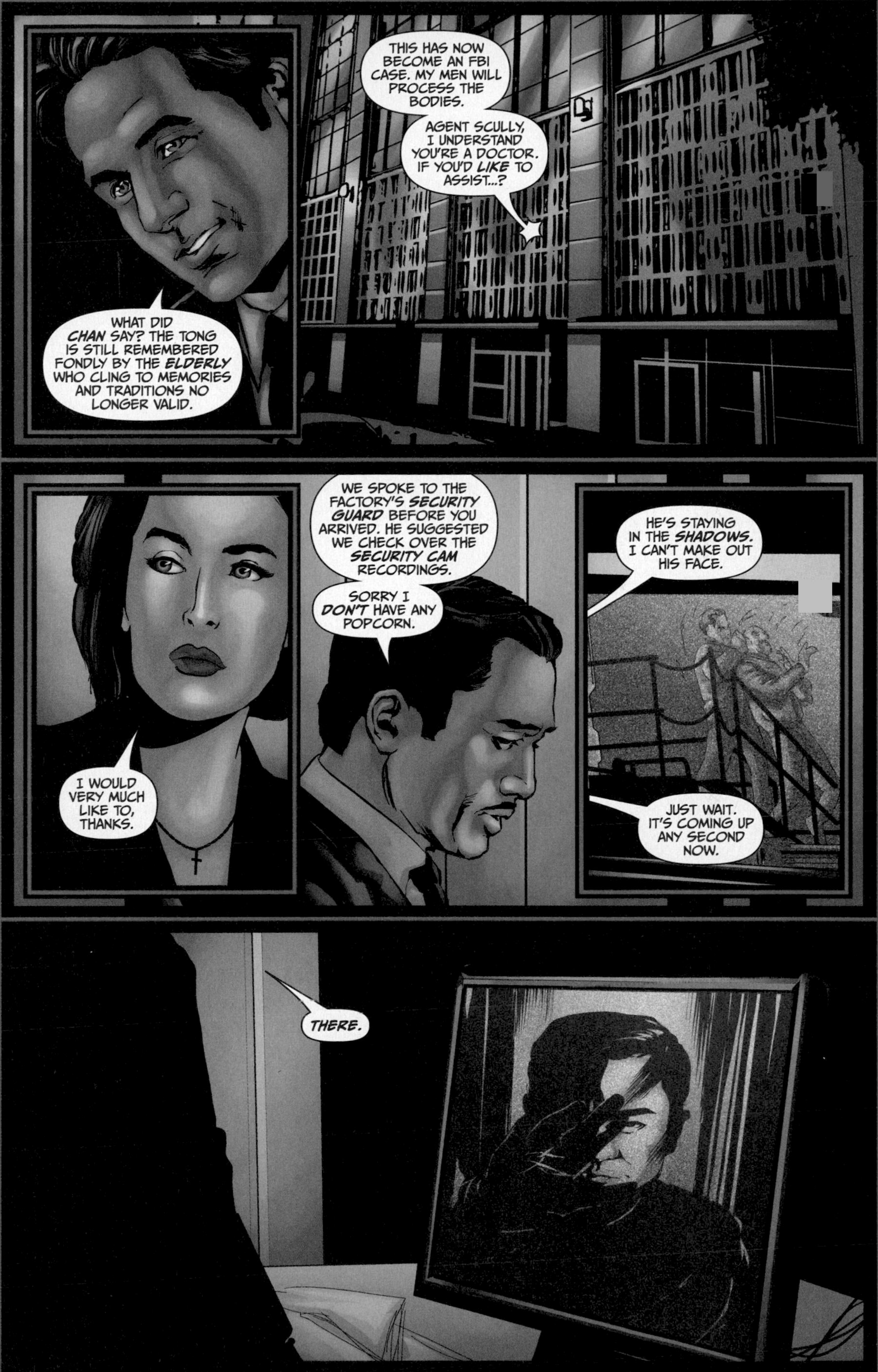
THIS HAS NOW BECOME AN FBI CASE. MY MEN WILL PROCESS THE BODIES.
AGENT SCULLY, I UNDERSTAND YOU'RE A DOCTOR. IF YOU'D *LIKE* TO ASSIST...?
WHAT DID *CHAN* SAY? THE TONG IS STILL REMEMBERED FONDLY BY THE *ELDERLY* WHO CLING TO MEMORIES AND TRADITIONS NO LONGER VALID.
I WOULD VERY MUCH LIKE TO, THANKS.
WE SPOKE TO THE FACTORY'S *SECURITY GUARD* BEFORE YOU ARRIVED. HE SUGGESTED WE CHECK OVER THE *SECURITY CAM* RECORDINGS.
SORRY I *DON'T* HAVE ANY POPCORN.
HE'S STAYING IN THE *SHADOWS*. I CAN'T MAKE OUT HIS FACE.
JUST WAIT. IT'S COMING UP ANY SECOND NOW.
THERE.

I'VE *ALMOST* GOT IT, AGENT OH.

I STILL CAN'T MAKE HIM OUT. CAN YOU GET A *COMPUTER ENHANCEMENT?*

THE *LAB BOYS* ARE WORKING ON IT. C'MON.

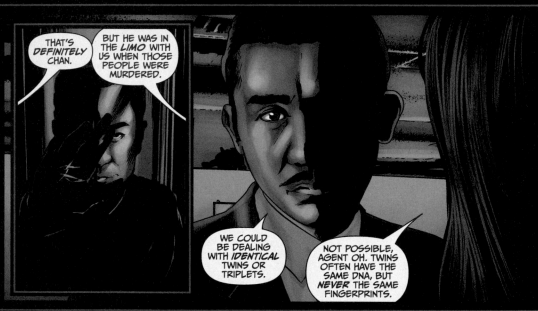

THAT'S *DEFINITELY* CHAN.

BUT HE WAS IN THE *LIMO* WITH US WHEN THOSE PEOPLE WERE MURDERED.

WE COULD BE DEALING WITH *IDENTICAL* TWINS OR TRIPLETS.

NOT POSSIBLE, AGENT OH. TWINS OFTEN HAVE THE SAME DNA, BUT *NEVER* THE SAME FINGERPRINTS.

THE REAL ANSWER MAY NOT BE SO CUT AND DRIED. WE COULD BE DEALING WITH *CHINESE MYSTICISM.*

AH. THE X-FILES DISCUSSION. THE TRUTH IS SOME PLACE OUT THERE. *THAT'S* THE NOTHING GOOD I HEARD ABOUT.

YOU DON'T KNOW THE *HALF* OF IT, AGENT OH.

AND YOU DON'T WANT TO KNOW THE *OTHER* HALF.

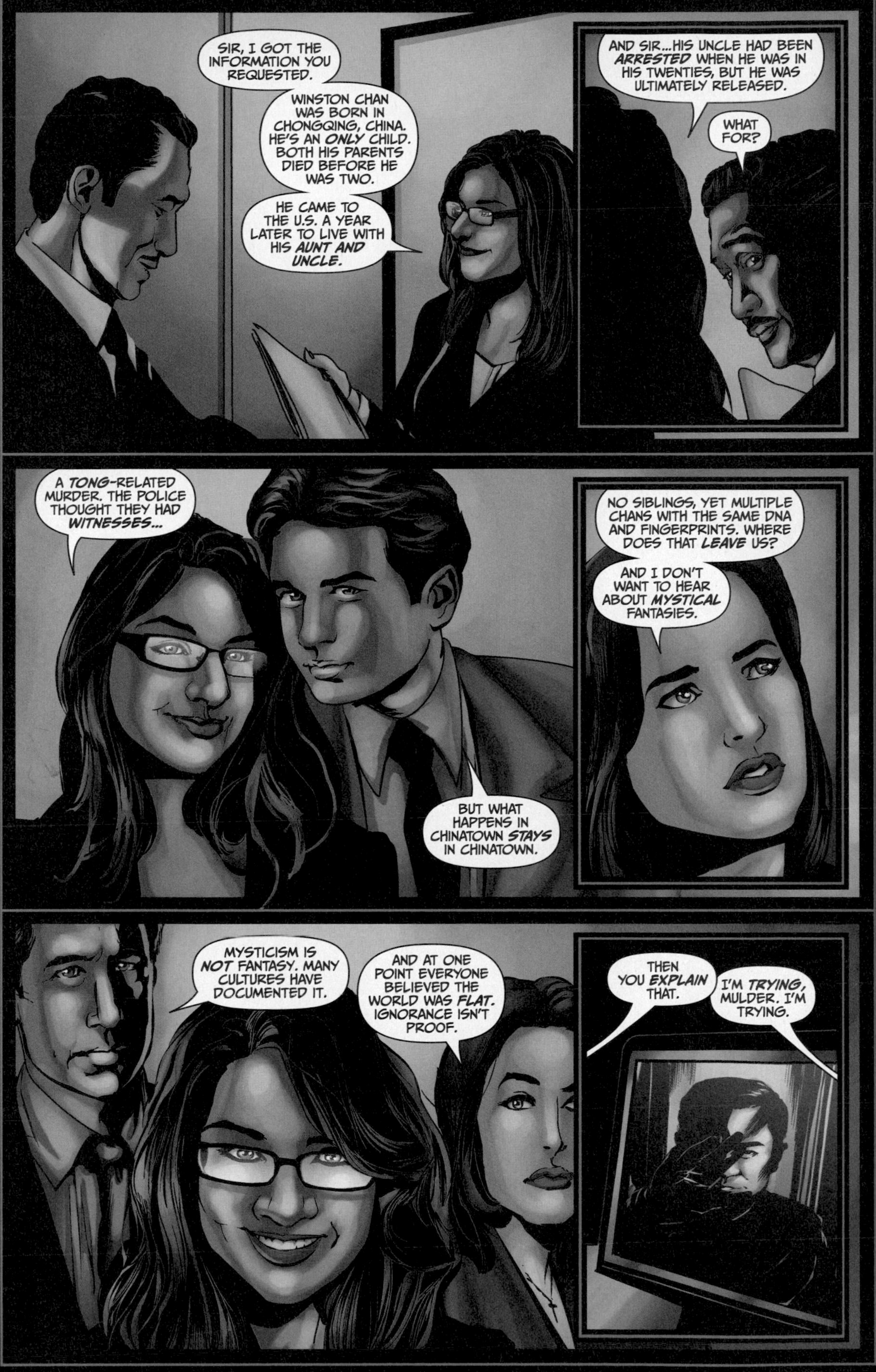

SIR, I GOT THE INFORMATION YOU REQUESTED.
WINSTON CHAN WAS BORN IN CHONGQING, CHINA. HE'S AN *ONLY* CHILD. BOTH HIS PARENTS DIED BEFORE HE WAS TWO.
HE CAME TO THE U.S. A YEAR LATER TO LIVE WITH HIS *AUNT AND UNCLE.*
AND SIR...HIS UNCLE HAD BEEN *ARRESTED* WHEN HE WAS IN HIS TWENTIES, BUT HE WAS ULTIMATELY RELEASED.
WHAT FOR?
A *TONG*-RELATED MURDER. THE POLICE THOUGHT THEY HAD *WITNESSES...*
BUT WHAT HAPPENS IN CHINATOWN *STAYS* IN CHINATOWN.
NO SIBLINGS, YET MULTIPLE CHANS WITH THE SAME DNA AND FINGERPRINTS. WHERE DOES THAT *LEAVE* US?
AND I DON'T WANT TO HEAR ABOUT *MYSTICAL* FANTASIES.
MYSTICISM IS *NOT* FANTASY. MANY CULTURES HAVE DOCUMENTED IT.
AND AT ONE POINT EVERYONE BELIEVED THE WORLD WAS *FLAT.* IGNORANCE ISN'T PROOF.
THEN YOU *EXPLAIN* THAT.
I'M *TRYING,* MULDER. I'M TRYING.

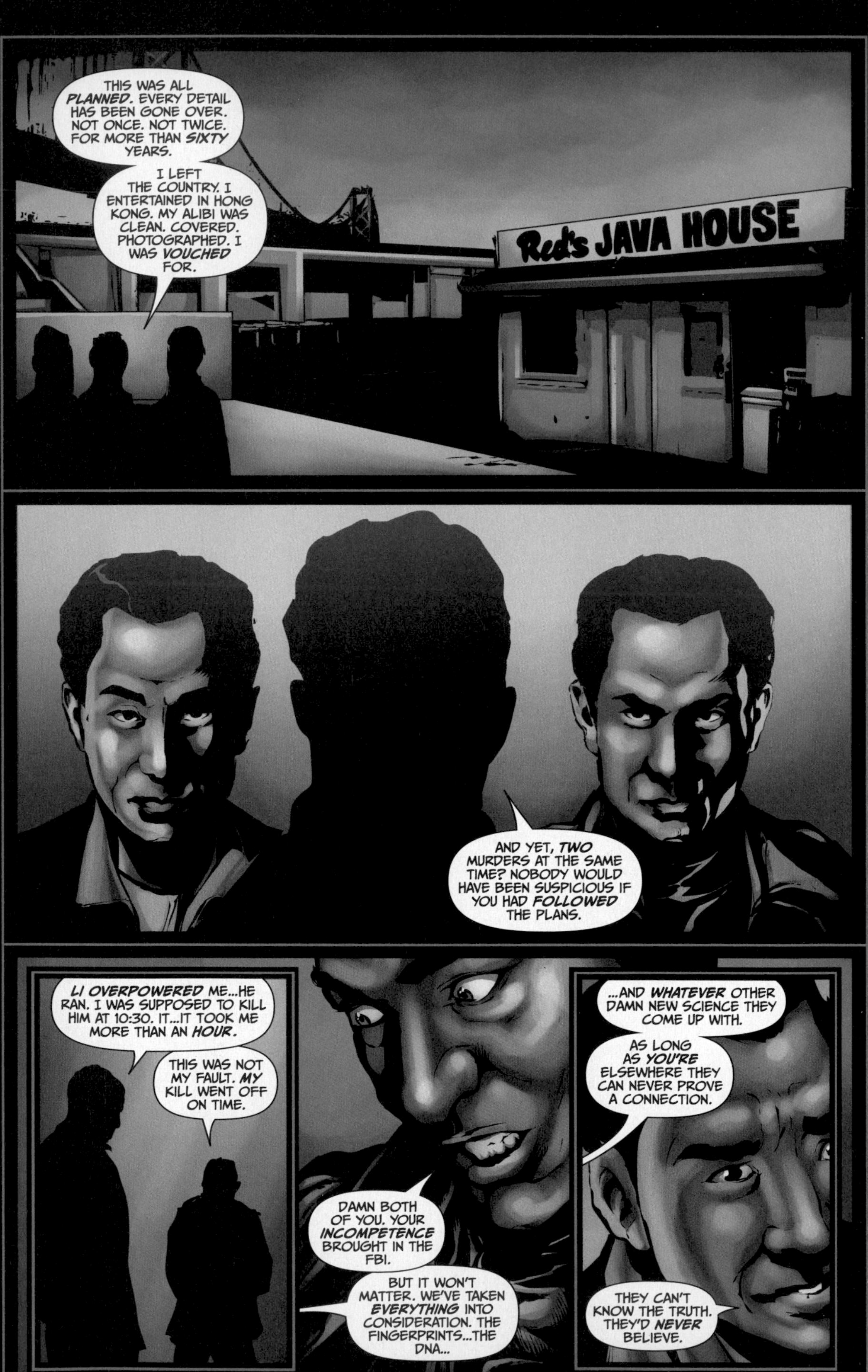
THIS WAS ALL PLANNED. EVERY DETAIL HAS BEEN GONE OVER. NOT ONCE. NOT TWICE. FOR MORE THAN SIXTY YEARS.
I LEFT THE COUNTRY. I ENTERTAINED IN HONG KONG. MY ALIBI WAS CLEAN. COVERED. PHOTOGRAPHED. I WAS VOUCHED FOR.
Red's JAVA HOUSE
AND YET, TWO MURDERS AT THE SAME TIME? NOBODY WOULD HAVE BEEN SUSPICIOUS IF YOU HAD FOLLOWED THE PLANS.
LI OVERPOWERED ME...HE RAN. I WAS SUPPOSED TO KILL HIM AT 10:30. IT...IT TOOK ME MORE THAN AN HOUR.
THIS WAS NOT MY FAULT. MY KILL WENT OFF ON TIME.
DAMN BOTH OF YOU. YOUR INCOMPETENCE BROUGHT IN THE FBI.
BUT IT WON'T MATTER. WE'VE TAKEN EVERYTHING INTO CONSIDERATION. THE FINGERPRINTS...THE DNA...
...AND WHATEVER OTHER DAMN NEW SCIENCE THEY COME UP WITH.
AS LONG AS YOU'RE ELSEWHERE THEY CAN NEVER PROVE A CONNECTION.
THEY CAN'T KNOW THE TRUTH. THEY'D NEVER BELIEVE.

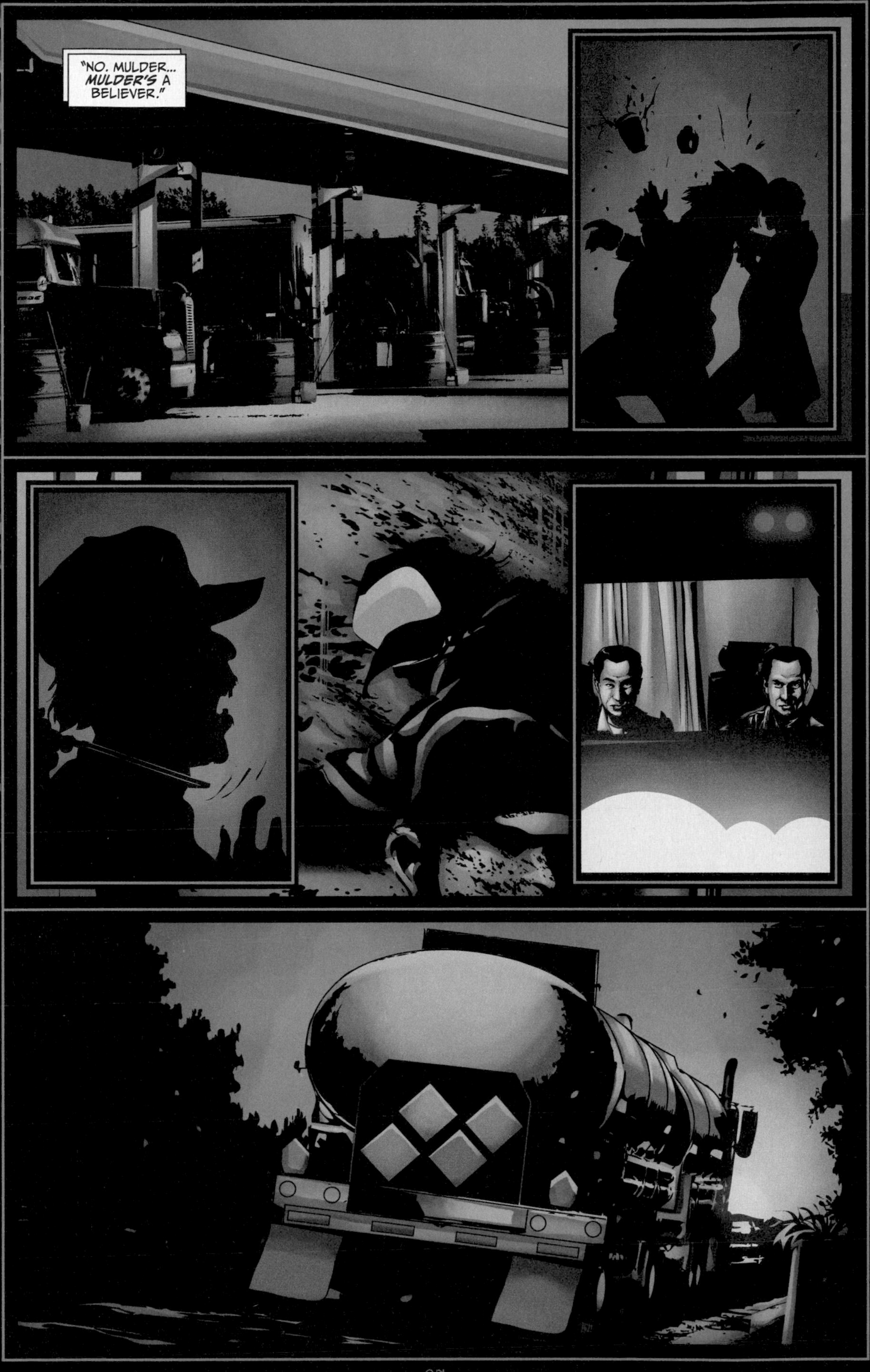
"NO. MULDER... MULDER'S A BELIEVER."

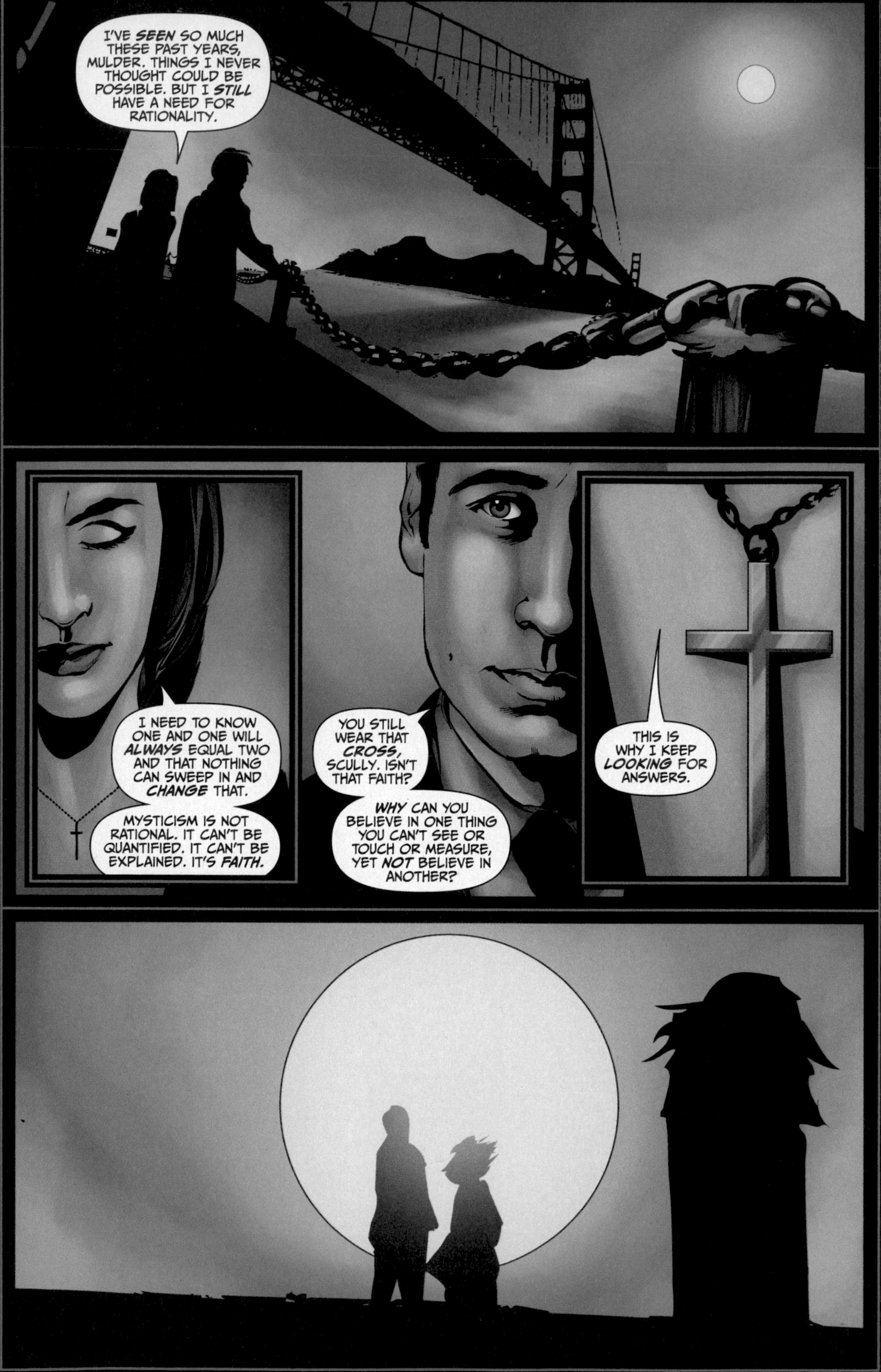
I'VE SEEN SO MUCH THESE PAST YEARS, MULDER. THINGS I NEVER THOUGHT COULD BE POSSIBLE. BUT I STILL HAVE A NEED FOR RATIONALITY.
I NEED TO KNOW ONE AND ONE WILL ALWAYS EQUAL TWO AND THAT NOTHING CAN SWEEP IN AND CHANGE THAT.
MYSTICISM IS NOT RATIONAL. IT CAN'T BE QUANTIFIED. IT CAN'T BE EXPLAINED. IT'S FAITH.
YOU STILL WEAR THAT CROSS, SCULLY. ISN'T THAT FAITH?
WHY CAN YOU BELIEVE IN ONE THING YOU CAN'T SEE OR TOUCH OR MEASURE, YET NOT BELIEVE IN ANOTHER?
THIS IS WHY I KEEP LOOKING FOR ANSWERS.

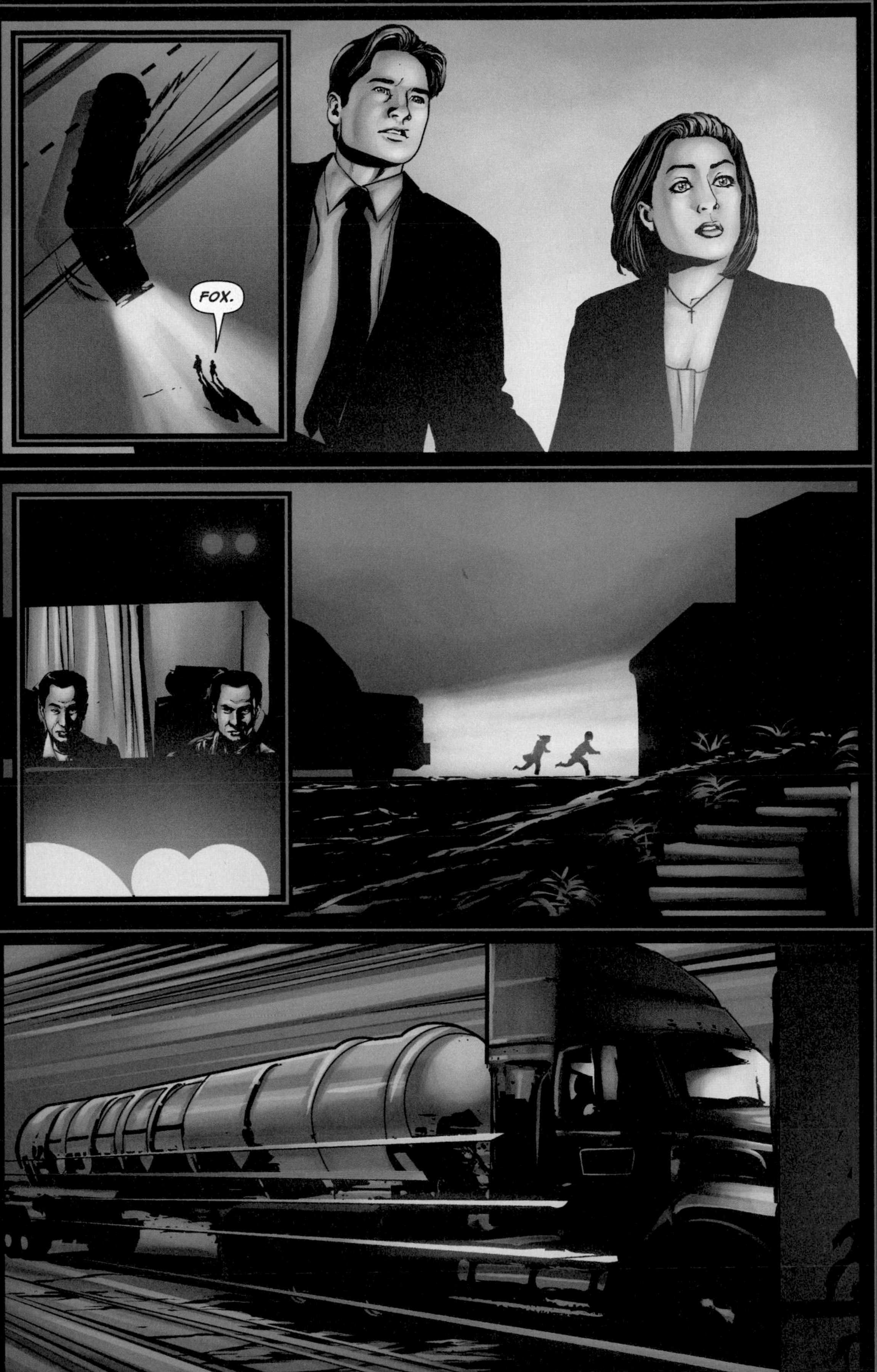
FOX.

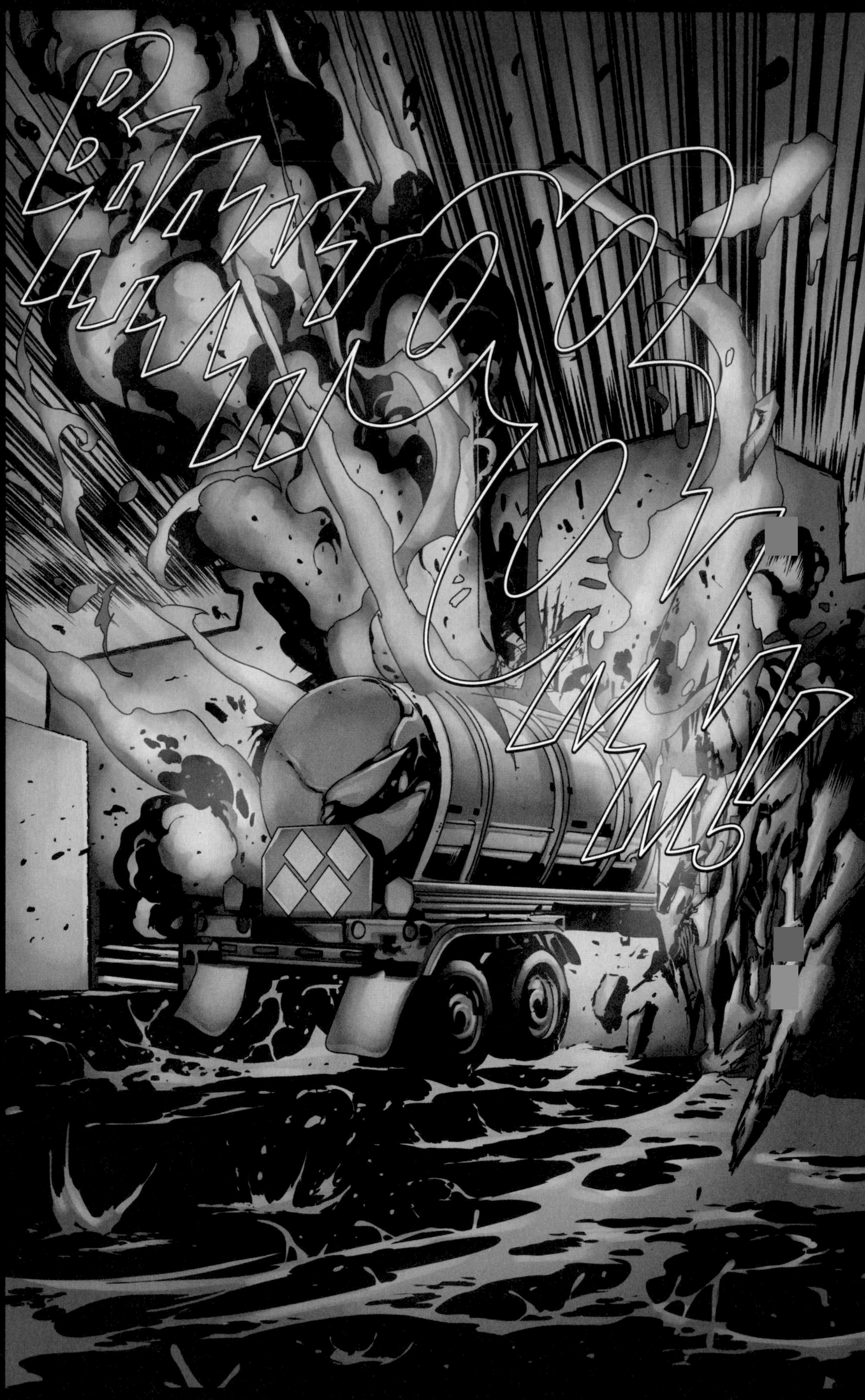

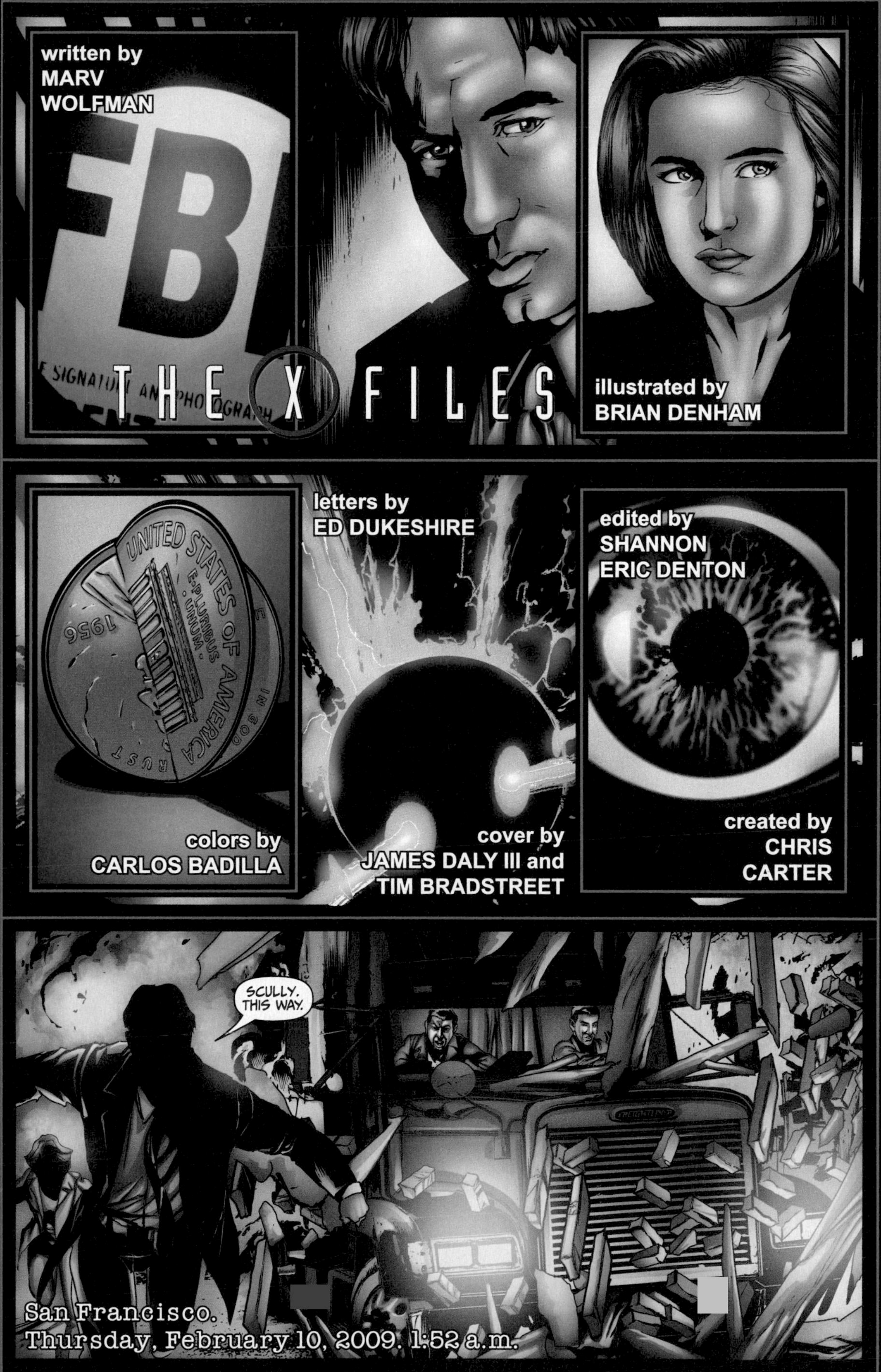
written by
MARV
WOLFMAN
THE X FILES
illustrated by
BRIAN DENHAM
letters by
ED DUKESHIRE
edited by
SHANNON
ERIC DENTON
UNITED STATES OF AMERICA
E·PLURIBUS UNUM
1956
colors by
CARLOS BADILLA
cover by
JAMES DALY III and
TIM BRADSTREET
created by
CHRIS
CARTER
SCULLY. THIS WAY.
San Francisco.
Thursday, February 10, 2009. 1:52 a.m.

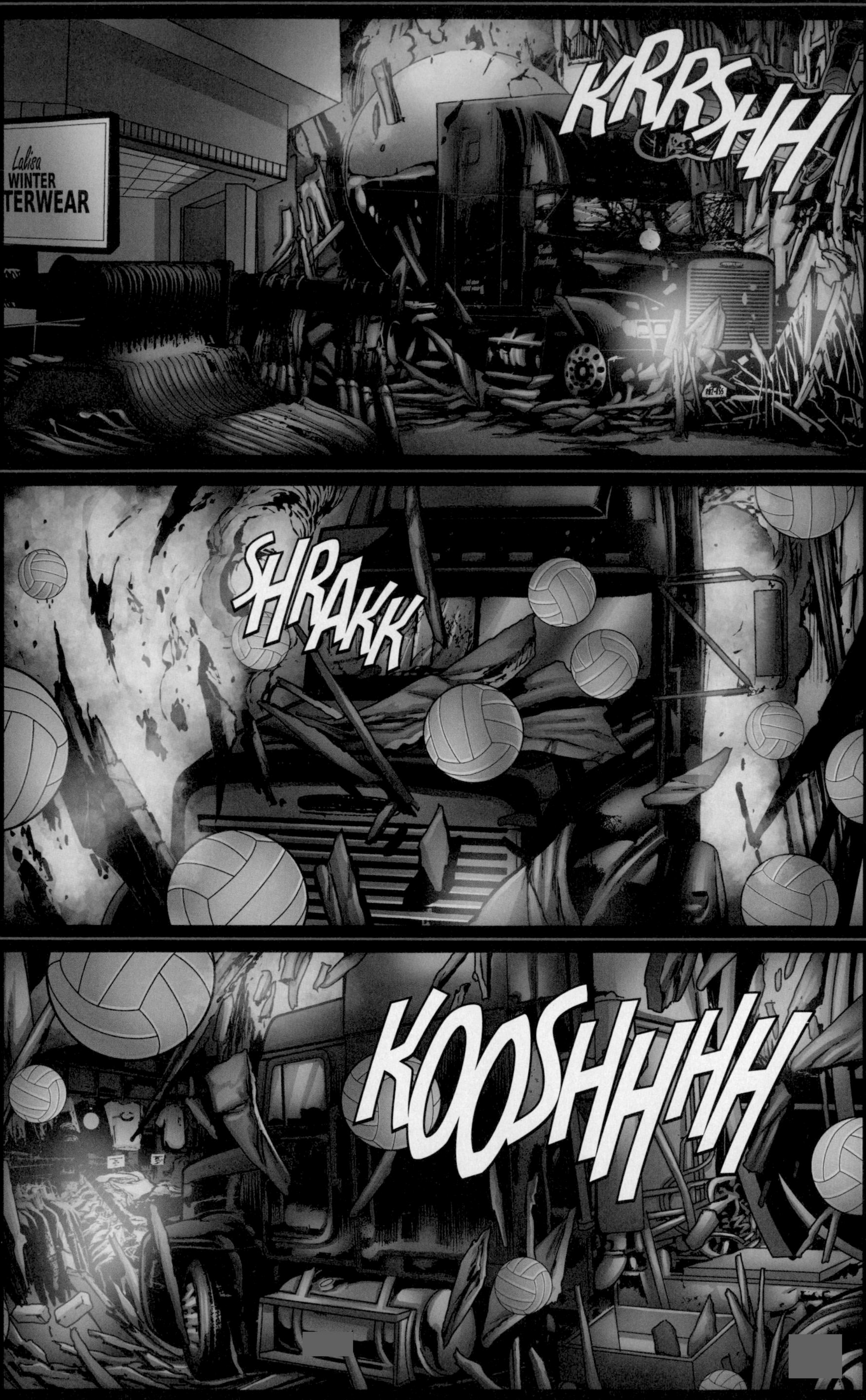
Lalisa
WINTER
TERWEAR
KRRSHH
SHRAKK
KOOSHHHH

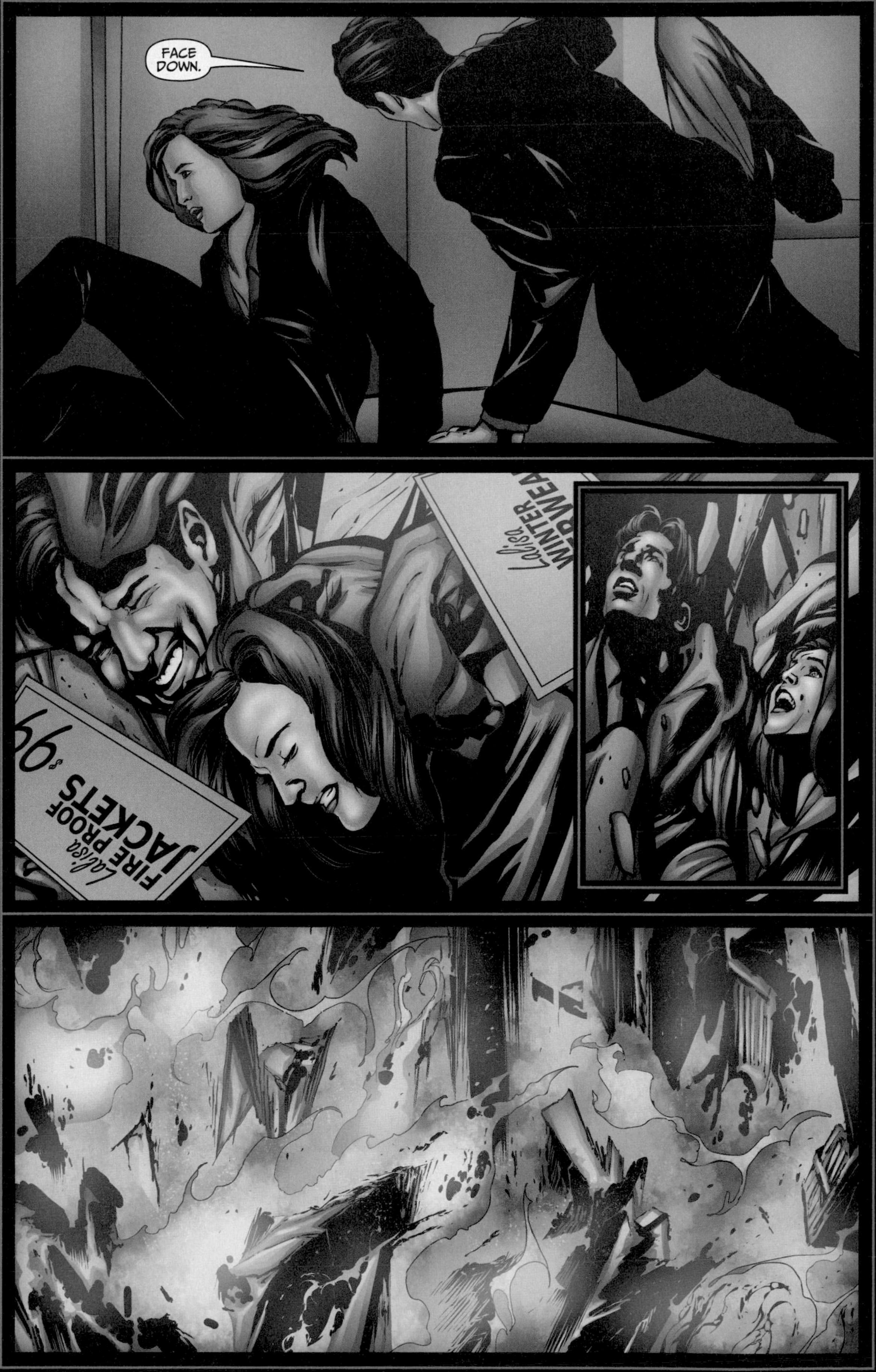
FACE DOWN.
FIRE PROOF JACKETS

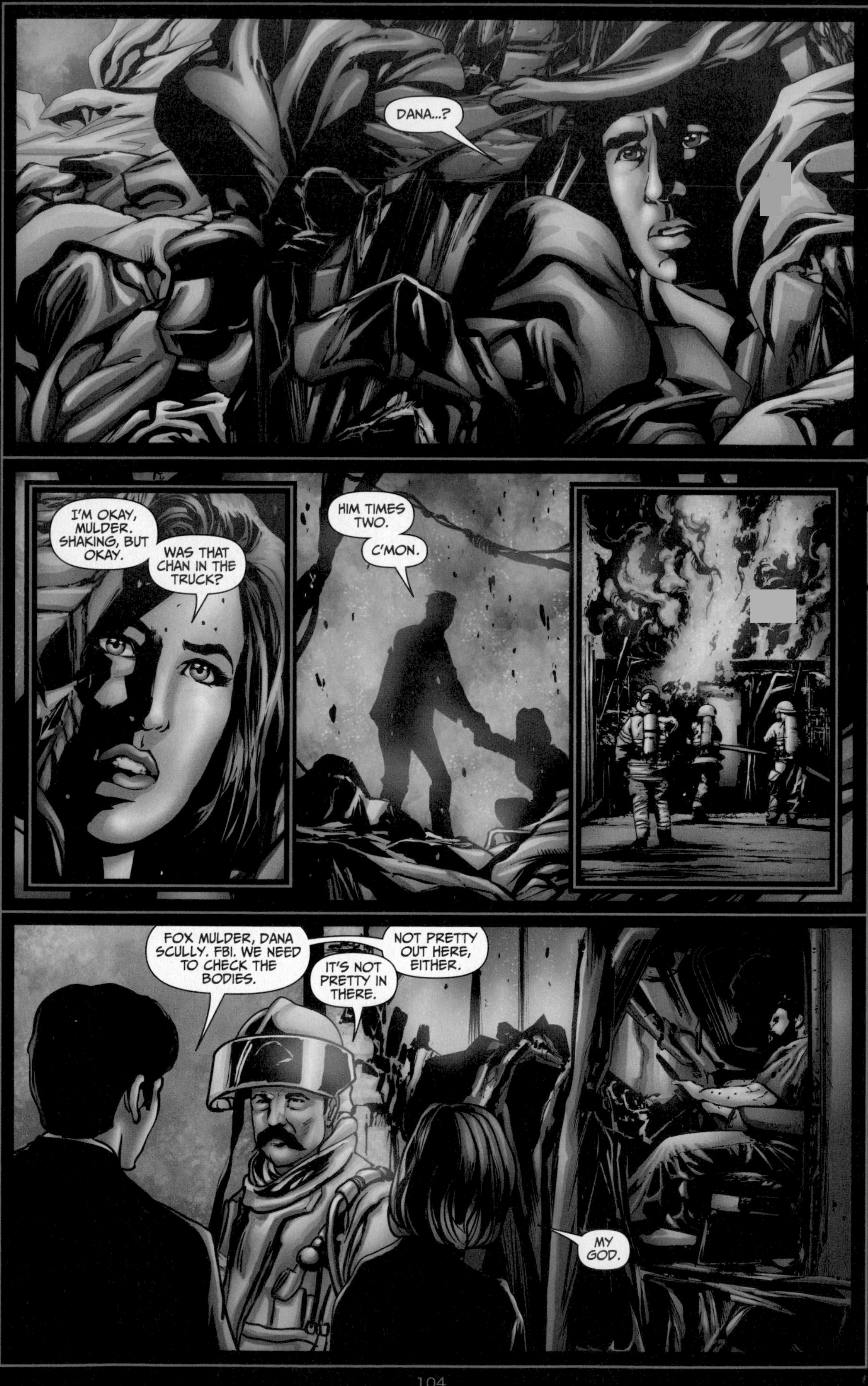
DANA...?
I'M OKAY, MULDER. SHAKING, BUT OKAY.
WAS THAT CHAN IN THE TRUCK?
HIM TIMES TWO.
C'MON.
FOX MULDER, DANA SCULLY. FBI. WE NEED TO CHECK THE BODIES.
IT'S NOT PRETTY IN THERE.
NOT PRETTY OUT HERE, EITHER.
MY GOD.

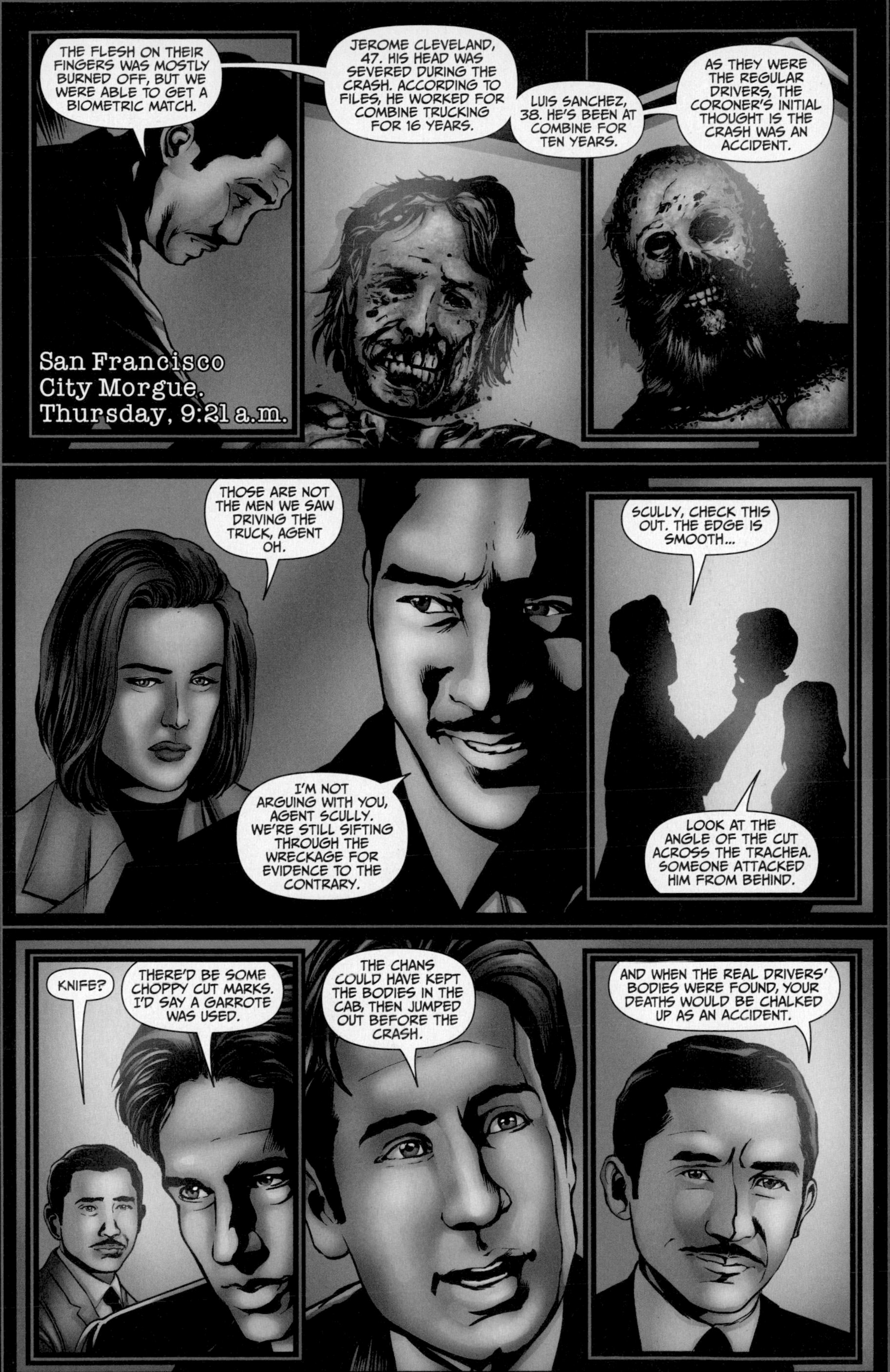
THE FLESH ON THEIR FINGERS WAS MOSTLY BURNED OFF, BUT WE WERE ABLE TO GET A BIOMETRIC MATCH.
JEROME CLEVELAND, 47. HIS HEAD WAS SEVERED DURING THE CRASH. ACCORDING TO FILES, HE WORKED FOR COMBINE TRUCKING FOR 16 YEARS.
San Francisco
City Morgue.
Thursday, 9:21 a.m.
LUIS SANCHEZ, 38. HE'S BEEN AT COMBINE FOR TEN YEARS.
AS THEY WERE THE REGULAR DRIVERS, THE CORONER'S INITIAL THOUGHT IS THE CRASH WAS AN ACCIDENT.
THOSE ARE NOT THE MEN WE SAW DRIVING THE TRUCK, AGENT OH.
I'M NOT ARGUING WITH YOU, AGENT SCULLY. WE'RE STILL SIFTING THROUGH THE WRECKAGE FOR EVIDENCE TO THE CONTRARY.
SCULLY, CHECK THIS OUT. THE EDGE IS SMOOTH...
LOOK AT THE ANGLE OF THE CUT ACROSS THE TRACHEA. SOMEONE ATTACKED HIM FROM BEHIND.
KNIFE?
THERE'D BE SOME CHOPPY CUT MARKS. I'D SAY A GARROTE WAS USED.
THE CHANS COULD HAVE KEPT THE BODIES IN THE CAB, THEN JUMPED OUT BEFORE THE CRASH.
AND WHEN THE REAL DRIVERS' BODIES WERE FOUND, YOUR DEATHS WOULD BE CHALKED UP AS AN ACCIDENT.

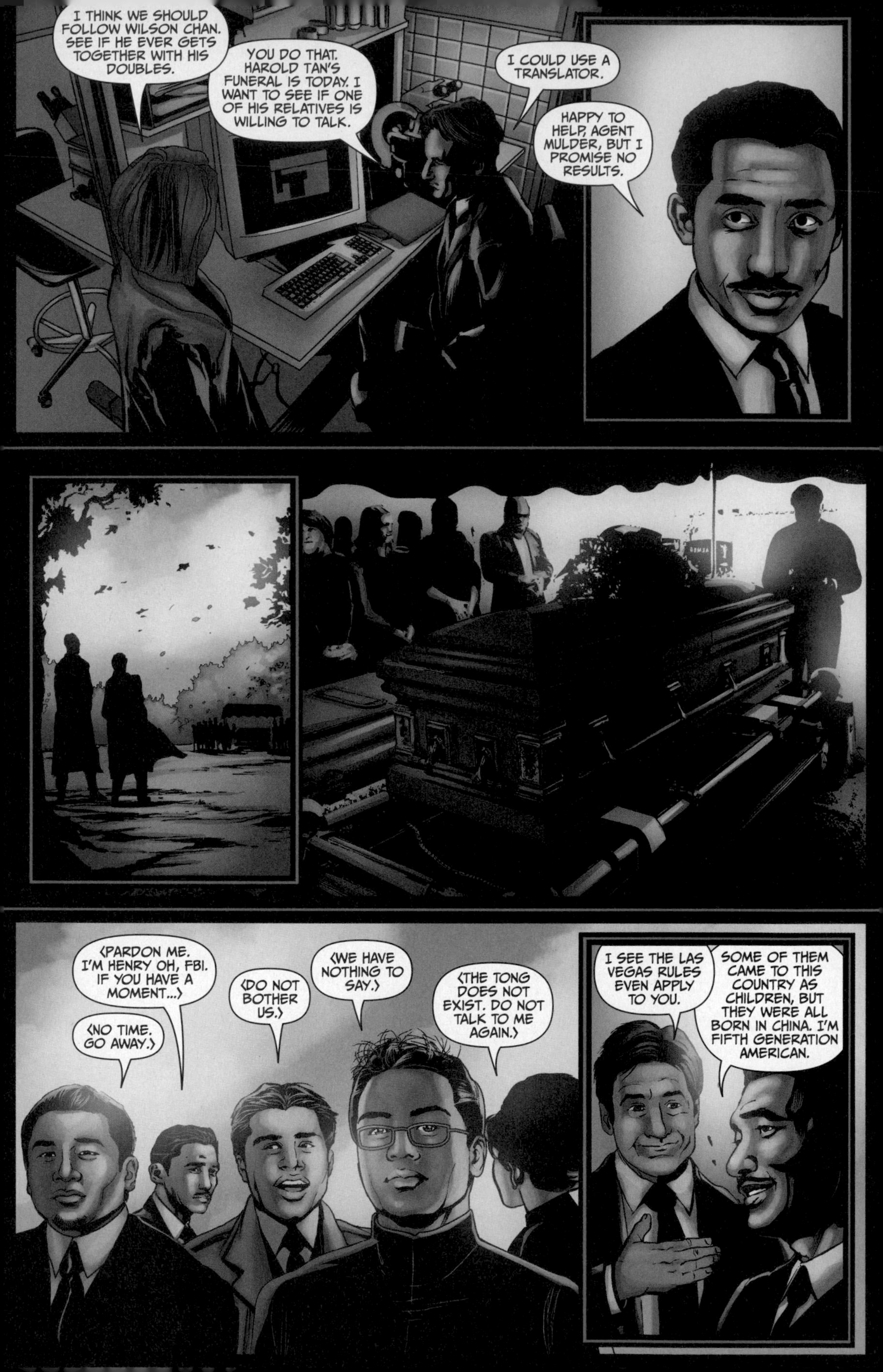
I THINK WE SHOULD FOLLOW WILSON CHAN. SEE IF HE EVER GETS TOGETHER WITH HIS DOUBLES.
YOU DO THAT. HAROLD TAN'S FUNERAL IS TODAY. I WANT TO SEE IF ONE OF HIS RELATIVES IS WILLING TO TALK.
I COULD USE A TRANSLATOR.
HAPPY TO HELP, AGENT MULDER, BUT I PROMISE NO RESULTS.
‹PARDON ME. I'M HENRY OH, FBI. IF YOU HAVE A MOMENT...›
‹NO TIME. GO AWAY.›
‹DO NOT BOTHER US.›
‹WE HAVE NOTHING TO SAY.›
‹THE TONG DOES NOT EXIST. DO NOT TALK TO ME AGAIN.›
I SEE THE LAS VEGAS RULES EVEN APPLY TO YOU.
SOME OF THEM CAME TO THIS COUNTRY AS CHILDREN, BUT THEY WERE ALL BORN IN CHINA. I'M FIFTH GENERATION AMERICAN.

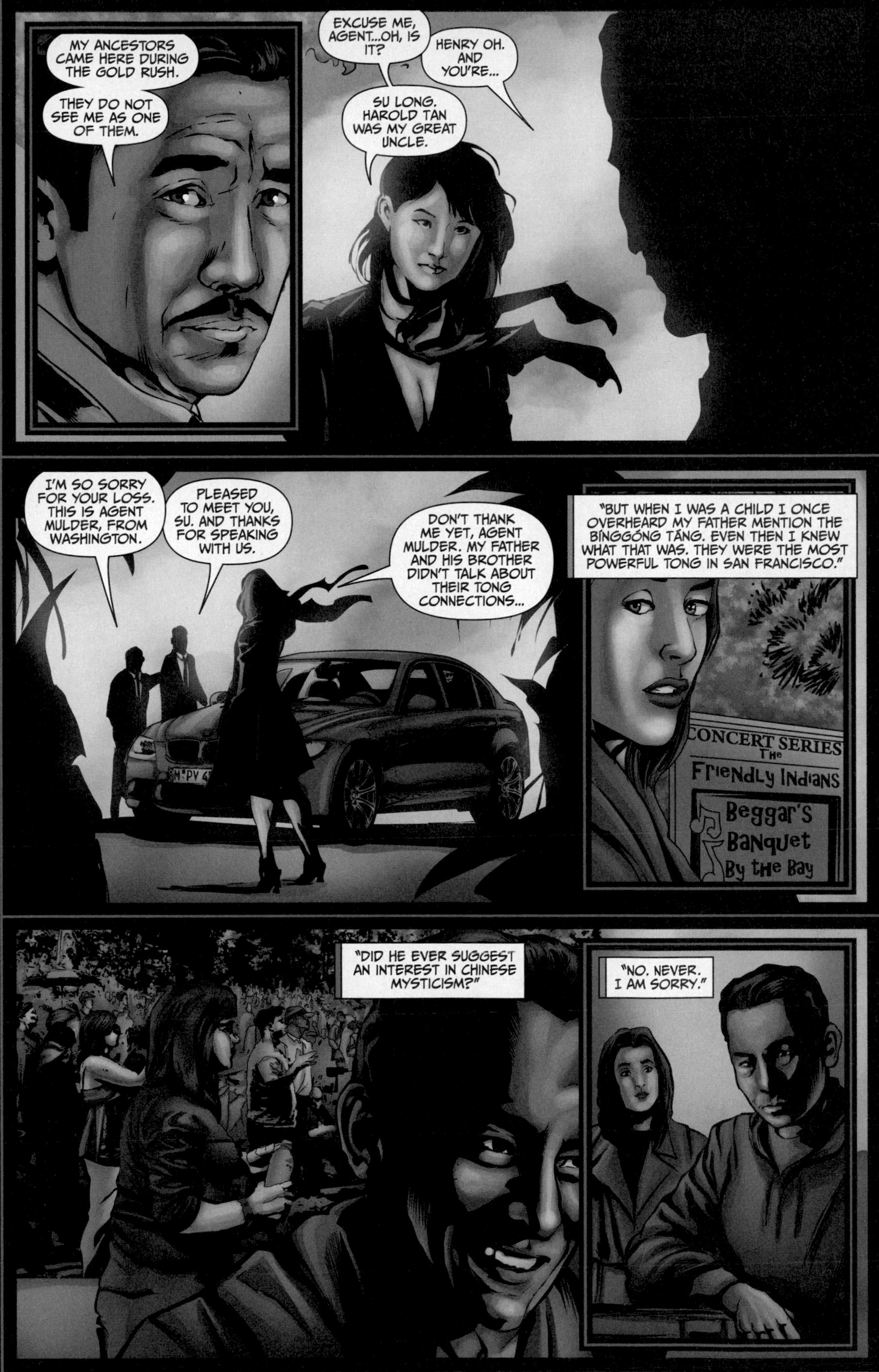
MY ANCESTORS CAME HERE DURING THE GOLD RUSH.
THEY DO NOT SEE ME AS ONE OF THEM.
EXCUSE ME, AGENT...OH, IS IT?
HENRY OH. AND YOU'RE...
SU LONG. HAROLD TAN WAS MY GREAT UNCLE.
I'M SO SORRY FOR YOUR LOSS. THIS IS AGENT MULDER, FROM WASHINGTON.
PLEASED TO MEET YOU, SU. AND THANKS FOR SPEAKING WITH US.
DON'T THANK ME YET, AGENT MULDER. MY FATHER AND HIS BROTHER DIDN'T TALK ABOUT THEIR TONG CONNECTIONS...
"BUT WHEN I WAS A CHILD I ONCE OVERHEARD MY FATHER MENTION THE BÍNGGÓNG TÁNG. EVEN THEN I KNEW WHAT THAT WAS. THEY WERE THE MOST POWERFUL TONG IN SAN FRANCISCO."
CONCERT SERIES
The Friendly Indians
Beggar's Banquet By the Bay
"DID HE EVER SUGGEST AN INTEREST IN CHINESE MYSTICISM?"
"NO. NEVER. I AM SORRY."

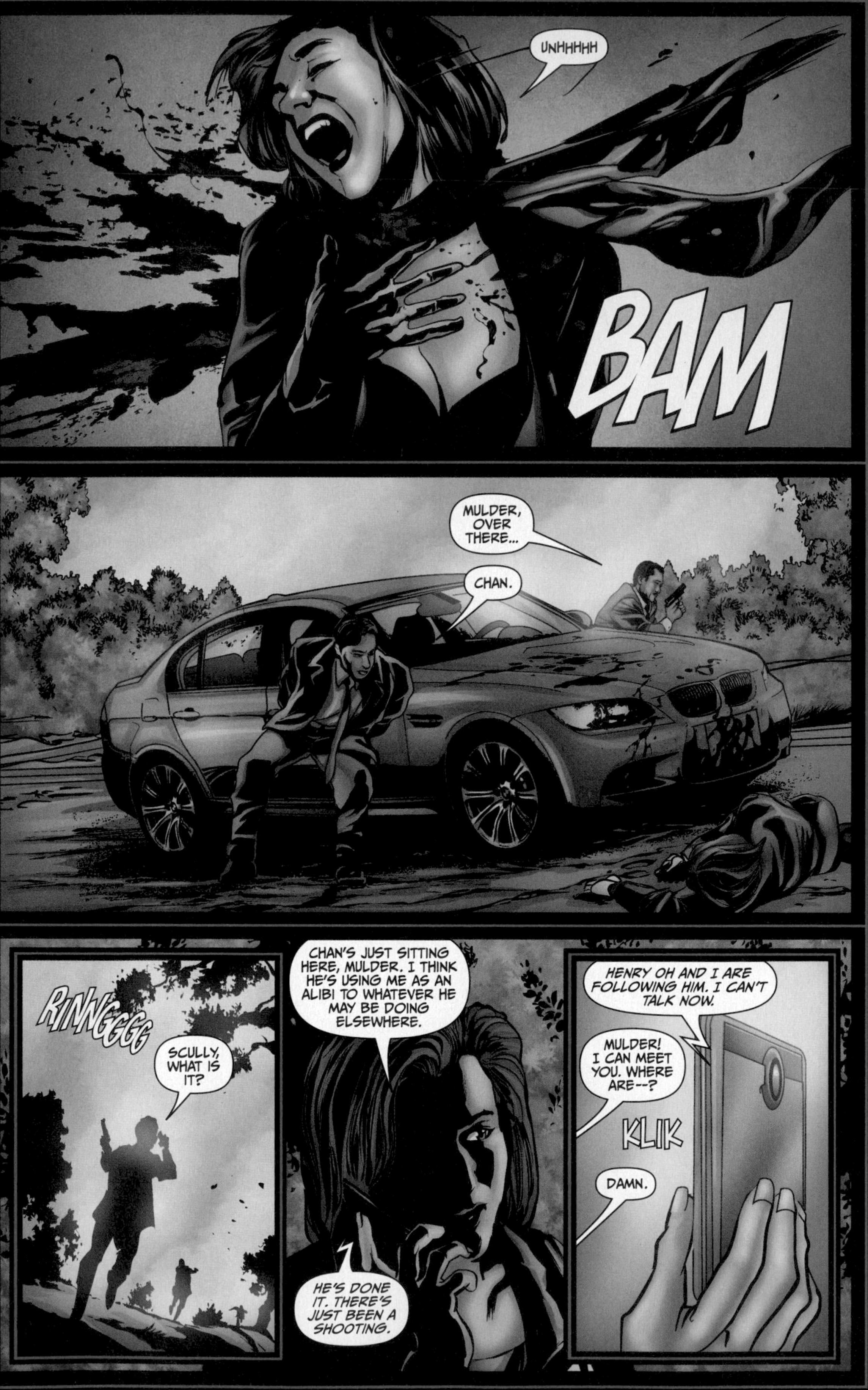
UNHHHHH
BAM
MULDER, OVER THERE...
CHAN.
RINNGGGG
SCULLY, WHAT IS IT?
CHAN'S JUST SITTING HERE, MULDER. I THINK HE'S USING ME AS AN ALIBI TO WHATEVER HE MAY BE DOING ELSEWHERE.
HE'S DONE IT. THERE'S JUST BEEN A SHOOTING.
HENRY OH AND I ARE FOLLOWING HIM. I CAN'T TALK NOW.
MULDER! I CAN MEET YOU. WHERE ARE--?
KLIK
DAMN.

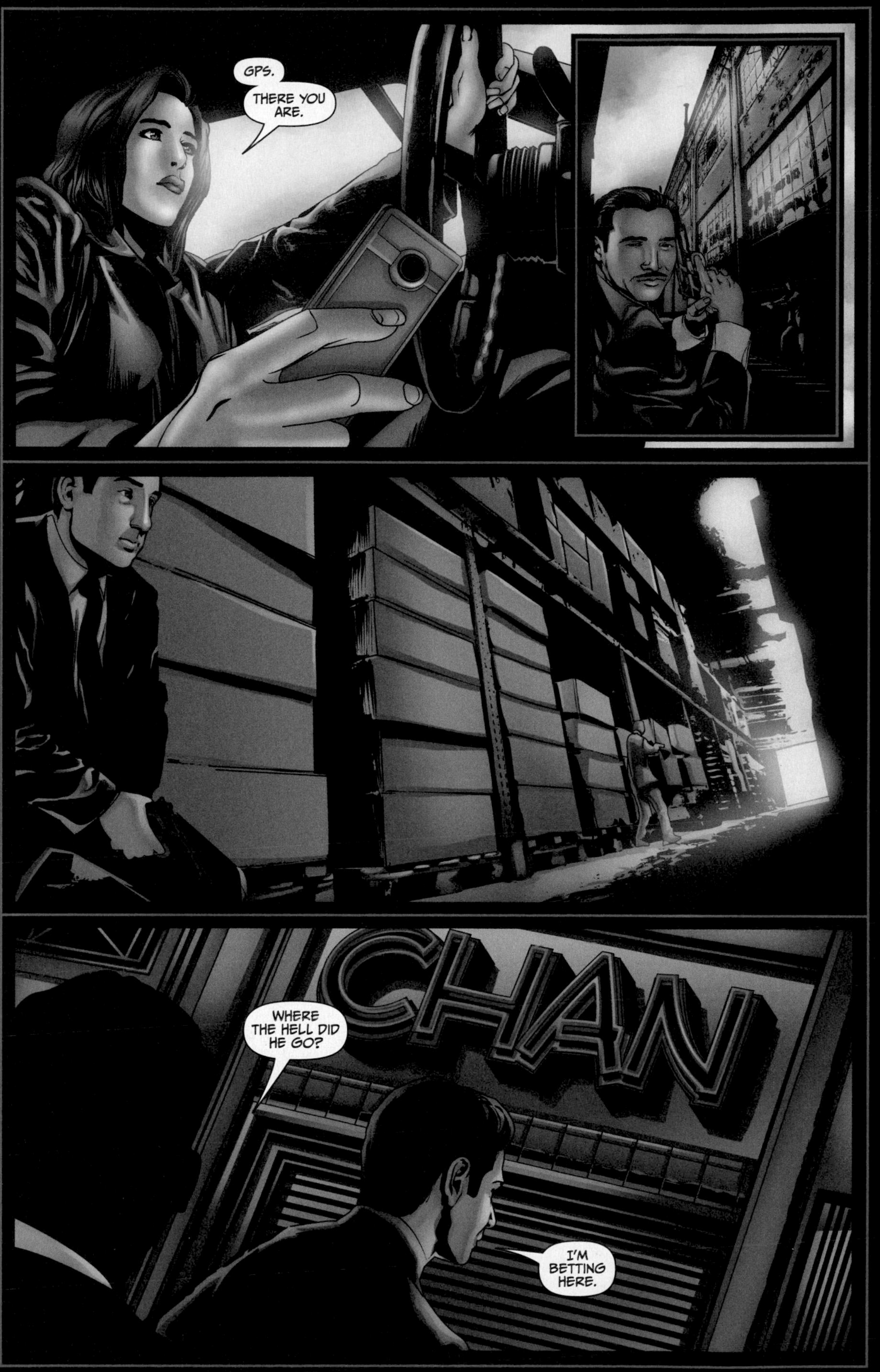
GPS.
THERE YOU ARE.
CHAN
WHERE THE HELL DID HE GO?
I'M BETTING HERE.

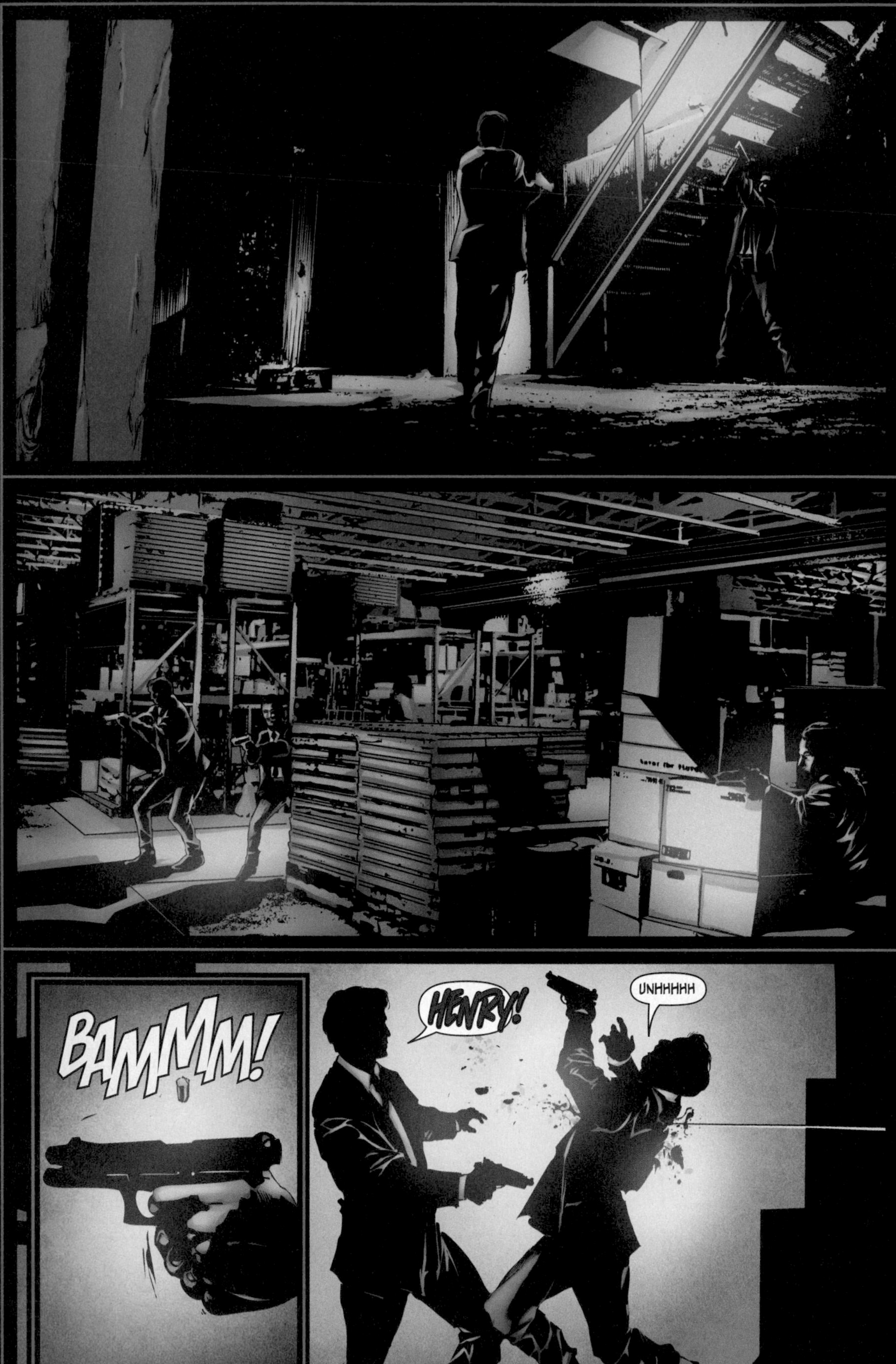
BAMMM!
HENRY!
UNHHHHH

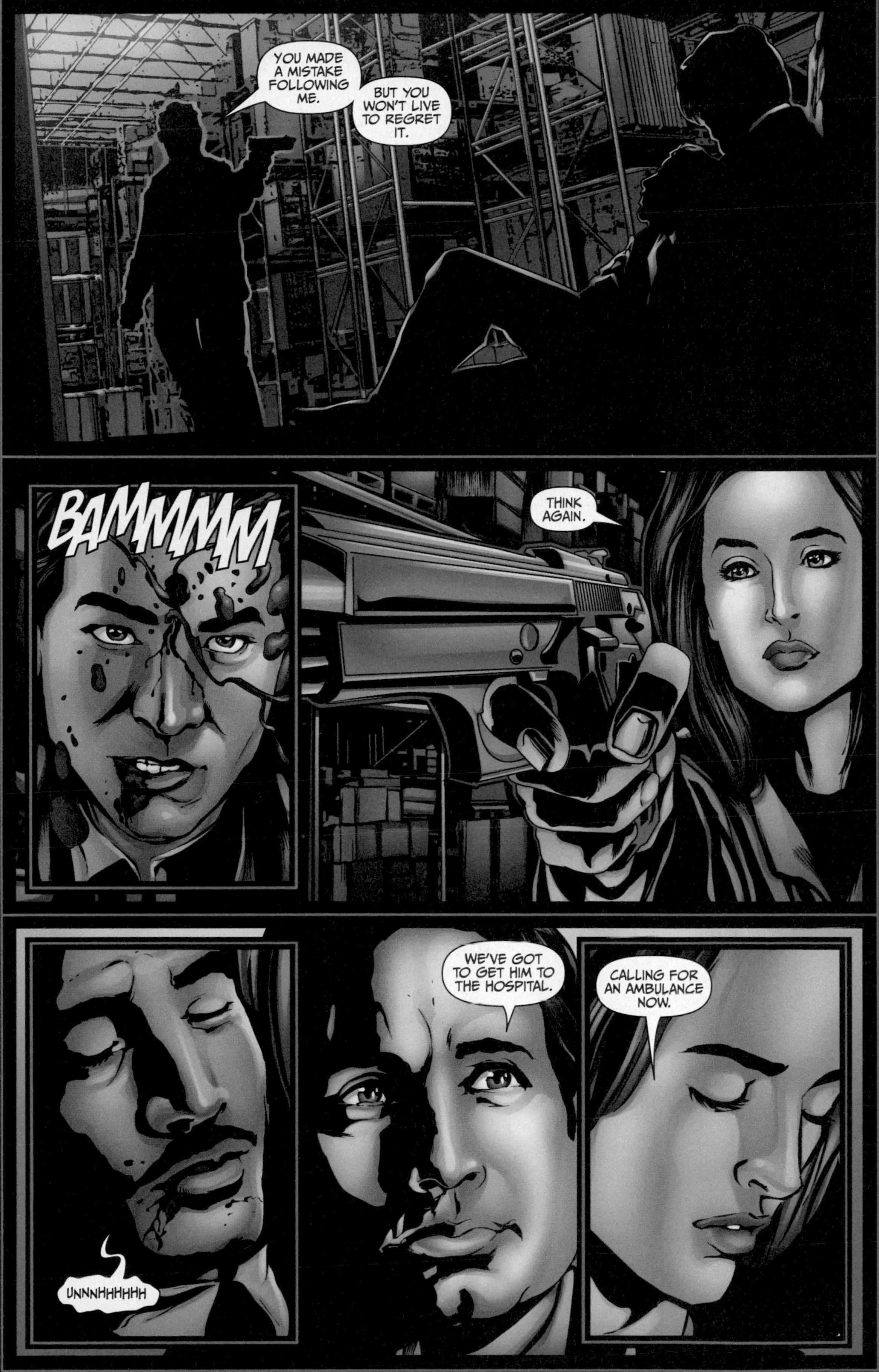
YOU MADE A MISTAKE FOLLOWING ME.
BUT YOU WON'T LIVE TO REGRET IT.
BAMMMM
THINK AGAIN.
WE'VE GOT TO GET HIM TO THE HOSPITAL.
CALLING FOR AN AMBULANCE NOW.
UNNNHHHHHH

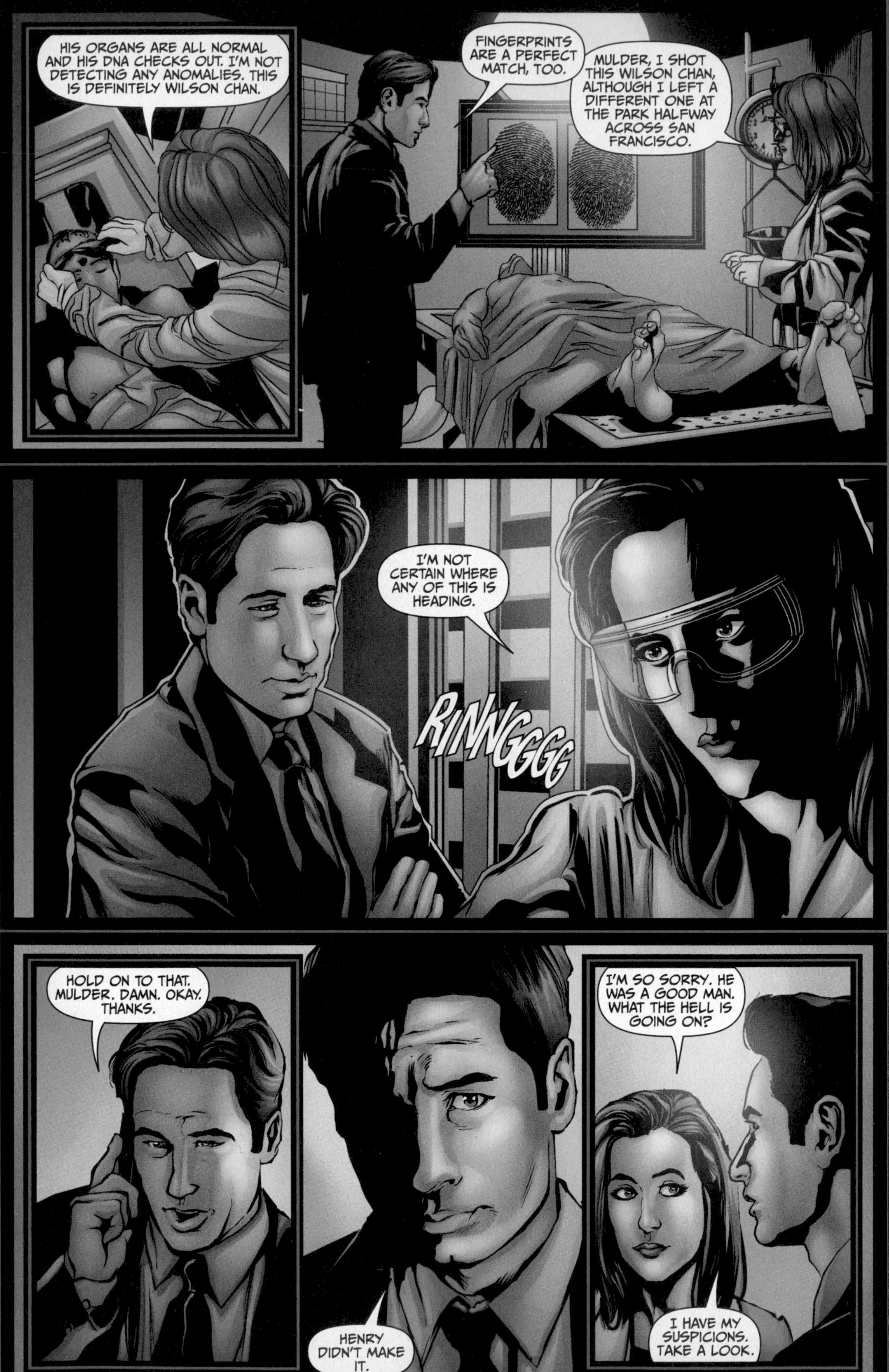
HIS ORGANS ARE ALL NORMAL AND HIS DNA CHECKS OUT. I'M NOT DETECTING ANY ANOMALIES. THIS IS DEFINITELY WILSON CHAN.
FINGERPRINTS ARE A PERFECT MATCH, TOO.
MULDER, I SHOT THIS WILSON CHAN, ALTHOUGH I LEFT A DIFFERENT ONE AT THE PARK HALFWAY ACROSS SAN FRANCISCO.
I'M NOT CERTAIN WHERE ANY OF THIS IS HEADING.
RINNGGGG
HOLD ON TO THAT. MULDER. DAMN. OKAY. THANKS.
HENRY DIDN'T MAKE IT.
I'M SO SORRY. HE WAS A GOOD MAN. WHAT THE HELL IS GOING ON?
I HAVE MY SUSPICIONS. TAKE A LOOK.

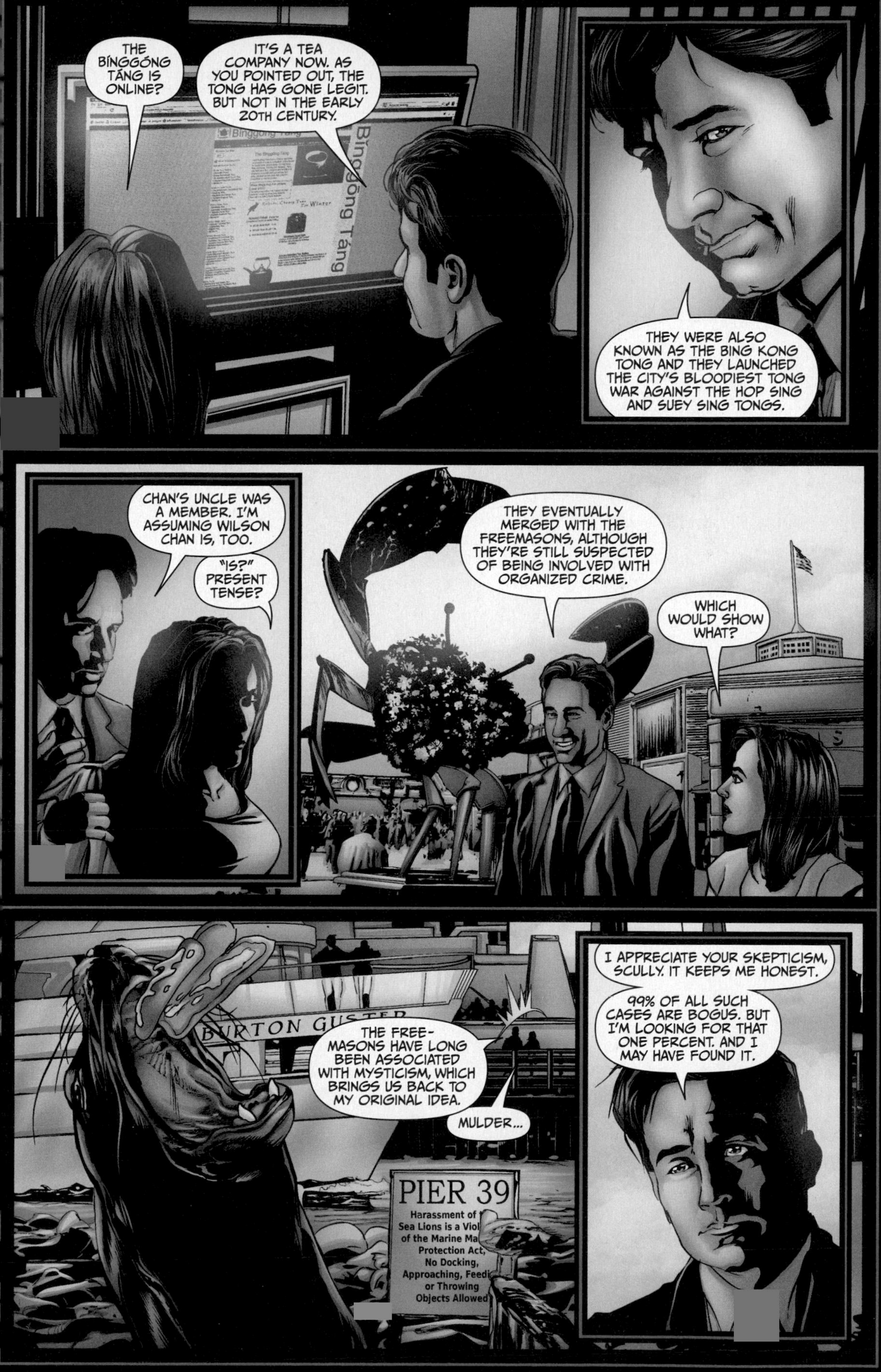
THE BÍNGGÓNG TÁNG IS ONLINE?
IT'S A TEA COMPANY NOW. AS YOU POINTED OUT, THE TONG HAS GONE LEGIT. BUT NOT IN THE EARLY 20TH CENTURY.
Bínggōng Táng
THEY WERE ALSO KNOWN AS THE BING KONG TONG AND THEY LAUNCHED THE CITY'S BLOODIEST TONG WAR AGAINST THE HOP SING AND SUEY SING TONGS.
CHAN'S UNCLE WAS A MEMBER. I'M ASSUMING WILSON CHAN IS, TOO.
"IS?" PRESENT TENSE?
THEY EVENTUALLY MERGED WITH THE FREEMASONS, ALTHOUGH THEY'RE STILL SUSPECTED OF BEING INVOLVED WITH ORGANIZED CRIME.
WHICH WOULD SHOW WHAT?
BURTON GUSTER
THE FREE-MASONS HAVE LONG BEEN ASSOCIATED WITH MYSTICISM, WHICH BRINGS US BACK TO MY ORIGINAL IDEA.
MULDER...
PIER 39
Harassment of t Sea Lions is a Viol of the Marine Ma Protection Act, No Docking, Approaching, Feedi or Throwing Objects Allowed
I APPRECIATE YOUR SKEPTICISM, SCULLY. IT KEEPS ME HONEST.
99% OF ALL SUCH CASES ARE BOGUS. BUT I'M LOOKING FOR THAT ONE PERCENT. AND I MAY HAVE FOUND IT.

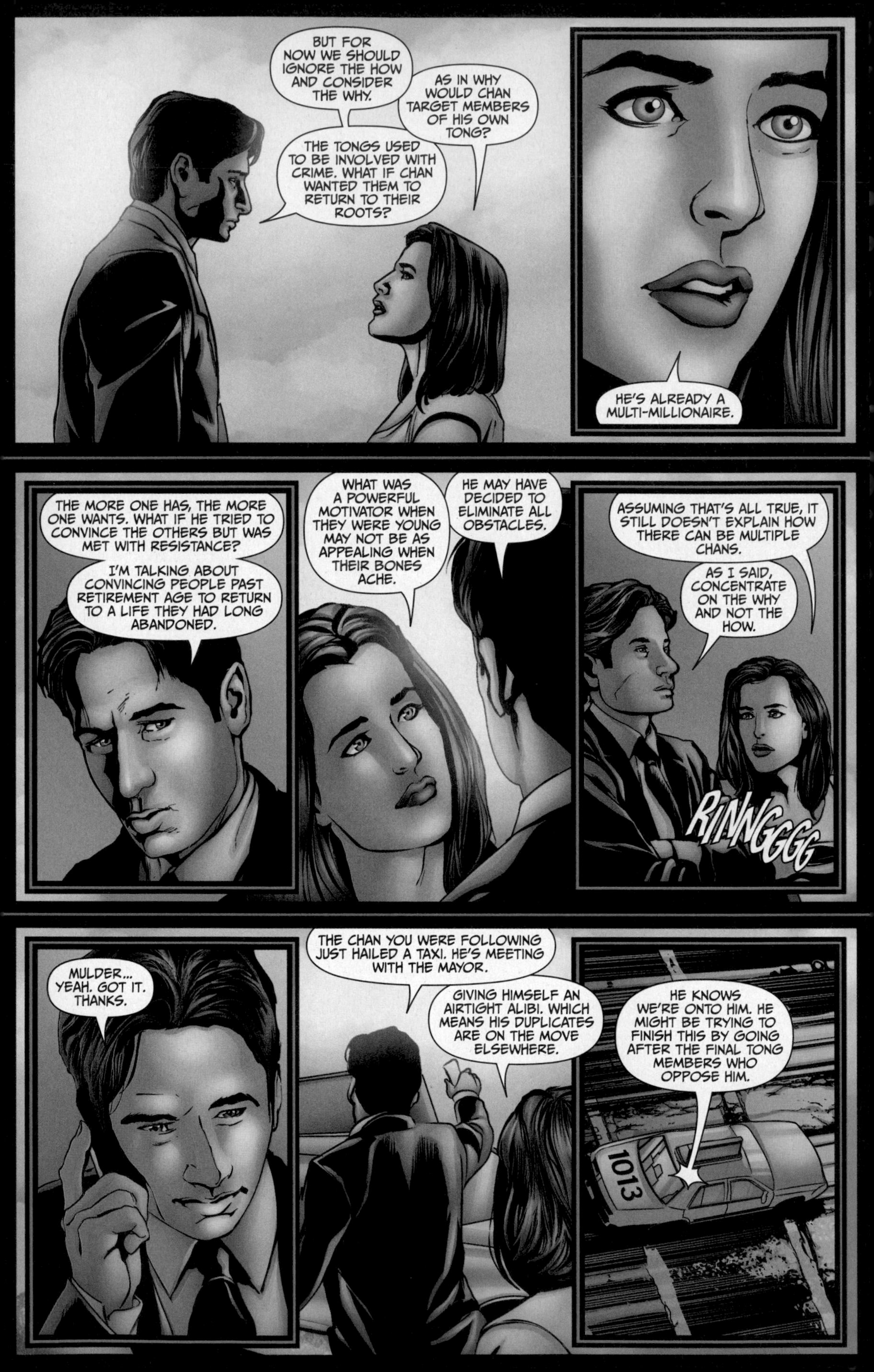
BUT FOR NOW WE SHOULD IGNORE THE HOW AND CONSIDER THE WHY.
THE TONGS USED TO BE INVOLVED WITH CRIME. WHAT IF CHAN WANTED THEM TO RETURN TO THEIR ROOTS?
AS IN WHY WOULD CHAN TARGET MEMBERS OF HIS OWN TONG?
HE'S ALREADY A MULTI-MILLIONAIRE.
THE MORE ONE HAS, THE MORE ONE WANTS. WHAT IF HE TRIED TO CONVINCE THE OTHERS BUT WAS MET WITH RESISTANCE?
I'M TALKING ABOUT CONVINCING PEOPLE PAST RETIREMENT AGE TO RETURN TO A LIFE THEY HAD LONG ABANDONED.
WHAT WAS A POWERFUL MOTIVATOR WHEN THEY WERE YOUNG MAY NOT BE AS APPEALING WHEN THEIR BONES ACHE.
HE MAY HAVE DECIDED TO ELIMINATE ALL OBSTACLES.
ASSUMING THAT'S ALL TRUE, IT STILL DOESN'T EXPLAIN HOW THERE CAN BE MULTIPLE CHANS.
AS I SAID, CONCENTRATE ON THE WHY AND NOT THE HOW.
RINNGGGG
MULDER... YEAH. GOT IT. THANKS.
THE CHAN YOU WERE FOLLOWING JUST HAILED A TAXI. HE'S MEETING WITH THE MAYOR.
GIVING HIMSELF AN AIRTIGHT ALIBI. WHICH MEANS HIS DUPLICATES ARE ON THE MOVE ELSEWHERE.
HE KNOWS WE'RE ONTO HIM. HE MIGHT BE TRYING TO FINISH THIS BY GOING AFTER THE FINAL TONG MEMBERS WHO OPPOSE HIM.
1013

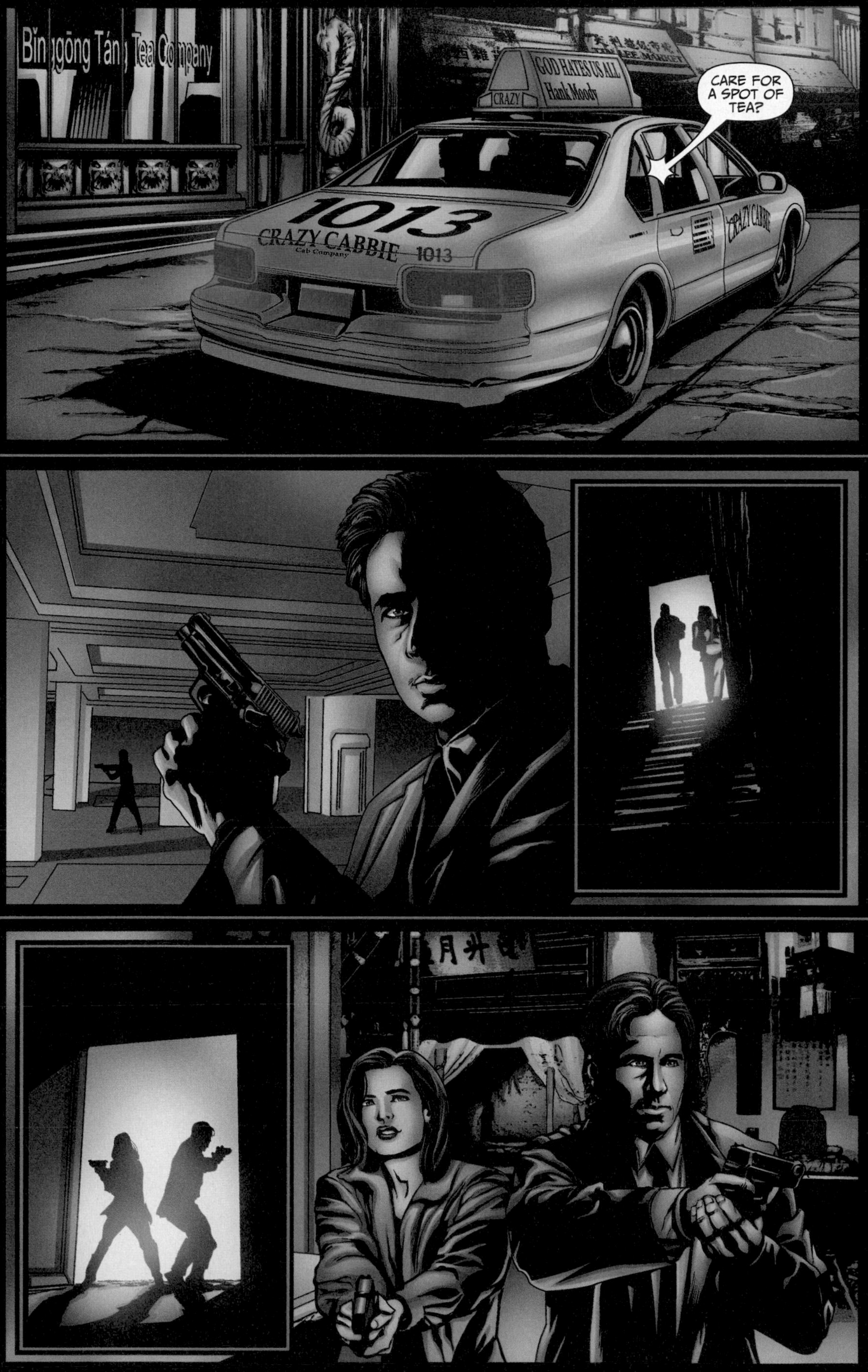
GOD HATES US ALL
Hank Moody
CRAZY
CARE FOR A SPOT OF TEA?
1013
CRAZY CABBIE
Cab Company
1013
CRAZY CABBIE

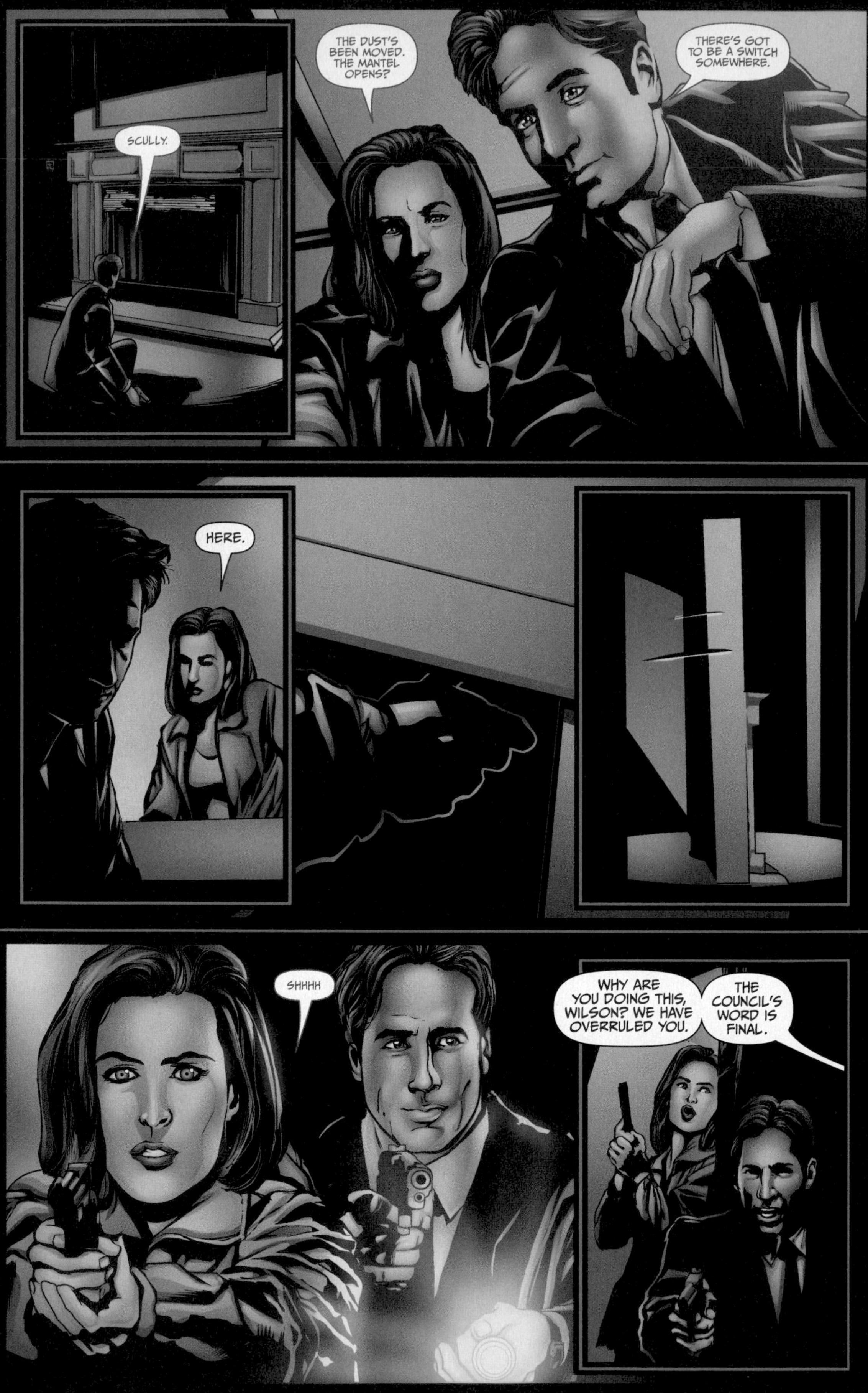
SCULLY.
THE DUST'S BEEN MOVED. THE MANTEL OPENS?
THERE'S GOT TO BE A SWITCH SOMEWHERE.
HERE.
SHHHH
WHY ARE YOU DOING THIS, WILSON? WE HAVE OVERRULED YOU.
THE COUNCIL'S WORD IS FINAL.

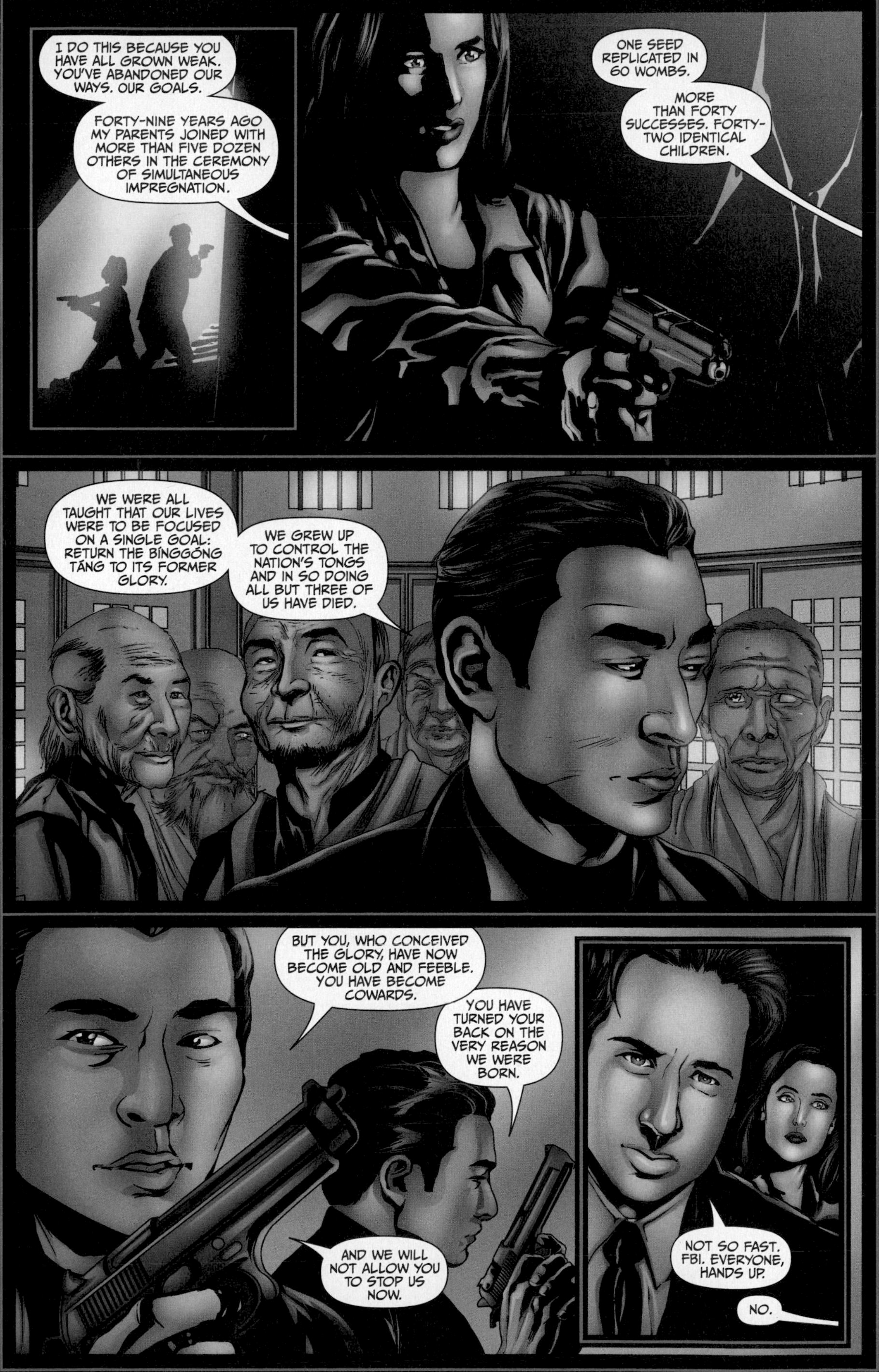
I DO THIS BECAUSE YOU HAVE ALL GROWN WEAK. YOU'VE ABANDONED OUR WAYS. OUR GOALS.
FORTY-NINE YEARS AGO MY PARENTS JOINED WITH MORE THAN FIVE DOZEN OTHERS IN THE CEREMONY OF SIMULTANEOUS IMPREGNATION.
ONE SEED REPLICATED IN 60 WOMBS.
MORE THAN FORTY SUCCESSES. FORTY-TWO IDENTICAL CHILDREN.
WE WERE ALL TAUGHT THAT OUR LIVES WERE TO BE FOCUSED ON A SINGLE GOAL: RETURN THE BÍNGGŌNG TÁNG TO ITS FORMER GLORY.
WE GREW UP TO CONTROL THE NATION'S TONGS AND IN SO DOING ALL BUT THREE OF US HAVE DIED.
BUT YOU, WHO CONCEIVED THE GLORY, HAVE NOW BECOME OLD AND FEEBLE. YOU HAVE BECOME COWARDS.
YOU HAVE TURNED YOUR BACK ON THE VERY REASON WE WERE BORN.
AND WE WILL NOT ALLOW YOU TO STOP US NOW.
NOT SO FAST. FBI. EVERYONE, HANDS UP.
NO.

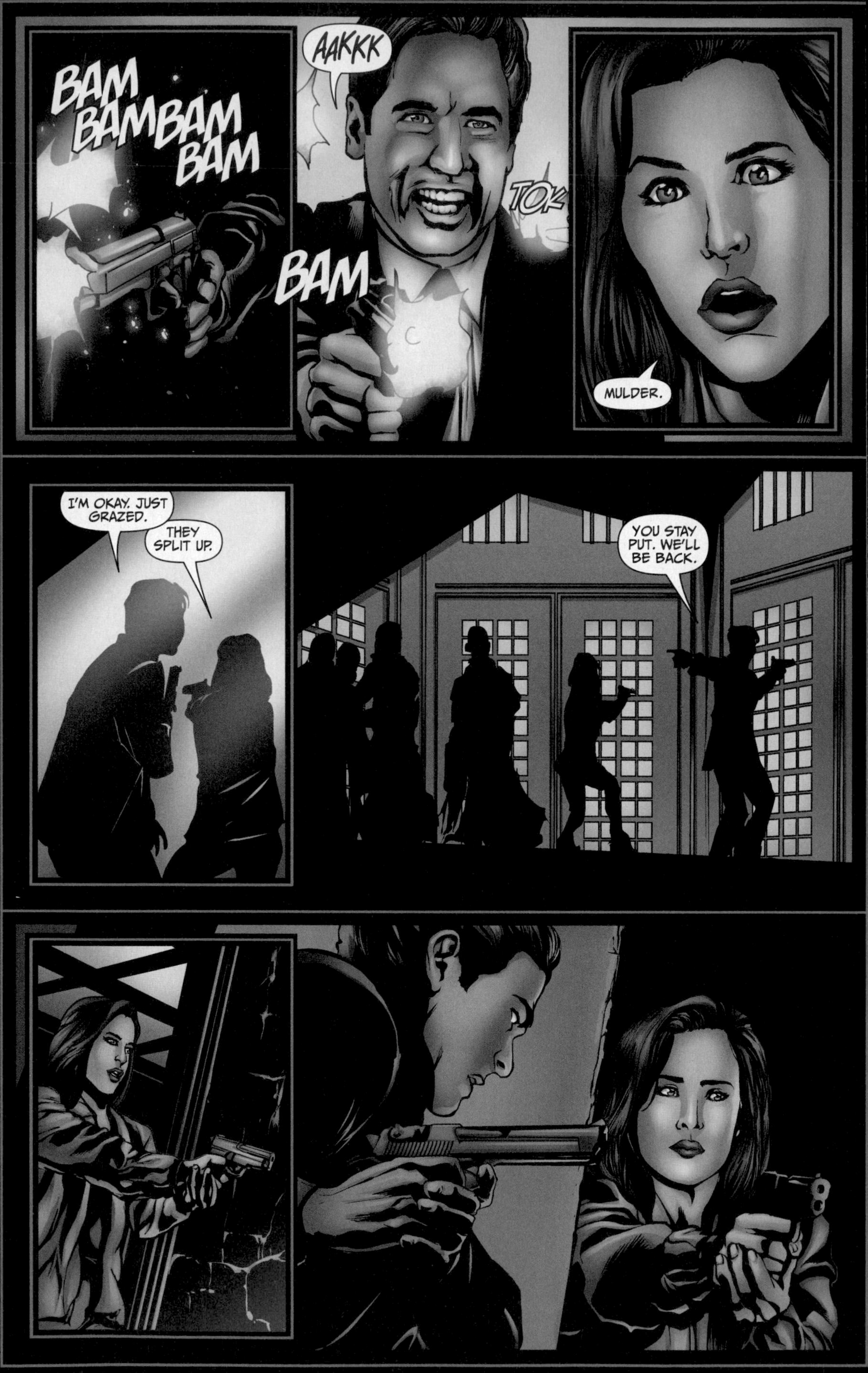

BAM
BAMBAMBAM
BAM
AAKKK
TOK
BAM
MULDER.
I'M OKAY. JUST GRAZED.
THEY SPLIT UP.
YOU STAY PUT. WE'LL BE BACK.

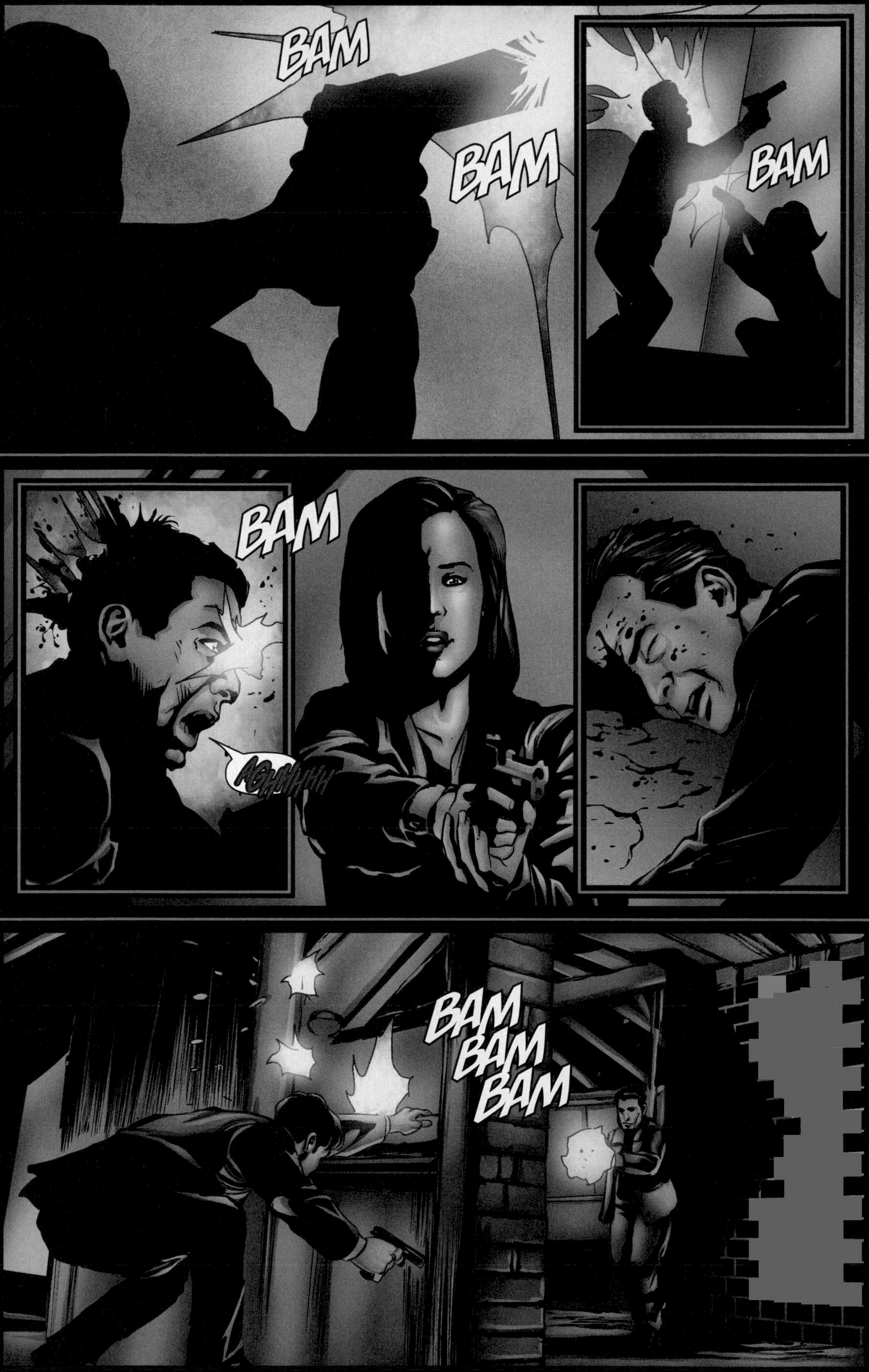
BAM
BAM
BAM
BAM
AGHHHHH
BAM
BAM
BAM

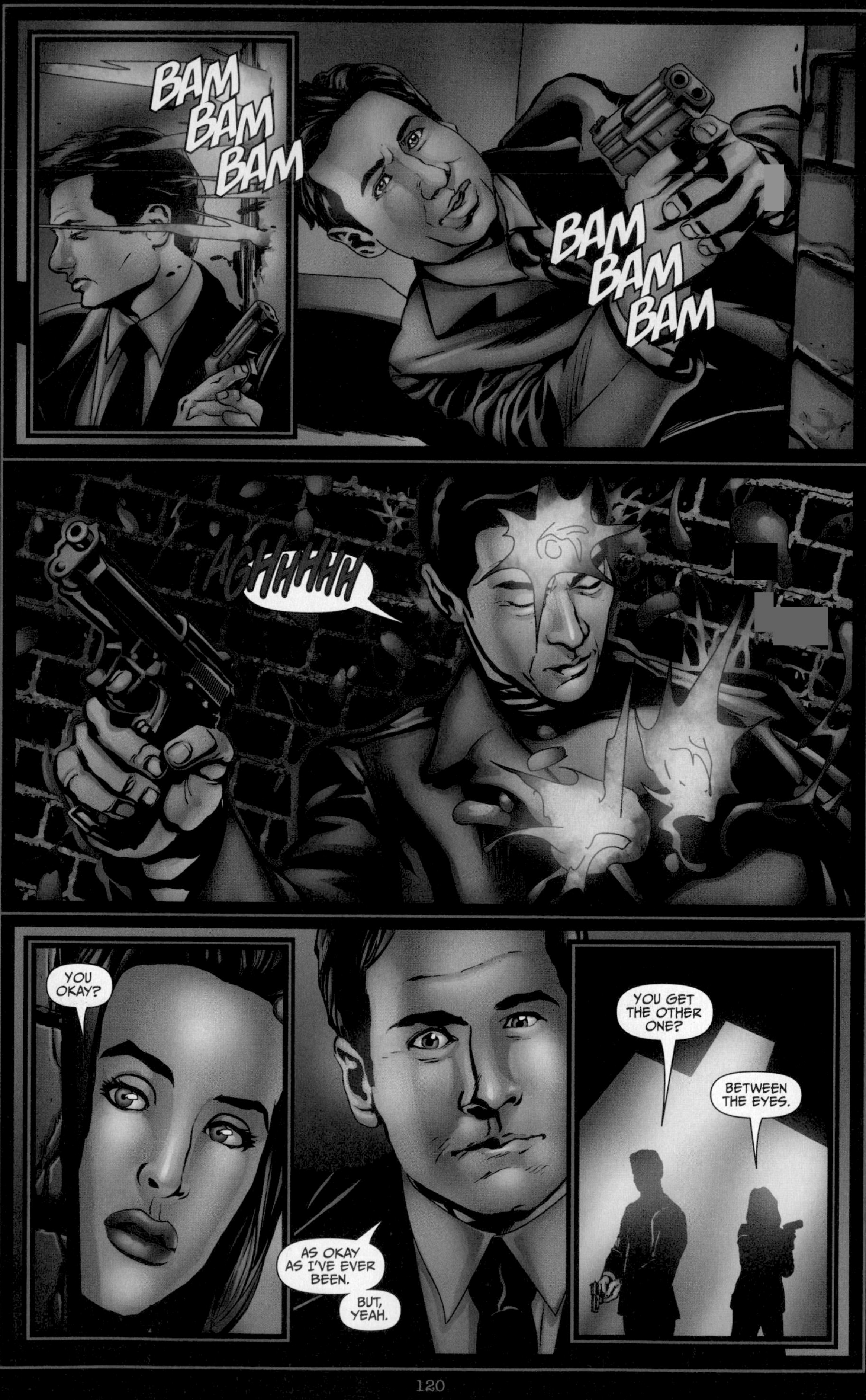
BAM
BAM
BAM
BAM
BAM
BAM
AGHHHHH
YOU OKAY?
AS OKAY AS I'VE EVER BEEN.
BUT, YEAH.
YOU GET THE OTHER ONE?
BETWEEN THE EYES.

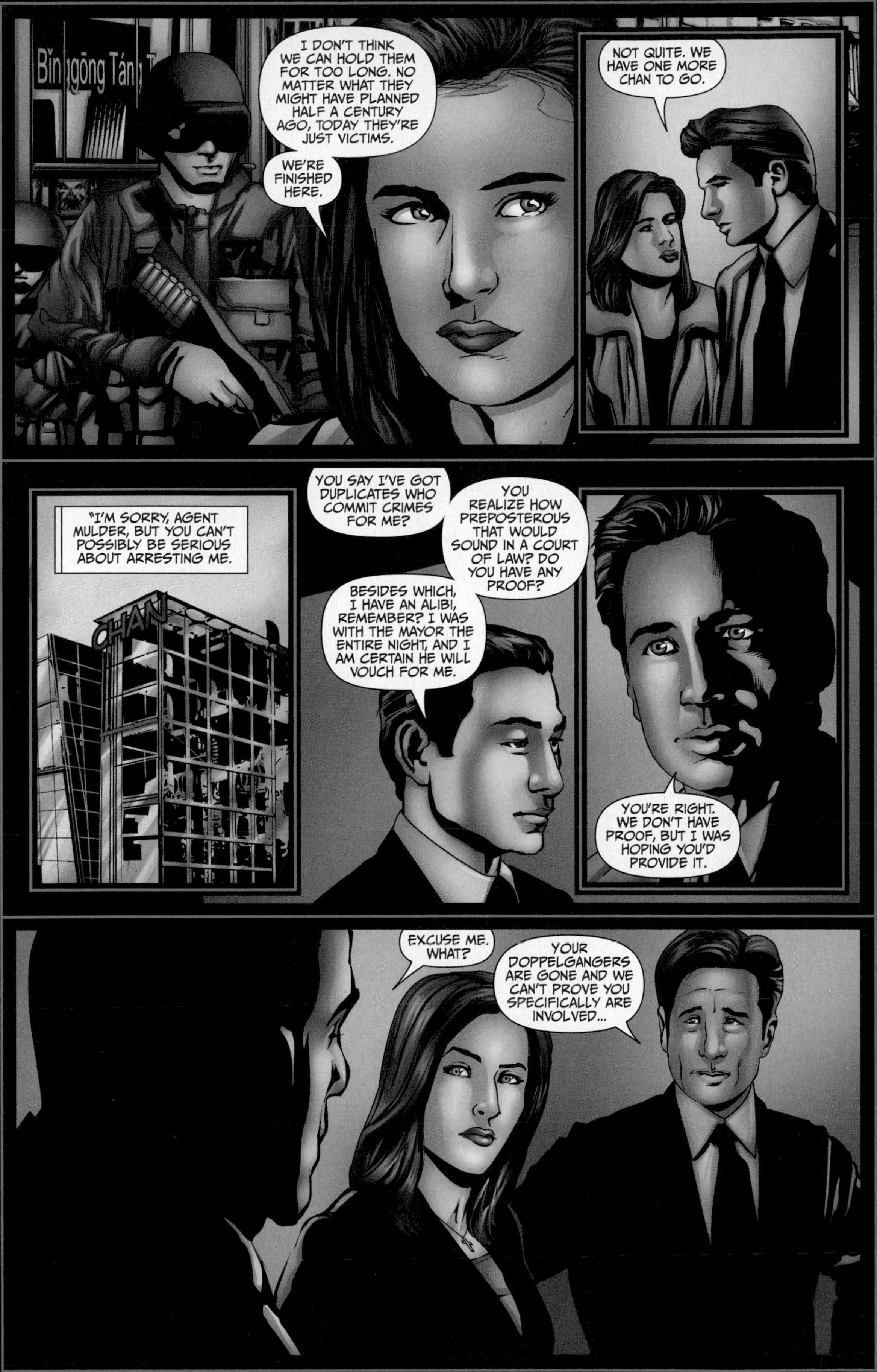
Bǐngōng Táng
I DON'T THINK WE CAN HOLD THEM FOR TOO LONG. NO MATTER WHAT THEY MIGHT HAVE PLANNED HALF A CENTURY AGO, TODAY THEY'RE JUST VICTIMS.
WE'RE FINISHED HERE.
NOT QUITE. WE HAVE ONE MORE CHAN TO GO.
"I'M SORRY, AGENT MULDER, BUT YOU CAN'T POSSIBLY BE SERIOUS ABOUT ARRESTING ME.
CHAN
YOU SAY I'VE GOT DUPLICATES WHO COMMIT CRIMES FOR ME?
YOU REALIZE HOW PREPOSTEROUS THAT WOULD SOUND IN A COURT OF LAW? DO YOU HAVE ANY PROOF?
BESIDES WHICH, I HAVE AN ALIBI, REMEMBER? I WAS WITH THE MAYOR THE ENTIRE NIGHT, AND I AM CERTAIN HE WILL VOUCH FOR ME.
YOU'RE RIGHT. WE DON'T HAVE PROOF, BUT I WAS HOPING YOU'D PROVIDE IT.
EXCUSE ME. WHAT?
YOUR DOPPELGANGERS ARE GONE AND WE CAN'T PROVE YOU SPECIFICALLY ARE INVOLVED...

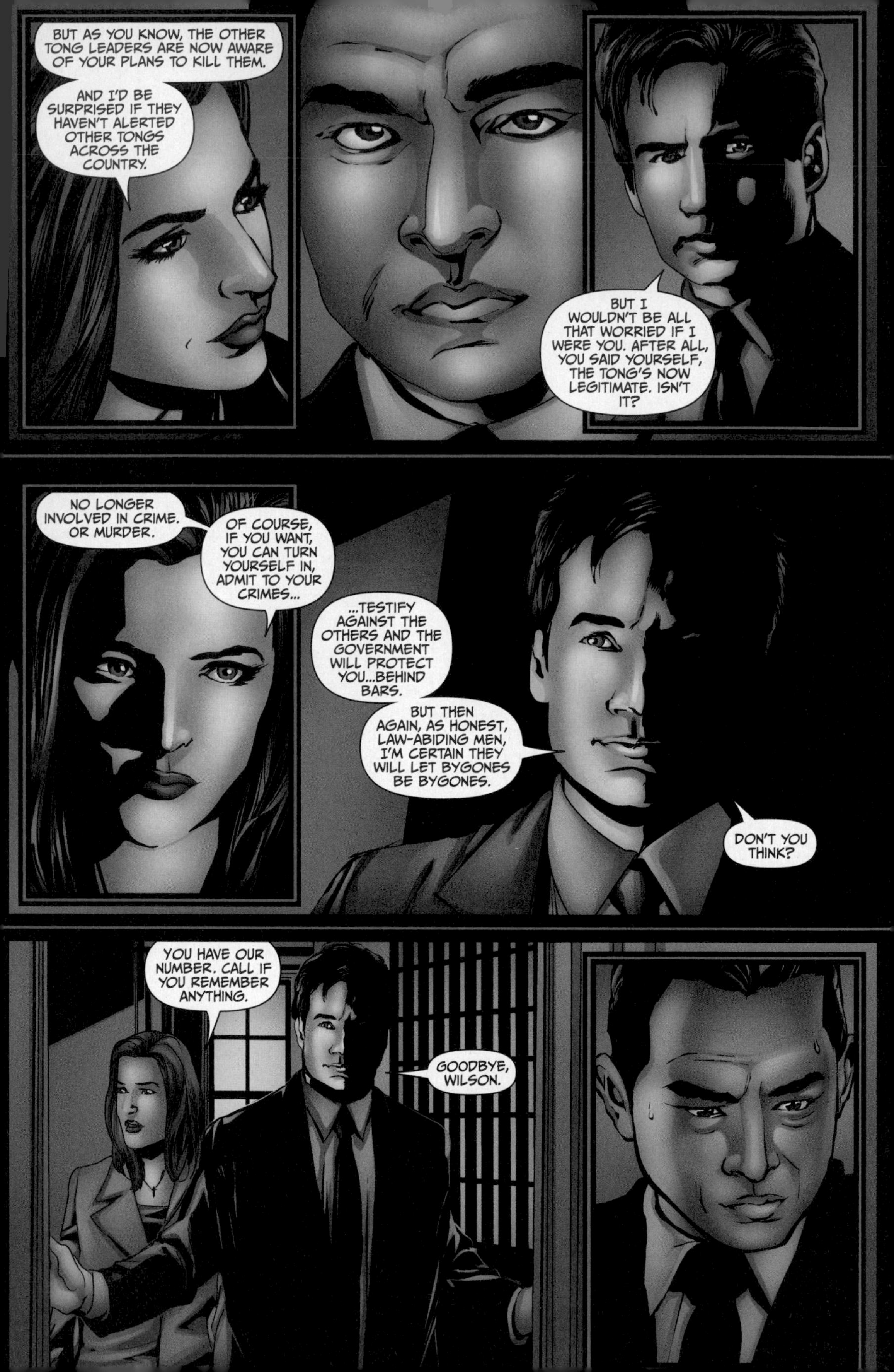
BUT AS YOU KNOW, THE OTHER TONG LEADERS ARE NOW AWARE OF YOUR PLANS TO KILL THEM.
AND I'D BE SURPRISED IF THEY HAVEN'T ALERTED OTHER TONGS ACROSS THE COUNTRY.
BUT I WOULDN'T BE ALL THAT WORRIED IF I WERE YOU. AFTER ALL, YOU SAID YOURSELF, THE TONG'S NOW LEGITIMATE. ISN'T IT?
NO LONGER INVOLVED IN CRIME. OR MURDER.
OF COURSE, IF YOU WANT, YOU CAN TURN YOURSELF IN, ADMIT TO YOUR CRIMES...
...TESTIFY AGAINST THE OTHERS AND THE GOVERNMENT WILL PROTECT YOU...BEHIND BARS.
BUT THEN AGAIN, AS HONEST, LAW-ABIDING MEN, I'M CERTAIN THEY WILL LET BYGONES BE BYGONES.
DON'T YOU THINK?
YOU HAVE OUR NUMBER. CALL IF YOU REMEMBER ANYTHING.
GOODBYE, WILSON.

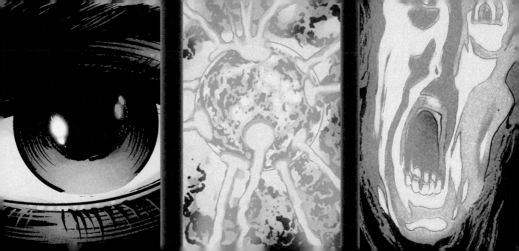

Chapter Four

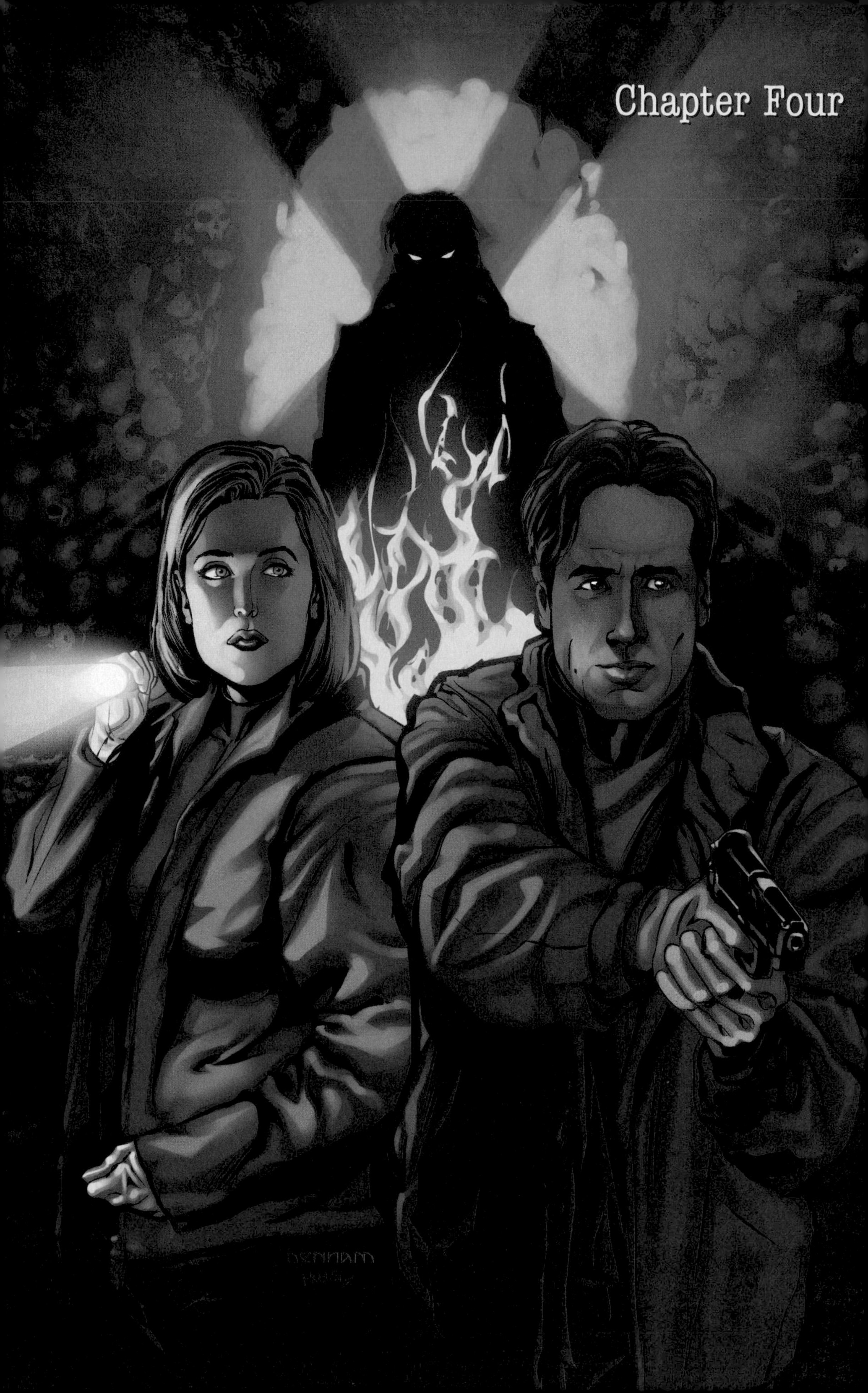

written by
DOUG MOENCH

illustrated by
BRIAN DENHAM

THE X FILES

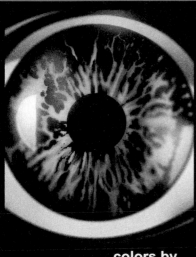

colors by
CARLOS BADILLA

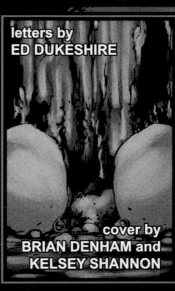

letters by
ED DUKESHIRE

cover by
BRIAN DENHAM and
KELSEY SHANNON

edited by
**SHANNON
ERIC DENTON**

created by
**CHRIS
CARTER**

Y-YOU...! I...I'VE SEEN YOU *BEFORE*... THREE TIMES SNEAKING AROUND OUT THERE...IN THE *NIGHT*.

The Badlands, South Dakota,
2:32 a.m., three years ago

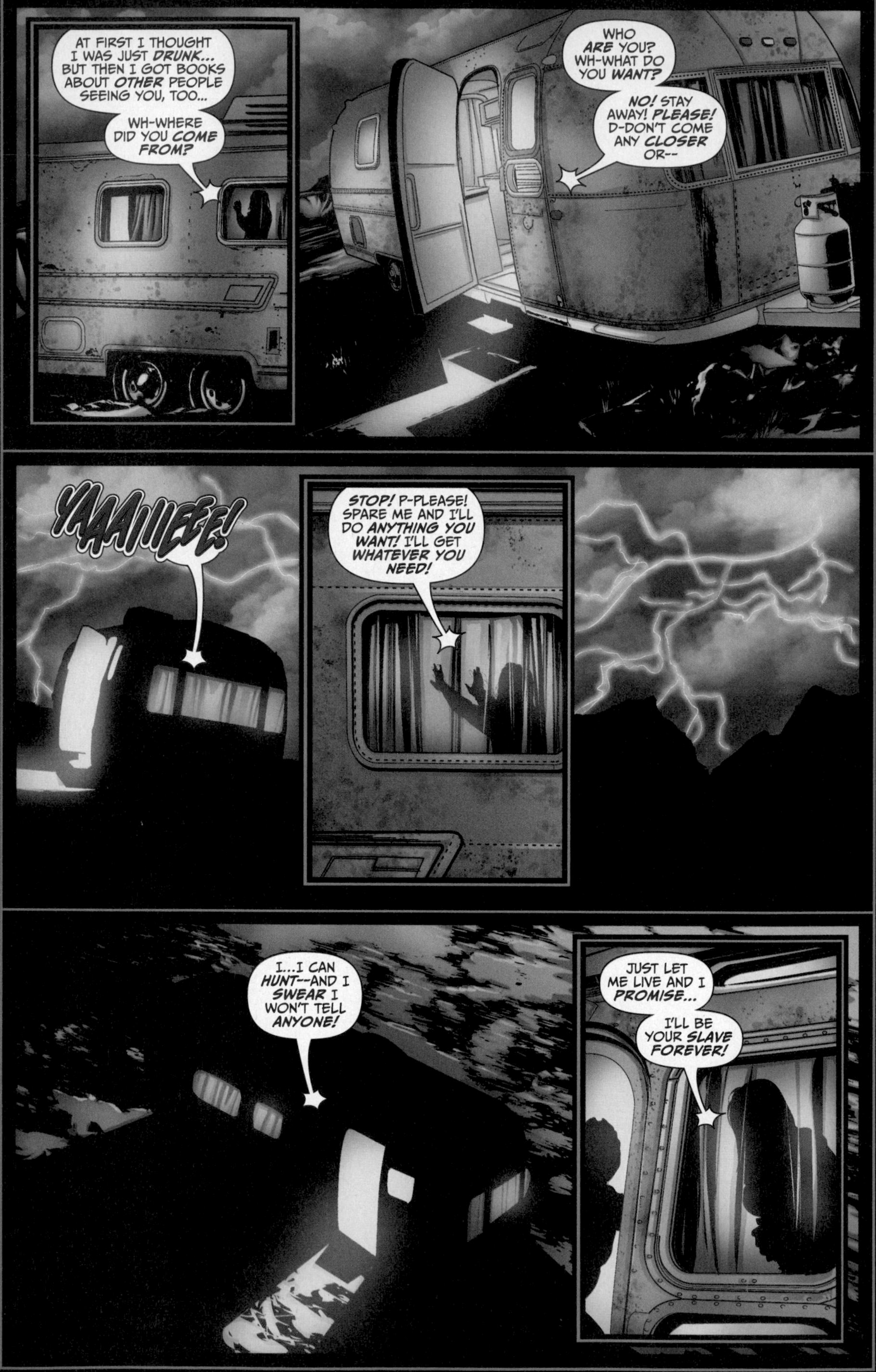
AT FIRST I THOUGHT I WAS JUST DRUNK... BUT THEN I GOT BOOKS ABOUT OTHER PEOPLE SEEING YOU, TOO...
WH-WHERE DID YOU COME FROM?
WHO ARE YOU? WH-WHAT DO YOU WANT?
NO! STAY AWAY! PLEASE! D-DON'T COME ANY CLOSER OR--
YAAAIIIEEE!
STOP! P-PLEASE! SPARE ME AND I'LL DO ANYTHING YOU WANT! I'LL GET WHATEVER YOU NEED!
I...I CAN HUNT--AND I SWEAR I WON'T TELL ANYONE!
JUST LET ME LIVE AND I PROMISE...
I'LL BE YOUR SLAVE FOREVER!

--THREE-YEAR STRING OF MISSING PERSONS, ALL *WOMEN*, IN THE VICINITY OF RED SHIRT, SOUTH DAKOTA.

FBI Headquarters, 9:17 a.m., today

THAT'D BE THE *BADLANDS*.

VERY BAD, JUDGING BY THE NOTES SENT TO LOCAL AUTHORITIES-- SIGNED *"DANTE."*

ANOTHER SERIAL KILLER?

The office of Assistant Director Skinner

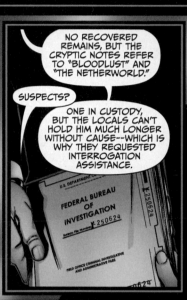

NO RECOVERED REMAINS, BUT THE CRYPTIC NOTES REFER TO "BLOODLUST" AND "THE NETHERWORLD."

SUSPECTS?

ONE IN CUSTODY, BUT THE LOCALS CAN'T HOLD HIM MUCH LONGER WITHOUT CAUSE--WHICH IS WHY THEY REQUESTED INTERROGATION ASSISTANCE.

U.S. DEPARTMENT

FEDERAL BUREAU OF INVESTIGATION

Bureau File Number ¥ 250624

FIELD OFFICE CRIMINAL INVESTIGATIVE AND ADMINISTRATIVE FILES

I CAN TAKE SCULLY--BUT *WHY US?*

BECAUSE OUR ANALYSTS RECOMMEND THE "SPOOKY MULDER PERSPECTIVE" GIVEN THE SUSPECT'S CLAIMS OF "CONTROL BY NASTY ONES FROM DOWN UNDER."

POSSESSED BY AUSSIES? OR A REFERENCE TO PERSISTENT BADLANDS SIGHTINGS OF GHOSTS, "PALE PEOPLE," DEMONS...

DEMONS SOUNDS RIGHT, ALTHOUGH THE SUSPECT HIMSELF SAYS HE DOESN'T *BELIEVE* IN DEMONIC POSSESSION.

ON THE OTHER HAND, HE CLAIMS "THE ONLY HOPE IS TO FEED EVIL."

AFTER A LONG FAST--NOW *BROKEN.*

REPORTS OF SPIRITS AND DEMONS HAUNTING THE BADLANDS TRACE FROM *INDIAN LEGENDS* ALL THE WAY TO THE POINT AT WHICH THEY *STOPPED...*

THREE YEARS AGO.

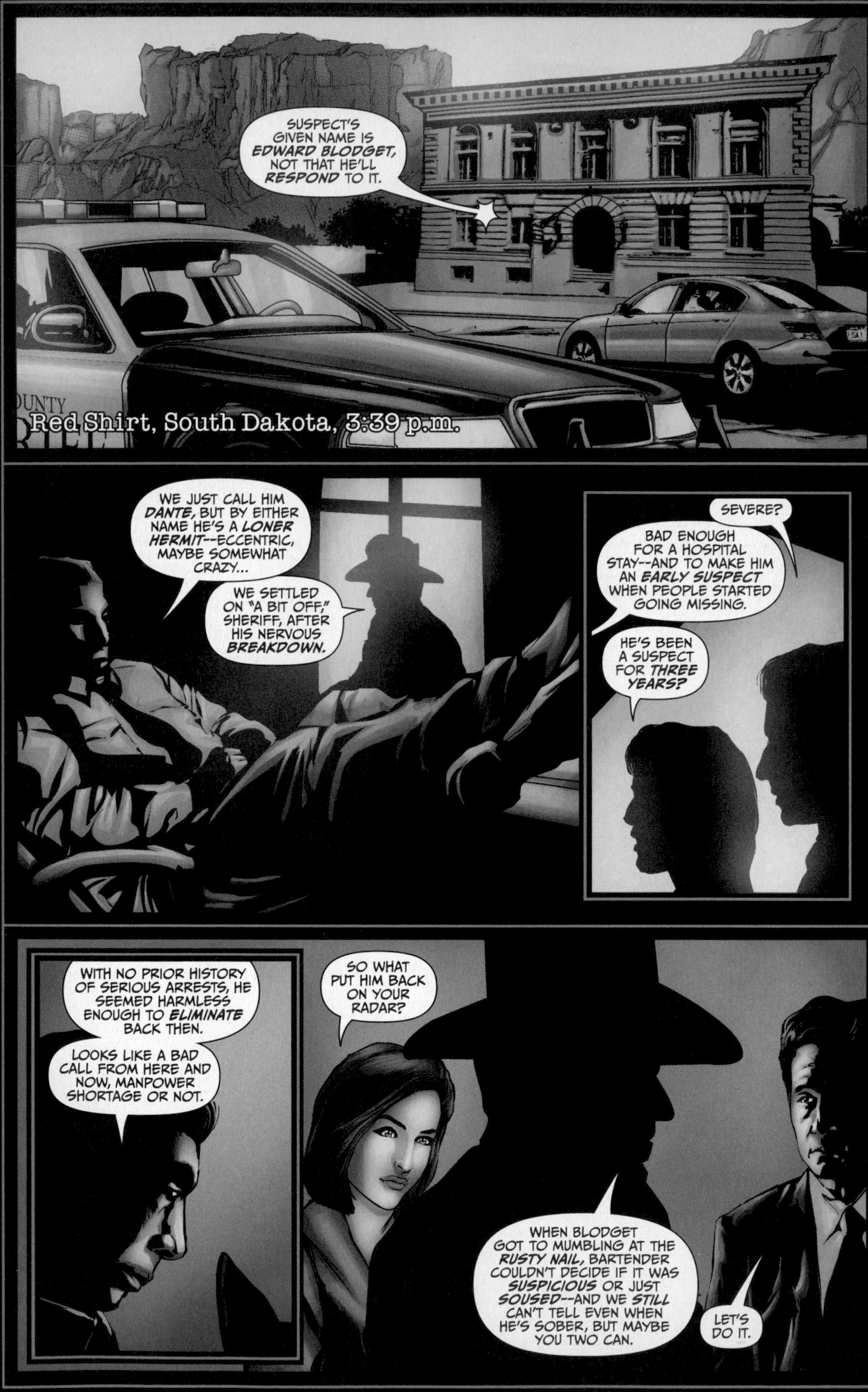
SUSPECT'S GIVEN NAME IS EDWARD BLODGET, NOT THAT HE'LL RESPOND TO IT.
Red Shirt, South Dakota, 3:39 p.m.
WE JUST CALL HIM DANTE, BUT BY EITHER NAME HE'S A LONER HERMIT--ECCENTRIC, MAYBE SOMEWHAT CRAZY...
WE SETTLED ON "A BIT OFF," SHERIFF, AFTER HIS NERVOUS BREAKDOWN.
SEVERE?
BAD ENOUGH FOR A HOSPITAL STAY--AND TO MAKE HIM AN EARLY SUSPECT WHEN PEOPLE STARTED GOING MISSING.
HE'S BEEN A SUSPECT FOR THREE YEARS?
WITH NO PRIOR HISTORY OF SERIOUS ARRESTS, HE SEEMED HARMLESS ENOUGH TO ELIMINATE BACK THEN.
LOOKS LIKE A BAD CALL FROM HERE AND NOW, MANPOWER SHORTAGE OR NOT.
SO WHAT PUT HIM BACK ON YOUR RADAR?
WHEN BLODGET GOT TO MUMBLING AT THE RUSTY NAIL, BARTENDER COULDN'T DECIDE IF IT WAS SUSPICIOUS OR JUST SOUSED--AND WE STILL CAN'T TELL EVEN WHEN HE'S SOBER, BUT MAYBE YOU TWO CAN.
LET'S DO IT.

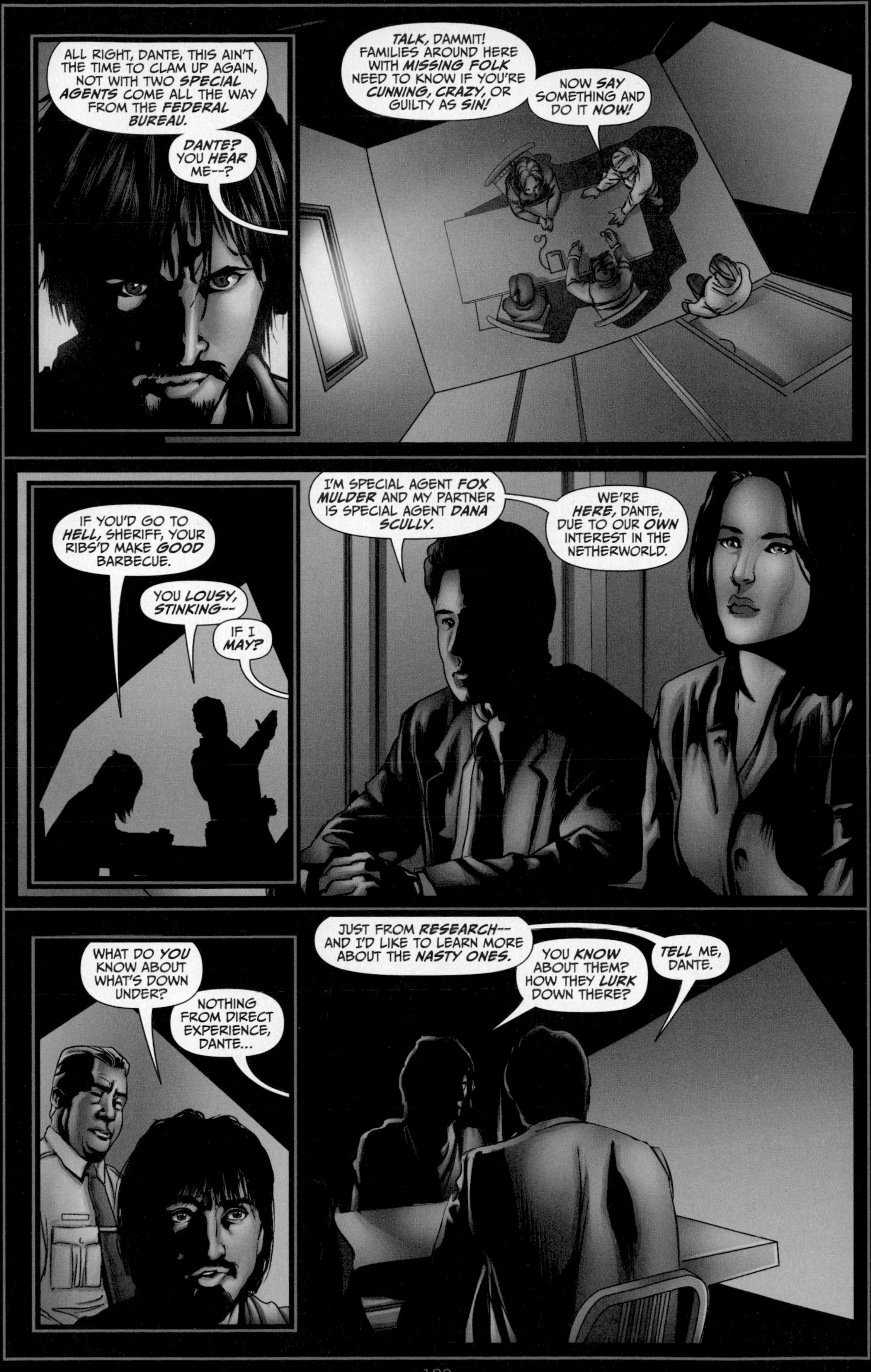
ALL RIGHT, DANTE, THIS AIN'T THE TIME TO CLAM UP AGAIN, NOT WITH TWO SPECIAL AGENTS COME ALL THE WAY FROM THE FEDERAL BUREAU.
DANTE? YOU HEAR ME--?
TALK, DAMMIT! FAMILIES AROUND HERE WITH MISSING FOLK NEED TO KNOW IF YOU'RE CUNNING, CRAZY, OR GUILTY AS SIN!
NOW SAY SOMETHING AND DO IT NOW!
IF YOU'D GO TO HELL, SHERIFF, YOUR RIBS'D MAKE GOOD BARBECUE.
YOU LOUSY, STINKING--
IF I MAY?
I'M SPECIAL AGENT FOX MULDER AND MY PARTNER IS SPECIAL AGENT DANA SCULLY.
WE'RE HERE, DANTE, DUE TO OUR OWN INTEREST IN THE NETHERWORLD.
WHAT DO YOU KNOW ABOUT WHAT'S DOWN UNDER?
NOTHING FROM DIRECT EXPERIENCE, DANTE...
JUST FROM RESEARCH-- AND I'D LIKE TO LEARN MORE ABOUT THE NASTY ONES.
YOU KNOW ABOUT THEM? HOW THEY LURK DOWN THERE?
TELL ME, DANTE.

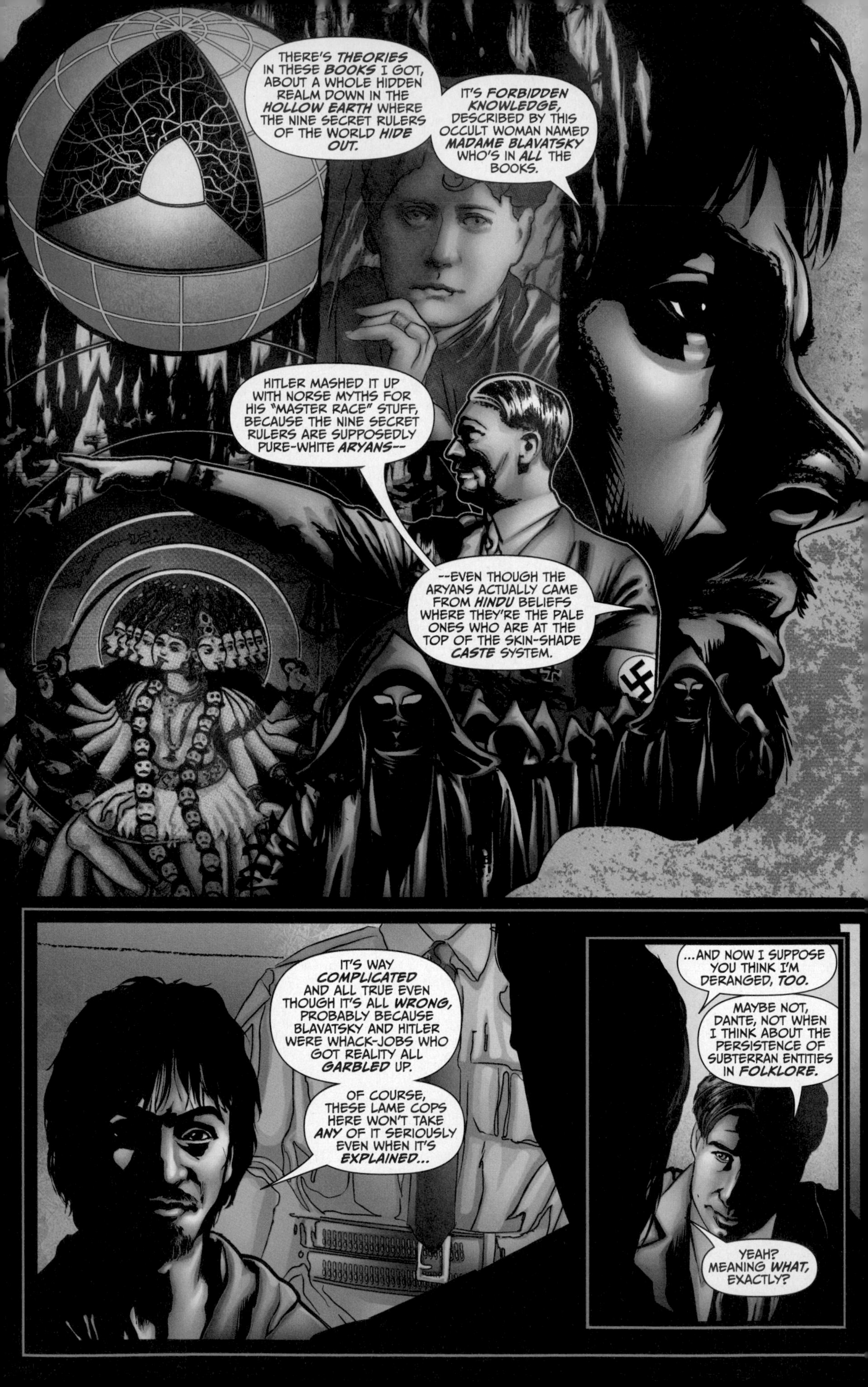

THERE'S THEORIES IN THESE BOOKS I GOT, ABOUT A WHOLE HIDDEN REALM DOWN IN THE HOLLOW EARTH WHERE THE NINE SECRET RULERS OF THE WORLD HIDE OUT.
IT'S FORBIDDEN KNOWLEDGE, DESCRIBED BY THIS OCCULT WOMAN NAMED MADAME BLAVATSKY WHO'S IN ALL THE BOOKS.
HITLER MASHED IT UP WITH NORSE MYTHS FOR HIS "MASTER RACE" STUFF, BECAUSE THE NINE SECRET RULERS ARE SUPPOSEDLY PURE-WHITE ARYANS--
--EVEN THOUGH THE ARYANS ACTUALLY CAME FROM HINDU BELIEFS WHERE THEY'RE THE PALE ONES WHO ARE AT THE TOP OF THE SKIN-SHADE CASTE SYSTEM.
IT'S WAY COMPLICATED AND ALL TRUE EVEN THOUGH IT'S ALL WRONG, PROBABLY BECAUSE BLAVATSKY AND HITLER WERE WHACK-JOBS WHO GOT REALITY ALL GARBLED UP.
OF COURSE, THESE LAME COPS HERE WON'T TAKE ANY OF IT SERIOUSLY EVEN WHEN IT'S EXPLAINED...
...AND NOW I SUPPOSE YOU THINK I'M DERANGED, TOO.
MAYBE NOT, DANTE, NOT WHEN I THINK ABOUT THE PERSISTENCE OF SUBTERRAN ENTITIES IN FOLKLORE.
YEAH? MEANING WHAT, EXACTLY?

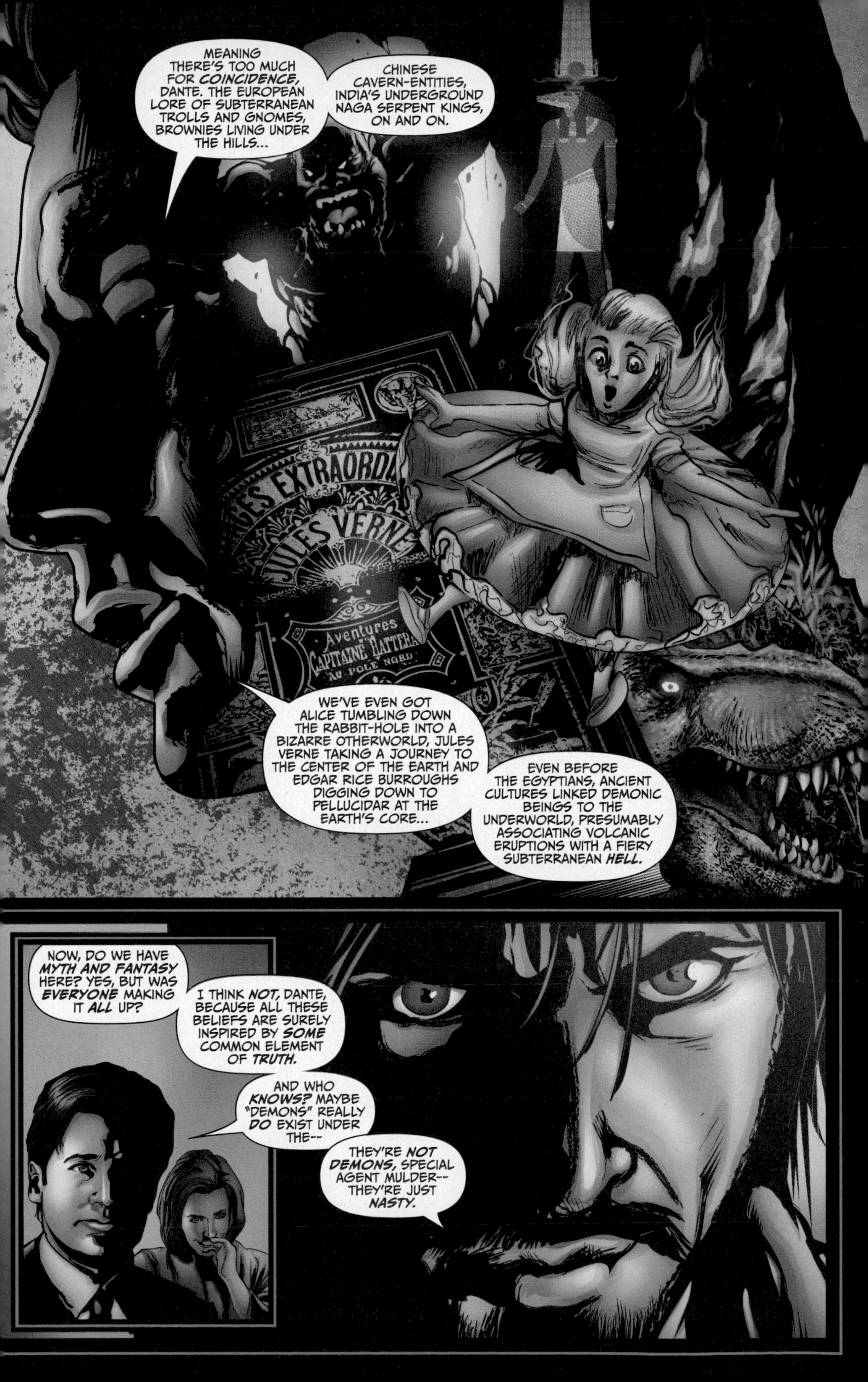
MEANING THERE'S TOO MUCH FOR COINCIDENCE, DANTE. THE EUROPEAN LORE OF SUBTERRANEAN TROLLS AND GNOMES, BROWNIES LIVING UNDER THE HILLS...
CHINESE CAVERN-ENTITIES, INDIA'S UNDERGROUND NAGA SERPENT KINGS, ON AND ON.
AVENTURES CAPITAINE HATTERAS AU POLE NORD
JULES VERNE
WE'VE EVEN GOT ALICE TUMBLING DOWN THE RABBIT-HOLE INTO A BIZARRE OTHERWORLD, JULES VERNE TAKING A JOURNEY TO THE CENTER OF THE EARTH AND EDGAR RICE BURROUGHS DIGGING DOWN TO PELLUCIDAR AT THE EARTH'S CORE...
EVEN BEFORE THE EGYPTIANS, ANCIENT CULTURES LINKED DEMONIC BEINGS TO THE UNDERWORLD, PRESUMABLY ASSOCIATING VOLCANIC ERUPTIONS WITH A FIERY SUBTERRANEAN HELL.
NOW, DO WE HAVE MYTH AND FANTASY HERE? YES, BUT WAS EVERYONE MAKING IT ALL UP?
I THINK NOT, DANTE, BECAUSE ALL THESE BELIEFS ARE SURELY INSPIRED BY SOME COMMON ELEMENT OF TRUTH.
AND WHO KNOWS? MAYBE "DEMONS" REALLY DO EXIST UNDER THE--
THEY'RE NOT DEMONS, SPECIAL AGENT MULDER-- THEY'RE JUST NASTY.

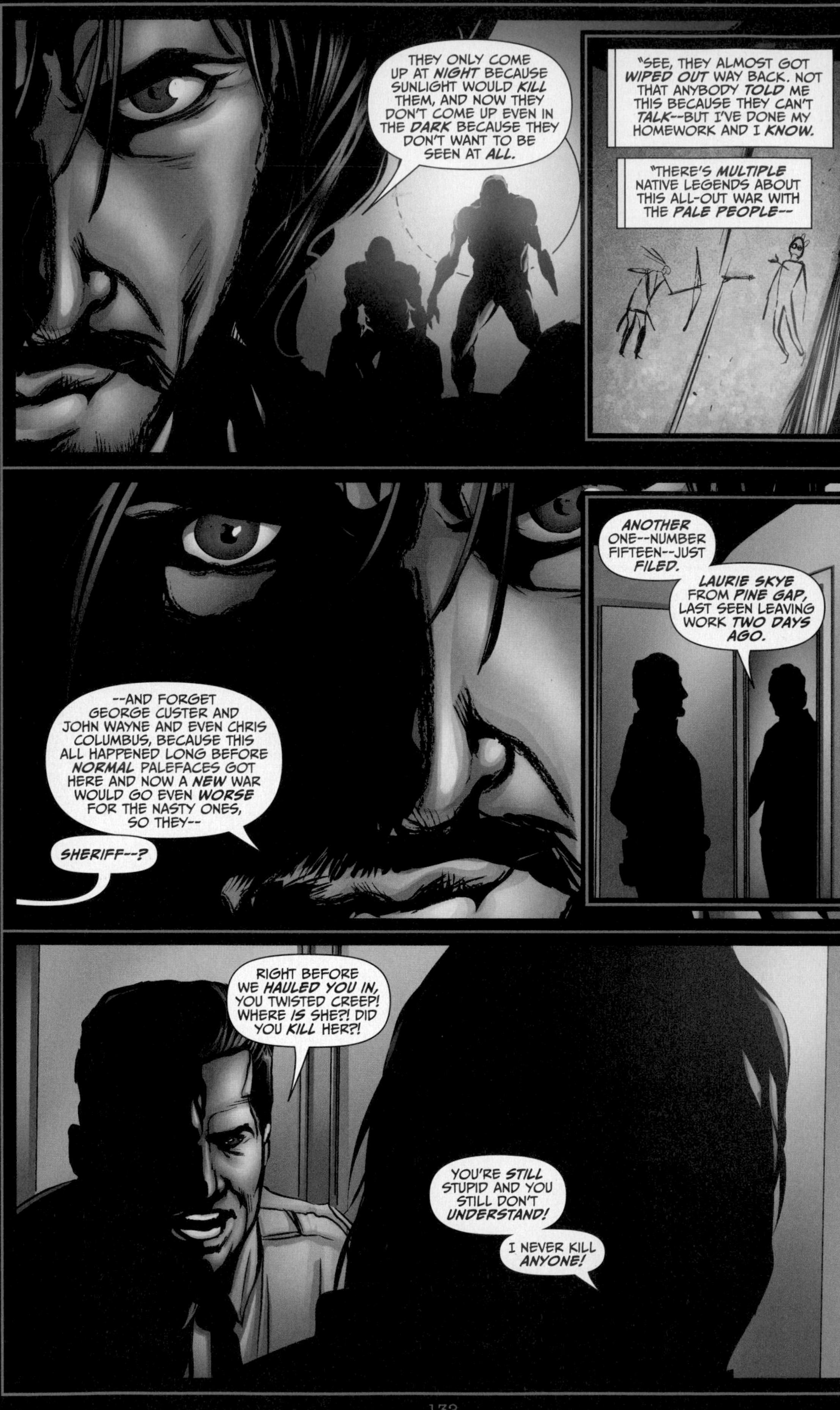
THEY ONLY COME UP AT NIGHT BECAUSE SUNLIGHT WOULD KILL THEM, AND NOW THEY DON'T COME UP EVEN IN THE DARK BECAUSE THEY DON'T WANT TO BE SEEN AT ALL.
"SEE, THEY ALMOST GOT WIPED OUT WAY BACK. NOT THAT ANYBODY TOLD ME THIS BECAUSE THEY CAN'T TALK--BUT I'VE DONE MY HOMEWORK AND I KNOW.
"THERE'S MULTIPLE NATIVE LEGENDS ABOUT THIS ALL-OUT WAR WITH THE PALE PEOPLE--
--AND FORGET GEORGE CUSTER AND JOHN WAYNE AND EVEN CHRIS COLUMBUS, BECAUSE THIS ALL HAPPENED LONG BEFORE NORMAL PALEFACES GOT HERE AND NOW A NEW WAR WOULD GO EVEN WORSE FOR THE NASTY ONES, SO THEY--
SHERIFF--?
ANOTHER ONE--NUMBER FIFTEEN--JUST FILED.
LAURIE SKYE FROM PINE GAP, LAST SEEN LEAVING WORK TWO DAYS AGO.
RIGHT BEFORE WE HAULED YOU IN, YOU TWISTED CREEP! WHERE IS SHE?! DID YOU KILL HER?!
YOU'RE STILL STUPID AND YOU STILL DON'T UNDERSTAND!
I NEVER KILL ANYONE!

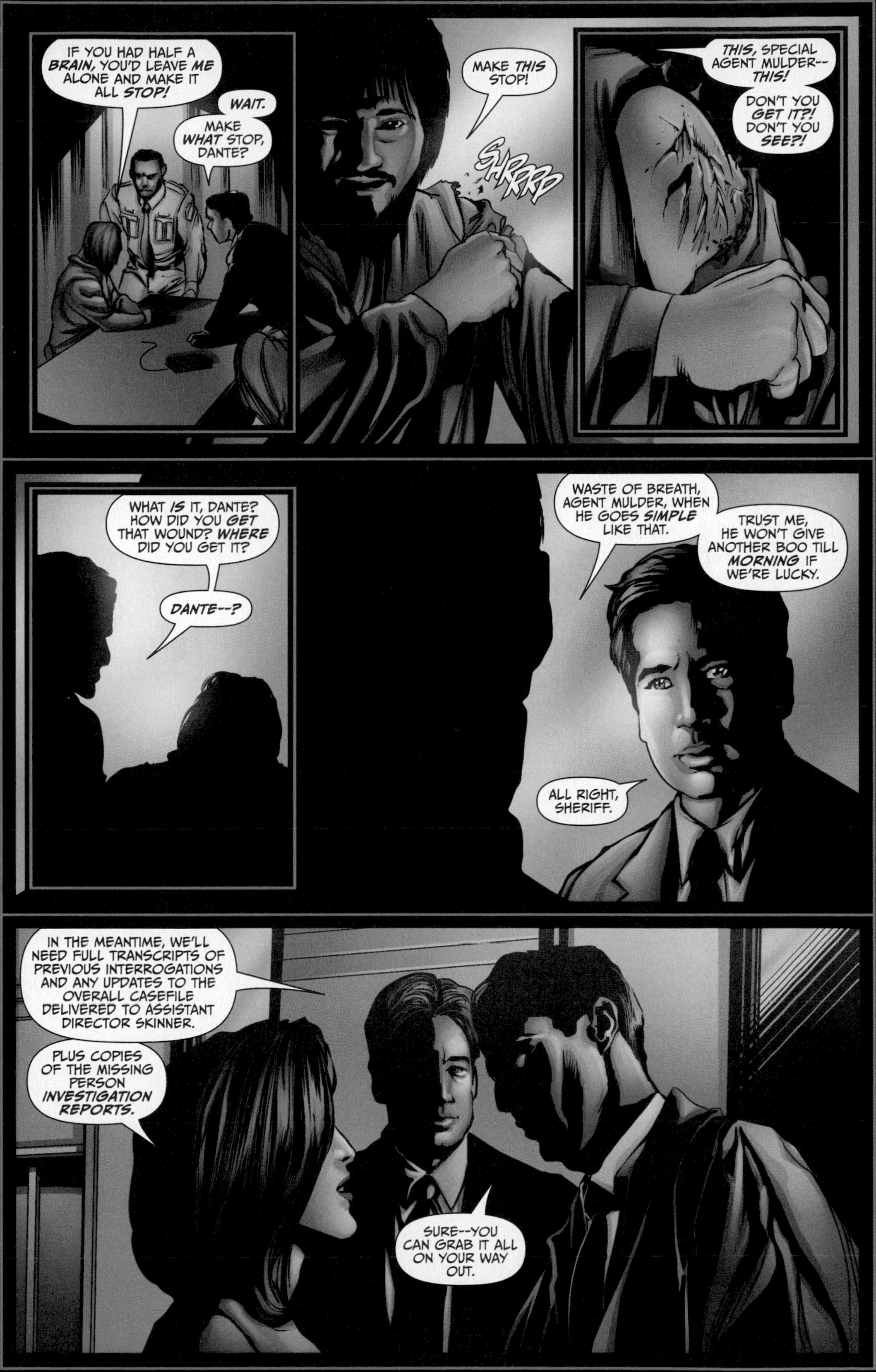
IF YOU HAD HALF A BRAIN, YOU'D LEAVE ME ALONE AND MAKE IT ALL STOP!
WAIT.
MAKE WHAT STOP, DANTE?
MAKE THIS STOP!
SHRRRP
THIS, SPECIAL AGENT MULDER-- THIS!
DON'T YOU GET IT?! DON'T YOU SEE?!
WHAT IS IT, DANTE? HOW DID YOU GET THAT WOUND? WHERE DID YOU GET IT?
DANTE--?
WASTE OF BREATH, AGENT MULDER, WHEN HE GOES SIMPLE LIKE THAT.
TRUST ME, HE WON'T GIVE ANOTHER BOO TILL MORNING IF WE'RE LUCKY.
ALL RIGHT, SHERIFF.
IN THE MEANTIME, WE'LL NEED FULL TRANSCRIPTS OF PREVIOUS INTERROGATIONS AND ANY UPDATES TO THE OVERALL CASEFILE DELIVERED TO ASSISTANT DIRECTOR SKINNER.
PLUS COPIES OF THE MISSING PERSON INVESTIGATION REPORTS.
SURE--YOU CAN GRAB IT ALL ON YOUR WAY OUT.

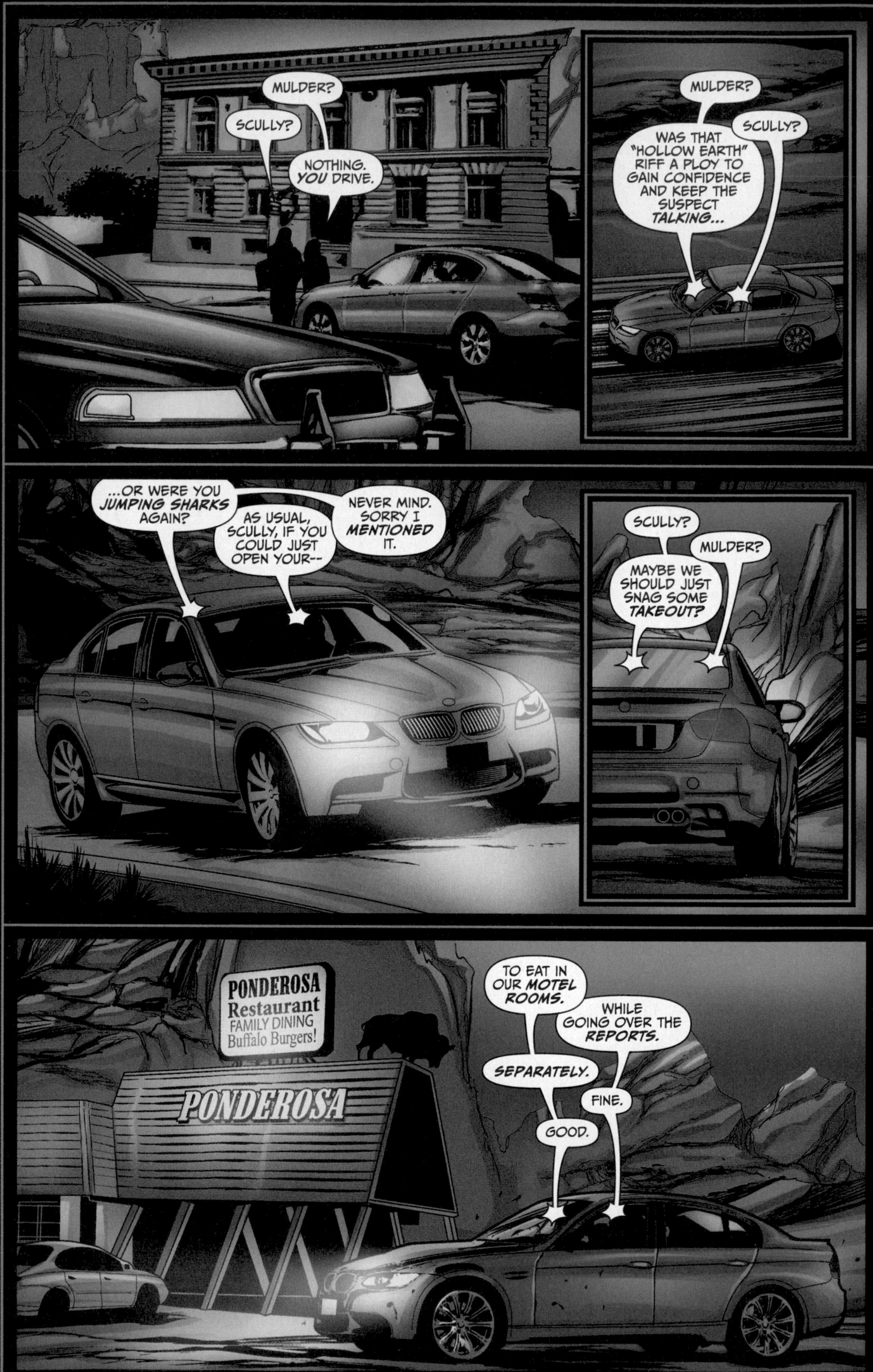
MULDER?
SCULLY?
NOTHING. YOU DRIVE.
MULDER?
SCULLY?
WAS THAT "HOLLOW EARTH" RIFF A PLOY TO GAIN CONFIDENCE AND KEEP THE SUSPECT TALKING...
...OR WERE YOU JUMPING SHARKS AGAIN?
AS USUAL, SCULLY, IF YOU COULD JUST OPEN YOUR--
NEVER MIND. SORRY I MENTIONED IT.
SCULLY?
MULDER?
MAYBE WE SHOULD JUST SNAG SOME TAKEOUT?
PONDEROSA Restaurant FAMILY DINING Buffalo Burgers!
PONDEROSA
TO EAT IN OUR MOTEL ROOMS.
WHILE GOING OVER THE REPORTS.
SEPARATELY.
FINE.
GOOD.

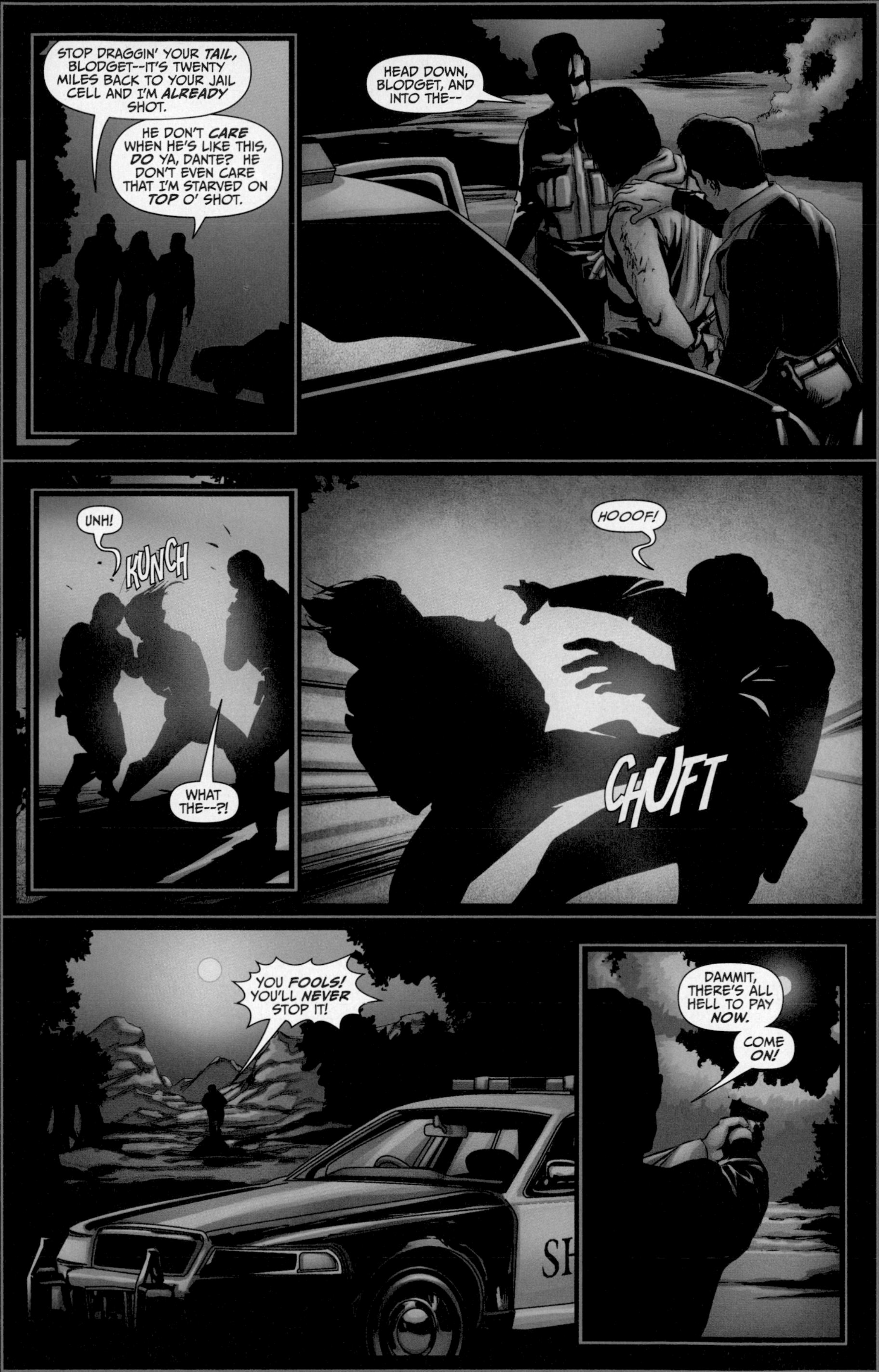

STOP DRAGGIN' YOUR TAIL, BLODGET--IT'S TWENTY MILES BACK TO YOUR JAIL CELL AND I'M ALREADY SHOT.
HE DON'T CARE WHEN HE'S LIKE THIS, DO YA, DANTE? HE DON'T EVEN CARE THAT I'M STARVED ON TOP O' SHOT.
HEAD DOWN, BLODGET, AND INTO THE--
UNH!
KUNCH
WHAT THE--?!
HOOOF!
CHUFT
YOU FOOLS! YOU'LL NEVER STOP IT!
SH
DAMMIT, THERE'S ALL HELL TO PAY NOW.
COME ON!

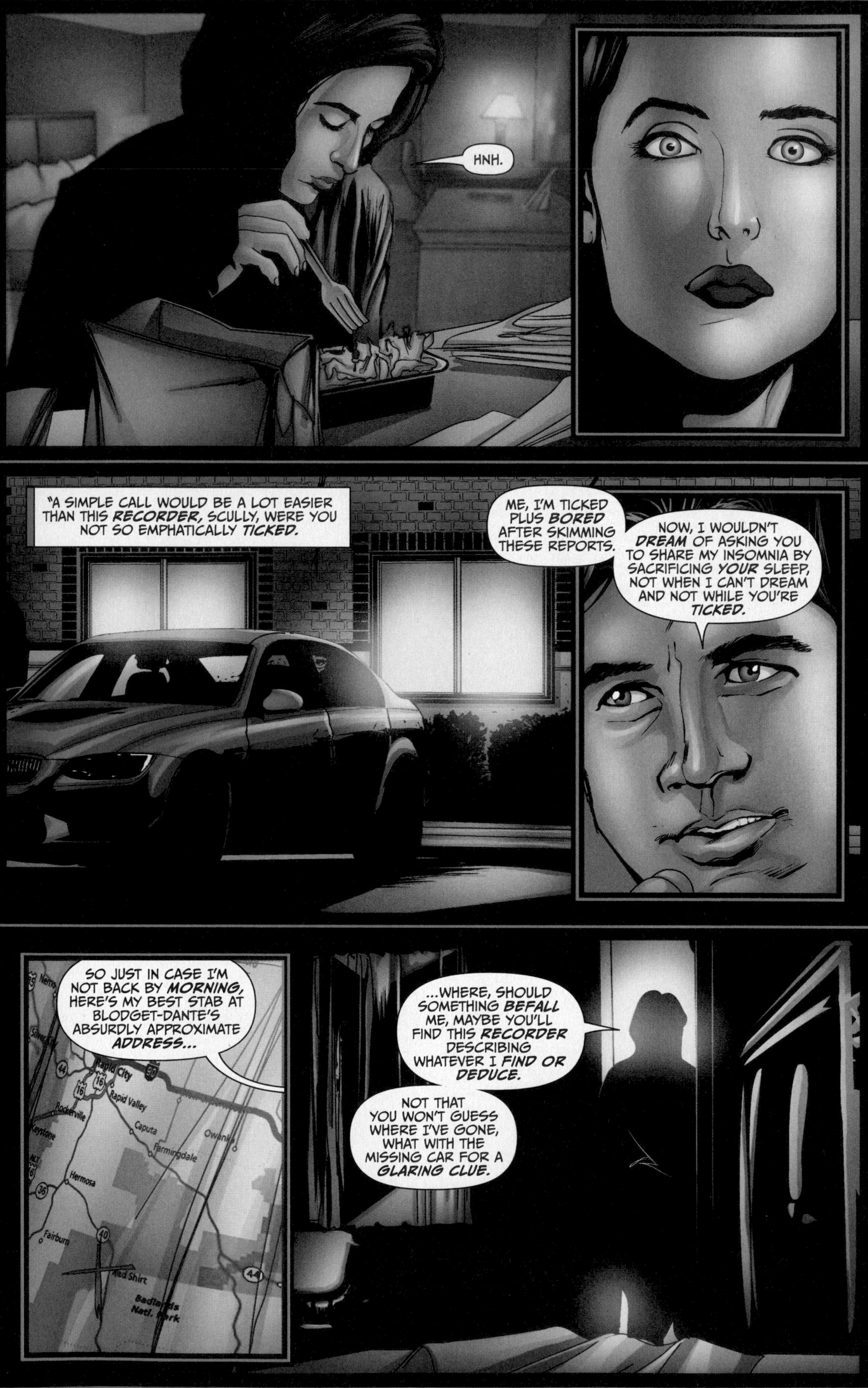
HNH.
"A SIMPLE CALL WOULD BE A LOT EASIER THAN THIS RECORDER, SCULLY, WERE YOU NOT SO EMPHATICALLY TICKED.
ME, I'M TICKED PLUS BORED AFTER SKIMMING THESE REPORTS.
NOW, I WOULDN'T DREAM OF ASKING YOU TO SHARE MY INSOMNIA BY SACRIFICING YOUR SLEEP, NOT WHEN I CAN'T DREAM AND NOT WHILE YOU'RE TICKED.
SO JUST IN CASE I'M NOT BACK BY MORNING, HERE'S MY BEST STAB AT BLODGET-DANTE'S ABSURDLY APPROXIMATE ADDRESS...
Rapid City
Rapid Valley
Rockerville
Keystone
Caputa
Owanka
Farmingdale
Hermosa
Fairburn
Red Shirt
...WHERE, SHOULD SOMETHING BEFALL ME, MAYBE YOU'LL FIND THIS RECORDER DESCRIBING WHATEVER I FIND OR DEDUCE.
NOT THAT YOU WON'T GUESS WHERE I'VE GONE, WHAT WITH THE MISSING CAR FOR A GLARING CLUE.

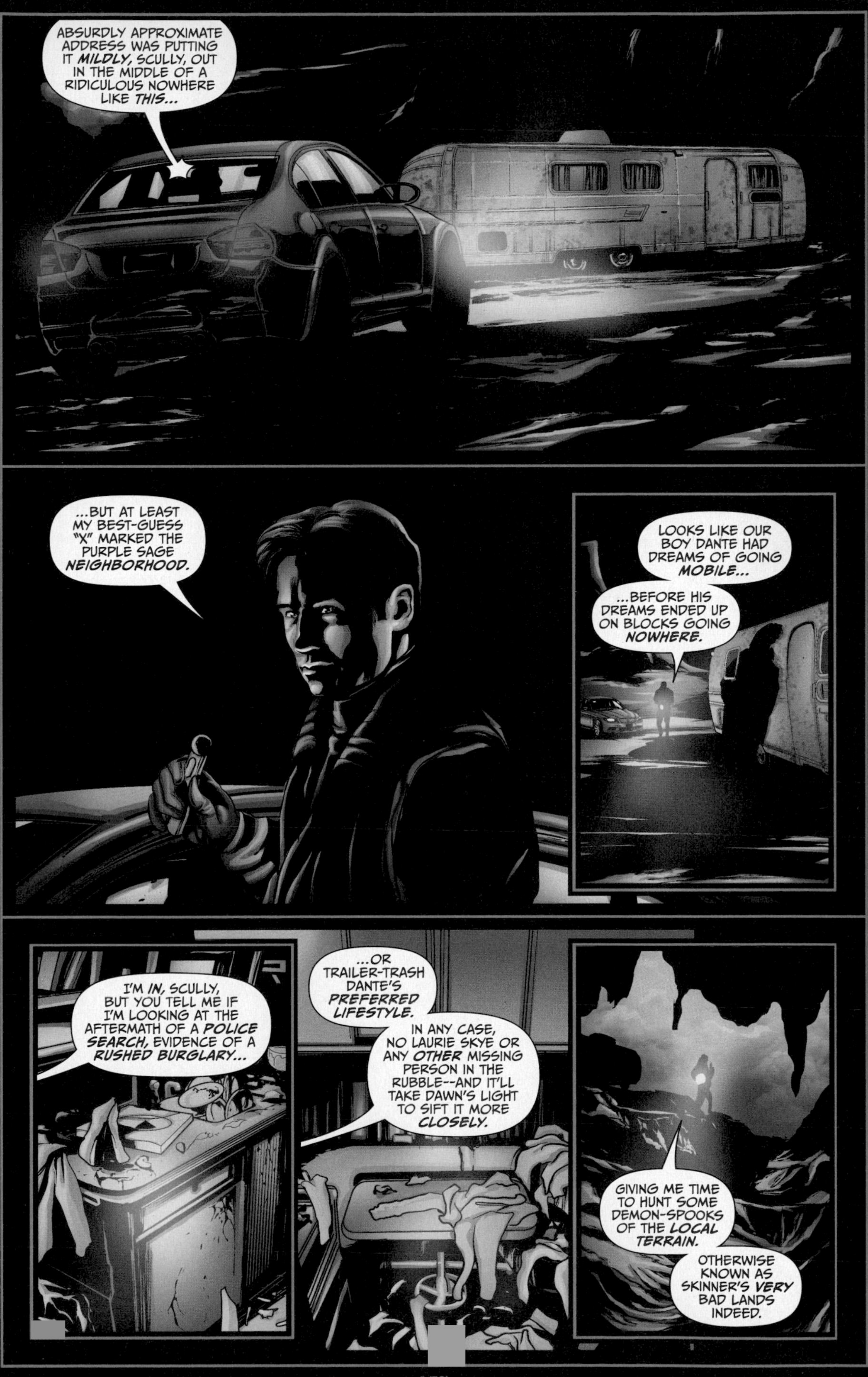
ABSURDLY APPROXIMATE ADDRESS WAS PUTTING IT MILDLY, SCULLY, OUT IN THE MIDDLE OF A RIDICULOUS NOWHERE LIKE THIS...
...BUT AT LEAST MY BEST-GUESS "X" MARKED THE PURPLE SAGE NEIGHBORHOOD.
LOOKS LIKE OUR BOY DANTE HAD DREAMS OF GOING MOBILE...
...BEFORE HIS DREAMS ENDED UP ON BLOCKS GOING NOWHERE.
I'M IN, SCULLY, BUT YOU TELL ME IF I'M LOOKING AT THE AFTERMATH OF A POLICE SEARCH, EVIDENCE OF A RUSHED BURGLARY...
...OR TRAILER-TRASH DANTE'S PREFERRED LIFESTYLE.
IN ANY CASE, NO LAURIE SKYE OR ANY OTHER MISSING PERSON IN THE RUBBLE--AND IT'LL TAKE DAWN'S LIGHT TO SIFT IT MORE CLOSELY.
GIVING ME TIME TO HUNT SOME DEMON-SPOOKS OF THE LOCAL TERRAIN.
OTHERWISE KNOWN AS SKINNER'S VERY BAD LANDS INDEED.

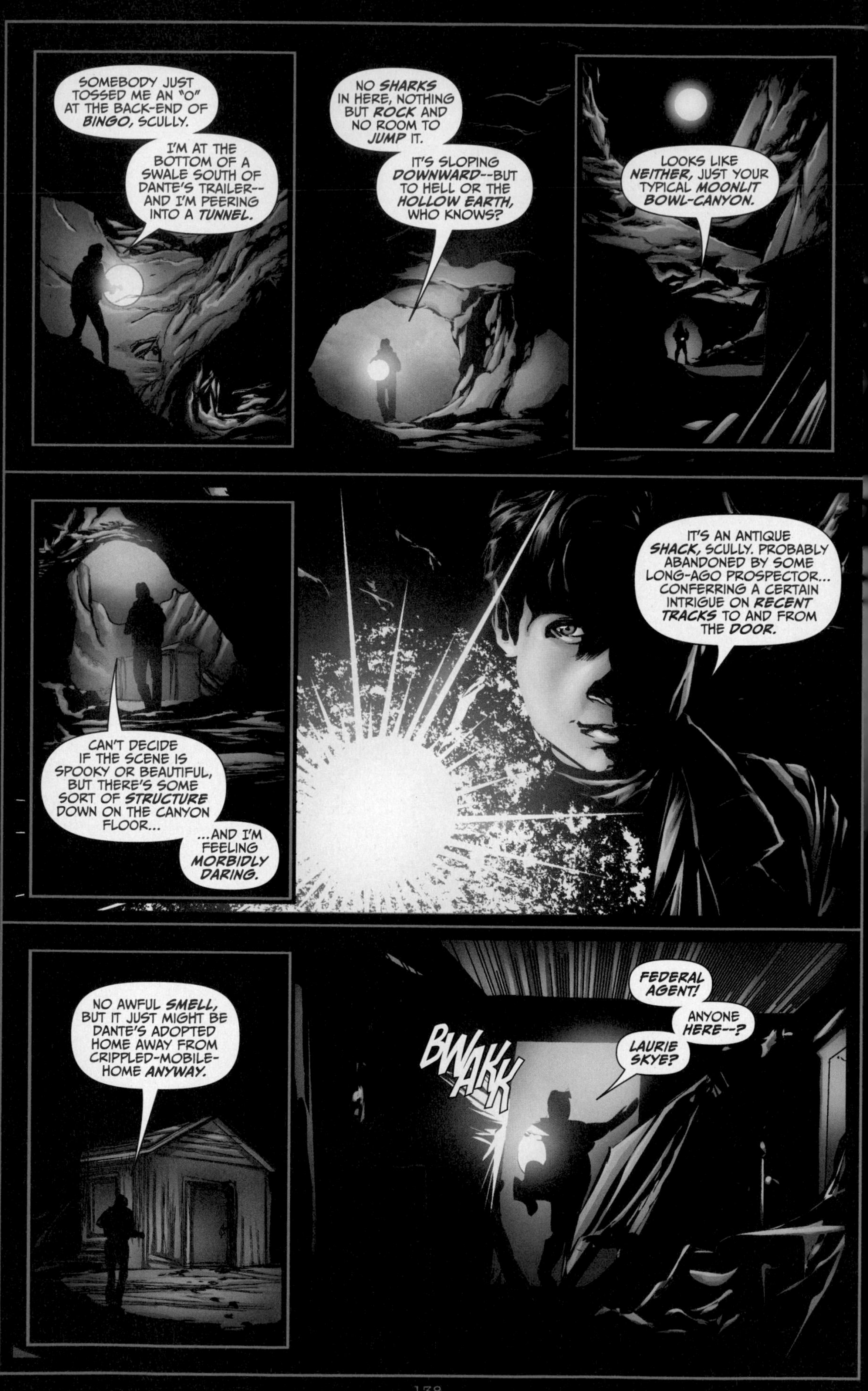
SOMEBODY JUST TOSSED ME AN "O" AT THE BACK-END OF BINGO, SCULLY.
I'M AT THE BOTTOM OF A SWALE SOUTH OF DANTE'S TRAILER-- AND I'M PEERING INTO A TUNNEL.
NO SHARKS IN HERE, NOTHING BUT ROCK AND NO ROOM TO JUMP IT.
IT'S SLOPING DOWNWARD--BUT TO HELL OR THE HOLLOW EARTH, WHO KNOWS?
LOOKS LIKE NEITHER, JUST YOUR TYPICAL MOONLIT BOWL-CANYON.
CAN'T DECIDE IF THE SCENE IS SPOOKY OR BEAUTIFUL, BUT THERE'S SOME SORT OF STRUCTURE DOWN ON THE CANYON FLOOR...
...AND I'M FEELING MORBIDLY DARING.
IT'S AN ANTIQUE SHACK, SCULLY. PROBABLY ABANDONED BY SOME LONG-AGO PROSPECTOR... CONFERRING A CERTAIN INTRIGUE ON RECENT TRACKS TO AND FROM THE DOOR.
NO AWFUL SMELL, BUT IT JUST MIGHT BE DANTE'S ADOPTED HOME AWAY FROM CRIPPLED-MOBILE-HOME ANYWAY.
BWAKK
FEDERAL AGENT!
ANYONE HERE--?
LAURIE SKYE?

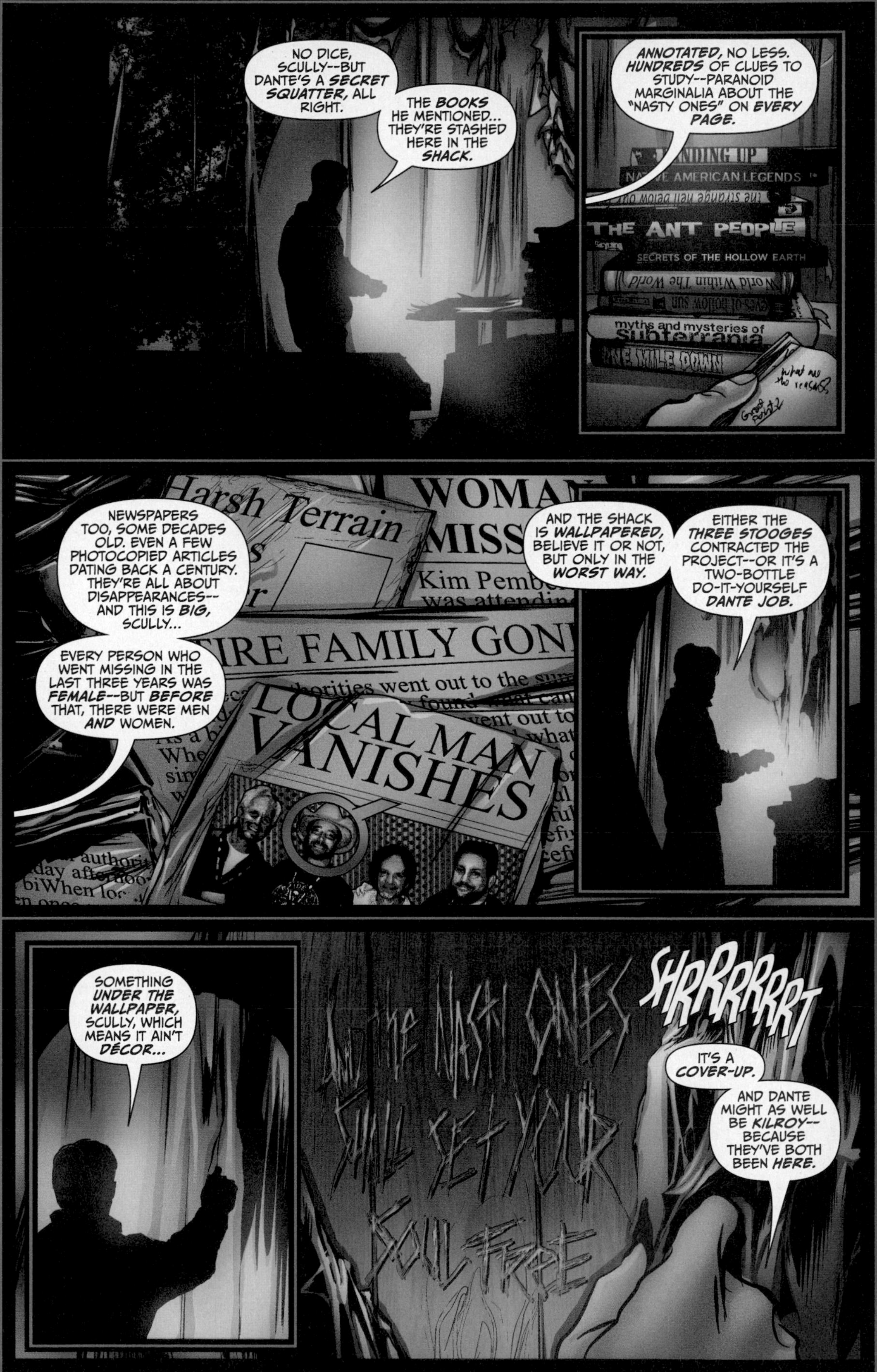

NO DICE, SCULLY--BUT DANTE'S A *SECRET SQUATTER*, ALL RIGHT.
THE *BOOKS* HE MENTIONED... THEY'RE STASHED HERE IN THE *SHACK*.
ANNOTATED, NO LESS. *HUNDREDS* OF CLUES TO STUDY--PARANOID MARGINALIA ABOUT THE "NASTY ONES" ON *EVERY PAGE*.
THE ANT PEOPLE
SECRETS OF THE HOLLOW EARTH
myths and mysteries of subterrania
NEWSPAPERS TOO, SOME DECADES OLD. EVEN A FEW PHOTOCOPIED ARTICLES DATING BACK A CENTURY. THEY'RE ALL ABOUT DISAPPEARANCES--AND THIS IS *BIG*, SCULLY...
EVERY PERSON WHO WENT MISSING IN THE LAST THREE YEARS WAS *FEMALE*--BUT *BEFORE* THAT, THERE WERE MEN *AND* WOMEN.
Harsh Terrain
LOCAL MAN VANISHES
AND THE SHACK IS *WALLPAPERED*, BELIEVE IT OR NOT, BUT ONLY IN THE *WORST WAY*.
EITHER THE *THREE STOOGES* CONTRACTED THE PROJECT--OR IT'S A TWO-BOTTLE DO-IT-YOURSELF *DANTE JOB*.
SOMETHING *UNDER THE WALLPAPER*, SCULLY, WHICH MEANS IT AIN'T *DÉCOR*...
SHRRRRRRT
IT'S A *COVER-UP*.
AND DANTE MIGHT AS WELL BE *KILROY*--BECAUSE THEY'VE BOTH BEEN *HERE*.

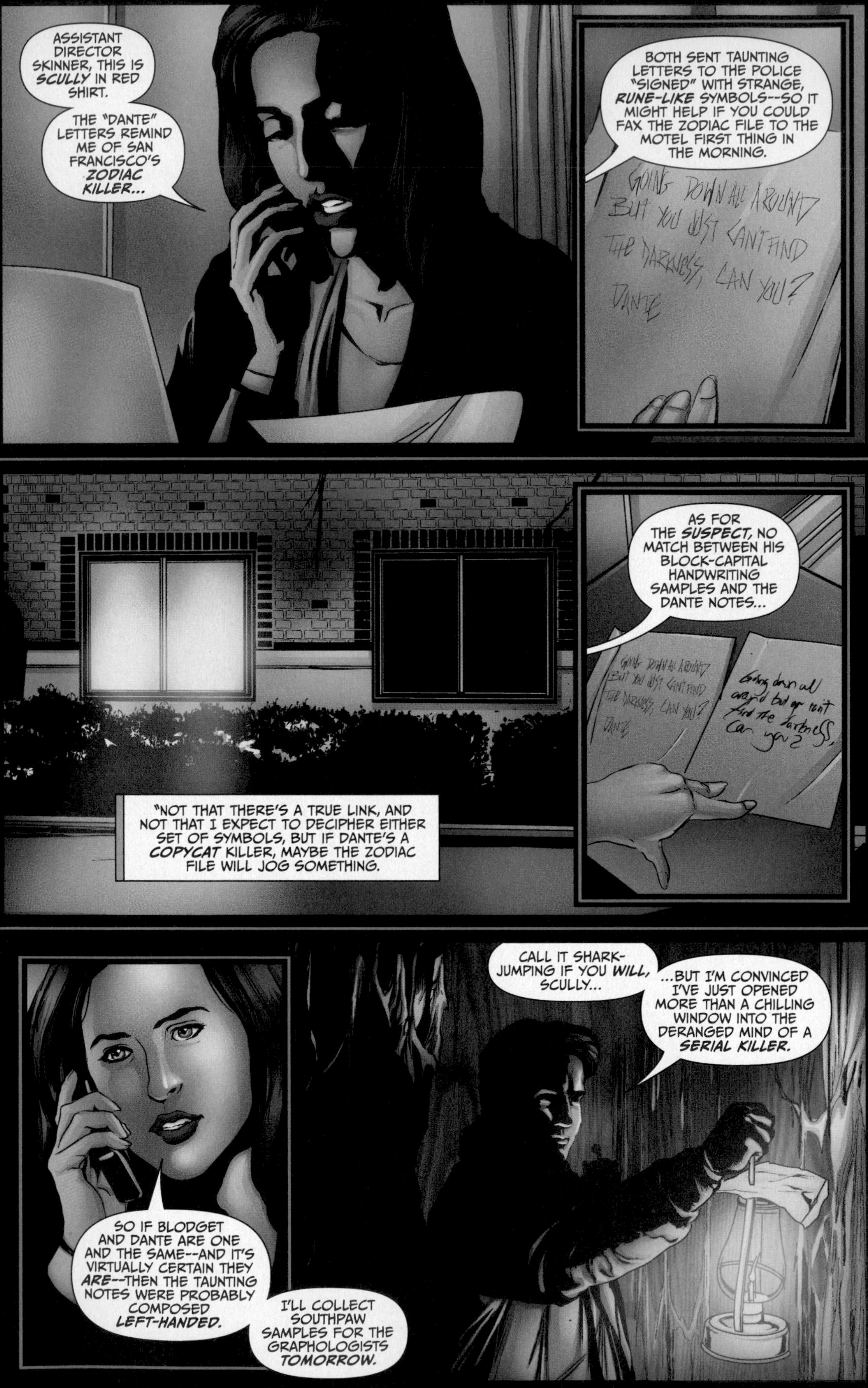
ASSISTANT DIRECTOR SKINNER, THIS IS SCULLY IN RED SHIRT.
THE "DANTE" LETTERS REMIND ME OF SAN FRANCISCO'S ZODIAC KILLER...
BOTH SENT TAUNTING LETTERS TO THE POLICE "SIGNED" WITH STRANGE, RUNE-LIKE SYMBOLS--SO IT MIGHT HELP IF YOU COULD FAX THE ZODIAC FILE TO THE MOTEL FIRST THING IN THE MORNING.
GOING DOWN ALL AROUND BUT YOU JUST CAN'T FIND THE DARKNESS, CAN YOU? DANTE
AS FOR THE SUSPECT, NO MATCH BETWEEN HIS BLOCK-CAPITAL HANDWRITING SAMPLES AND THE DANTE NOTES...
"NOT THAT THERE'S A TRUE LINK, AND NOT THAT I EXPECT TO DECIPHER EITHER SET OF SYMBOLS, BUT IF DANTE'S A COPYCAT KILLER, MAYBE THE ZODIAC FILE WILL JOG SOMETHING.
SO IF BLODGET AND DANTE ARE ONE AND THE SAME--AND IT'S VIRTUALLY CERTAIN THEY ARE--THEN THE TAUNTING NOTES WERE PROBABLY COMPOSED LEFT-HANDED.
I'LL COLLECT SOUTHPAW SAMPLES FOR THE GRAPHOLOGISTS TOMORROW.
CALL IT SHARK-JUMPING IF YOU WILL, SCULLY...
...BUT I'M CONVINCED I'VE JUST OPENED MORE THAN A CHILLING WINDOW INTO THE DERANGED MIND OF A SERIAL KILLER.

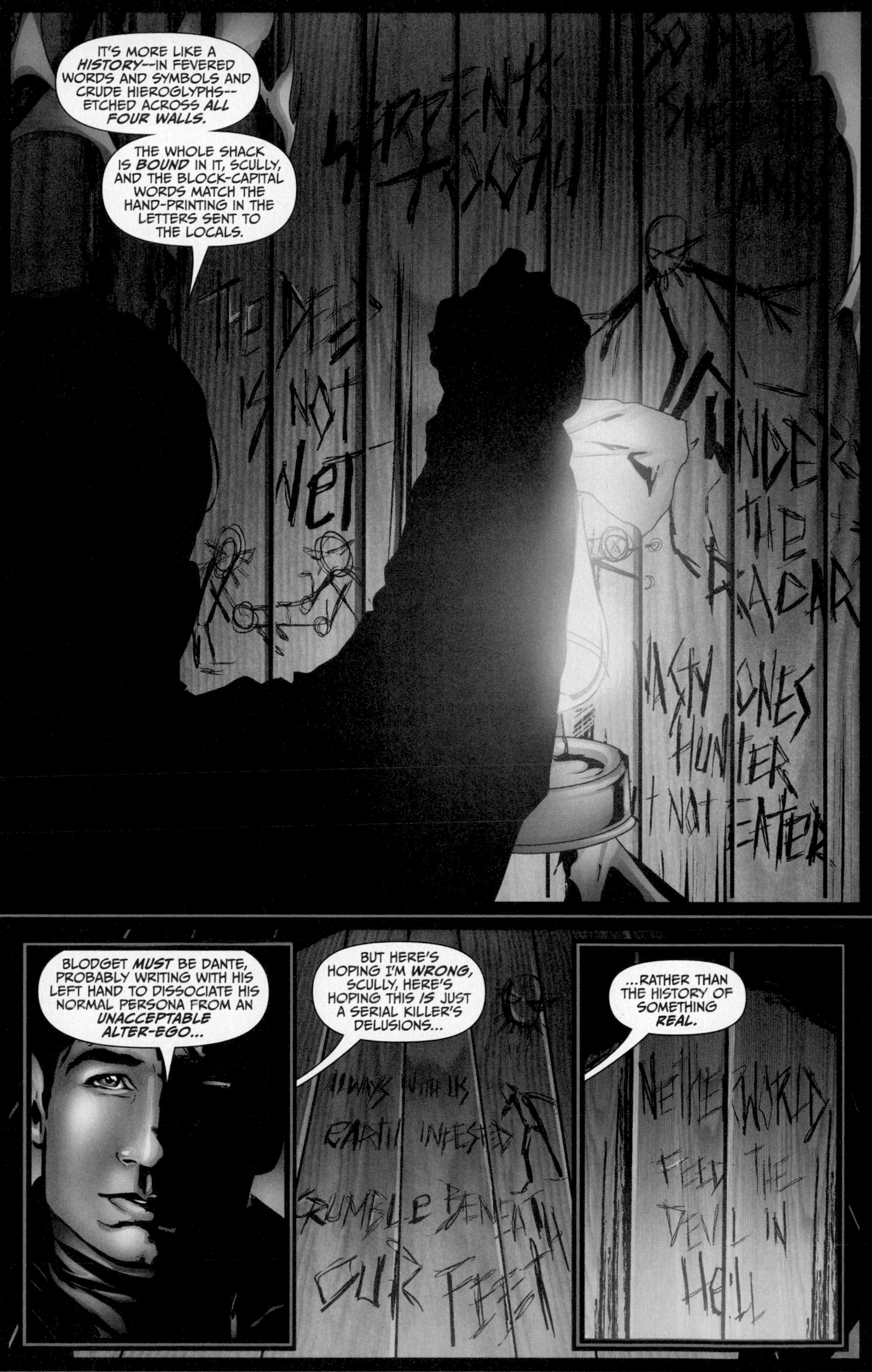
IT'S MORE LIKE A HISTORY--IN FEVERED WORDS AND SYMBOLS AND CRUDE HIEROGLYPHS--ETCHED ACROSS ALL FOUR WALLS.
THE WHOLE SHACK IS BOUND IN IT, SCULLY, AND THE BLOCK-CAPITAL WORDS MATCH THE HAND-PRINTING IN THE LETTERS SENT TO THE LOCALS.
BLODGET MUST BE DANTE, PROBABLY WRITING WITH HIS LEFT HAND TO DISSOCIATE HIS NORMAL PERSONA FROM AN UNACCEPTABLE ALTER-EGO...
BUT HERE'S HOPING I'M WRONG, SCULLY, HERE'S HOPING THIS IS JUST A SERIAL KILLER'S DELUSIONS...
ALWAYS WITH US
EARTH INFESTED
CRUMBLE BENEATH
OUR FEET
...RATHER THAN THE HISTORY OF SOMETHING REAL.
NETHERWORLD
FEED THE DEVIL IN HELL

"HOLD ON, SCULLY, I'M *HEARING* SOMETHING...LIKE... MUFFLED *SCUFFING*...AND THE *SOURCE* IS MORE THAN A TRIFLE CREEPY...

"AS IN, THE SOUNDS ARE COMING FROM BELOW...*UNDER THE SHACK*.

AND *BINGO* REDUX.

FOUND A SECTION OF LOOSE *FLOORBOARDS*... MAKESHIFT *TRAP-DOOR*.

LAURIE SKYE--? FEDERAL AGENT--I'M HERE TO HELP!

SHE'S *HERE*, SCULLY, BUT NO RESPONSE--NO MOVEMENT AT ALL.

EITHER UNCONSCIOUS OR DEAD, NEITHER OF WHICH EXPLAINS HOW SHE MADE THE *SOUNDS* I JUST--

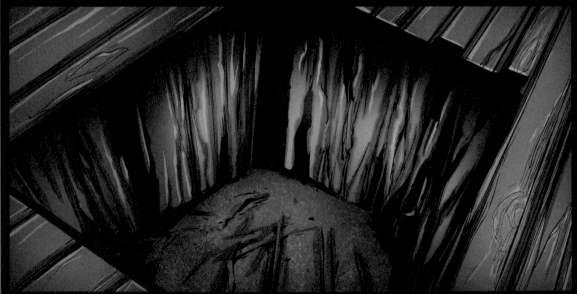

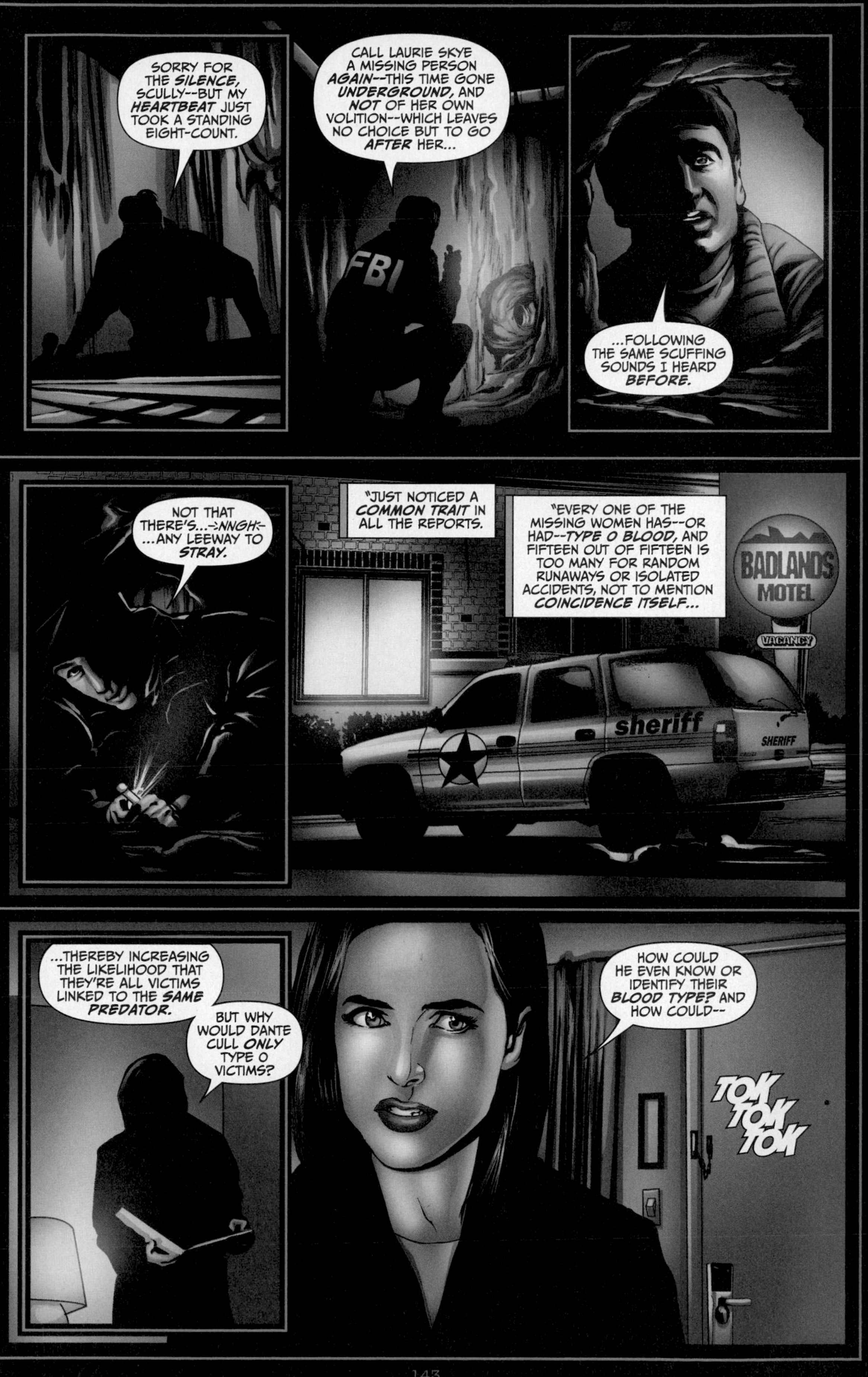
SORRY FOR THE SILENCE, SCULLY--BUT MY HEARTBEAT JUST TOOK A STANDING EIGHT-COUNT.
CALL LAURIE SKYE A MISSING PERSON AGAIN--THIS TIME GONE UNDERGROUND, AND NOT OF HER OWN VOLITION--WHICH LEAVES NO CHOICE BUT TO GO AFTER HER...
FBI
...FOLLOWING THE SAME SCUFFING SOUNDS I HEARD BEFORE.
NOT THAT THERE'S...-NNGH- ...ANY LEEWAY TO STRAY.
"JUST NOTICED A COMMON TRAIT IN ALL THE REPORTS.
"EVERY ONE OF THE MISSING WOMEN HAS--OR HAD--TYPE O BLOOD, AND FIFTEEN OUT OF FIFTEEN IS TOO MANY FOR RANDOM RUNAWAYS OR ISOLATED ACCIDENTS, NOT TO MENTION COINCIDENCE ITSELF...
BADLANDS MOTEL
VACANCY
sheriff
SHERIFF
...THEREBY INCREASING THE LIKELIHOOD THAT THEY'RE ALL VICTIMS LINKED TO THE SAME PREDATOR.
BUT WHY WOULD DANTE CULL ONLY TYPE O VICTIMS?
HOW COULD HE EVEN KNOW OR IDENTIFY THEIR BLOOD TYPE? AND HOW COULD--
TOK TOK TOK

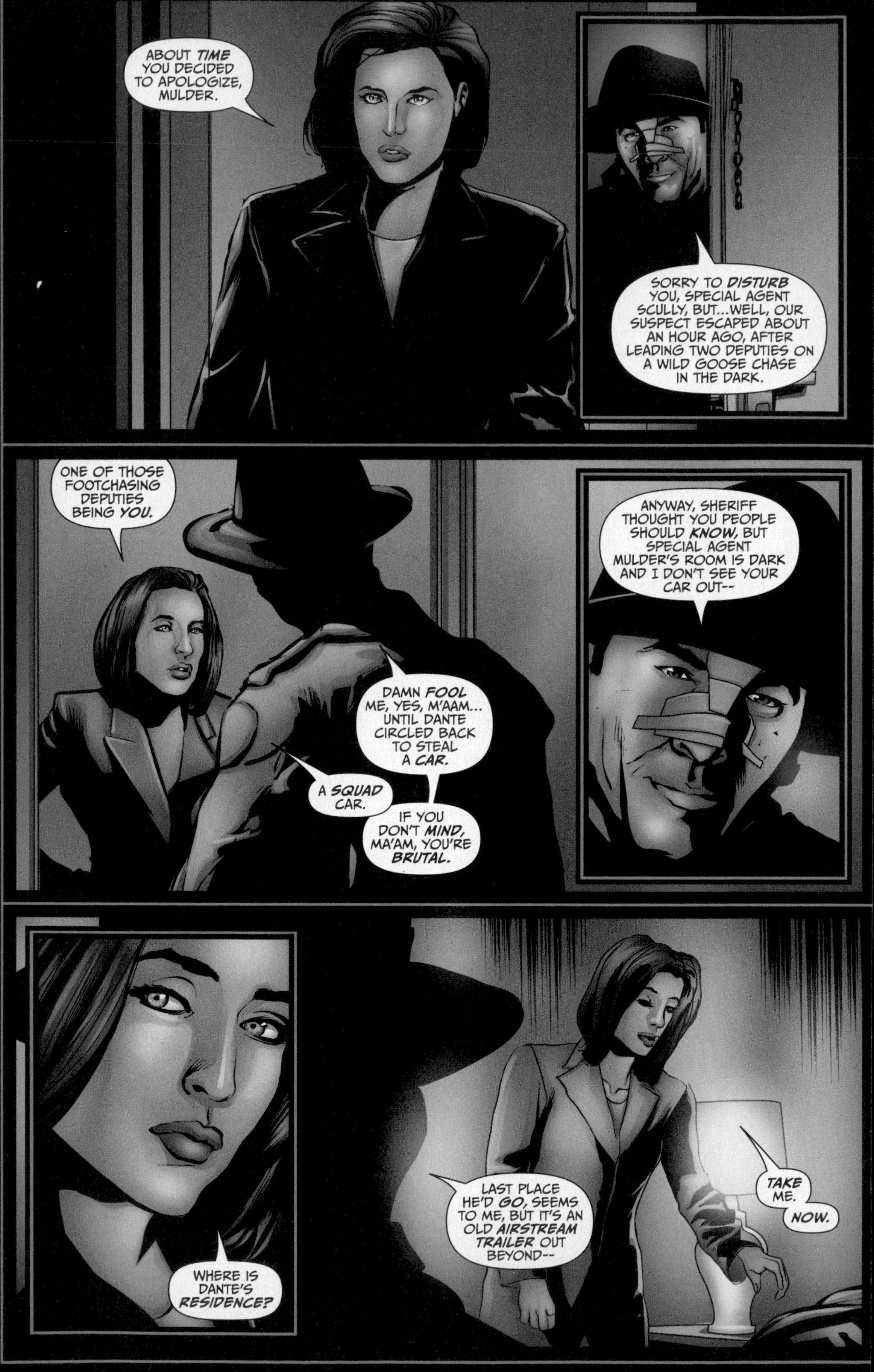
ABOUT TIME YOU DECIDED TO APOLOGIZE, MULDER.
SORRY TO DISTURB YOU, SPECIAL AGENT SCULLY, BUT...WELL, OUR SUSPECT ESCAPED ABOUT AN HOUR AGO, AFTER LEADING TWO DEPUTIES ON A WILD GOOSE CHASE IN THE DARK.
ONE OF THOSE FOOTCHASING DEPUTIES BEING YOU.
DAMN FOOL ME, YES, M'AAM... UNTIL DANTE CIRCLED BACK TO STEAL A CAR.
A SQUAD CAR.
IF YOU DON'T MIND, MA'AM, YOU'RE BRUTAL.
ANYWAY, SHERIFF THOUGHT YOU PEOPLE SHOULD KNOW, BUT SPECIAL AGENT MULDER'S ROOM IS DARK AND I DON'T SEE YOUR CAR OUT--
WHERE IS DANTE'S RESIDENCE?
LAST PLACE HE'D GO, SEEMS TO ME, BUT IT'S AN OLD AIRSTREAM TRAILER OUT BEYOND--
TAKE ME.
NOW.

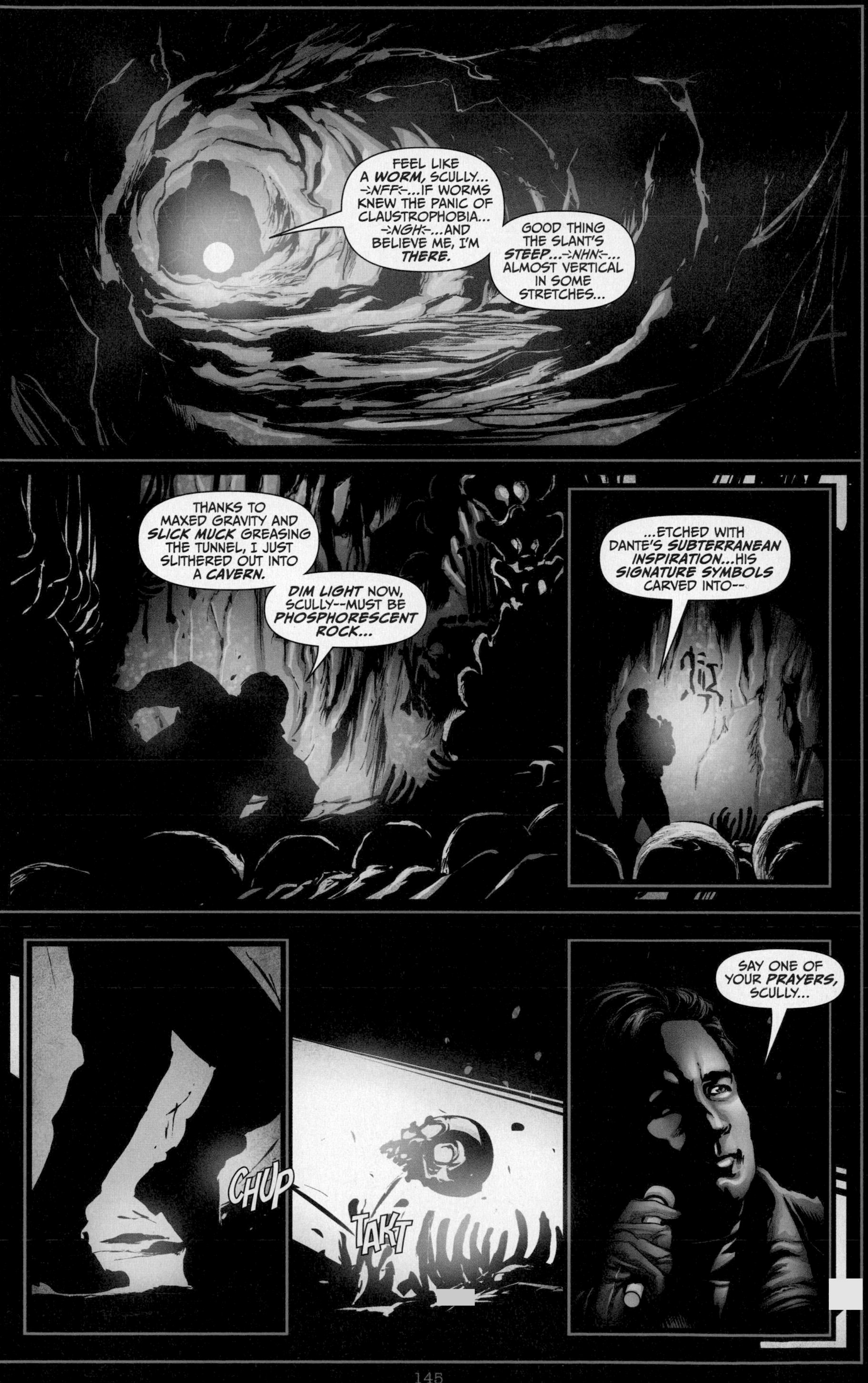

FEEL LIKE A WORM, SCULLY... -NFF-...IF WORMS KNEW THE PANIC OF CLAUSTROPHOBIA... -NGH-...AND BELIEVE ME, I'M THERE.
GOOD THING THE SLANT'S STEEP...-NHN-... ALMOST VERTICAL IN SOME STRETCHES...
THANKS TO MAXED GRAVITY AND SLICK MUCK GREASING THE TUNNEL, I JUST SLITHERED OUT INTO A CAVERN.
DIM LIGHT NOW, SCULLY--MUST BE PHOSPHORESCENT ROCK...
...ETCHED WITH DANTE'S SUBTERRANEAN INSPIRATION...HIS SIGNATURE SYMBOLS CARVED INTO--
CHUP
TAKT
SAY ONE OF YOUR PRAYERS, SCULLY...

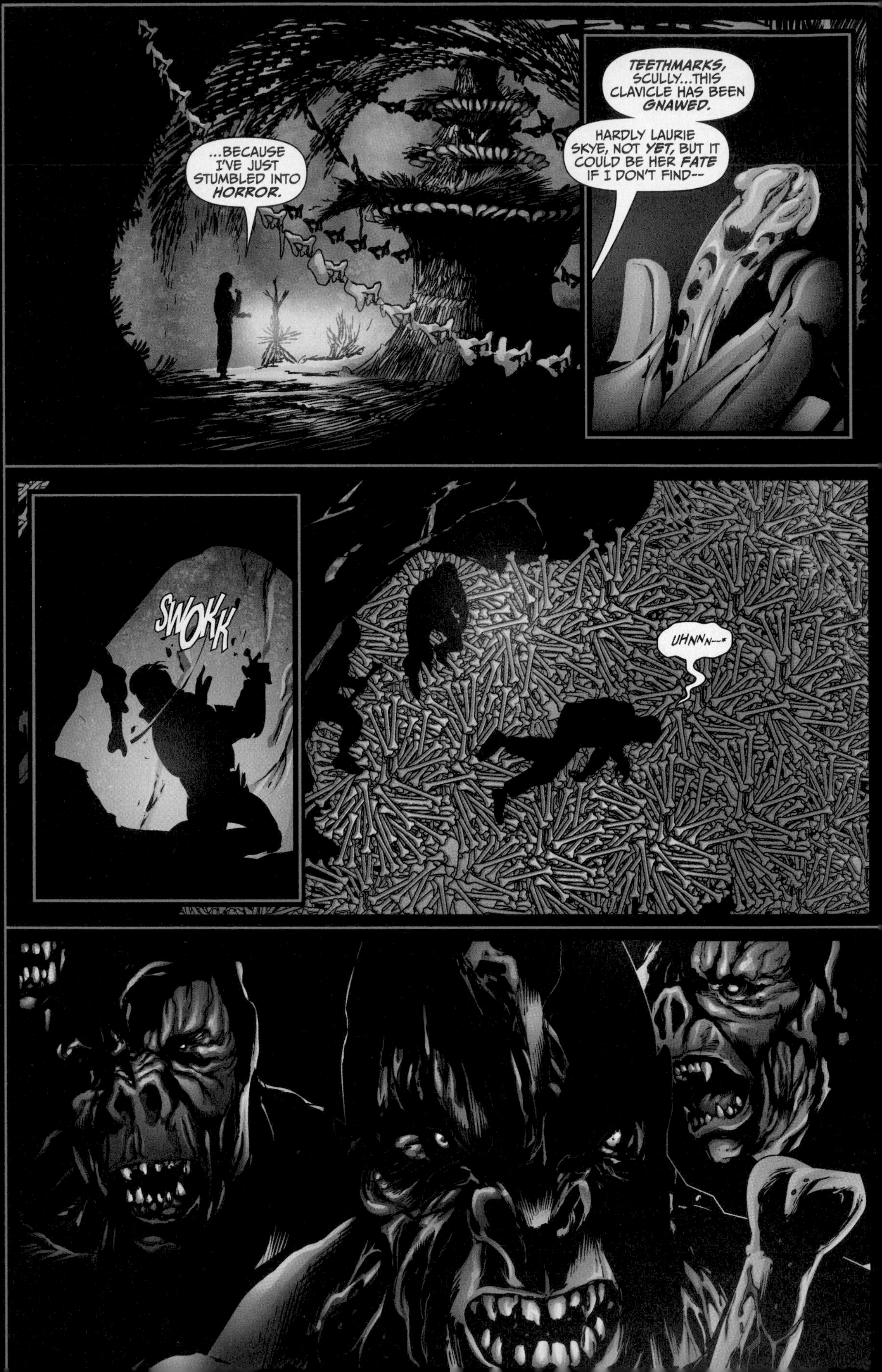
...BECAUSE I'VE JUST STUMBLED INTO HORROR.
TEETHMARKS, SCULLY...THIS CLAVICLE HAS BEEN GNAWED.
HARDLY LAURIE SKYE, NOT YET, BUT IT COULD BE HER FATE IF I DON'T FIND--
SWOKK
UHNNN--*

written by
DOUG MOENCH

THE X FILES

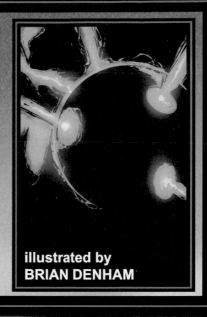

illustrated by
BRIAN DENHAM

colors by
CARLOS BADILLA

letters by
ED DUKESHIRE

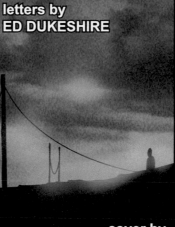

cover by
**BRIAN DENHAM and
KELSEY SHANNON**

edited by
**SHANNON
ERIC DENTON**

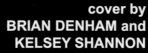

THE TRUTH IS OUT THERE

created by
CHRIS CARTER

~NHNNN~
WH-WHERE...?

Under the Badlands, South Dakota, 11:53 p.m.

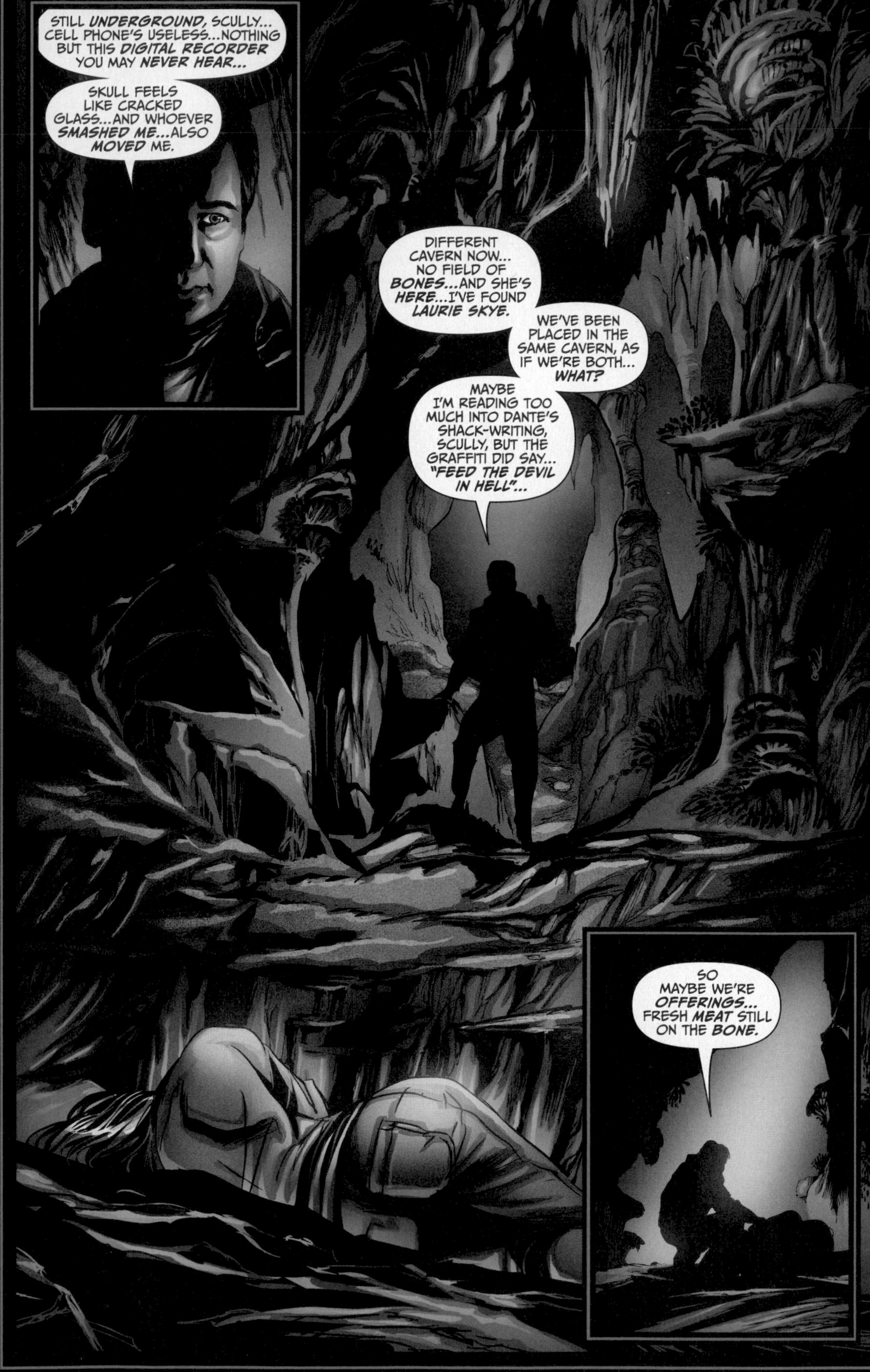
STILL UNDERGROUND, SCULLY... CELL PHONE'S USELESS...NOTHING BUT THIS DIGITAL RECORDER YOU MAY NEVER HEAR...
SKULL FEELS LIKE CRACKED GLASS...AND WHOEVER SMASHED ME...ALSO MOVED ME.
DIFFERENT CAVERN NOW... NO FIELD OF BONES...AND SHE'S HERE...I'VE FOUND LAURIE SKYE.
WE'VE BEEN PLACED IN THE SAME CAVERN, AS IF WE'RE BOTH... WHAT?
MAYBE I'M READING TOO MUCH INTO DANTE'S SHACK-WRITING, SCULLY, BUT THE GRAFFITI DID SAY... "FEED THE DEVIL IN HELL"...
SO MAYBE WE'RE OFFERINGS... FRESH MEAT STILL ON THE BONE.

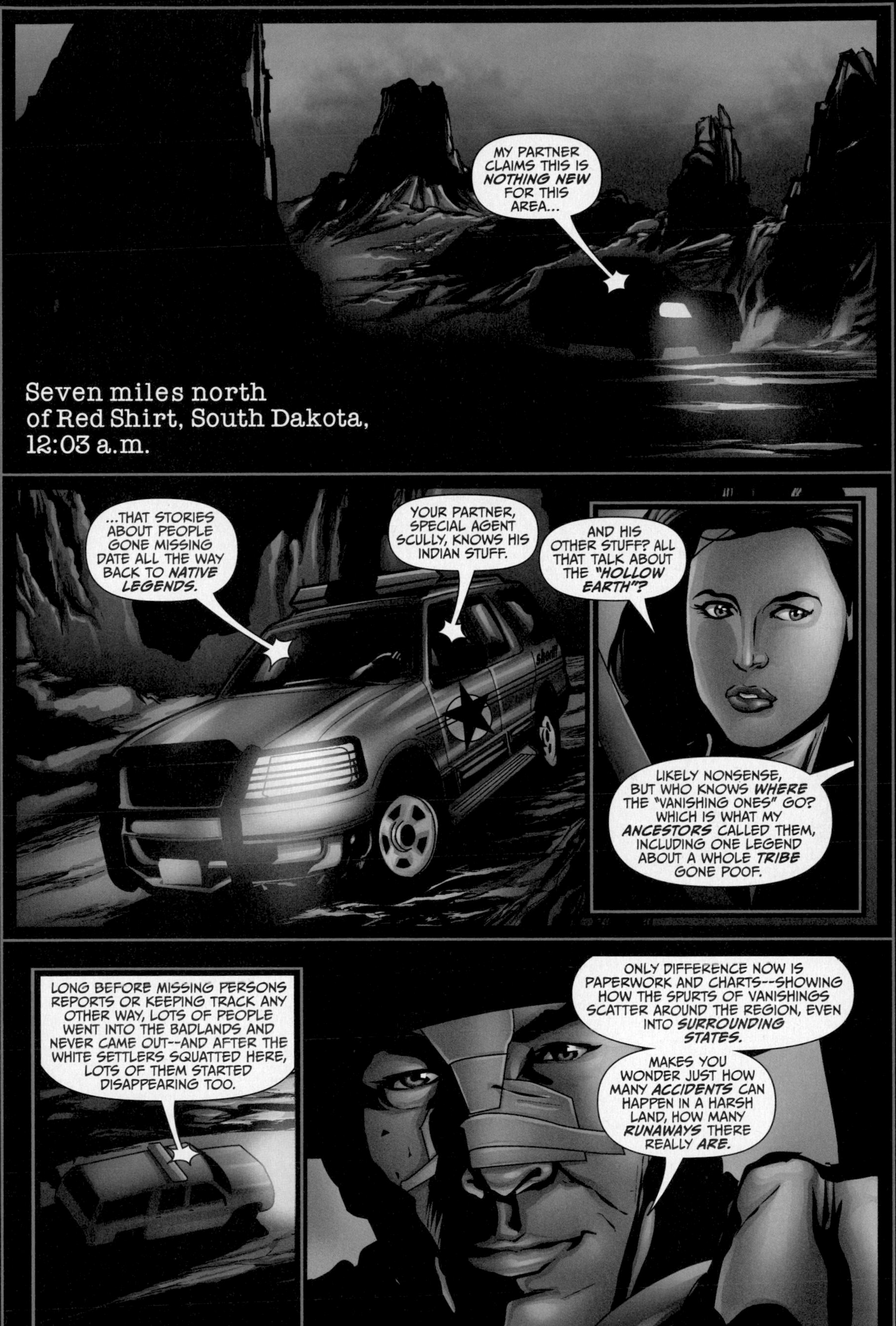

MY PARTNER CLAIMS THIS IS NOTHING NEW FOR THIS AREA...
Seven miles north of Red Shirt, South Dakota, 12:03 a.m.
...THAT STORIES ABOUT PEOPLE GONE MISSING DATE ALL THE WAY BACK TO NATIVE LEGENDS.
YOUR PARTNER, SPECIAL AGENT SCULLY, KNOWS HIS INDIAN STUFF.
AND HIS OTHER STUFF? ALL THAT TALK ABOUT THE "HOLLOW EARTH"?
LIKELY NONSENSE, BUT WHO KNOWS WHERE THE "VANISHING ONES" GO? WHICH IS WHAT MY ANCESTORS CALLED THEM, INCLUDING ONE LEGEND ABOUT A WHOLE TRIBE GONE POOF.
LONG BEFORE MISSING PERSONS REPORTS OR KEEPING TRACK ANY OTHER WAY, LOTS OF PEOPLE WENT INTO THE BADLANDS AND NEVER CAME OUT--AND AFTER THE WHITE SETTLERS SQUATTED HERE, LOTS OF THEM STARTED DISAPPEARING TOO.
ONLY DIFFERENCE NOW IS PAPERWORK AND CHARTS--SHOWING HOW THE SPURTS OF VANISHINGS SCATTER AROUND THE REGION, EVEN INTO SURROUNDING STATES.
MAKES YOU WONDER JUST HOW MANY ACCIDENTS CAN HAPPEN IN A HARSH LAND, HOW MANY RUNAWAYS THERE REALLY ARE.

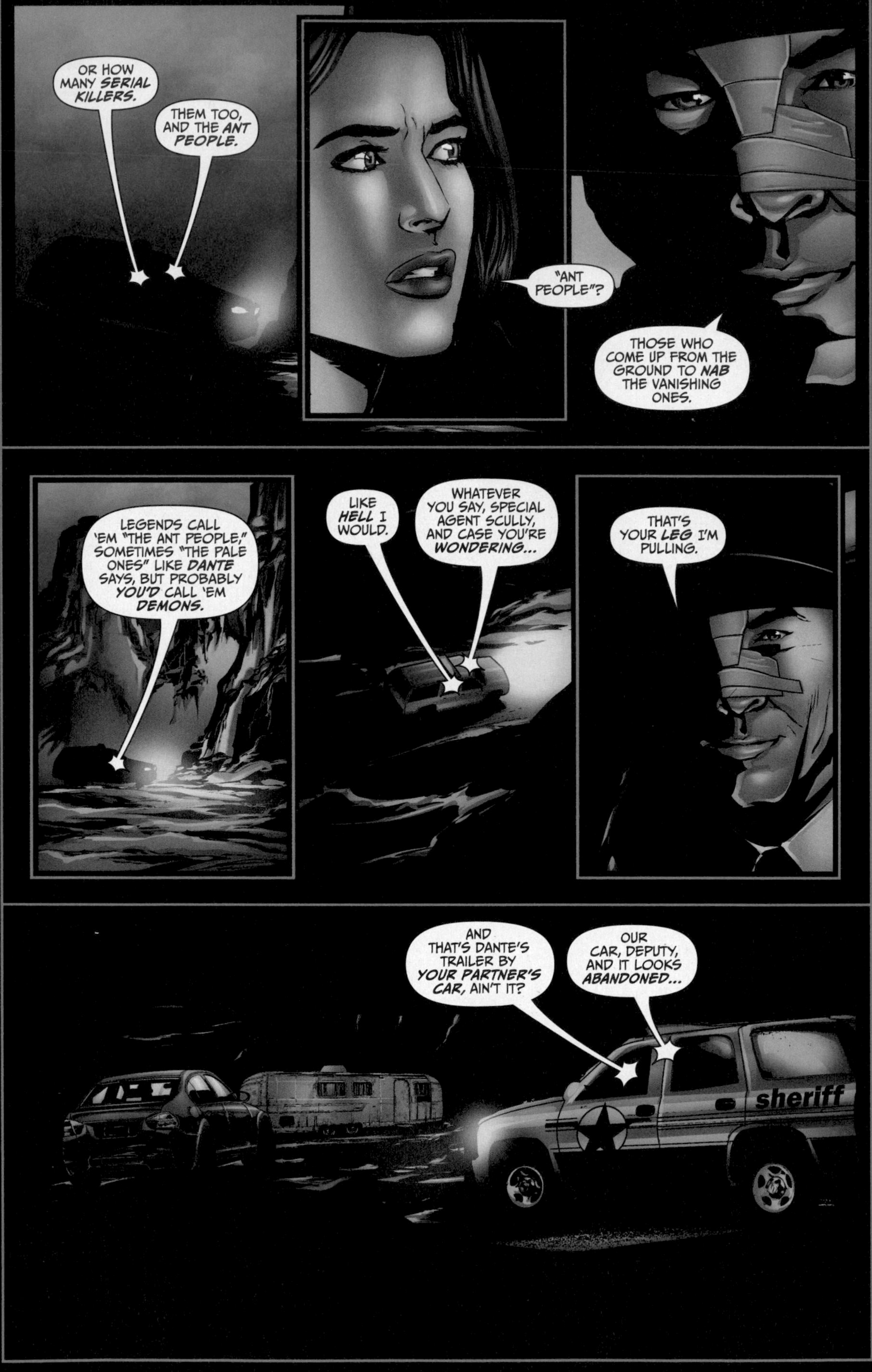

OR HOW MANY SERIAL KILLERS.
THEM TOO, AND THE ANT PEOPLE.
"ANT PEOPLE"?
THOSE WHO COME UP FROM THE GROUND TO NAB THE VANISHING ONES.
LEGENDS CALL 'EM "THE ANT PEOPLE," SOMETIMES "THE PALE ONES" LIKE DANTE SAYS, BUT PROBABLY YOU'D CALL 'EM DEMONS.
LIKE HELL I WOULD.
WHATEVER YOU SAY, SPECIAL AGENT SCULLY, AND CASE YOU'RE WONDERING...
THAT'S YOUR LEG I'M PULLING.
AND THAT'S DANTE'S TRAILER BY YOUR PARTNER'S CAR, AIN'T IT?
OUR CAR, DEPUTY, AND IT LOOKS ABANDONED...
sheriff

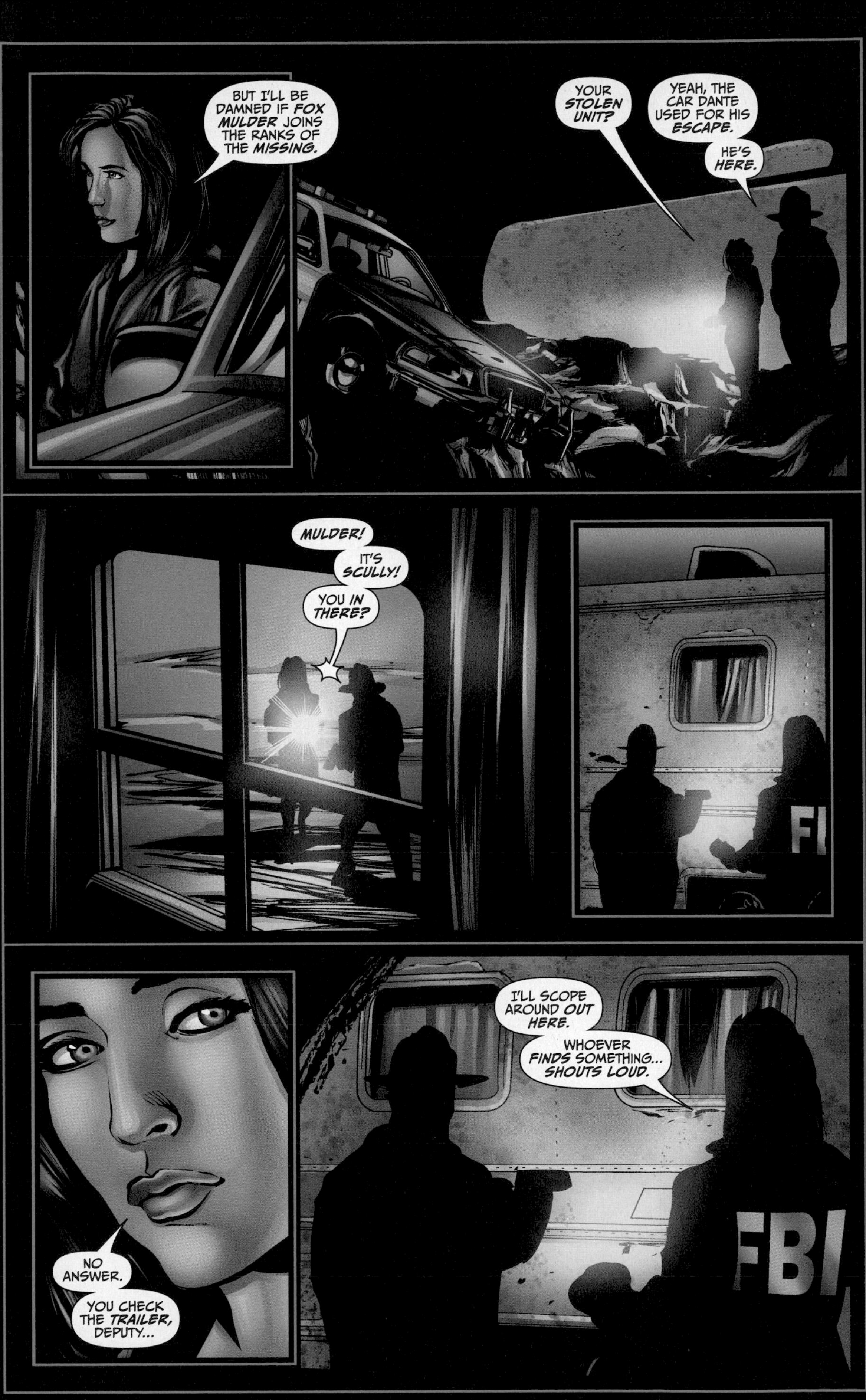

BUT I'LL BE DAMNED IF FOX MULDER JOINS THE RANKS OF THE MISSING.
YOUR STOLEN UNIT?
YEAH, THE CAR DANTE USED FOR HIS ESCAPE.
HE'S HERE.
MULDER!
IT'S SCULLY!
YOU IN THERE?
FBI
NO ANSWER.
YOU CHECK THE TRAILER, DEPUTY...
I'LL SCOPE AROUND OUT HERE.
WHOEVER FINDS SOMETHING... SHOUTS LOUD.
FBI

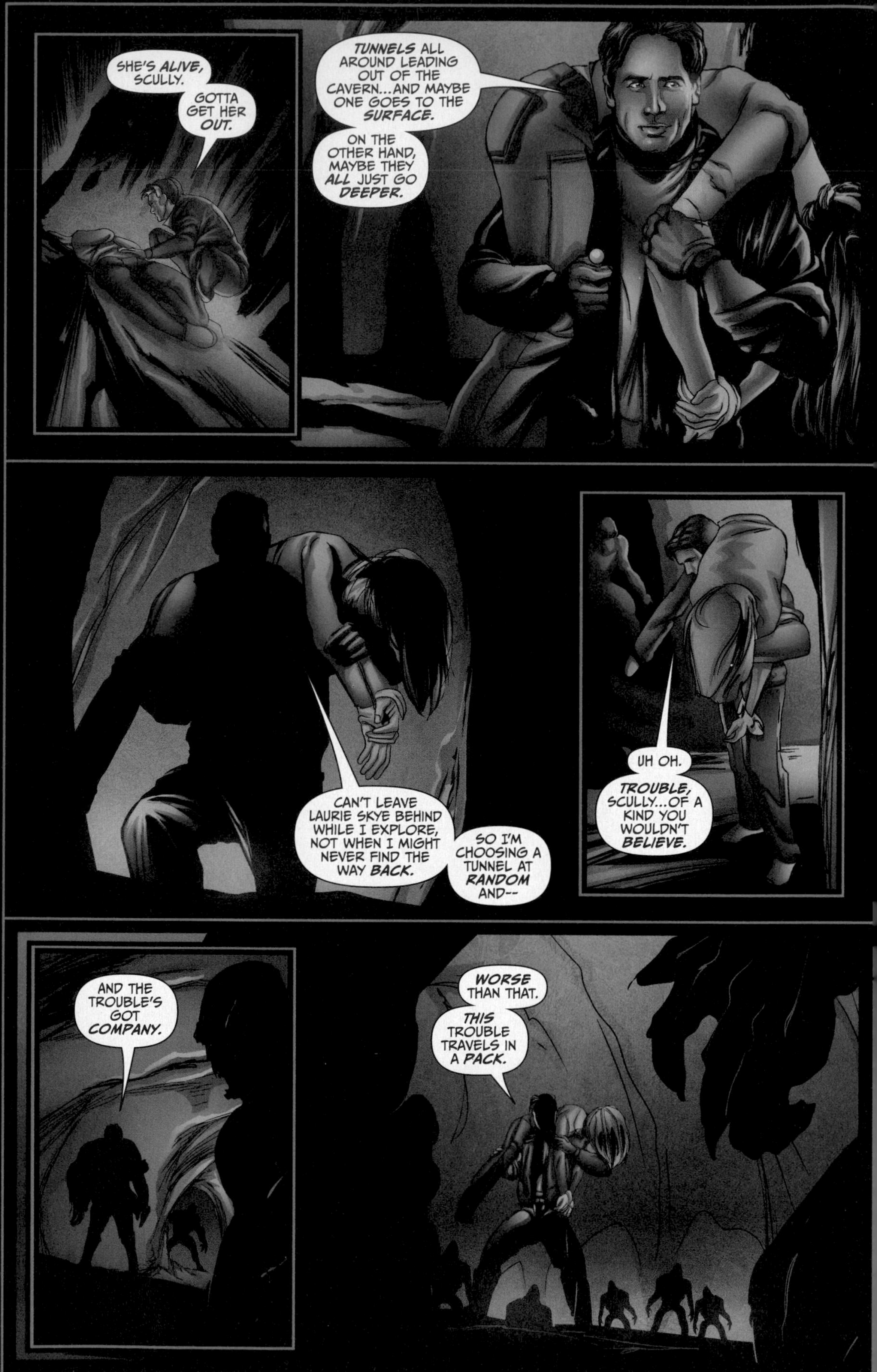

SHE'S ALIVE, SCULLY.
GOTTA GET HER OUT.
TUNNELS ALL AROUND LEADING OUT OF THE CAVERN...AND MAYBE ONE GOES TO THE SURFACE.
ON THE OTHER HAND, MAYBE THEY ALL JUST GO DEEPER.
CAN'T LEAVE LAURIE SKYE BEHIND WHILE I EXPLORE, NOT WHEN I MIGHT NEVER FIND THE WAY BACK.
SO I'M CHOOSING A TUNNEL AT RANDOM AND--
UH OH.
TROUBLE, SCULLY...OF A KIND YOU WOULDN'T BELIEVE.
AND THE TROUBLE'S GOT COMPANY.
WORSE THAN THAT.
THIS TROUBLE TRAVELS IN A PACK.

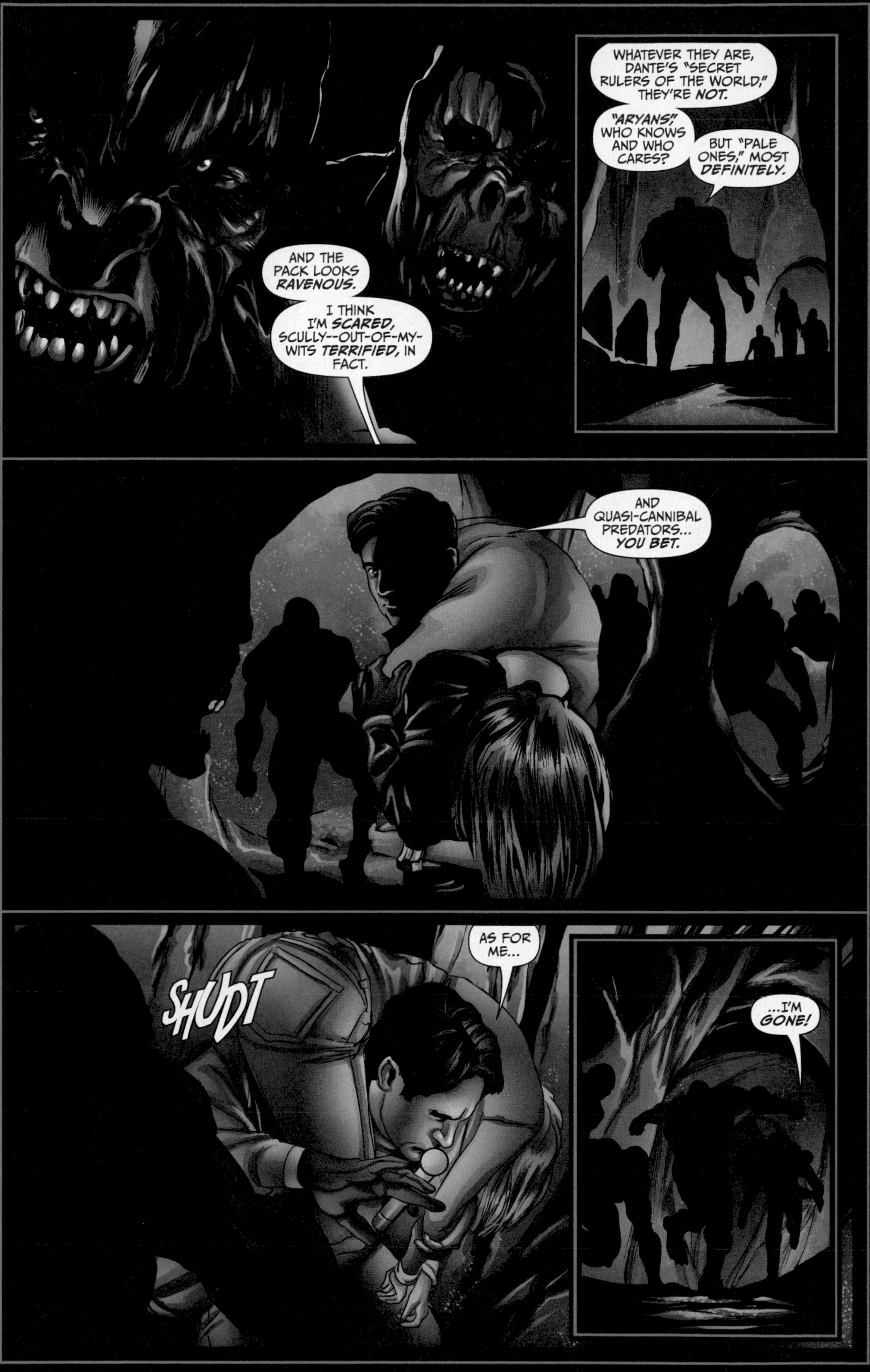

WHATEVER THEY ARE, DANTE'S "SECRET RULERS OF THE WORLD," THEY'RE *NOT.*
"ARYANS," WHO KNOWS AND WHO CARES?
BUT "PALE ONES," MOST *DEFINITELY.*
AND THE PACK LOOKS *RAVENOUS.*
I THINK I'M *SCARED,* SCULLY--OUT-OF-MY-WITS *TERRIFIED,* IN FACT.
AND QUASI-CANNIBAL PREDATORS... *YOU BET.*
SHUDT
AS FOR ME...
...I'M *GONE!*

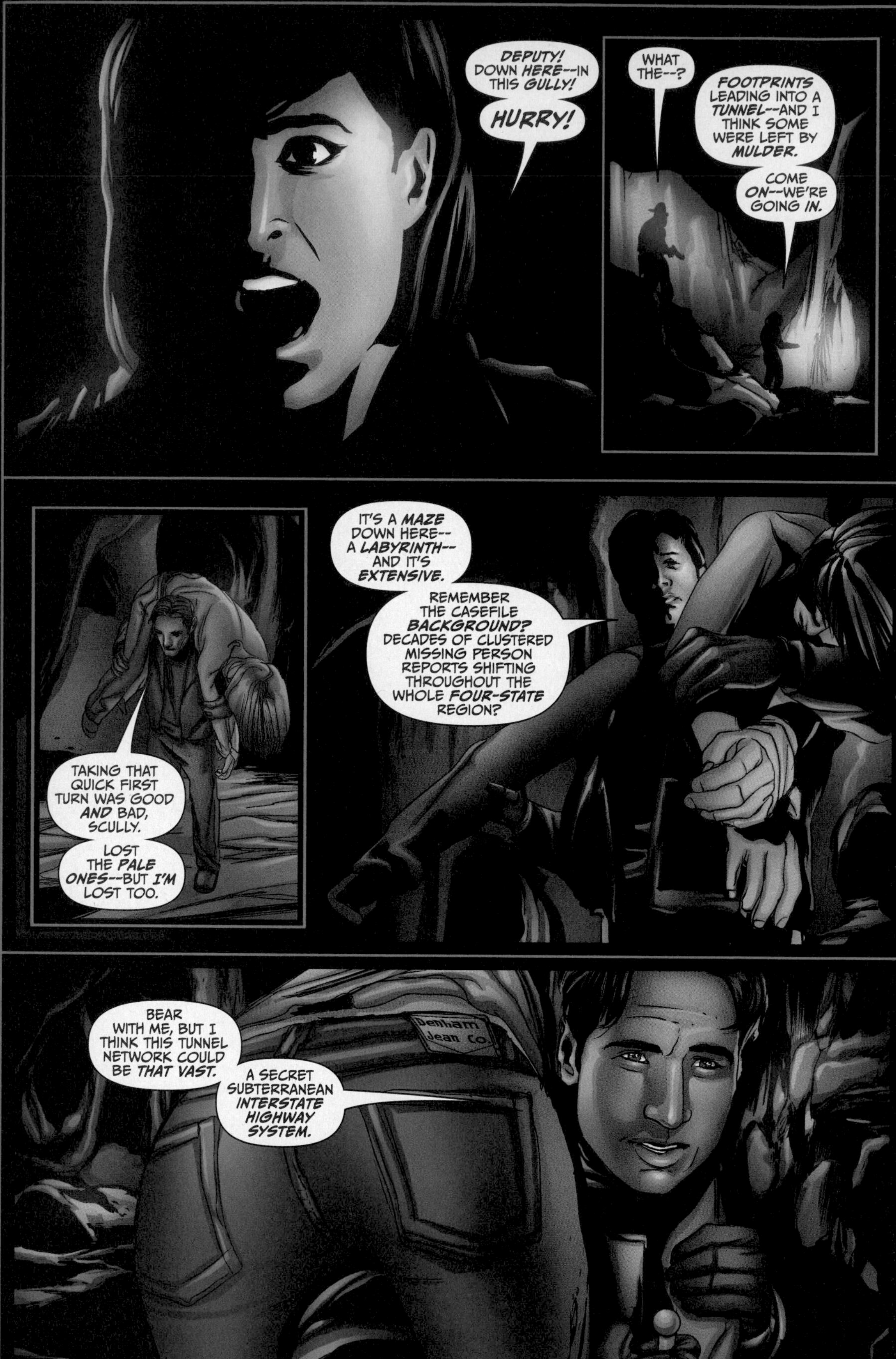
DEPUTY! DOWN HERE--IN THIS GULLY!
HURRY!
WHAT THE--?
FOOTPRINTS LEADING INTO A TUNNEL--AND I THINK SOME WERE LEFT BY MULDER.
COME ON--WE'RE GOING IN.
TAKING THAT QUICK FIRST TURN WAS GOOD AND BAD, SCULLY.
LOST THE PALE ONES--BUT I'M LOST TOO.
IT'S A MAZE DOWN HERE--A LABYRINTH--AND IT'S EXTENSIVE.
REMEMBER THE CASEFILE BACKGROUND? DECADES OF CLUSTERED MISSING PERSON REPORTS SHIFTING THROUGHOUT THE WHOLE FOUR-STATE REGION?
BEAR WITH ME, BUT I THINK THIS TUNNEL NETWORK COULD BE THAT VAST.
A SECRET SUBTERRANEAN INTERSTATE HIGHWAY SYSTEM.
Denham Jean Co.

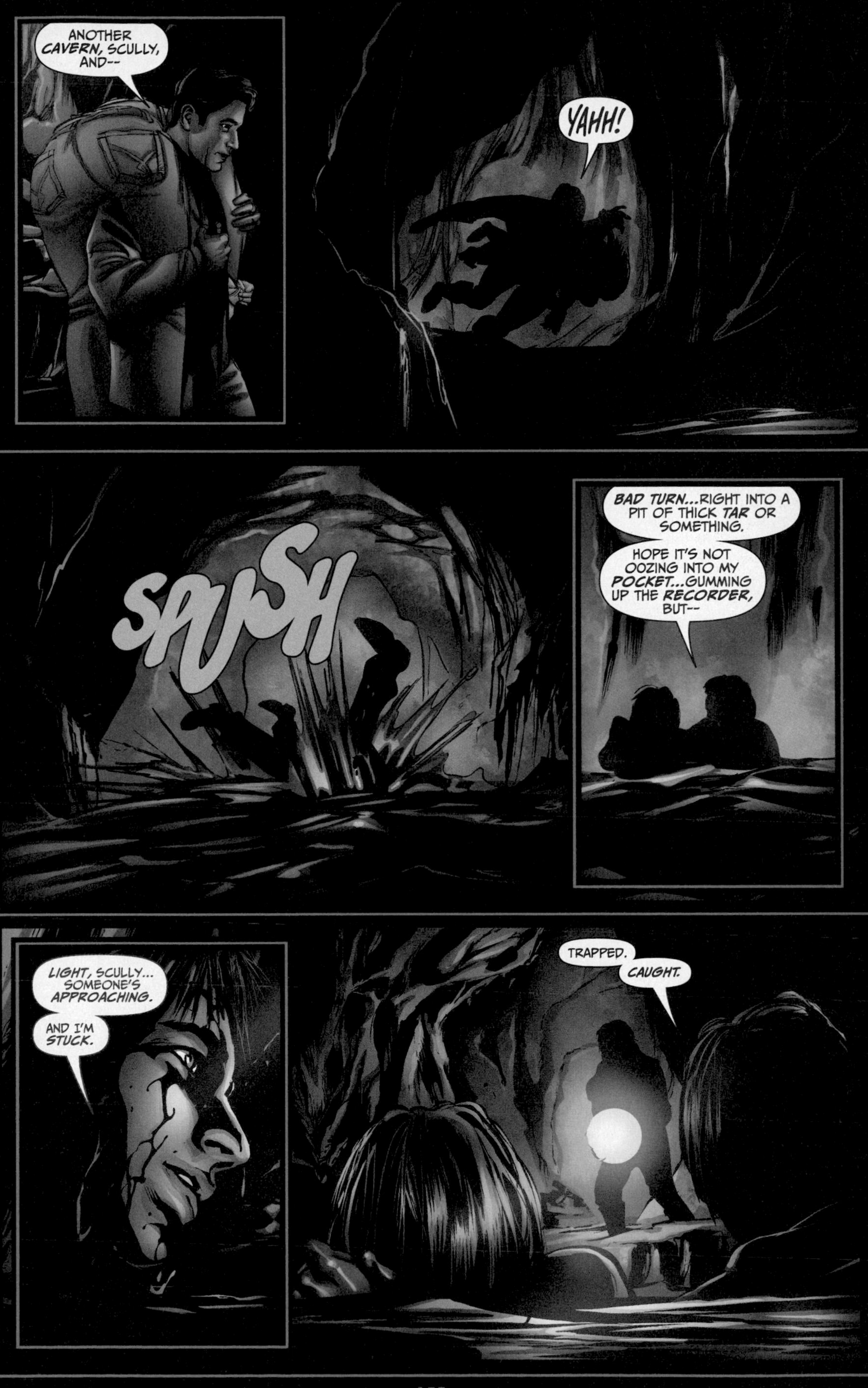

ANOTHER CAVERN, SCULLY, AND--
YAHH!
SPLUSH
BAD TURN...RIGHT INTO A PIT OF THICK TAR OR SOMETHING.
HOPE IT'S NOT OOZING INTO MY POCKET...GUMMING UP THE RECORDER, BUT--
LIGHT, SCULLY... SOMEONE'S APPROACHING.
AND I'M STUCK.
TRAPPED.
CAUGHT.

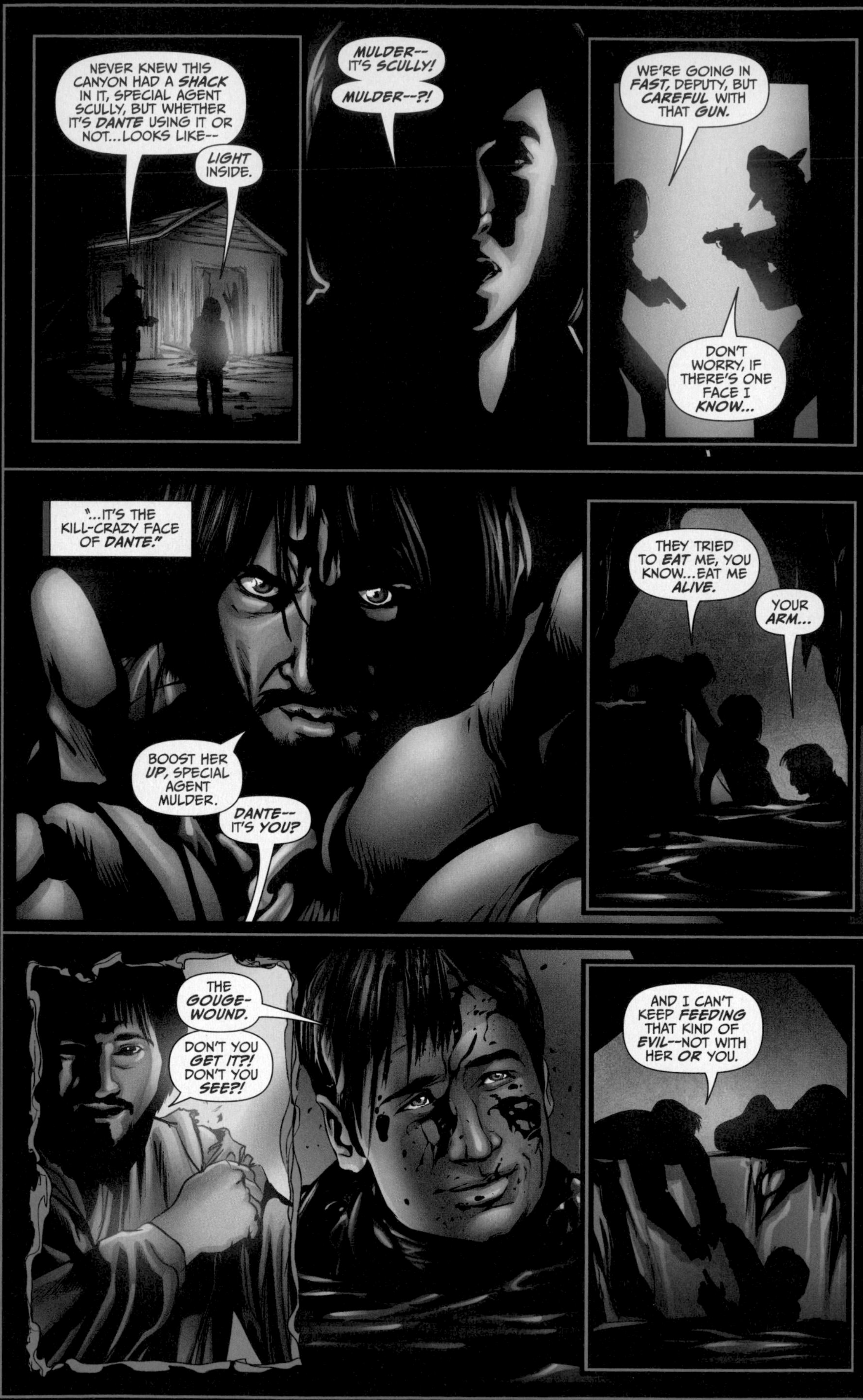
NEVER KNEW THIS CANYON HAD A SHACK IN IT, SPECIAL AGENT SCULLY, BUT WHETHER IT'S DANTE USING IT OR NOT...LOOKS LIKE--
LIGHT INSIDE.
MULDER-- IT'S SCULLY!
MULDER--?!
WE'RE GOING IN FAST, DEPUTY, BUT CAREFUL WITH THAT GUN.
DON'T WORRY, IF THERE'S ONE FACE I KNOW...
"...IT'S THE KILL-CRAZY FACE OF DANTE."
BOOST HER UP, SPECIAL AGENT MULDER.
DANTE-- IT'S YOU?
THEY TRIED TO EAT ME, YOU KNOW...EAT ME ALIVE.
YOUR ARM...
THE GOUGE-WOUND.
DON'T YOU GET IT?! DON'T YOU SEE?!
AND I CAN'T KEEP FEEDING THAT KIND OF EVIL--NOT WITH HER OR YOU.

IT'S NOT RIGHT, SPECIAL AGENT MULDER.
YOU MADE ME SEE THAT, MADE ME THINK... EXORCIZED MY SOUL.
YOU ESCAPED, DANTE...AND THEN YOU CAME HERE?
BECAUSE YOU BELIEVED IN ME, WHEN I NEEDED REDEMPTION.
INSTEAD OF JUST CALLING ME CRAZY, YOU BROKE THE SPELL.
FBI
FBI
YOU'RE SAYING THE PALE PEOPLE PUT A SPELL ON YOU, DANTE?
NOT A REAL SPELL, SPECIAL AGENT MULDER, ALTHOUGH I PROBABLY HYPNOTIZED MYSELF.
LIVING ALONE, YOU GOT NOTHING BUT YOUR OWN BRAIN-- WHICH I'M NOT SURE CAN BE TRUSTED ON ITS OWN.
MAYBE I WAS ALREADY STRANGE WHEN THEY CAME TO ME THAT NIGHT...THE NASTY ONES, SPECIAL AGENT MULDER, THE ONE WHO STARTED ALL THE STORIES ABOUT THE HOLLOW EARTH.
IT AIN'T REALLY HOLLOW, OF COURSE, BUT THERE'S TUNNELS DOWN HERE THEY USE LIKE HUMAN SNAKES.
MY GUESS IS THEY PREY IN ONE AREA FOR A WHILE AND THEN TRAVEL UNDERGROUND TO FATTEN UP SOMEWHERE ELSE...
AND THREE YEARS AGO, WHEN THEY CYCLED BACK TO THIS AREA...
...I ALMOST BECAME A MIDNIGHT SNACK.

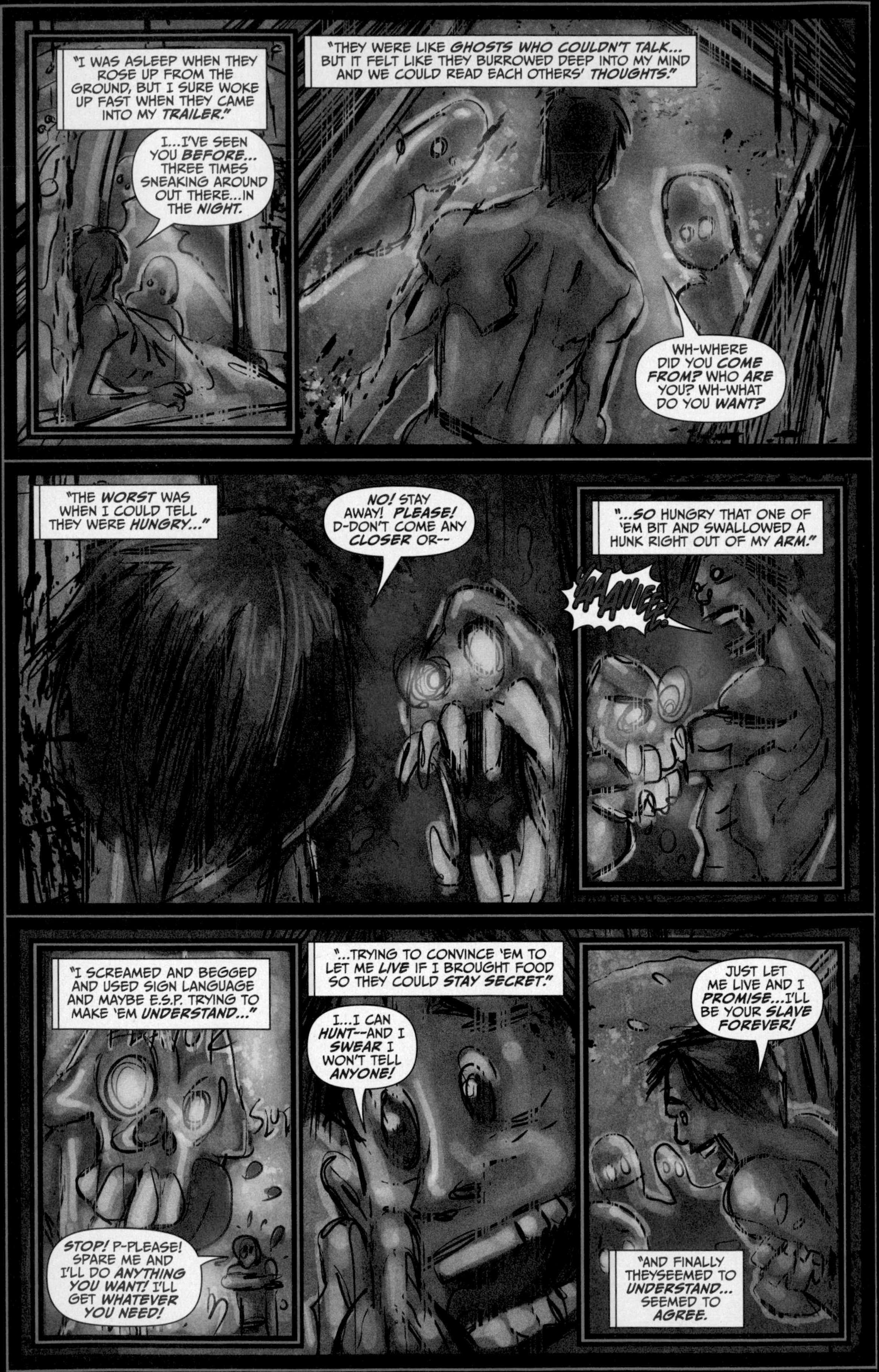
"I WAS ASLEEP WHEN THEY ROSE UP FROM THE GROUND, BUT I SURE WOKE UP FAST WHEN THEY CAME INTO MY TRAILER."
I...I'VE SEEN YOU BEFORE... THREE TIMES SNEAKING AROUND OUT THERE...IN THE NIGHT.
"THEY WERE LIKE GHOSTS WHO COULDN'T TALK... BUT IT FELT LIKE THEY BURROWED DEEP INTO MY MIND AND WE COULD READ EACH OTHERS' THOUGHTS."
WH-WHERE DID YOU COME FROM? WHO ARE YOU? WH-WHAT DO YOU WANT?
"THE WORST WAS WHEN I COULD TELL THEY WERE HUNGRY..."
NO! STAY AWAY! PLEASE! D-DON'T COME ANY CLOSER OR--
"...SO HUNGRY THAT ONE OF 'EM BIT AND SWALLOWED A HUNK RIGHT OUT OF MY ARM."
YAAAAIIEEE!
"I SCREAMED AND BEGGED AND USED SIGN LANGUAGE AND MAYBE E.S.P. TRYING TO MAKE 'EM UNDERSTAND..."
STOP! P-PLEASE! SPARE ME AND I'LL DO ANYTHING YOU WANT! I'LL GET WHATEVER YOU NEED!
"...TRYING TO CONVINCE 'EM TO LET ME LIVE IF I BROUGHT FOOD SO THEY COULD STAY SECRET."
I...I CAN HUNT--AND I SWEAR I WON'T TELL ANYONE!
JUST LET ME LIVE AND I PROMISE...I'LL BE YOUR SLAVE FOREVER!
"AND FINALLY THEYSEEMED TO UNDERSTAND... SEEMED TO AGREE.

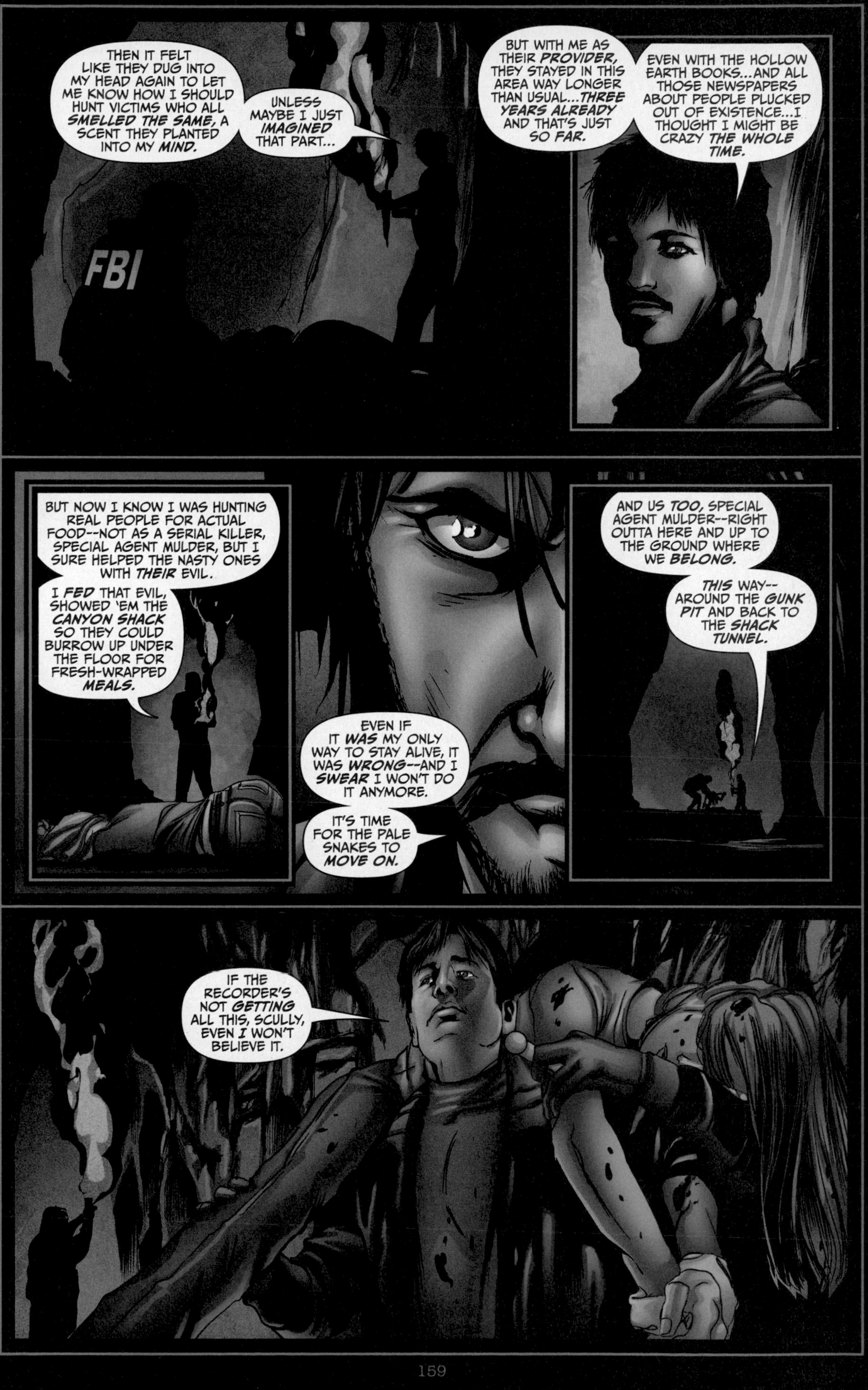
THEN IT FELT LIKE THEY DUG INTO MY HEAD AGAIN TO LET ME KNOW HOW I SHOULD HUNT VICTIMS WHO ALL SMELLED THE SAME, A SCENT THEY PLANTED INTO MY MIND.
UNLESS MAYBE I JUST IMAGINED THAT PART...
FBI
BUT WITH ME AS THEIR PROVIDER, THEY STAYED IN THIS AREA WAY LONGER THAN USUAL...THREE YEARS ALREADY AND THAT'S JUST SO FAR.
EVEN WITH THE HOLLOW EARTH BOOKS...AND ALL THOSE NEWSPAPERS ABOUT PEOPLE PLUCKED OUT OF EXISTENCE...I THOUGHT I MIGHT BE CRAZY THE WHOLE TIME.
BUT NOW I KNOW I WAS HUNTING REAL PEOPLE FOR ACTUAL FOOD--NOT AS A SERIAL KILLER, SPECIAL AGENT MULDER, BUT I SURE HELPED THE NASTY ONES WITH THEIR EVIL.
I FED THAT EVIL, SHOWED 'EM THE CANYON SHACK SO THEY COULD BURROW UP UNDER THE FLOOR FOR FRESH-WRAPPED MEALS.
EVEN IF IT WAS MY ONLY WAY TO STAY ALIVE, IT WAS WRONG--AND I SWEAR I WON'T DO IT ANYMORE.
IT'S TIME FOR THE PALE SNAKES TO MOVE ON.
AND US TOO, SPECIAL AGENT MULDER--RIGHT OUTTA HERE AND UP TO THE GROUND WHERE WE BELONG.
THIS WAY--AROUND THE GUNK PIT AND BACK TO THE SHACK TUNNEL.
IF THE RECORDER'S NOT GETTING ALL THIS, SCULLY, EVEN I WON'T BELIEVE IT.

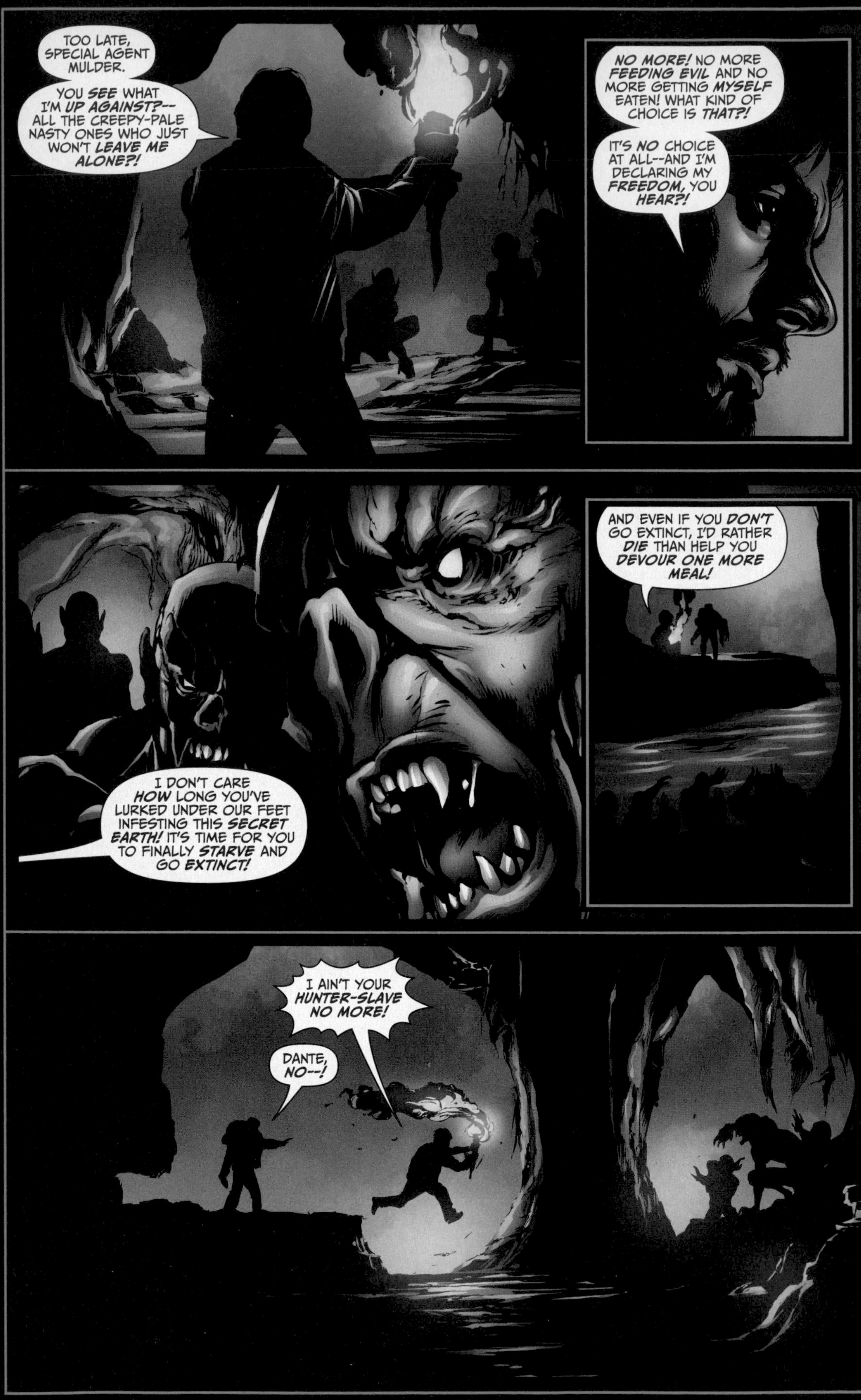
TOO LATE, SPECIAL AGENT MULDER.
YOU SEE WHAT I'M UP AGAINST?--ALL THE CREEPY-PALE NASTY ONES WHO JUST WON'T LEAVE ME ALONE?!
NO MORE! NO MORE FEEDING EVIL AND NO MORE GETTING MYSELF EATEN! WHAT KIND OF CHOICE IS THAT?!
IT'S NO CHOICE AT ALL--AND I'M DECLARING MY FREEDOM, YOU HEAR?!
I DON'T CARE HOW LONG YOU'VE LURKED UNDER OUR FEET INFESTING THIS SECRET EARTH! IT'S TIME FOR YOU TO FINALLY STARVE AND GO EXTINCT!
AND EVEN IF YOU DON'T GO EXTINCT, I'D RATHER DIE THAN HELP YOU DEVOUR ONE MORE MEAL!
I AIN'T YOUR HUNTER-SLAVE NO MORE!
DANTE, NO--!

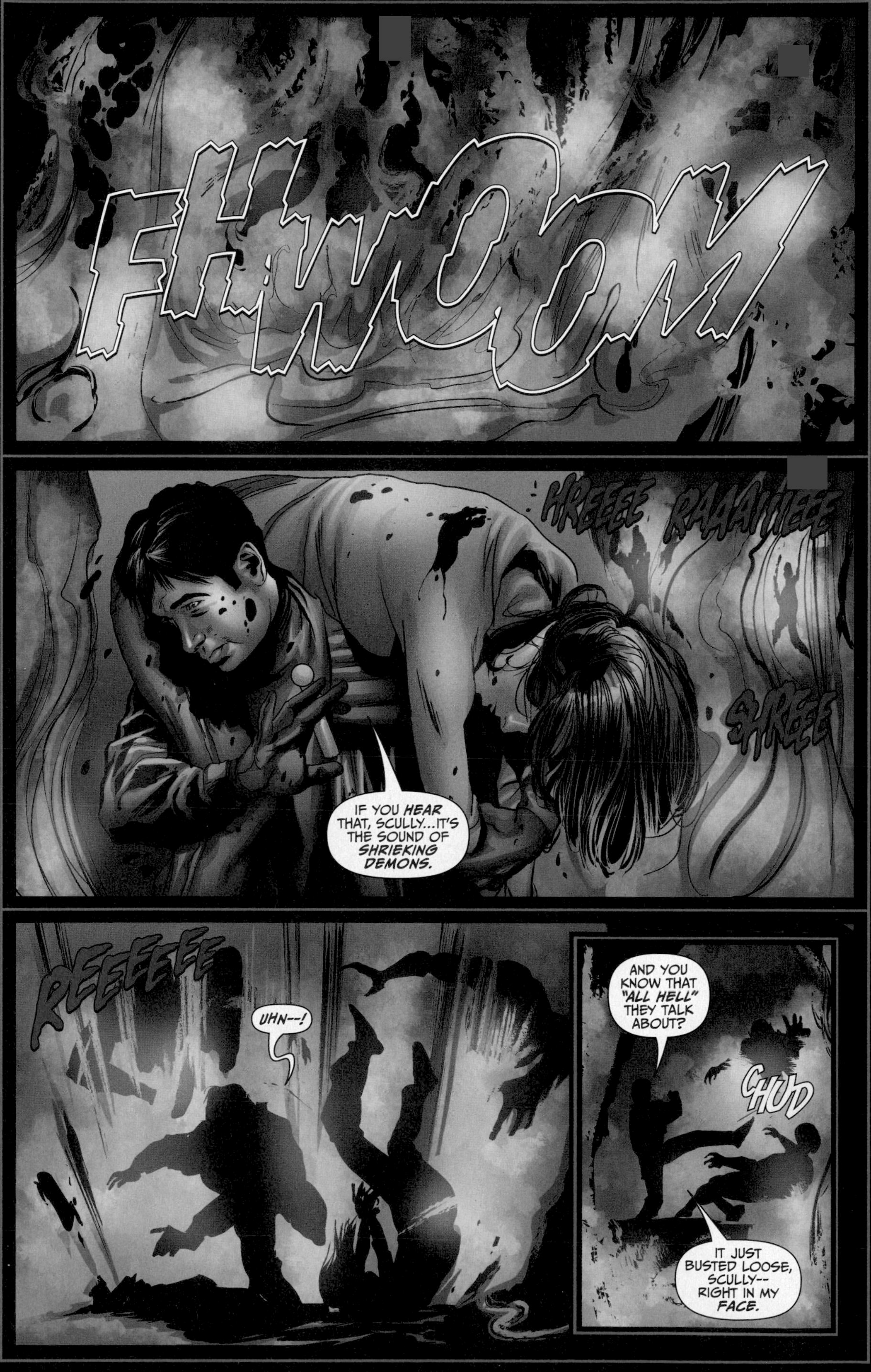
FHWOOM
HREEEE
RAAAIIIEEE
SHREEE
IF YOU *HEAR* THAT, SCULLY...IT'S THE SOUND OF *SHRIEKING DEMONS.*
REEEEEE
UHN--!
AND YOU KNOW THAT *"ALL HELL"* THEY TALK ABOUT?
CHUD
IT JUST BUSTED LOOSE, SCULLY-- RIGHT IN MY *FACE.*

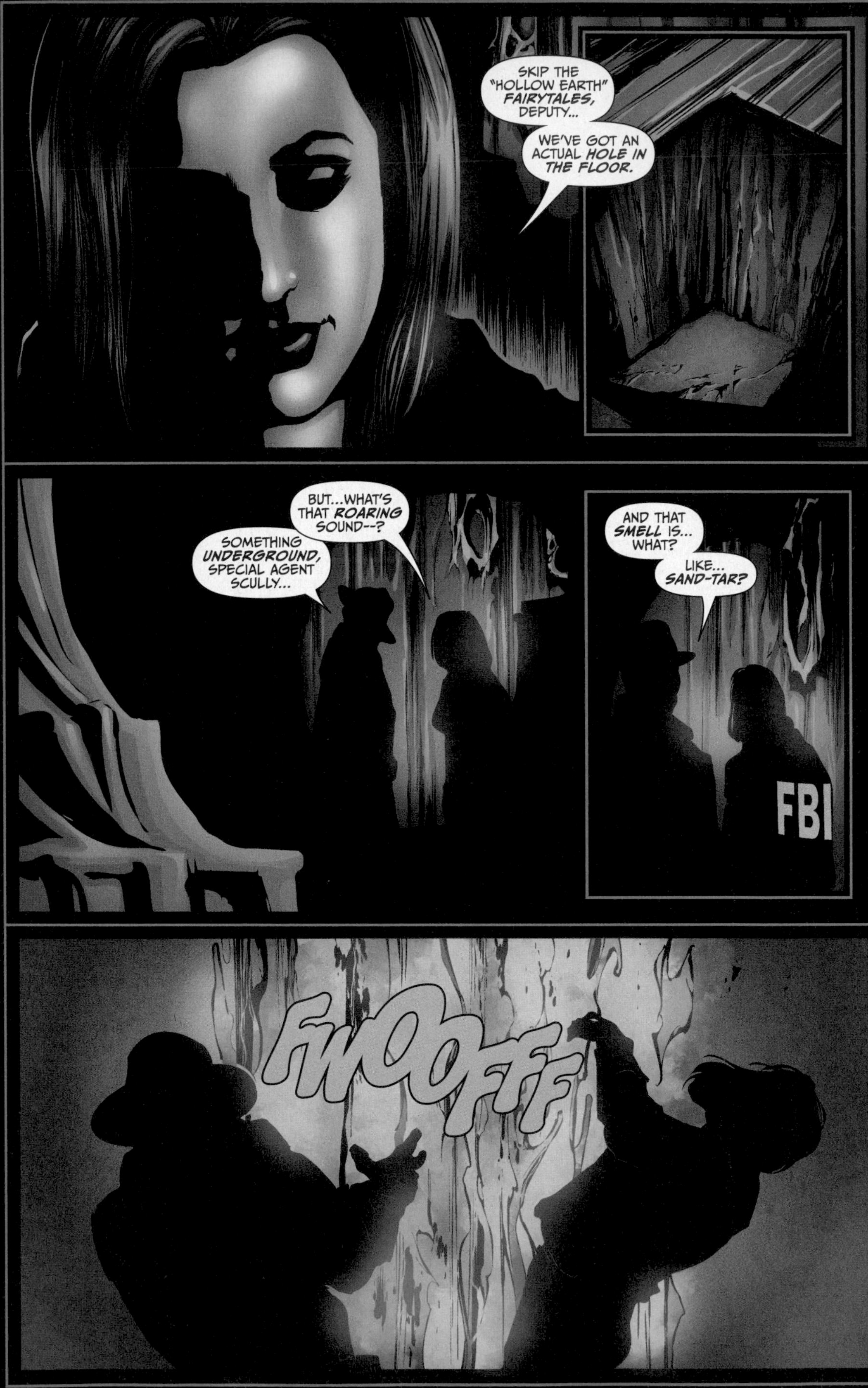
SKIP THE "HOLLOW EARTH" FAIRYTALES, DEPUTY...
WE'VE GOT AN ACTUAL HOLE IN THE FLOOR.
BUT...WHAT'S THAT ROARING SOUND--?
SOMETHING UNDERGROUND, SPECIAL AGENT SCULLY...
AND THAT SMELL IS... WHAT?
LIKE... SAND-TAR?
FBI
FWOOFFF

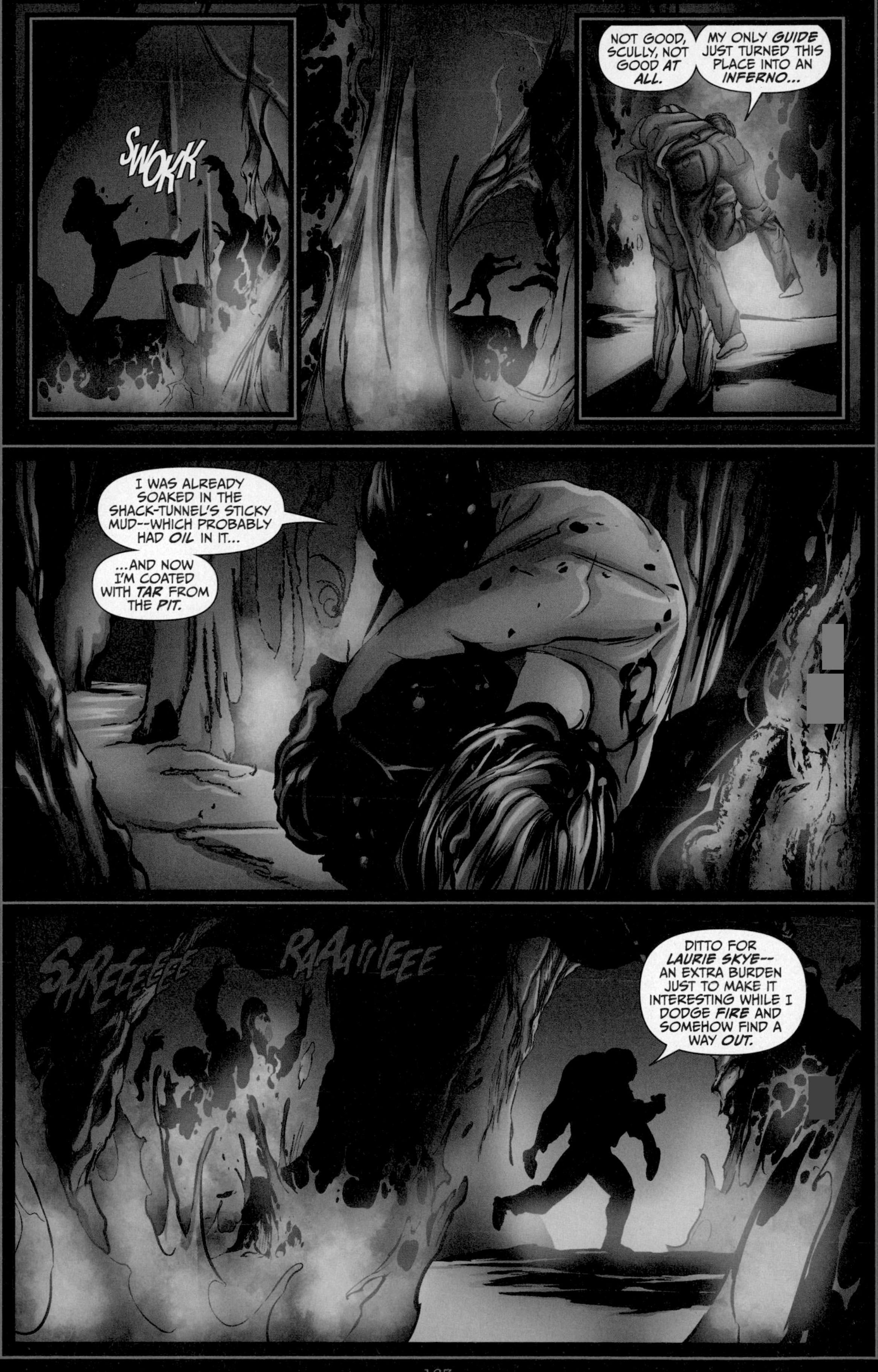
SWOKK
NOT GOOD, SCULLY, NOT GOOD AT ALL.
MY ONLY GUIDE JUST TURNED THIS PLACE INTO AN INFERNO...
I WAS ALREADY SOAKED IN THE SHACK-TUNNEL'S STICKY MUD--WHICH PROBABLY HAD OIL IN IT...
...AND NOW I'M COATED WITH TAR FROM THE PIT.
SHREEEEEE
RAAAIIIEEE
DITTO FOR LAURIE SKYE-- AN EXTRA BURDEN JUST TO MAKE IT INTERESTING WHILE I DODGE FIRE AND SOMEHOW FIND A WAY OUT.

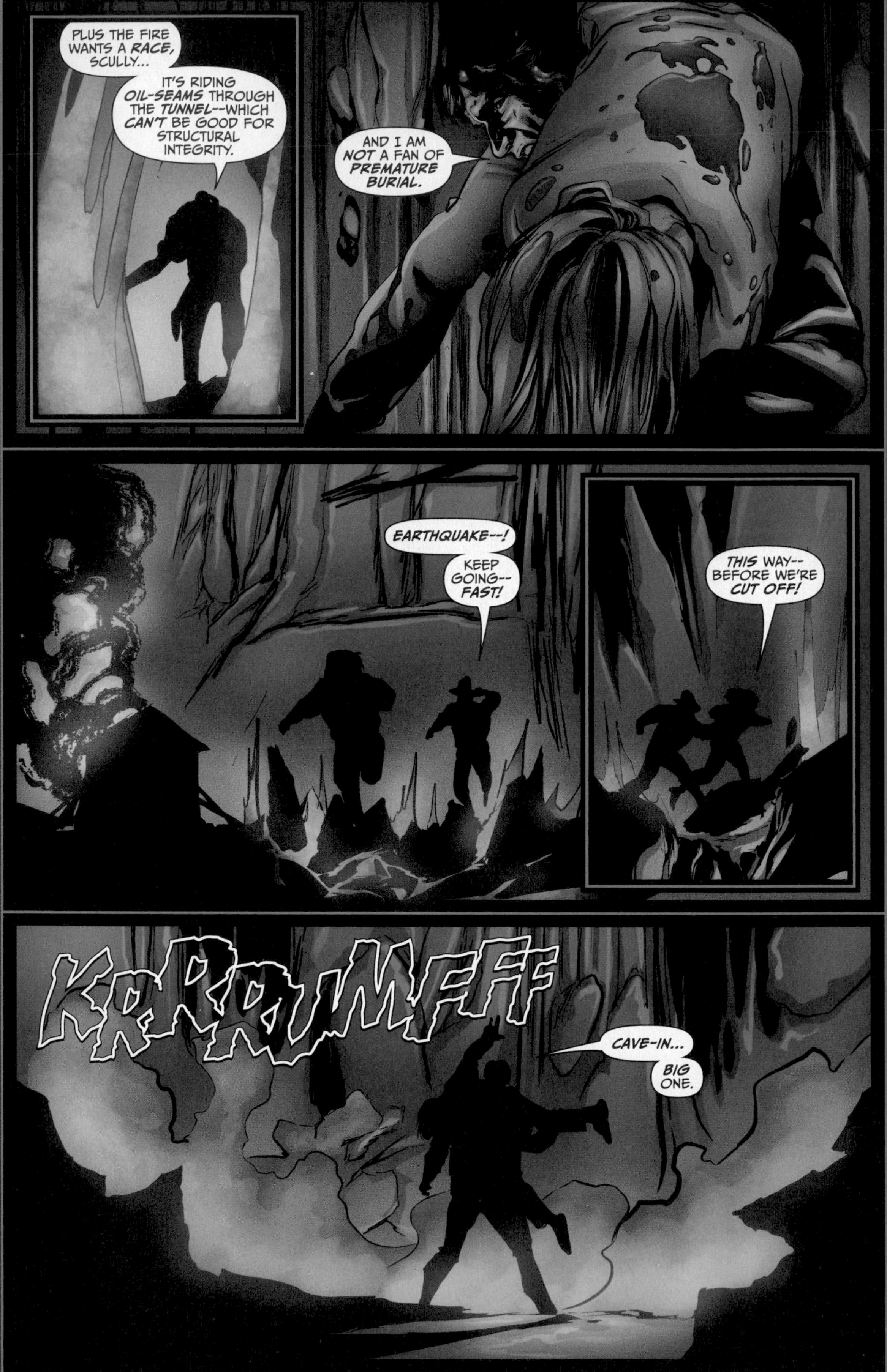
PLUS THE FIRE WANTS A RACE, SCULLY...
IT'S RIDING OIL-SEAMS THROUGH THE TUNNEL--WHICH CAN'T BE GOOD FOR STRUCTURAL INTEGRITY.
AND I AM NOT A FAN OF PREMATURE BURIAL.
EARTHQUAKE--!
KEEP GOING--FAST!
THIS WAY--BEFORE WE'RE CUT OFF!
KRRUMFFF
CAVE-IN...
BIG ONE.

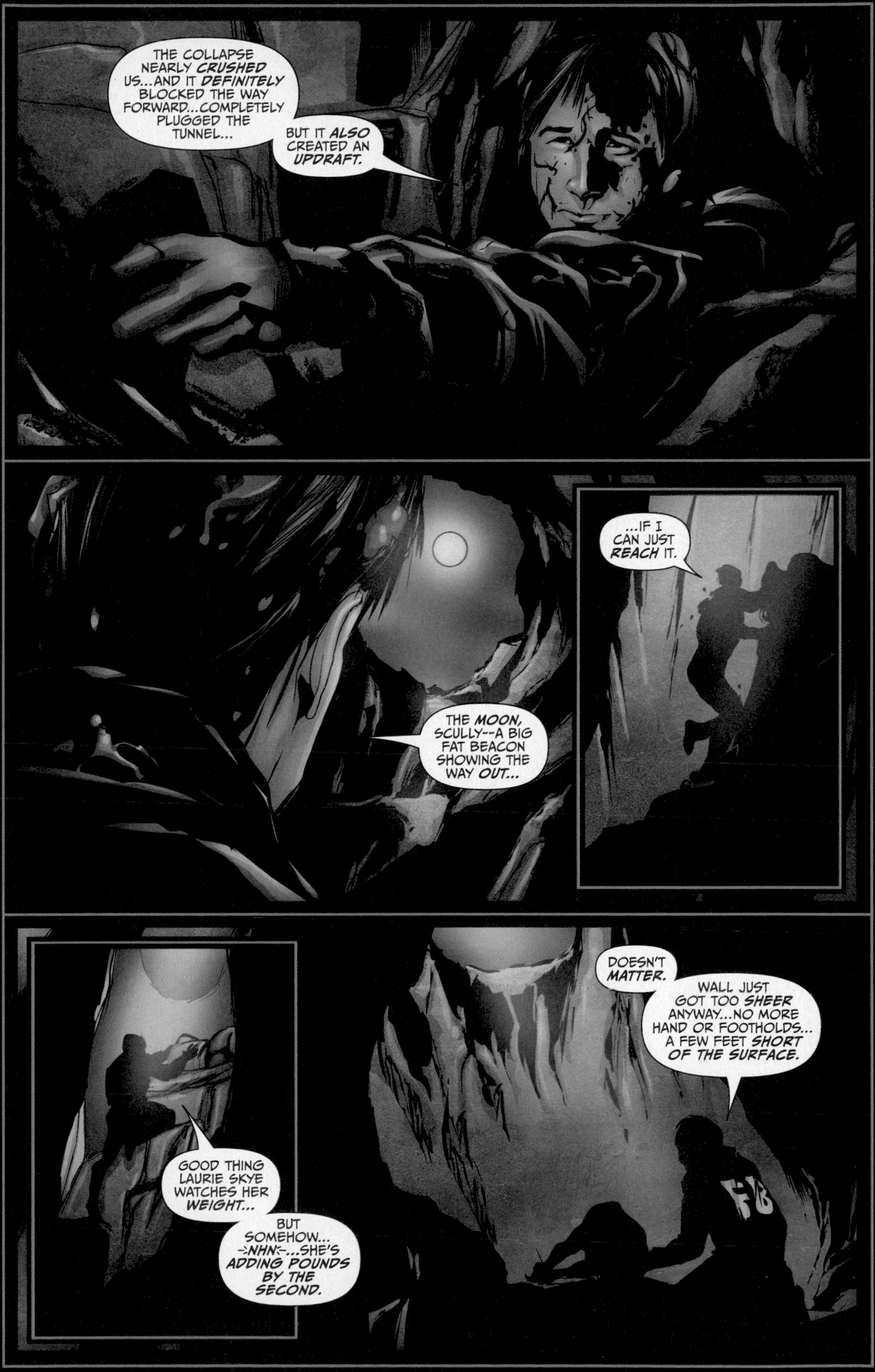
THE COLLAPSE NEARLY CRUSHED US...AND IT DEFINITELY BLOCKED THE WAY FORWARD...COMPLETELY PLUGGED THE TUNNEL...
BUT IT ALSO CREATED AN UPDRAFT.
THE MOON, SCULLY--A BIG FAT BEACON SHOWING THE WAY OUT...
...IF I CAN JUST REACH IT.
GOOD THING LAURIE SKYE WATCHES HER WEIGHT...
BUT SOMEHOW... -NHN-...SHE'S ADDING POUNDS BY THE SECOND.
DOESN'T MATTER.
WALL JUST GOT TOO SHEER ANYWAY...NO MORE HAND OR FOOTHOLDS... A FEW FEET SHORT OF THE SURFACE.
FB

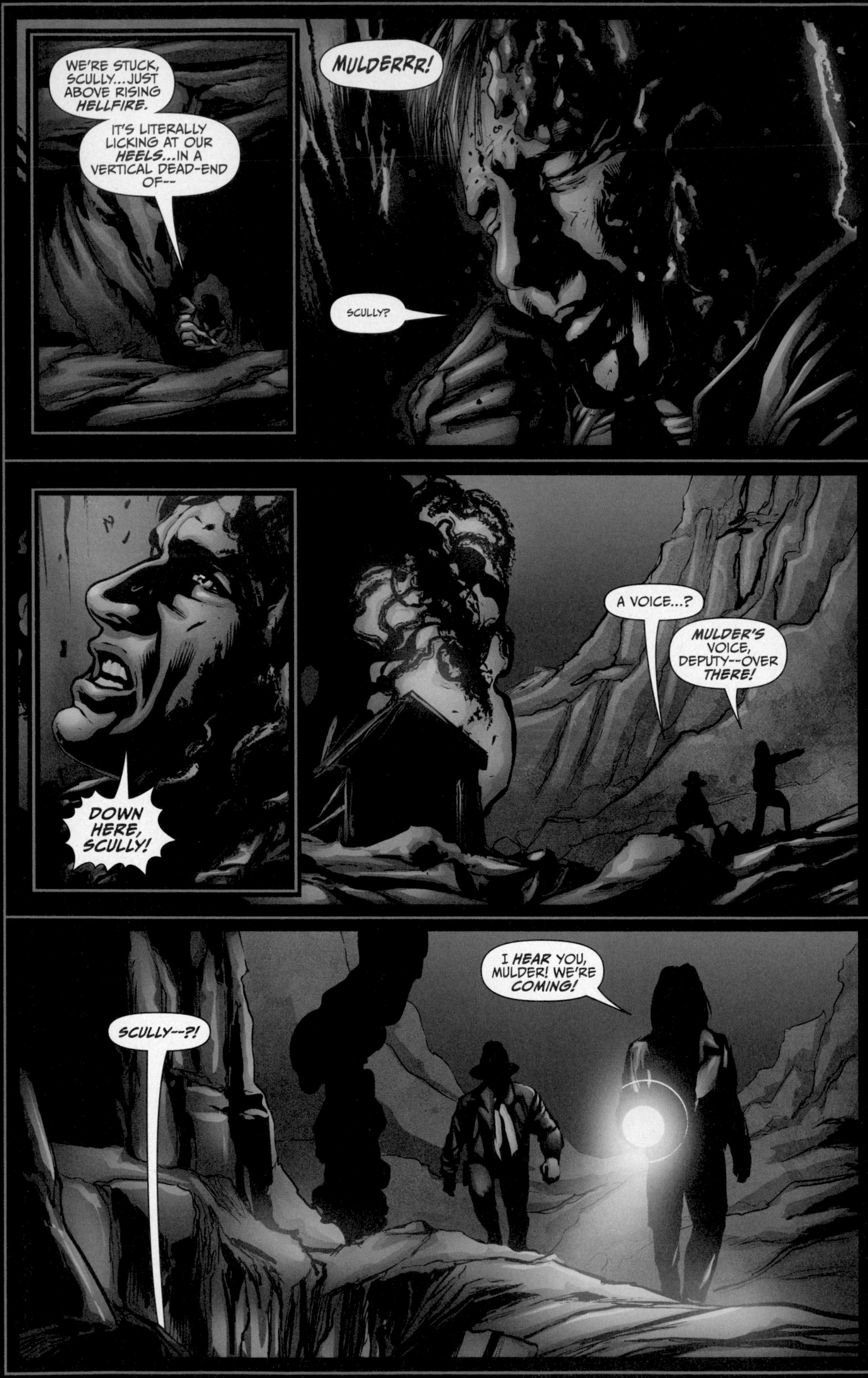
WE'RE STUCK, SCULLY...JUST ABOVE RISING HELLFIRE.
IT'S LITERALLY LICKING AT OUR HEELS...IN A VERTICAL DEAD-END OF--
MULDERRR!
SCULLY?
DOWN HERE, SCULLY!
A VOICE...?
MULDER'S VOICE, DEPUTY--OVER THERE!
SCULLY--?!
I HEAR YOU, MULDER! WE'RE COMING!

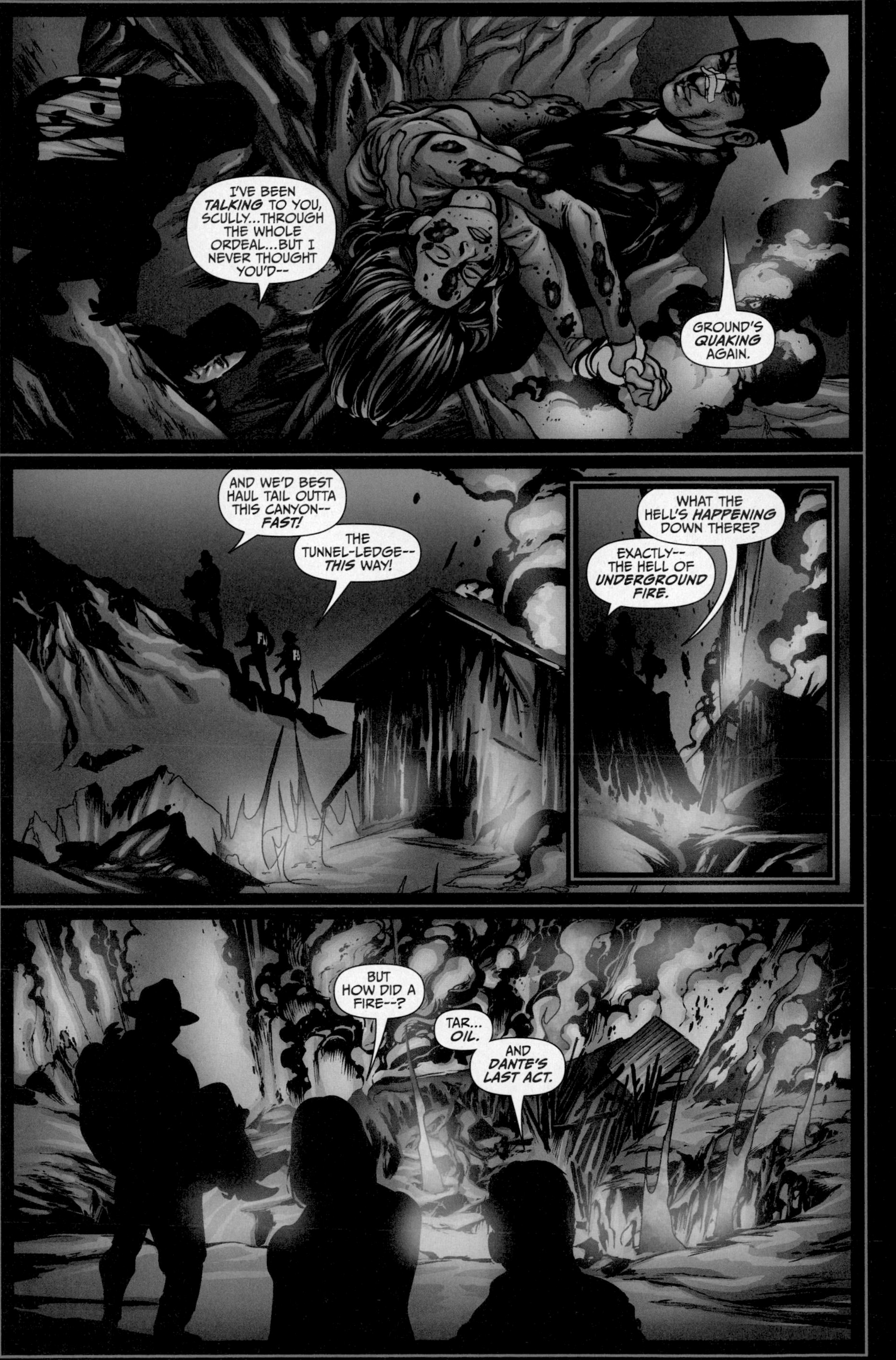
I'VE BEEN TALKING TO YOU, SCULLY...THROUGH THE WHOLE ORDEAL...BUT I NEVER THOUGHT YOU'D--
GROUND'S QUAKING AGAIN.
AND WE'D BEST HAUL TAIL OUTTA THIS CANYON-- FAST!
THE TUNNEL-LEDGE-- THIS WAY!
WHAT THE HELL'S HAPPENING DOWN THERE?
EXACTLY-- THE HELL OF UNDERGROUND FIRE.
BUT HOW DID A FIRE--?
TAR... OIL.
AND DANTE'S LAST ACT.

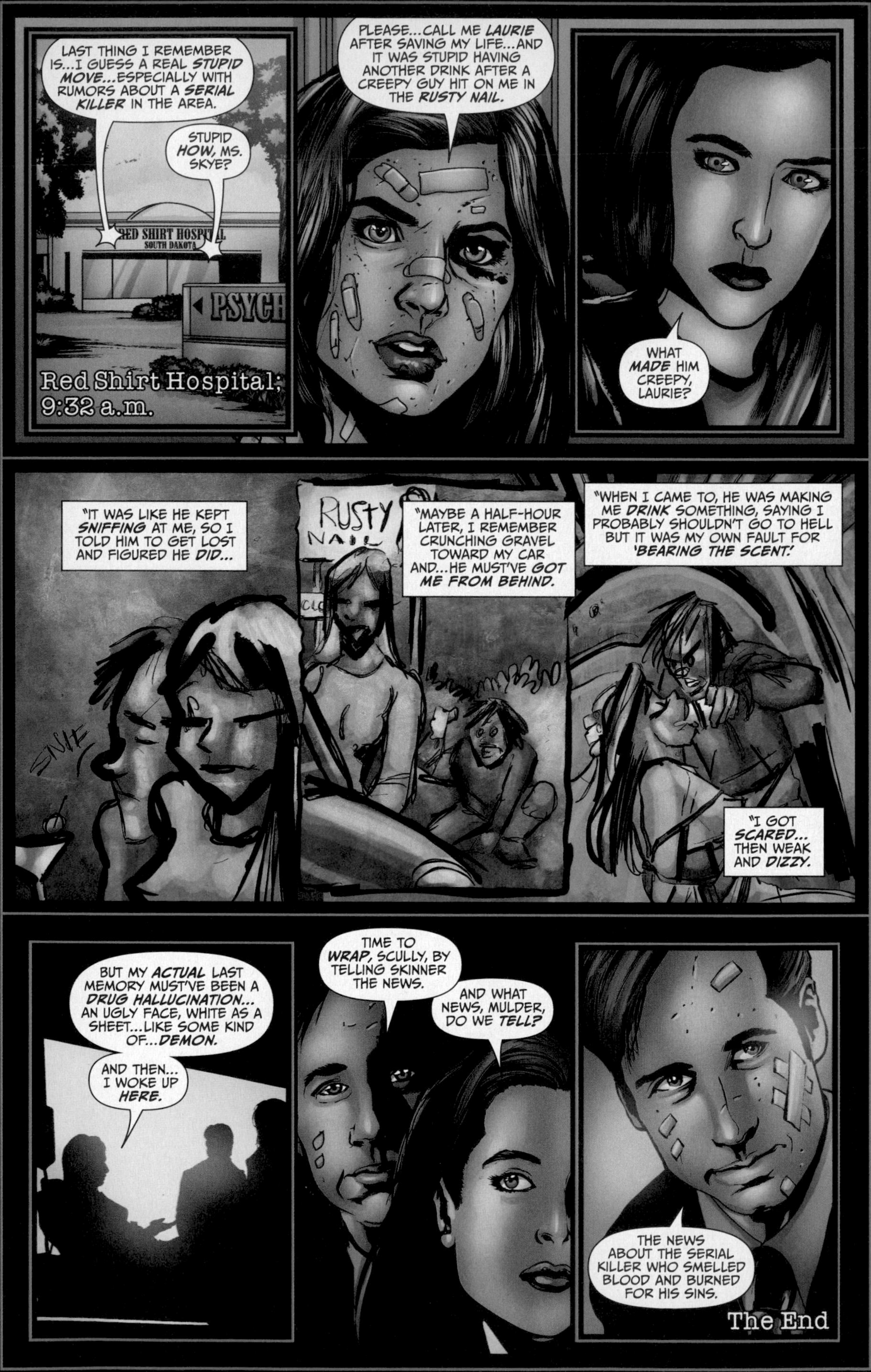
LAST THING I REMEMBER IS...I GUESS A REAL STUPID MOVE...ESPECIALLY WITH RUMORS ABOUT A SERIAL KILLER IN THE AREA.
STUPID HOW, MS. SKYE?
RED SHIRT HOSPITAL
SOUTH DAKOTA
PSYCH
Red Shirt Hospital; 9:32 a.m.
PLEASE...CALL ME LAURIE AFTER SAVING MY LIFE...AND IT WAS STUPID HAVING ANOTHER DRINK AFTER A CREEPY GUY HIT ON ME IN THE RUSTY NAIL.
WHAT MADE HIM CREEPY, LAURIE?
"IT WAS LIKE HE KEPT SNIFFING AT ME, SO I TOLD HIM TO GET LOST AND FIGURED HE DID...
RUSTY NAIL
"MAYBE A HALF-HOUR LATER, I REMEMBER CRUNCHING GRAVEL TOWARD MY CAR AND...HE MUST'VE GOT ME FROM BEHIND.
"WHEN I CAME TO, HE WAS MAKING ME DRINK SOMETHING, SAYING I PROBABLY SHOULDN'T GO TO HELL BUT IT WAS MY OWN FAULT FOR 'BEARING THE SCENT.'
"I GOT SCARED... THEN WEAK AND DIZZY.
BUT MY ACTUAL LAST MEMORY MUST'VE BEEN A DRUG HALLUCINATION... AN UGLY FACE, WHITE AS A SHEET...LIKE SOME KIND OF...DEMON.
AND THEN... I WOKE UP HERE.
TIME TO WRAP, SCULLY, BY TELLING SKINNER THE NEWS.
AND WHAT NEWS, MULDER, DO WE TELL?
THE NEWS ABOUT THE SERIAL KILLER WHO SMELLED BLOOD AND BURNED FOR HIS SINS.
The End

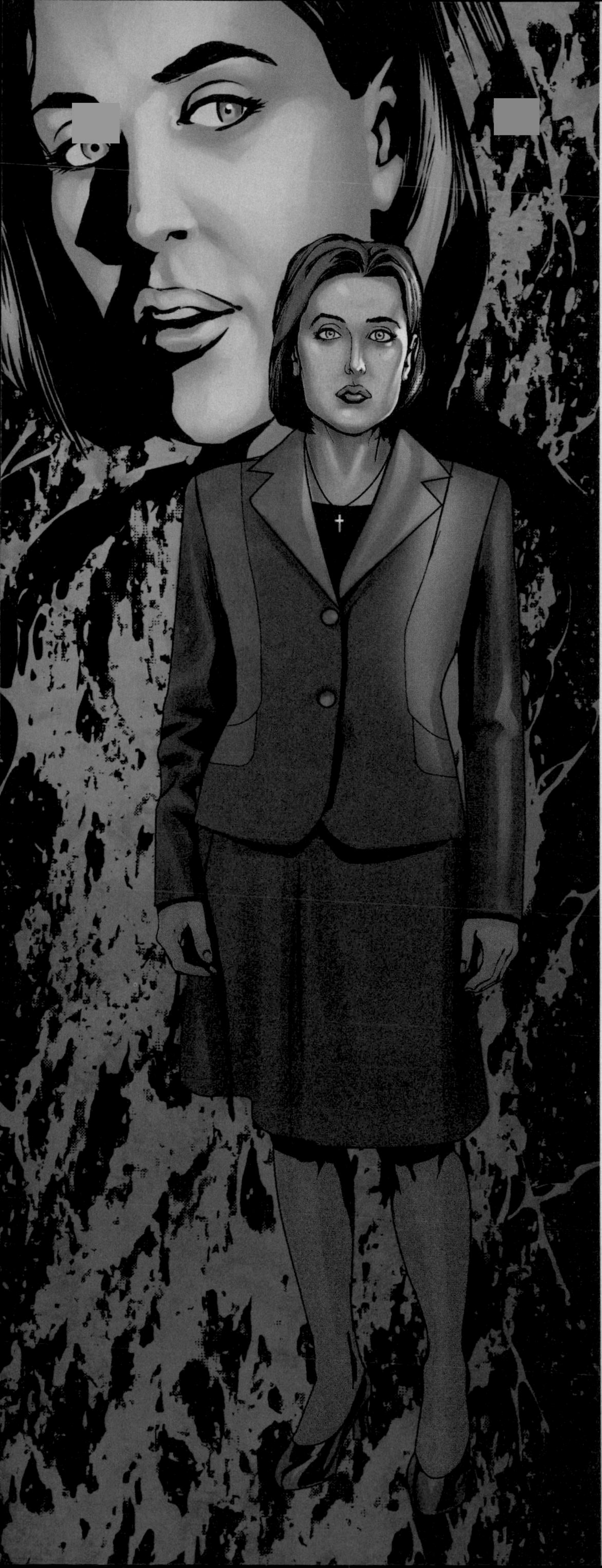

FEDERAL AGENT
Dana Scully

Raised Catholic in a Navy family, Scully studied physics as an undergraduate before attending medical school, where she was recruited by the FBI. Eager to distinguish herself, she ended up drawing an assignment that would stymie her ambitions at the FBI–partnering with Mulder with the assigned secret intent of debunking him and his work on the X-Files, which was considered a potential source of embarrassment to the Bureau. Far from debunking Mulder, Scully ended up strengthening his work. Scully's scientific mind and relentless intellect quickly became indispensable to him.

Art: Brian Denham & Kelsey Shannon

FEDERAL AGENT
Fox Mulder

The central event of Mulder's life was the mysterious disappearance of his sister, Samantha, from their childhood home in Chilmark, Massachusetts. At the time, it was unexplained, but years later, Mulder underwent regression hypnosis and "recovered" a memory of her having been taken by aliens. This discovery destroyed a promising career at the FBI. After studying psychology at Oxford, Mulder entered the FBI Academy in Quantico, Virginia, and quickly helped catch a notorious serial killer by writing a monograph on serial killers and the occult. But after becoming convinced of his sister's abduction, his priorities rapidly changed. He learned of the existence of the bureau's long-neglected "X-Files," and moved to the basement of the FBI to pursue his interest in crimes connected to aliens and other unexplained phenomena.

Art: Brian Denham & Kelsey Shannon

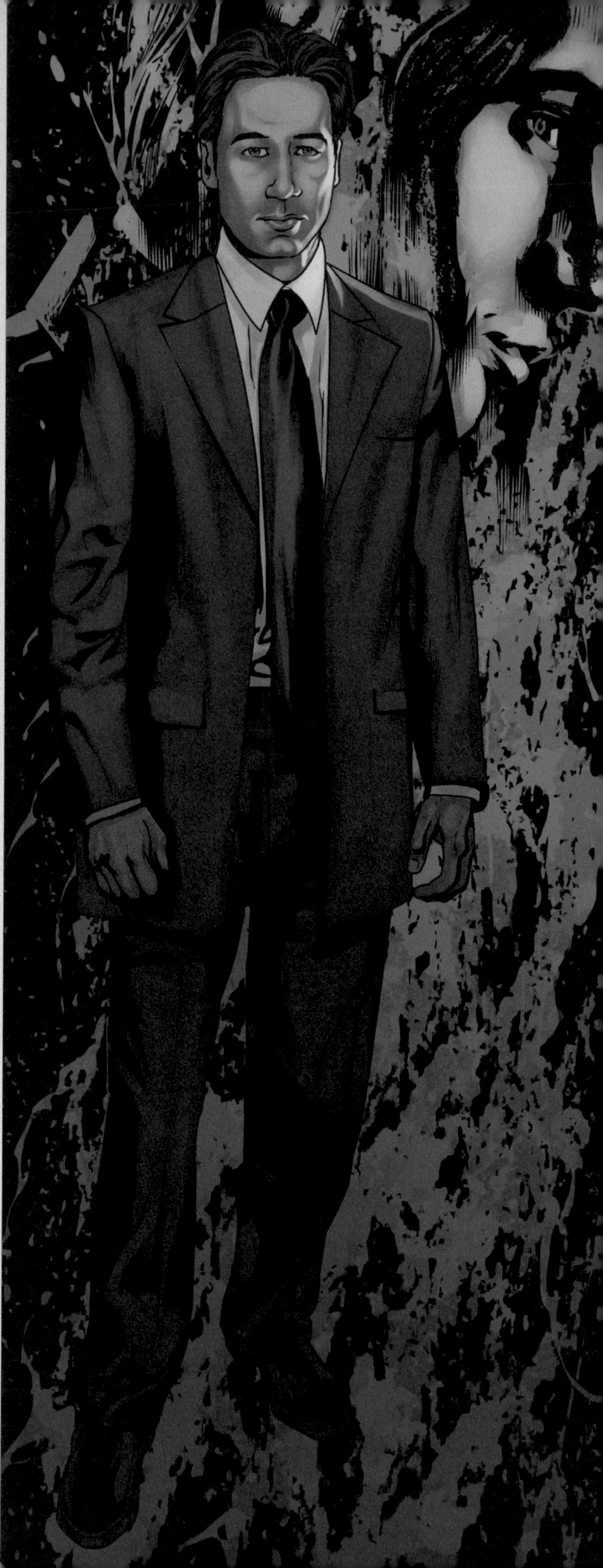

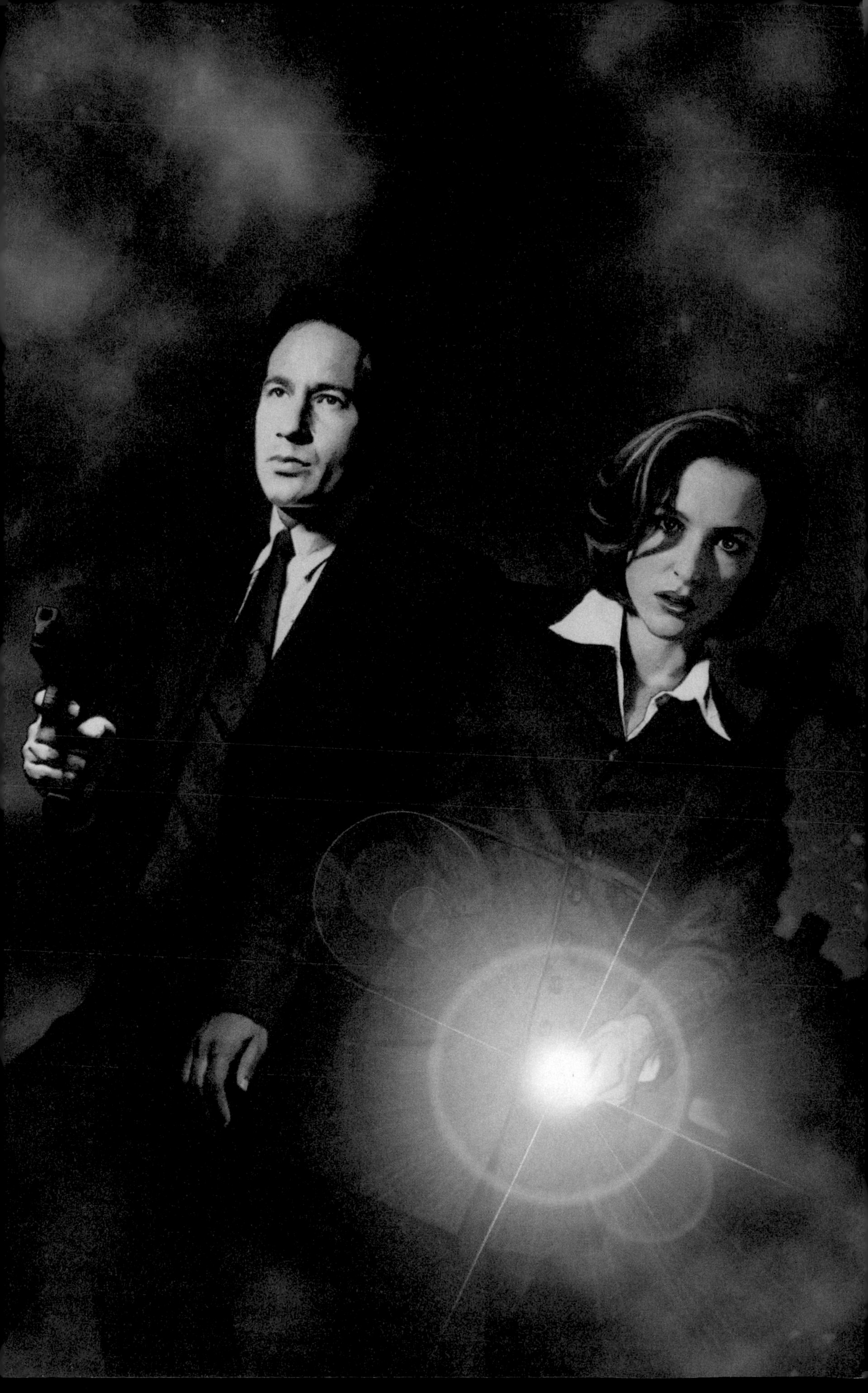

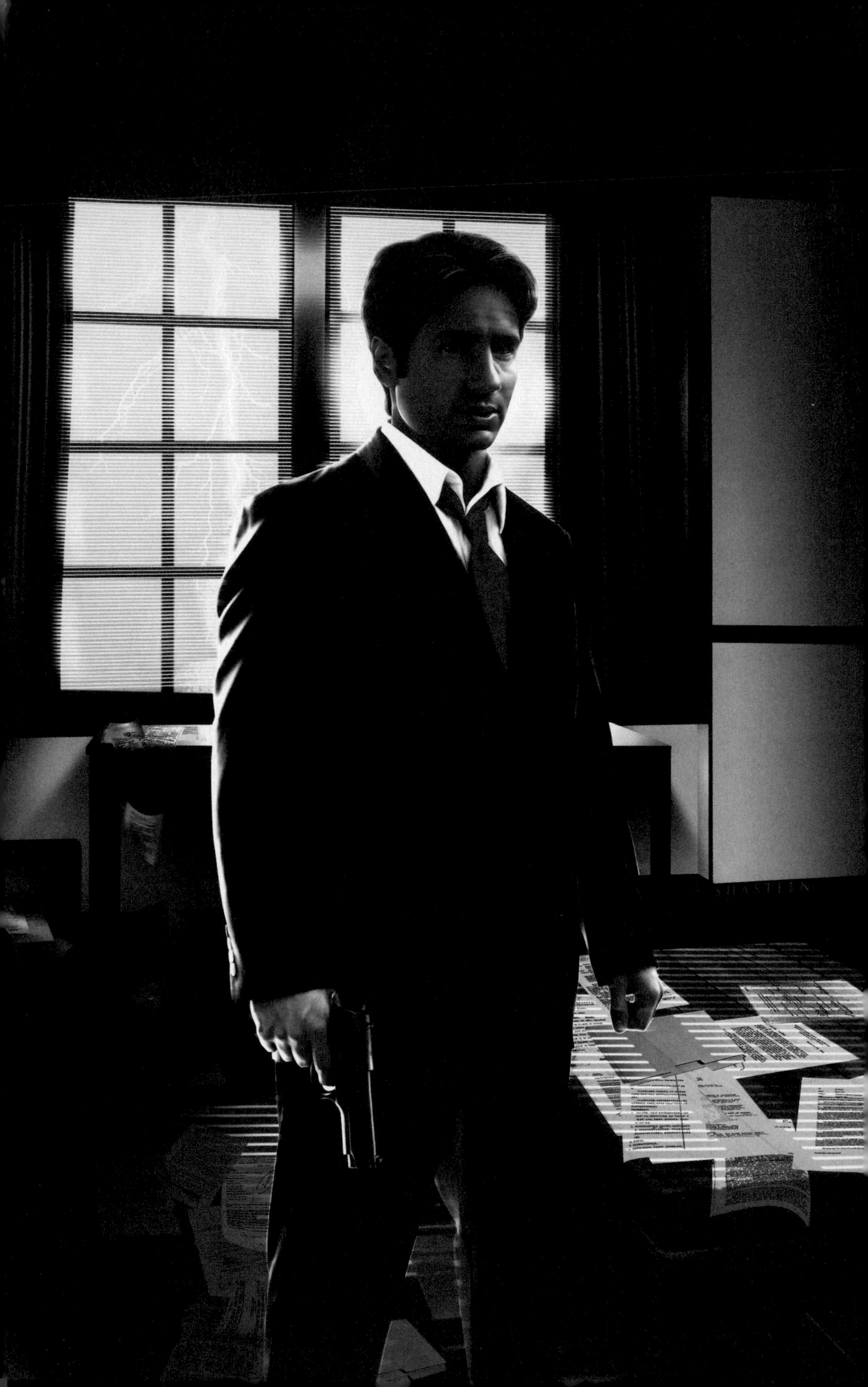
SHASTEEN

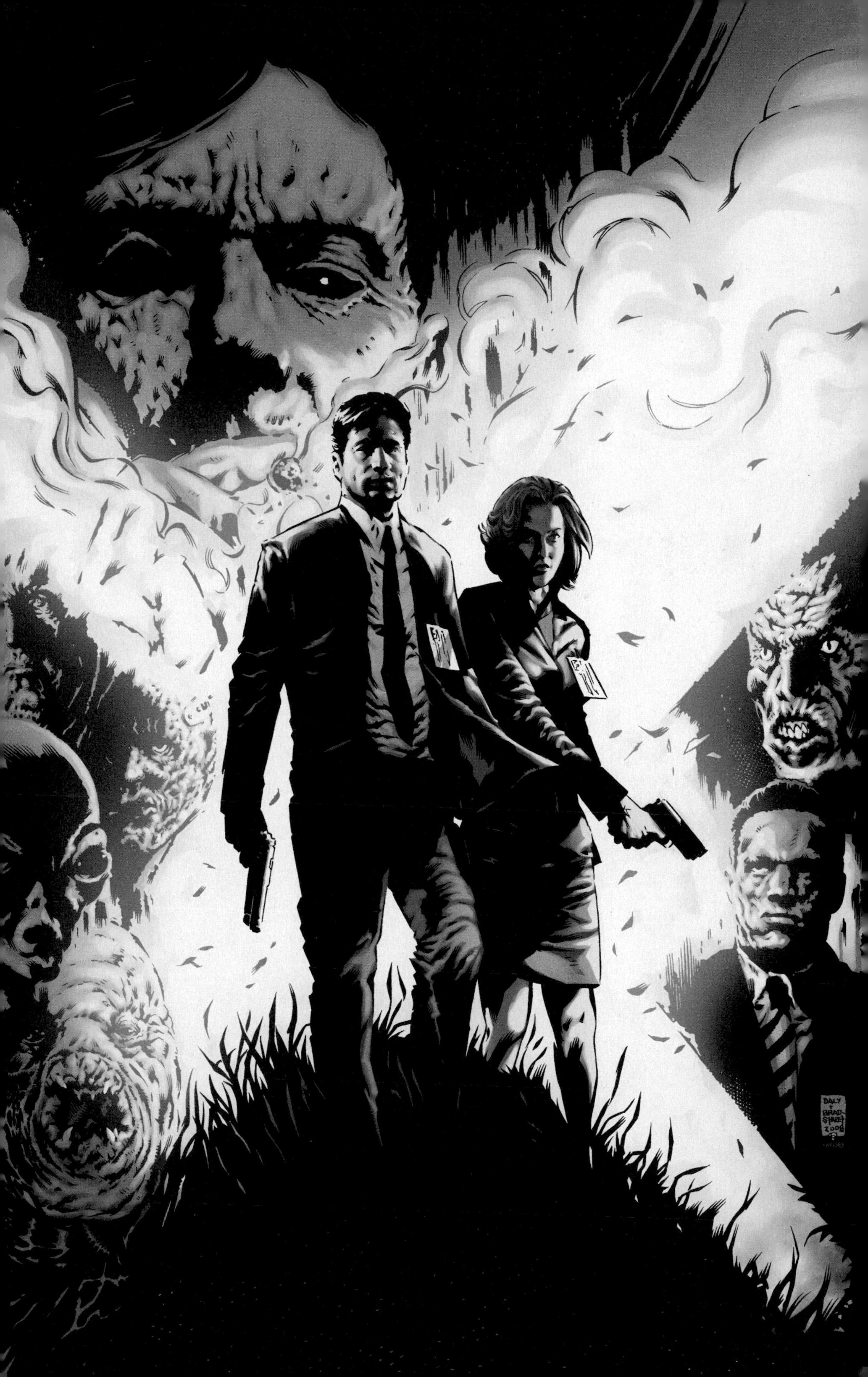
DALY + BRAD- STREET 2008

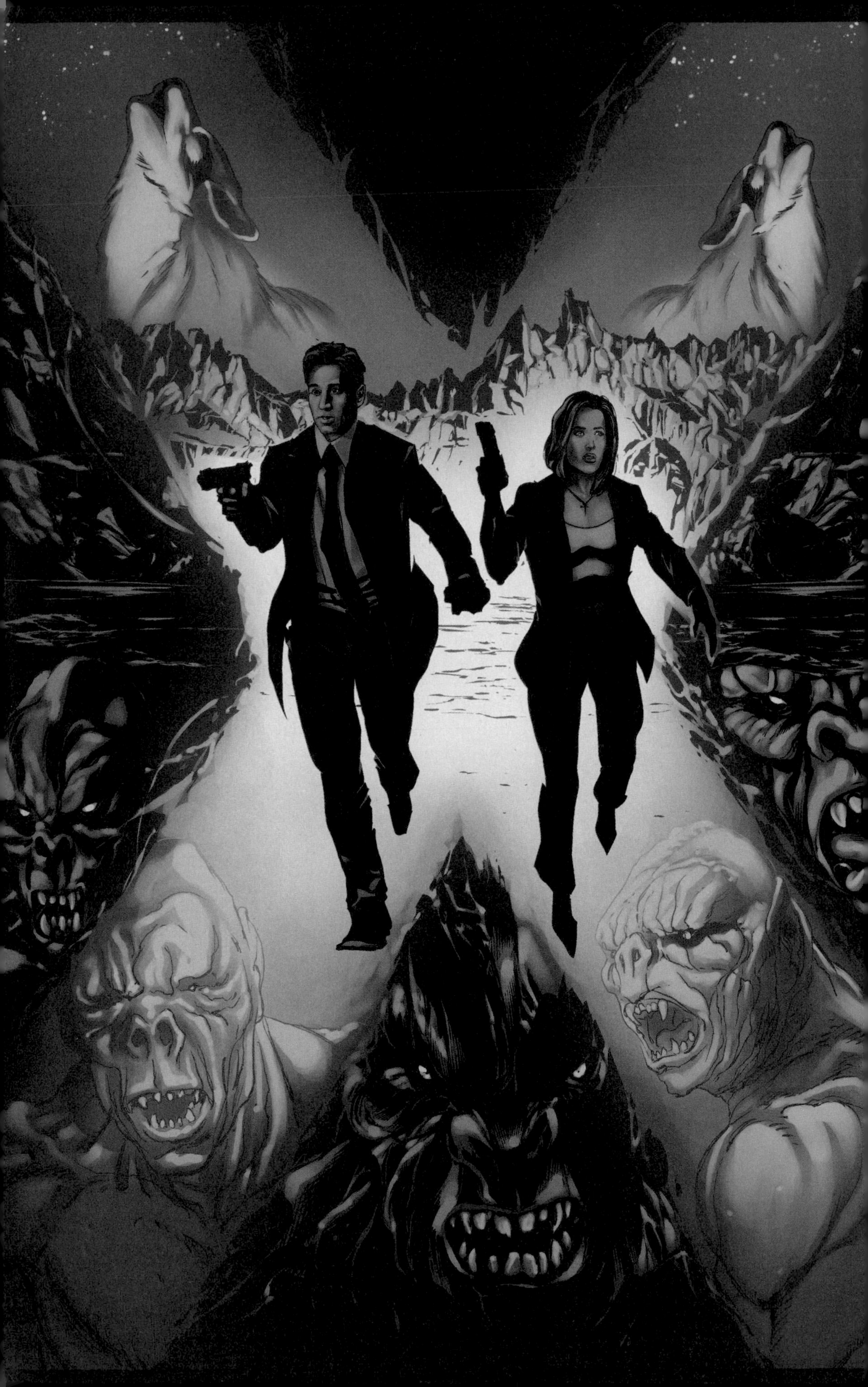

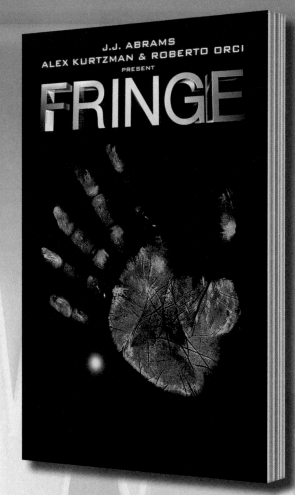

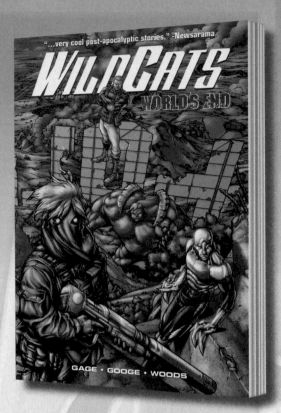
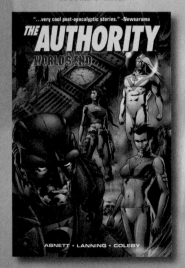